A volume in the Hyperion reprint series
RUSSIAN STUDIES

RUSSIAN-AMERICAN RELATIONS

March, 1917 — March, 1920

DOCUMENTS AND PAPERS

COMPILED AND EDITED BY

C. K. CUMMING AND WALTER W. PETTIT

UNDER THE DIRECTION OF

JOHN A. RYAN, D.D.
J. HENRY SCATTERGOOD
WILLIAM ALLEN WHITE

AT THE REQUEST OF THE

LEAGUE OF FREE NATIONS ASSOCIATION

HYPERION PRESS, INC.
Westport, Connecticut

Published in 1920 by Harcourt, Brace and Howe, New York
Copyright, 1920, By The League of Free Nations Association
Hyperion reprint edition 1977
Reproduced from a copy in the collection of The University
of Illinois Library
Library of Congress Catalog Number 75-39049
ISBN 0-88355-428-3 (cloth ed.)
Printed in the United States of America

Library of Congress Cataloging in Publication Data
Foreign Policy Association.
    Russian-American relations, March, 1917-March, 1920.
    (Russian studies)
    Reprint of the 1920 ed. published by Harcourt, Brace
and Howe, New York.
    Includes index.
    1. United States—Foreign relations—Russia—Sources.
2. Russia—Foreign relations—United States—Sources.
I. Cumming, Caroline King. II. Pettit, Walter
William, 1882-   III. Title.   IV. Series.
E183.8.R9F57   1977   327.73'047   75-39049
ISBN 0-88355-428-3

FOREWORD

The League of Free Nations Association, through encouragement of research by competent scholars, through the organization of study groups and open forums in all parts of the country, and by means of its own publications, is working for a liberal and constructive American foreign policy. It stands for America's entrance into the present League of Nations with the object of aiding its development into a truly democratic and world-inclusive organization.

It is axiomatic that upon the re-establishment of normal cultural, commercial, and political relations with the Russian people depends any adequate solution of the problems of food supply and the revival of industry and trade which involve the whole world. In the belief that the first requisite for the renewal of these essential relationships between the United States and Russia is a fuller knowledge of our Government's Russian policy during the past three years, this Association on August 2, 1919, invited Dr. John A. Ryan, Mr. J. Henry Scattergood, and Mr. William Allen White to direct a study of Russian-American relations since the overthrow of the tsar.

The result is this volume of documents which, because of its objective and non-partisan character will, we believe, contribute towards the formation of an enlightened public opinion on this most important aspect of our foreign relations.

This Association plans to conduct, as one of its activities, further investigations of similar character into other phases of our foreign policy.

JAMES G. MCDONALD,
Chairman of the League of Free Nations Association.

130 West 42nd Street,
   New York City,
March 1, 1920.

PREFACE

This collection of documents and papers is the result of a decision taken last summer by the Executive Committee of the League of Free Nations Association to undertake an inquiry into the relations between the United States and Russia since the Revolution of March, 1917. The responsibility for such an historical study was given to a committee of three. The general purport and spirit of the inquiry are indicated by the following extract from the letter written by the Chairman of the Association, asking members to serve on this committee:

"It is not intended that this study should go into the question of the relative merits of Bolshevism or of the forces fighting Bolshevism in Russia, but that it should be merely an attempt to make clear to the American people what the actual facts have been in our governmental dealings with the various groups in what was the Russian Empire."

Those responsible for the work do not pretend that even the limited objective suggested by the Chairman has been attained in any degree of fullness. The story told by this compilation is necessarily fragmentary and incomplete. Many important facts are doubtless embodied in documents which are not accessible and it is to be hoped that this collection may be supplemented by others from authoritative quarters. The documents which have been included vary greatly in value and significance—some are official and some unofficial; and the inequality in the volume of materials available for different periods gives a certain effect of disproportion to the study as a whole.

Yet it may well be claimed that these documents, here brought together for the first time, throw light on many important aspects of our recent relations with Russia. Every such piece of work, seriously and dispassionately undertaken, may be regarded as a contribution to the task of interpretation and appraisement which awaits the future historian of our Russian policy during this critical period.

The documents fall into three main categories:

(1) Documents already published in English in Senate Reports, State Department publications, *The New York Times,* the *Current History Magazine* (the monthly published by the New York Times Company), *The Nation,* etc.;
(2) Original translations from various Russian official and unofficial newspapers;
(3) Materials hitherto unpublished, contributed by Colonel Raymond Robins and others.

The arrangement followed has been a simple chronological one, save in a few instances where clearness and continuity could be better secured by a slight departure from that plan. The documents have been allowed to speak for themselves with only such annotation as seemed absolutely required. Uniformity in the spelling of Russian names and in such matters as capitalization throughout the book has not been attempted. A minimum of punctuation has been introduced into the cables and telegrams in order to render them intelligible to the reader.

               (signed)   JOHN A. RYAN,
                               J. HENRY SCATTERGOOD,
                               WILLIAM ALLEN WHITE.

March 1, 1920.

CONTENTS

	PAGE
FOREWORD	iii
PREFACE	v
INTRODUCTION	xiii

DOCUMENT
1. Statement by the Provisional Government of Russia, March 16, 1917 1
2. Address by Paul N. Miliukov, Minister of Foreign Affairs, to the Representatives of the Allies, cabled to all Russian Diplomats abroad, March 18, 1917 2
3. Manifesto by the Provisional Government of Russia to the People, March 20, 1917 4
4. Statement conveying Recognition of the Provisional Government by the United States and the Provisional Government's Reply, March 22, 1917 6
5. Proclamation by the Petrograd Soviet to the Peoples of the World, March 27, 1917 7
6. Statement by the Provisional Government regarding the War, April 9, 1917 9
7. Communication by P. N. Miliukov, Minister of Foreign Affairs, to the Russian Diplomats in the Allied Countries, May 1, 1917 . 11
8. Explanation of P. N. Miliukov's Communication to the Russian Diplomats in Allied Countries, furnished by the Provisional Government to the Soviet of Workers' and Soldiers' Deputies, May 4, 1917 12
9. Appeal by the Executive Committee of the Soviet of Workers' and Soldiers' Deputies, May 4, 1917 13
10. Cable from Samuel Gompers, President of the American Federation of Labor, to the Executive Committee of the Petrograd Soviet of Workers' and Soldiers' Deputies, May 7, 1917 . . 14
11. Appeal by the Petrograd Soviet of Workers' and Soldiers' Deputies to the Socialists of all Countries, May 15, 1917 . . . 16
12. Declaration by the Second Provisional Government, May 18, 1917 19
13. Call by the Petrograd Soviet for an International Congress, June 2, 1917 22
14. Note from President Wilson to the Russian Government, May 26, 1917 23
15. Note from the Provisional Government to the Allies, published June 16, 1917 26
16. Note from Secretary Lansing, explaining the Aims of the American Extraordinary Mission to Russia, published June 19, 1917 27
17. Address delivered by the Honorable Elihu Root, to the Russian Provisional Government, June 15, 1917 28
18. Address by President Wilson, welcoming Boris A. Bakhmeteff, the new Russian Ambassador to the United States, July 5, 1917 31
19. Statement by Mr. Root on the Work of the Mission, July 10, 1917 32
20. Statement by the Provisional Government to the Allied Powers, August 1, 1917 33
21. Speech by Mr. Root in New York, August 12, 1917 . . . 34

CONTENTS

DOCUMENT	PAGE
22. Message from President Wilson to the National Conference in Moscow, August 26, 1917	36
23. Statement by the Provisional Government, October 8, 1917	36
24. Kerensky's Interview with The Associated Press, November 1, 1917	39
25. Decree of Peace	41
26. Soviet Government's First Note to Allied Ambassadors, November 22, 1917	44
27. Note from Soviet Government to Representatives of the following Neutral Countries Norway, the Netherlands, Spain, land, Denmark, and Sweden, November 23, 1917	45
28. Replies to the Soviet Note of November 23	46
29. Letter from General Judson to the Chief of the Russian General Staff, November 25, 1917	47
30. Statement issued to the Press by Colonel William Boyce Thompson, with regard to American Supplies, November 27, 1917	48
31. Second Letter from General Judson to the Chief of the Russian General Staff, November 28, 1917	48
32. Statement by Allied Military Attachés at the Russian Staff Headquarters, November. 23, 1917	49
33. Statement by the Chief of the French Military Mission, General Berthelot, addressed to General Dukhonin, Commander-in-Chief of the Russian Armies, November 25, 1917	50
34. Note from the Soviet Government to the Diplomatic Representatives of Allied Countries regarding the Beginning of Armistice Negotiations, November 28, 1917	51
35. Statement by the British Embassy, November 29, 1917	51
36. Reply of the Soviet Government to the Statement of the British Embassy, November 30, 1917	52
37. Statement by Lieutenant-Colonel Kerth to General Dukhonin, November 27, 1917	53
38. Statement by Trotsky regarding the Note of Lieutenant-Colonel Kerth, December 1, 1917	54
39. Statement by the People's Commissariat of Foreign Affairs, regarding the Visit of General Judson to Trotsky, December 1, 1917	55
40. Note from Trotsky to the Allied Ambassadors, December 6, 1917	56
41. Cable from Edgar G. Sisson to George Creel, December 18, 1917	57
42. Denial by the American Military Mission of the Presence of American Officers with General Kaledin	58
43. Communication from Captain Juan of the French Military Mission to the Russian Commander-in-Chief, December 22, 1917	59
44. Cable from Colonel Raymond Robins to Henry P. Davison, sent through the American Embassy, Petrograd, December 26, 1917	60
45. Cable from Henry P. Davison to Colonel Robins, January 6, 1918	60
46. Note from Trotsky to the Peoples and Governments of Allied Countries regarding Peace Negotiations, December 29, 1917	61
47. Document given by Ambassador Francis to Colonel Robins, January 2, 1918 (No. I)	65
48. Document given by Ambassador Francis to Colonel Robins, January 2, 1918 (No. II)	66
49. Cable from Edgar G. Sisson to George Creel, January 3, 1918	67
50. President Wilson's Address to Congress, January 8, 1918	68
51. Cable from Edgar G. Sisson to George Creel, January 13, 1918	74
52. Protest of the Diplomatic Corps in Petrograd regarding the Arrest of the Rumanian Minister in Petrograd, January 14, 1918	75

CONTENTS

DOCUMENT	PAGE
53. Resolution Adopted by Constituent Assembly, January 18, 1918	75
54. Cable from Colonel Robins to Colonel William Boyce Thompson, January 23, 1918	76
55. Text of Decree repudiating Russia's Debts, February 8, 1918	77
56. Protest by the Diplomatic Corps in Russia against the Repudiation of State Debts	78
57. Cable from Colonel Robins to Colonel William B. Thompson, February 15, 1918	79
58. Telegram from Colonel Robins to Lenin and Lenin's Reply, February 28, 1918	80
59. Note from the Soviet Government, given by Trotsky to Colonel Robins for transmission to the American Government, March 5, 1918	81
60. Cable from R. H. Bruce Lockhart to the British Foreign Office, March 5, 1918	82
61. Cable from the American Ambassador to the State Department, March 9, 1918 (I)	84
62. Cable from the American Ambassador to the State Department, March 9, 1918 (II)	85
63. Telegram from Colonel Robins to Trotsky, March 9, 1918	86
64. Telegram from Tchicherin to Colonel Robins, received March 9, 1918	87
65. Cable sent by President Wilson to the All-Russian Congress of Soviets at Moscow, March 14-16, 1918	87
66. Cable sent by Samuel Gompers, President of the American Federation of Labor, to the All-Russian Congress of Soviets, March 14-16, 1918	88
67. Resolution adopted by the All-Russian Congress of Soviets in reply to President Wilson, March 14-16, 1918	89
68. Speech by Mr. Balfour, British Secretary of State for Foreign Affairs, in Parliament, March 14, 1918	89
69. Statement by the Prime Ministers and Foreign Ministers of the Entente, March 19, 1918	92
70. Interview with Mr. Francis, the American Ambassador, March 15, 1918	94
71. Certificate given by the American Ambassador to Colonel Robins, March 10, 1918	95
72. Correspondence between the American Ambassador, David R. Francis, and Colonel Robins, March 11-May 14, 1918	96
73. Paraphrase of Cipher Message received from Mr. MacGowan at Irkutsk by Ambassador Francis, March 15, 1918	164
74. Armed War Prisoner Investigation Siberia: Record of Captain Webster's and Captain Hick's Special Mission	165
75. Report of English and American Officers in regard to arming of Prisoners of War in Siberia, April 26, 1918	177
76. Communication from Tchicherin to Colonel Robins with Two Enclosures, March 21, 1918	186
77. Cable from Colonel Robins to Henry P. Davison, March 26, 1918	188
78. Statement given by Soviet Government to Colonel Robins, regarding Red Cross Activities in Russia	188
79. Telegram from Henry P. Davison to Colonel Robins, sent through the American Ambassador in Paris, April 4, 1918	189
80. Telegram from Colonel Robins to Henry P. Davison, April 5, 1918	189
81. Address by President Wilson at Baltimore, April 6, 1918	190
82. Soviet Government Statement regarding the Attack on Russia from the East	194
83. Statement by Ambassador Francis, April 16, 1918	196

x   CONTENTS

DOCUMENT   PAGE
 84. Cable from Henry P. Davison to Colonel Robins sent through the
        American Ambassador in Paris   196
 85. Letter from Tchicherin to Colonel Robins with Enclosure, April
        25, 1918   197
 86. Cable from Colonel Robins to Henry P. Davison, April 25, 1918 202
 87. Cable from Henry P. Davison to Colonel Robins, sent through the
        American Ambassador in Paris   202
 88. Letter from R. H. Bruce Lockhart to Colonel Robins, May 5, 1918 202
 89. Cable from the Secretary of State to Colonel Robins, May 9, 1918 203
 90. Cable from Colonel Robins to Henry P. Davison, May 9, 1918 204
 91. Plan for Russian-American Commercial Relations, sent by Lenin
        to Colonel Robins, May 14, 1918   204
 92. Report presented by Colonel Raymond Robins to the Secretary
        of State, July 1, 1918   212
 93. Statement by Ambassador Francis, given out by the Committee
        on Public Information, May 31, 1918   219
 94. Statement cabled by Mr. Lansing to Ambassador Francis, and
        given out by the Committee on Public Information, May 31,
        1918   221
 95. Statement by the American Ambassador—supplied to the Press
        by the Committee on Public Information, June 1, 1918 . . 223
 96. Note from the Soviet Government regarding the Czechoslovaks,
        June 13, 1918   224
 97. Note handed by Tchicherin to R. H. Bruce Lockhart, British Representative,
        June 28, 1918   226
 98. Note sent by Tchicherin to R. H. Bruce Lockhart, June 30,
        1918   227
 99. Protest by Tchicherin against the Movement of British Troops 229
100. Note from Tchicherin to the United States   229
101. Statement by the Allied Consuls   230
102. Message sent to Tchicherin by Ambassador Francis, July 25,
        1918   231
103. Agreement between the Allies and the Murmansk Soviet, concluded
        July 17, 1918   232
104. Statement issued by the Czechoslovak National Council at Washington,
        July 27, 1918   235
105. Official Announcement issued at Washington, August 3, 1918 . 237
106. Declaration by the Japanese Government, August 3, 1918 .   239
107. Statement issued by the Russian Embassy at Washington, August 5, 1918   241
108. Proclamation by the Provisional Government of the Country of
        the North, August 7, 1918   242
109. Declaration of the British Government to the Peoples of Russia,
        August 8, 1918   243
110. Address by Ambassador Francis to the Russian People, August 9,
        1918   244
111. Note from Tchicherin to Dewitt C. Poole, Jr., American Consul,
        August 6, 1918   246
112. Note from Tchicherin regarding the Departure from Russia of
        French and British, August 20, 1918   248
113. Statement by Trotsky, August 23, 1918   249
114. Resolution adopted at a Meeting of the All-Russian Central
        Executive Committee on September 2, 1918 250
115. Official Statement by Soviet Government   252
116. Statement by Tchicherin, September 7, 1918   253
117. Note from the British Foreign Secretary to Tchicherin, September 6, 1918   255

CONTENTS

DOCUMENT	PAGE
118. Note from American Government to all the Associated and Neutral Governments, September 21, 1918	256
119. Appeal by the All-Russian Provisional Government to President Wilson, November 7, 1918	257
120. Letter from the Russian Soviet Government to President Wilson, dated October 24, 1918	258
121. Statement by Tchicherin to Provisional Czechoslovak Government, November 1, 1918	267
122. Protest by Tchicherin against intervention, sent out by Wireless, December 2, 1918	268
123. Appeal by Litvinov to President Wilson, December 24, 1918	270
124. Statement by M. Pichon, French Minister of Foreign Affairs, in the Chamber of Deputies, December 29, 1918	273
125. Letter from Litvinov and Vorovsky to Dr. Ludwig Meyer of Christiania: Semi-Official Statement with regard to Peace, January 10, 1919	274
126. Documents referring to the plan for Allied Supervision of the Chinese Eastern and Trans-Siberian Railways	276
127. Reply by French Foreign Minister to the British Government's Suggestion with regard to Russia, January 5, 1919	280
128. Note from Tchicherin to the American State Department, January 12, 1919	282
129. Notes on Conversations held in the Office of M. Pichon at the Quai D'Orsay, on January 16, 1919: preliminary discussion regarding the Situation in Russia	284
130. Secretaries' Notes of a Conversation held in M. Pichon's Room at the Quai d'Orsay on Tuesday, January 21, 1919, regarding Situation in Russia	289
131. President Wilson's Prinkipo Proposal at the Meeting of the Peace Conference, January 22, 1919	297
132. Note from the Soviet Government in reply to Prinkipo Invitation, February 4, 1919	298
133. Replies of Non-Bolshevik Russian Governments to Prinkipo Invitation	303
134. Announcement of recognition of Poland by State Department, January 29, 1919	306
135. Note from the Russian Soviet Government to Italy, February 14, 1919	306
136. Text of Projected Peace Proposal prepared by Representatives of the Soviet Government, March 14, 1919	317
137. Translation of Credentials sent by L. C. A. K. Martens to the State Department, March 19, 1919	320
138. Memorandum sent to the State Department by L. C. A. K. Martens, March 19, 1919	321
139. Letter from Dr. Nansen to President Wilson, April 3, 1919	329
140. Reply of President Wilson, Premiers Clemenceau, Lloyd-George, and Orlando to Dr. Nansen, April 17, 1919	330
141. The Soviet Government's Reply to the Nansen Offer	332
142. Statement by Secretary Lansing conveying recognition of Finland, May 7, 1919	336
143. Note from the Supreme Council to Admiral Kolchak, May 26, 1919	337
144. Admiral Kolchak's Reply to the Supreme Council, June 4, 1919	340
145. Acknowledgment by Supreme Council of Admiral Kolchak's Reply, June 12, 1919	343
146. Reply of President Wilson to a Senate Resolution concerning the American troops in Siberia, June 26, 1919	343

CONTENTS

DOCUMENT PAGE
147. Protest from Russian Soviet Government to the State Department, received through Swedish Channels, June 24, 1919 . . 346
148. Reply to Russian Protest cabled by Mr. Phillips, Assistant Secretary of State, to American Legation at Stockholm, July 1, 1919 347
149. Letter from Secretary Lansing to the Lithuanian National Council, on the Question of Recognition, October 15, 1919 . . . 348
150. Note from the Allies to the German Government, inviting Germany to participate in the Blockade of Bolshevik Russia . 349
151. Reply by Mr. Phillips, Assistant Secretary of State, to Senator Wadsworth, November 4, 1919 351
152. Resolution of Congress of Soviets, December 5, 1919 . . . 353
153. Letter from Secretary Lansing to the Lithuanian Executive Committee, January 7, 1920 354
154. Statement by the Secretary of State regarding the Withdrawal of American Military Forces from Siberia, January 16, 1920 . 355
155. Announcement by the Supreme Council on Trade with Russia, January 16, 1920 358
156. Supreme Council's Note to the Representatives of the Russian Central Cooperative Union regarding the Partial Lifting of the Blockade, January 26, 1920 359
157. Authorization given by the Soviet Government to the Central Union of Russian Cooperatives to trade with Foreign Countries, February 2, 1920 360
158. Statement by the Supreme Council, February 24, 1920 . . 361

INDEX 363

INTRODUCTION

The documents and papers contained in this volume cover three years. They begin wtih the first declaration issued by the Provisional Government of Russia after the revolution on March 16, 1917, and end with the statement made by the supreme Council at Paris on February 24, 1920. While they by no means constitute in themselves complete materials for the history of the relations between the United States and Russia during the three years, they suggest and illustrate many salient facts of that history. In a lesser degree they throw light on the relations between Russia and the Allies over the same period, although documents referring especially to the Allies have been included only when they supply some essential element in the background or have a real, if indirect, bearing on some aspect of American policy.

For the purpose of this short analysis we may find it convenient to divide the documents into five groups on a chronological basis: (1) from the revolution in March, 1917, to the revolution in November; (2) from the Bolshevik revolution to the peace of Brest-Litovsk in March, 1918; (3) from Brest-Litovsk to definitive intervention by the Allies and the United States in the summer of 1918; (4) from intervention to the discussions on Russia in the Peace Conference in January, 1919; (5) from Prinkipo to the announcement of a new Russian policy by the Supreme Council in February, 1920, with which the record comes to a close. These divisions are arbitrary, but useful as points of departure. The periods thus indicated are each signalized by an historic event of the first importance from which many of the documents derive. Moreover, they roughly correspond with successive stages in Russia's foreign relations, viewed, in particular, from the standpoint of the United States.

I.

The first period opens with the revolution in March, 1917, welcomed abroad as adding strength to the Alliance against the Central Powers by the inclusion of a new democracy. At the outset we have the proclamations of the Provisional Government to the people.[1] On March 18, the Minister of Foreign Affairs, M. Miliukov, sends a Note to Russian diplomats, defining Russia's future foreign policy in terms of loyal adherence to the pact with the Allies and the continuance of the struggle "without cessation and without faltering."[2]

On March 27 the Petrograd Soviet of Workers' and Soldiers' Deputies issues its proclamation to "the peoples of the world,"[3] thereby revealing for the first time the portentous new force behind the revolution and the existence of internal conflict. The foreign policy of the Soviet is developed along two lines. On the one hand, the Soviet strives to impress its view of the immediate urgency of a general democratic peace upon successive Provisional Governments; on the other, it appeals over the heads of all Governments to the peoples.

The successful pursuance of the first aim is reflected in the pronouncement by the Government on April 9 for a peace without annexations and indemnities, on the basis of self-determination of peoples,[4] and in the reaffirmation of the statement after the decisive victory won by the Soviet over the old diplomacy as represented by Miliukov.[5] On May 18, the Second Provisional Government, reorganized and broadened by the inclusion of six Socialist members, once more affirms the famous formula and announces its intention of effecting an understanding with the Allies on that basis.[6] Meanwhile, the Soviet pursues its second line of advance by its appeal to "the Socialists of the world" (including those of the enemy countries) on May 15,[7] and its call for an international Socialist congress at Stockholm sent out on June 2.[8]

Contacts with the United States during this period take various forms. The dominant note is one of confidence, although a qualified confidence in some instances. On March 22, the new Government is given official recognition through Mr. Francis, the American Ambassador in Petrograd.[9] Mr. Gompers, President of the American Federation of Labor, sends a long cable to the Petrograd Soviet on May 7, declaring that the views of American and Russian workers on the ends of the war are

[1] Documents 1 and 3.
[2] Document 2.
[3] Document 5.
[4] Document 6.
[5] Documents 7, 8.
[6] Document 12.
[7] Document 11.
[8] Document 13.
[9] Document 4.

INTRODUCTION xv

fundamentally the same.[1] The visit of the American Mission to Russia, headed by Mr. Root, provides the occasion for two notes, one signed by President Wilson, the other by Mr. Lansing, published on June 10 and June 19 respectively,[2] expressing the goodwill and friendship of the American people and explaining America's war aims. On June 15, Mr. Root addresses the Provisional Government;[3] on July 10, while still in Russia, he issues a statement to the Press, referring to the success of the Mission and promising American help;[4] on August 12, after his return home, he delivers a speech in New York on eulogistic and hopeful lines.[5] The new Ambassador from Russia, appointed by the Provisional Government, is welcomed by President Wilson on July 5.[6] In August President Wilson sends a message of encouragement to the National Conference in Moscow.[7]

In Russia the situation grows increasingly more complicated and threatening. In June Tereshchenko, the Minister of Foreign Affairs, sends a Note to the Allies suggesting a conference for the revision of war aims,[8] and this suggestion frequently reappears. Throughout the summer and autumn troubles accumulate for the Government: the failure of the offensive, disorders in Petrograd, the fall of Riga, the Kornilov revolt. The note of anxiety and strain deepens.[9] The declaration issued on October 8 by the last Government under Kerensky represents the final effort to cope with insuperable difficulties.[10] It looks for hope to two things: the creation of the Constituent Assembly and revision of war aims in concert with the Allies. On November 1 Kerensky gives his famous interview to the Associated Press, with its reiteration of the fact that Russia is "worn out."[11] In spite of its guarded terms, in spite of official denials of implications which lie plain upon the surface, this interview gives clear warning of the crisis which is close at hand.

II.

The Bolshevik revolution is accomplished on November 6-7, 1917. The second period opens with the Decree of Peace adopted unanimously at the All-Russian Convention of Soviets

[1] Document 10.
[2] Documents 14, 16.
[3] Document 17.
[4] Document 19.
[5] Document 21.
[6] Document 18.
[7] Document 22.
[8] Document 15.
[9] Document 20.
[10] Document 23.
[11] Document 24:

xvi INTRODUCTION

on November 8, proposing immediate negotiations for a peace without annexations and without indemnities and announcing the Government's intention to publish all secret treaties.[1] The Government's proposals for an armistice and peace negotiations are formally communicated by Trotsky, the People's Commissary of Foreign Affairs, to the Ambassadors of the Allies and the United States on November 22.[2] The following day a communication on the subject is addressed to the representatives of neutral countries, requesting their aid.[3] The Spanish Ambassador sends a sympathetic reply.

A series of protests follow from the military and diplomatic representatives of the Allies against the action of the Soviet Government.[5] On November 27 an American military representative addresses a protest against any separate armistice to General Dukhonin.[6] He is informed in a caustic reply by Trotsky that General Dukhonin has been removed by the Government from the position of Commander-in-Chief.[7]

On November 28 Trotsky sends a Note to the representatives of the Allies, announcing the acceptance by the German Supreme Command of proposals for negotiations, and again inviting participation.[8] Armistice negotiations between Russia and the Central Powers begin on December 3. In a Note on December 6 Trotsky outlines the course negotiations have taken and announces their suspension for a week in order that the other belligerents may define their attitude.[9] Peace negotiations follow. On December 29 Trotsky announces a further suspension for an interval of ten days and passionately appeals to the peoples and Governments of the Allies to come in.[10]

A certain impression of confusion is given by the record of Russian-American relations during this period. But the first phase of bewildered readjustment is succeeded by one in which the note of hopefulness and sympathy still predominates. On November 25 General Judson, Chief of the American Military Mission in Russia sends a letter to the Chief of the Russian General Staff, with regard to the probable attitude of his Government towards the question of the continued shipment of American supplies to Russia.[11] Two days later, Colonel William Boyce Thompson, commanding the American Red Cross Mission,

[1] Document 25.
[2] Document 26.
[3] Document 27.
[4] Document 28
[5] Documents 32, 33, 35, 36.
[6] Document 37.
[7] Document 38.
[8] Document 34.
[9] Document 40.
[10] Document 46.
[11] Document 29.

INTRODUCTION xvii

gives a statement to the Press bearing on this point in so far as it affects the Red Cross.[1] On November 28 General Judson writes again to the Chief of the Russian General Staff, referring to American sympathy for the Russian people and expressing the opinion that Russia is within her rights in bringing up the question of a general peace.[2] On December 2, the *Izvestia* (now the official organ of the Soviet Government) gives an account of a friendly discussion between General Judson and Trotsky on the question of the negotiations, in which the former is quoted as saying: "The time of protest and threats addressed to the Soviet Government has passed, if that time ever existed." [3]

Early in December Colonel Raymond Robins succeeds Colonel Thompson in command of the American Red Cross Mission in Russia. On December 27 a cable goes from him to Mr. Davison, Director General of the Red Cross, then in Washington, asking him to urge upon the President the necessity for continued intercourse with the Bolshevik Government.[4] The cable is sent through the American Ambassador who approves its terms. Mr. Davison in his reply on January 6 reports the approval of the State Department.[5] On January 2 two documents are given by Mr. Francis to Colonel Robins for use in the event of certain contingencies.[6]

Cabling Mr. Thompson in New York in January 23, Colonel Robins urges the "prompt recognition of Bolshevik authority" and the immediate establishment of a "modus vivendi making possible generous and sympathetic co-operation." [7] This view, he says, is approved by Mr. Sisson, then in Russia at the head of the Committee on Public Information. In a cable to Mr. Thompson on February 15, after the rupture of negotiations at Brest-Litovsk, Colonel Robins emphasizes the danger of German commercial aggression and the immense importance of developing by every means commercial relations between the United States and Russia.[8]

Three cables from Mr. Sisson in Petrograd to Mr. Creel in Washington, dated December 18, 1917, and January 3 and 13, 1918, illustrate the activities of the Committee on Public Information during this period and its relations with the Soviet

[1] Document 30.
[2] Document 31.
[3] Document 39.
[4] Document 44.
[5] Document 45.
[6] Documents 47, 48.
[7] Document 54.
[8] Document 57.

xviii   INTRODUCTION

Government.[1] President Wilson's address to Congress on January 8[2] with its reference to the treatment of Russia by her sister nations as "the acid test" is given wide publicity.

Other documents are concerned with the Government's repudiation of Russia's debts[3] and the episode of the arrest of the Rumanian Minister.[4] The peace resolution, hastily passed by the frustrate Constituent Assembly on January 18, 1918, employs the old phrasing in calling on the Allies to define their terms and join in working for an immediate, general, democratic peace, but it also expresses readiness to carry forward the negotiations with the enemy which have been begun.[5]

III.

The third period is the period of rapprochement, although the strength of the forces working in the opposite direction is clearly apparent from the documents. The Soviet Government has not been recognized by the United States, but friendly relations are maintained through semi-official channels.

In this period we may include the group of documents related to and immediately preceding the ratification of the Brest peace. Colonel Robins inquires of Lenin with regard to the signing of peace on February 28, telegraphing from Vologda to which place the American Embassy has just moved.[6] Next we have the Note handed by Trotsky to Colonel Robins on March 5 for transmission to the American Government, asking what aid might be expected in the event of the refusal of ratification or the renewal of hostilities, and also what attitude would be taken by the Government of the United States in case of hostile Japanese action in Siberia.[7] No reply to this Note is recorded. The same day Mr. Lockhart, British High Commissioner, cables the British Foreign Office, urging assistance and warning against Japanese intervention.[8] Ambassador Francis on March 9 sends two cables to the State Department on similar lines,[9] and Colonel Robins informs Trotsky of the fact.[10] Tchicherin writes to Colonel Robins on March 9, expressing appreciation of the American Embassy's friendly attitude.[11]

[1] Documents 41, 49, 51.
[2] Document 50.
[3] Documents 55, 56.
[4] Document 52.
[5] Document 53.
[6] Document 58.
[7] Document 59.
[8] Document 60.
[9] Documents 61, 62.
[10] Document 63.
[11] Document 64.

INTRODUCTION

On March 12 the All-Russian Congress of Soviets meets at Moscow. President Wilson sends a cable expressing sympathy,[1] which is acknowledged in a resolution of the Congress.[2] Mr. Gompers also sends a message.[3] The peace is ratified. On March 19 a statement is issued by the Prime Ministers and Foreign Ministers of the Entente refusing to acknowledge the treaty.[4] About the same time an interview with Mr. Francis is published in which he declares that he will not leave Russia and that America must still be regarded as an ally of the Russian people.[5]

Meanwhile, on March 10, Colonel Robins has gone to Moscow with a special certificate from the Ambassador.[6] During the next two months a correspondence is carried on between the two, consisting of practically daily direct wire or ordinary telegraphic communications.[7] This correspondence overlaps in point of time with most of the documents included in the period. It touches upon a great variety of subjects: the Brest peace and the attitude to be observed towards the Soviet Government; Japanese intervention; Trotsky's reorganization of the Russian Army with the co-operation of Allied officers; the American Railway Mission; the rumored German control commission in Petrograd; the investigation by Captain Hicks of the British Military Mission and Captain Webster of the American Red Cross into the armed war-prisoner rumor in Siberia; the proposed purchase of platinum from the Soviet Government, etc., etc. Special attention may be directed to the State Department dispatch—communicated by Mr. Francis to Colonel Robins in which the United States pronounces against Japanese intervention.[8]

Other documents relate to the Japanese question. Mr. Balfour discusses it in the House of Commons on March 14.[9] On April 6 the landing of Japanese and British marines at Vladivostok is the occasion of an official statement by the Soviet Government.[10] In a statement on April 16, Mr. Francis declares that the incident is of purely local significance and in no sense the result of concerted action between the Allies.[11] On April 25 Tchicherin writes to Colonel Robins alleging the implication of the American consular officer at Vladivostok in a counter-

[1] Document 65.
[2] Document 67.
[3] Document 66.
[4] Document 69.
[5] Document 70.
[6] Document 71.
[7] Document 72.
[8] Document 72, No. 4.
[9] Document 68.
[10] Document 82.
[11] Document 83.

INTRODUCTION

revolutionary conspiracy, promoted by the newly-established Government of Autonomous Siberia.[1]

The story of the investigation (referred to above) made by an American and a British officer into the rumors of danger from armed prisoners of war in Siberia, is fully told in the series of telegrams recording the experiences and observations of the investigators[2] and in the comprehensive report, dated April 26, in which they set forth their conclusions.[3]

The degree of co-operation existing at this time between the Soviet Government and at least some representatives of the Allies is also shown by such documents as the letter from Mr. Lockhart, dated May 5, in which he instances to Colonel Robins a number of specific ways in which Trotsky has shown his willingness to work with the Allies.[4]

Several documents refer to the work of the Red Cross. A statement signed by Lenin and Tchicherin, dated March 29, emphasizes the importance attached to it by the Soviet Government.[5] In a series of telegrams Mr. Davison and Colonel Robins discuss the question of the continuance of the work, as well as other points of general policy.[6] A cable from Mr. Lansing, dated May 9,[7] suggests that Colonel Robins come home for consultation and the latter leaves Russia about the middle of May.

Colonel Robins takes with him a plan for Russian-American commercial relations sent him by Lenin on May 14.[8] After his return home he presents his own proposals for economic co-operation which he has stressed so emphatically throughout, in a report to the Secretary of State, dated July 1.[9]

IV.

No sharp line of demarkation separates the third from the fourth period on the face of these documents. Non-intervention seems to fade into intervention. Rapprochement is gradually transformed into alienation and hostility. In Russia, the Committee on Public Information issues on the last day of May a statement by the American Ambassador and one by Mr. Lansing, asserting that the American policy is one of friendship, non-

[1] Document 85.
[2] Document 74.
[3] Document 75.
[4] Document 88.
[5] Document 78.
[6] Documents 77, 79, 80, 84, 86, 87, 90.
[7] Document 89.
[8] Document 91.
[9] Document 92.

INTRODUCTION

intervention in Russia's internal affairs, and complete aloofness to the appeals for help from groups opposed to the Soviet Government.[1] Another statement by Mr. Francis on June 1 reiterates these points.[2]

Towards the end of May hostilities have begun between the Czechoslovak troops and the Soviet forces. On June 13 Tchicherin sends a Note to the British High Commissioner and the French, American, and Italian Consuls General giving his version of the facts of the conflict and protesting against the protecting attitude which he alleges has been assumed towards Czechoslovak aggression.[3]

Later in the month the Allied landing at Murmansk takes place, the forces landed including a small number of American marines. A series of protests follow from the Soviet Government, addressed to the representatives of the Allies, deepening in bitterness with the advance of the Allied troops.[4] On July 12 Tchicherin appeals to the Consul General of the United States in the name of that American friendship which is "so highly valued."[5] On July 17 an agreeemnt is concluded between the Allies and the Murman Regional Soviet.[6]

During the month the difficulties of the Soviet Government multiply. On July 25 the increasing tension of the situation results in the departure of the Allied Embassies from Vologda to Archangel. Mr. Francis sends a statement to Tchicherin, explaining the reasons for the step.[7] The American Consul General, Mr. Poole, announces the intention of himself and his fellow Consuls to remain in Moscow.[8]

In Washington the Czechoslovak National Council issues a statement on July 27.[9] This refers to the great military successes achieved by the Czechoslovak forces, mentions their lack of desire to "play policemen" in Russia, and dwells on their complete subordination to the orders of the Supreme War Council of the Allies.

On August 3 an official announcement is made of the policy of the American Government.[10] It pronounces against "such military intervention as has been most frequently proposed " and declares military action to be "admissible in Russia now only to render such protection and help as is possible to the

[1] Documents 93, 94.
[2] Document 95.
[3] Document 96.
[4] Documents 97, 98, 99.
[5] Document 100.
[6] Document 103.
[7] Document 102.
[8] Document 101.
[9] Document 104.
[10] Document 105.

Czechoslovaks against the armed Austrian and German prisoners who are attacking them, and to steady any efforts at self-government or self-defense in which the Russians themselves may be willing to accept assistance." To these ends, it states, the Government of the United States has proposed to the Government of Japan that each should send a force of a few thousand men to Vladivostok. The statement issued simultaneously by the Japanese Government is entirely concerned with the dangerous situation of the Czechoslovaks.[1]

On August 5 the Russian Embassy in Washington (still representing the Provisional Government which fell in November, 1917) issues a statement with regard to the groups which have revealed themselves in Siberia as the result of the "liberating" activities of the Czechoslovak forces and the disappearance of Soviets in their train—in particular, the "Temporary Government of Siberia."[2]

An uprising in Archangel on August 3 results in the overthrow of the Soviet. On August 7 a statement is issued by the Provisional Government of the Country of the North, organized under the protection of the Allies.[3] British representatives at Vladivostok, Murmansk, and Archangel on August 8 publish a declaration to the "Peoples of Russia" that the invaders come as friends to assist in the struggle against Germany.[4] Tchicherin on August 6 sends an appeal to Mr. Poole against the action of the Allies.[5] On August 9, Mr. Francis, in the name of the Diplomatic Corps, issues an address to the Russian people, disclaiming all intention of interfering in Russia's internal affairs, but declaring against recognition of any Government "which has not a national character, which disregards Russia's solemn bonds of alliance and which observes the Brest-Litovsk Treaty.[6]

A number of documents in this period reflect different aspects of the strained relations now existing between the Soviet Government and the Allies; the internment of French and British citizens and the conditions of their exchange;[7] the attack on the British Embassy;[8] the Soviet Government's charge of an Anglo-French conspiracy.[9] On August 23 Trotsky makes an indignant reply to the reference to the attacks by armed prisoners of war in the American statement of August 3.[10]

[1] Document 106.
[2] Document 107.
[3] Document 108.
[4] Document 109.
[5] Document 111.
[6] Document 110.
[7] Document 112.
[8] Document 117.
[9] Documents 115, 116.
[10] Document 113.

INTRODUCTION xxiii

The attack on Lenin's life is followed by a resolution adopted by the All-Russian Central Executive Committee on September 2, declaring for "mass terror" against counter-revolutionists.[1] The Government of the United States sends a Note on September 21 to all the associated and neutral Governments, asking them to protest against "the indiscriminate slaughter" of Russian citizens.[2]

Early in November the recently-established All-Russian Provisional Government at Omsk appeals for aid to President Wilson.[3] This moderate Socialist Government is overthrown by a coup d'état on November 18-19 and Admiral Kolchak is proclaimed Supreme Ruler.

Shortly before the armistice we find the first of a long series of appeals for peace addressed by the Soviet Government to the United States and the Allies—individually or collectively. On October 24 a long argumentative letter is sent by Tchicherin to President Wilson.[4] On December 2 a combined protest and peace proposal is sent out to Great Britain, France, Italy, and the United States.[5] On December 24 Litvinov from Stockholm sends a reasoned statement to President Wilson.[6] A semi-official approach is made on January 10, 1919, through a letter signed by Litvinov and Vorovsky to Dr. Meyer of Christiania, containing certain definite conditions which the Soviet Government would observe, including the abstention from propaganda in Allied countries.[7] On January 12 a statement by Tchicherin, dealing especially with the grounds advanced for the sending of American troops to Russia, is addressed to the State Department.[8] A Note to Italy, dated February 14, very fully reviews the whole situation up to that date, from the point of view of the Soviet Government.[9] On December 5, 1919, the Seventh Congress of Soviets in a resolution refers to earlier appeals and "once more confirms its unchanging desire for peace" by renewing the proposal for negotiations.[10]

V.

With the consideration of the Russian situation in the Peace Conference in January, 1919, begins what we roughly marked

[1] Document 114.
[2] Document 118.
[3] Document 119.
[4] Document 120.
[5] Document 122.
[6] Document 123.
[7] Document 125.
[8] Document 128.
[9] Document 135.
[10] Document 152.

off as the fifth period—the period of groping. In the search for a Russian policy by the Associated Powers, one plan after another is tried and discarded.

On December 29, 1918, M. Pichon restates as the inter-Allied plan of action the policy of economic encirclement of the Bolsheviks, enunciated by M. Clemenceau earlier in the month.[1] On January 11, 1919, his wholly unfavorable reply to a British proposal for re-establishing peace in Russia is published.[2] The whole Russian situation is discussed at a meeting of the Peace Conference on January 16.[3] Mr. Lloyd George explains his proposal, which he declares has been misunderstood by the French Government, gives his reasons for desiring to hear the views of all the Russian groups, and is supported by President Wilson. On January 21 the discussion is resumed.[4] President Wilson suggests a modification of the British proposal, viz., that the various Russian groups should be invited, on the condition of the cessation of hostilities, to send representatives to some place to be appointed (other than Paris) there to confer with representatives of the Associated Powers. This plan is agreed upon.

On January 22 President Wilson's proposal is announced in the definite form of an invitation to "every organized group that is now exercising or attempting to exercise political authority or military control" in Siberia or European Russia to send representatives to the Princes' Islands in the Sea of Marmora by February 15, a truce of arms to be operative meanwhile.[5] The reply of the Soviet Government, dated February 4, is in form an acceptance of the invitation, which, it states, it has learned of only through a radio review of the Press.[6] It expresses great anxiety for peace and suggests possible offers to the Allies in respect of assuming obligations for Russian loans, the guaranteeing of interest by raw materials, concessions in natural resources, and even territorial concessions. The question of a truce is not specifically mentioned. The Lettish and Esthonian Governments accept the invitation to the Princes' Islands, although postulating their complete independence of Russia. The Siberian, Archangel, and South Russian Governments categorically refuse to meet in any conference with the Bolsheviks.[7] The proposal falls to the ground.

[1] Document 124.
[2] Document 127.
[3] Document 129.
[4] Document 130.
[5] Document 131.
[6] Document 132.
[7] Document 133.

INTRODUCTION xxv

On February 22 Mr. Bullitt is sent to Russia by the American Commission to negotiate peace, arriving in Petrograd on March 8. Definite peace proposals are drafted by representatives of the Soviet Government and given to him for transmission to Paris.[1] No action is taken on them.

On April 3 Dr. Nansen writes to President Wilson and to Messrs. Clemenceau, Orlando, and Lloyd George, suggesting that a purely humanitarian and non-political commission of neutrals should be organized for the provisioning of Russia in view of the grave distress there.[2] President Wilson and the three Premiers reply on April 17, approving the suggestion and promising co-operation, but asserting that such a course must involve the complete cessation of hostilities in Russia, as relief without a state of peace would be futile.[3] Tchicherin, in a letter to Dr. Nansen dated May 7, expresses cordial appreciation of his proposal and would welcome it on a purely humanitarian basis, but states emphatically that the Soviet Government, in view of the constant subsidizing of its internal enemies by the Entente, could consider the question of the cessation of hostilities only in connection with the whole problem of its relations with the Associated Powers.[4]

Meanwhile, the Soviet Government has appointed Mr. Martens as its representative in the United States and on March 19 he presents his credentials to the State Department,[5] together with a long statement reviewing the situation, and dealing in particular with the commercial facilities his Government is prepared to offer in the event of the resumption of trade.[6] Tchicherin protests to the State Department on June 24 with regard to the treatment accorded to him, comparing it very unfavorably with that given to American representatives in Russia.[7] On July 1 the State Department replies with counter-recriminations.[8]

Early in February, 1919, following negotiations between the American and Japanese Governments, the United States formally accepts a plan for the supervision of the Chinese Eastern and Trans-Siberian railways by an inter-allied committee. It is agreed that the technical operation of the railways shall be in the hands of Mr. John F. Stevens.[9]

[1] Document 136.
[2] Document 139.
[3] Document 140.
[4] Document 141.
[5] Document 137.
[6] Document 138.
[7] Document 147.
[8] Document 148.
[9] Document 126.

INTRODUCTION

The Supreme Council at Paris sends a Note to Admiral Kolchak on May 26, stating that they are disposed to assist him and his associates to establish themselves as the Government of all Russia, on the acceptance of certain specified conditions, of which the first is the summoning of a Constituent Assembly, and requesting a reply as to his future policy.[1] Admiral Kolchak's reply, containing assurances on the points raised by the Supreme Council, is received on June 5.[2] On June 13 the Supreme Council sends an acknowledgment, declaring that the terms of the reply seem to be "in substantial agreement" with the conditions proposed and expressing willingness to extend support.[3]

In the United States increasing agitation with regard to the continued presence of American troops in Siberia results in a Senate resolution on June 23, asking for full information. President Wilson sends a long message in reply on June 25.[4] This points out that one of the conditions attached to the acceptance of the Siberian Railway plan was that adequate protection should be afforded, asserts that the duties of the American troops are solely confined to participation in that task, and emphasizes the dependence of the people of Siberia and the forces of Admiral Kolchak on the railways for necessary supplies.

The attitude of the State Department towards the future status of nationalities formerly comprised within the Russian Empire (other than Poland and Finland, recognized respectively on January 29 and May 7, 1919)[5] is indicated by a letter from Mr. Lansing to the Lithuanian National Council on October 15, in reply to communications asking for provisional recognition.[6] This is refused on the ground that, while the outcome of Admiral Kolchak's efforts to establish "orderly, constitutional government" in Russia is still uncertain, it is undesirable to prejudice in advance "the principle of Russian unity." This position is reaffirmed in a further letter on January 7, 1920, in which the State Department declines to recognize the Committee which has been appointed by the Lithuanian Provisional Government as its diplomatic agent in the United States, as possessing any diplomatic character.[7]

[1] Document 143.
[2] Document 144.
[3] Document 145.
[4] Document 146.
[5] Documents 134, 142.
[6] Document 149.
[7] Document 153.

INTRODUCTION

During the autumn the neutral Powers and Germany are asked by the Supreme Council to enter into an agreement to prevent their nationals from engaging in any commercial intercourse with Soviet Russia.[1] Mr. Phillips, the Acting Secretary of State, in a letter to Senator Wadsworth dated November 4, defends the policy of non-intercourse on two grounds: the "declared purpose" of the Bolsheviks "to carry revolution throughout the world"; and the control exercised by the Soviet Government, which prevents any commercial dealings except with the Bolshevik authorities.[2]

The last months of 1919 are filled with military events which the documents do not record, the tide flowing strongly in favor of the Soviet forces. On January 16, 1920, a Note from the United States to Japan, in reply to an inquiry from the Japanese Government on December 8, is made public.[3] This announces that, in consideration of the unfavorable development of the military situation in Siberia and also the fact that the main purposes for which American troops were sent are now at an end, all American military forces will be at once withdrawn, their withdrawal being accompanied by that of the American railway experts assisting in the operation of the Trans-Siberian and Chinese Eastern Railways.

The Supreme Council at Paris on the same day announces its decision to permit trade relations between the Russian people and Allied and neutral countries, through the medium of the Russian co-operative organizations—these arrangements implying "no change in the policies of the Allied Governments towards the Soviet Government."[4] The terms of the proposal to the Russian Central Co-operative Union are published on January 26[5] and the authorization to trade given the Union by the Soviet Government on February 2.[6]

On February 26, 1920, the Supreme Council issues a statement on Russian policy to this effect: the Allies cannot advise the communities bordering on Soviet Russia to continue to make war; they cannot enter into relations with the Soviet Government until convinced it is ready "to conform its methods and diplomatic conduct to those of all civilized Governments;" they consider commerce between Russia and the rest of Europe as essential; they regard it as "highly desirable to obtain impartial

[1] Document 150.
[2] Document 151.
[3] Document 154.
[4] Document 155.
[5] Document 156.
[6] Document 157.

and authoritative information" and recommend that a commission of investigation be sent to Russia by the Council of the League of Nations to find out the facts.[1]

C. K. C.

[1] Document 158.

RUSSIAN-AMERICAN RELATIONS
March, 1917—March, 1920

[1.]

Statement by the Provisional Government of Russia, March 16, 1917.[1]

(*New York Times Current History*, Vol. VI, Part 1, p. 7.)

Citizens:

The Executive Committee of the Duma, with the aid and support of the garrison of the capital and its inhabitants, has succeeded in triumphing over the obnoxious forces of the old régime in such a manner that we are now able to proceed to a more stable organization of the executive power, with men whose past political activity assures them the country's confidence.

The new Cabinet will base its policy on the following principles:

First—An immediate general amnesty for all political and religious offenses, including terrorist acts and military and agrarian offenses.

Second—Liberty of speech and of the press; freedom for alliances, unions and strikes, with the extension of these liberties to military officials, within the limits admitted by military requirements.

Third—Abolition of all social, religious, and national restrictions.

Fourth—To proceed forthwith to the preparation and con-

[1] The Tsar abdicated March 15, 1917. The new Provisional Government consisted of the following members: Prime Minister, Prince G. E. Lvov; Foreign Affairs, Paul N. Miliukov; War-Navy, A. I. Guchkov; Justice, A. F. Kerensky; Trade-Commerce, A. I. Konovalov; Agriculture, A. I. Shingariev; Communication, N. V. Nekrasov; Education, A. A. Maniulov; Finance, M. I. Tereshchenko; Comptroller, I. V. Godniev; Procurator of Holy Synod, V. N. Lvov.

1

organization guaranteeing respect for right and justice. She will fight by their side against the common enemy until the end, without cessation and without faltering.

The Government of which I form a part will devote all its energy to preparation of victory and will apply itself to the task of repairing as quickly as possible the errors of the past, which hitherto have paralyzed the aspirations and the self-sacrifice of the Russian people. I am firmly convinced that the marvelous enthusiasm, which to-day animates the whole nation, will multiply its strength in time and hasten the hour of the final triumph of a regenerated Russia and her valiant Allies.

I beg you to communicate to the Minister of Foreign Affairs [of the country to which the diplomat addressed is accredited] the contents of the present telegram.

[3.]

Manifesto by the Provisional Government of Russia to the People, March 20, 1917.

(*New York Times Current History*, Vol. VI, Part 1, p. 12.)

Citizens:

The great work has been accomplished. By a powerful stroke the Russian people have overthrown the old régime. A new Russia is born. This coup d'état has set the keystone upon long years of struggle.

Under pressure of awakened national forces, the act of October 30, 1905, promised Russia constitutional liberties, which were never put into execution. The First Duma, the mouthpiece of the national wishes, was dissolved. The Second Duma met the same fate, and the Government, being powerless to crush the national will, decided by the act of June 16, 1907, to deprive the people of part of the legislative rights promised them.

During the ensuing ten years the Government successively withdrew from the people all the rights they had won. The country was again thrown into the abyss of absolute ruin and administrative arbitrariness. All attempts to make the voice of reason heard were vain, and the great world struggle into which the country was plunged found it face to face with moral decadence and power not united with the people—power indifferent to the country's destinies and steeped in vices and infamy.

The heroic efforts of the Army, crushed under the cruel weight of internal disorganization, the appeals of the national representatives, who were united in view of the national danger, were powerless to lead the Emperor and his Government into the path of union with the people. Thus, when Russia, through the illegal and sinister acts of her governors, was confronted with the greatest disasters, the people had to take the power into their own hands.

With unanimous revolutionary spirit, the people, fully realizing the seriousness of the moment and the firm will of the Duma, established a Provisional Government, which considers that it is its sacred duty to realize the national desires and lead the country into the bright path of free civil organization. The Government believes that the lofty spirit of patriotism which the people have shown in the struggle against the old régime will also animate our gallant soldiers on the battlefields.

In its turn the Government will do its utmost to provide the Army with everything necessary to bring the war to a victorious conclusion. The Government will faithfully observe all alliances uniting us to other powers and all agreements made in the past.

While taking measures indispensable for the defense of the country against a foreign enemy, the Government will consider it its first duty to grant to the people every facility to express its will concerning the political administration, and will convoke as soon as possible the Constituent Assembly on the basis of universal suffrage, at the same time assuring the gallant defenders of the country their share in the Parliamentary elections.

The Constituent Assembly will issue fundamental laws, guaranteeing the country the immutable rights of equality and liberty.

Conscious of the burden of the political oppression weighing on the country and hindering the free creative forces of the people during years of painful hardships, the Provisional Government deems it necessary, before the Constituent Assembly, to announce to the country its principles, assuring political liberty and equality to all citizens, making free use of the spiritual forces in creative work for the benefit of the country. The Government will also take care to elaborate the principles assuring all citizens participation in communal elections, which will be carried out on a basis of universal suffrage.

At the moment of national emancipation, the whole country recalls with pious gratitude those who, in the struggle for their political and religious ideas, fell victims of the vengeance of the old power, and the Provisional Government will joyfully bring back from exile and prison all those who thus suffered for the good of their country.

In realizing these problems, the Provisional Government believes it is executing the national will and that the whole people will support it in its efforts to insure the happiness of Russia.

[4.]

Statement conveying Recognition of the Provisional Government by the United States and the Provisional Government's Reply, March 22, 1917.

(*New York Times Current History*, Vol. VI, Part 1, p. 293.)

On March 22 the Government of the United States, through its Ambassador in Petrograd, David R. Francis,[1] conveyed to the Council of Ministers its official recognition of the new Russian Government:

"I have the honor, as the Ambassador and Representative of the Government of the United States accredited to Russia, to state, in accordance with instructions, that the Government of the United States has recognized the new Government of Russia, and I, as Ambassador of the United States, will be pleased to continue intercourse with Russia through the medium of the new Government.

"May the cordial relations existing between the two countries continue to obtain. May they prove mutually satisfactory and beneficial."

The reply for the Provisional Government was made by P. N. Miliukov, Minister of Foreign Affairs:

"Permit me, in the name of the Provisional Government, to answer the act of recognition by the United States. You have been able to follow for yourself the events which have established the new order of affairs for free Russia. I have been more than once in your country and may bear witness that the ideals which are represented by the Provisional Government are the same as underlie the existence of your own country. I hope that this

---

[1] Mr. Francis was appointed American Ambassador to Russia in March, 1916.

great change which has come to Russia will do much to bring us closer together than we have ever been before.

"I must tell your Excellency that during the last few days I have received many congratulations from prominent men in your country, assuring me that the public opinion of the United States is in sympathy with us. Permit me to thank you. We are proud to be recognized first by a country whose ideals we cherish."

[5.]

Proclamation by the Petrograd Soviet to the Peoples of the World, March 27, 1917.[1]

(*Izvestia*,[2] March 28, 1917.)

Comrade proletarians and all laboring people of all countries:

We, Russian workingmen and soldiers, united in the Petrograd Soviet of Workers' and Soldiers' Deputies, are sending

[1] The Petrograd Soviet of Workers' and Soldiers' Deputies began to assert its power in the early days of the Revolution. E. H. Wilcox, an English correspondent, in his book entitled *Russia's Ruin*, gives an interesting account of what took place on March 12.

"Simultaneously with the meeting in No. 12 Committee Room, the Provisional Committee of the Duma had been constituting itself in another part of the building, and Prince Lvov's Cabinet was the result of negotiations between this body and the Executive Committee of the Soviet. Of the course of these negotiations very little has been revealed. It is known, however, that the Soviet leaders were urged to join the Cabinet but refused. . . ."

"From the very outset the Petrograd Soviet was the only body the authority of which was acknowledged by those who had supplied the element of physical force in bringing about the Revolution, that is to say the garrison and factory hands of the Capital" (pp. 154, 161).

In a report to the conference of Soviets in March, 1917, Steklov, then member of the Executive Committee of the Petrograd Soviet, said: "In the first days of the Revolution the Petrograd Soviet was in a position to take power into its own hands. It did not do so but left it to the State Duma to organize the Provisional Government. It even refused to participate in that Government but decided to influence it from without. . . . The Soviet decided to limit itself to presenting to the Provisional Government definite political demands, and without influencing directly the composition of the Cabinet, which means without recommending directly desirable candidates for ministers, to confine itself to the right to veto those candidates who are definitely undesirable and definitely opposed and dangerous to the Revolution" (*Izvestia*, No. 32).

[2] The *Izvestia* (Bulletins) of the Petrograd Soviet of Workers' and Soldiers' Deputies was the organ of that body. In August, 1917, it became also the organ of the All-Russian Central Executive Committee of the Soviets of Workers' and Soldiers' Deputies. It supported successive Provisional Governments. After the November revolution the *Izvestia* became the official organ of the Soviet Government.

you our fiery greetings and announce the great event. The Russian democracy threw down into the dust the age-long despotism of the Tsar, and is joining your family as an equal member and as a mighty force in the struggle for our common liberation. Our victory is a great victory of world freedom and democracy. The stronghold of world reaction and the "gendarme of Europe" is no more. Let the earth on its grave be like a heavy stone. Long live freedom! Long live the international solidarity of the proletariat and its struggle for final victory!

Our work is not finished yet: the shadows of the old order have not yet been scattered, and not a few enemies are gathering force against the Russian revolution. But our gains are tremendous. The peoples of Russia will express their will in the Constituent Assembly, which will be called as soon as is possible on the basis of universal, equal, direct, and secret suffrage. And already it may be said without a doubt that a democratic republic will triumph in Russia. The Russian people now possess full political liberty. They can now assert their mighty power in the internal affairs of the country and in its foreign policy. And, appealing to all the peoples, who are being destroyed and ruined in the monstrous war, we announce that the time has come to start a decisive struggle against the intentions of conquest on the part of the governments of all countries; the time has come for the peoples to take into their own hands the decision of the question of war and peace.

Conscious of its revolutionary power the Russian democracy announces that it will, by every means, resist the policy of conquest of its ruling classes, and it calls upon the peoples of Europe for concerted decisive actions in favor of peace.

And we are appealing to our brother-proletarians of the Austro-German coalition and first of all to the German proletariat. From the first days of the war you were assured that by raising arms against autocratic Russia, you were defending the culture of Europe from Asiatic despotism. Many of you saw in this a justification of that support which you were giving to the war. Now even this justification is gone: democratic Russia cannot be a threat to liberty and civilization.

We will firmly defend our own liberty from all reactionary attempts from within as well as from without. The Russian revolution will not retreat before the bayonets of conquerors and will not allow itself to be crushed by foreign military force. But we are calling to you: throw off the yoke of your semi-autocratic rule in the same way that the Russian people shook off the Tsar's autocracy; refuse to serve as an instrument of conquest and violence in the hands of kings, landowners, and bankers—and by co-ordinated efforts we will stop the horrible butchery, which is disgracing humanity and is beclouding the great days of the birth of Russian freedom.

Laboring people of all countries: We are stretching out in a brotherly fashion our hands to you over the mountains of corpses of our brothers, across rivers of innocent blood and tears, over the smoking ruins of cities and villages, over the wreckage of the treasures of culture,—we appeal to you for the re-establishment and strengthening of international unity. That will be the security for our future victories and the complete liberation of humanity.

Proletarians of all countries, unite!

PETROGRAD SOVIET OF WORKER'S AND SOLDIERS' DEPUTIES.

[6.]

Statement by the Provisional Government regarding the War, April 9, 1917.

(*Izvestia*, April 11, 1917.)

Citizens:

The Provisional Government after considering the military situation of the Russian state, in view of its duty to the country, decided to directly and openly tell the people the entire truth.

The Government which was overthrown left the defense of the country in a thoroughly disorganized condition. By its criminal inactivity and its inefficient methods it brought disorganization into our finances, into the work of food-supply and transportation, into the work of supplying the army. It has undermined our economic system.

The Provisional Government, with the active and vigorous assistance of the entire people, will make every effort to correct these burdensome consequences of the old régime. But time does not wait. The blood of numerous sons of the fatherland was flowing without measure during these two and a half long years of war, but the country still remains under the blows of a powerful enemy, which has occupied whole provinces of our country, and now, in the days of the birth of Russian freedom, is threatening us with a new decisive attack.

[13.]

Call by the Petrograd Soviet for an International Congress, June 2, 1917.

(*Izvestia*, June 3, 1917.)

The Executive Committee of the Petrograd Soviet of Workers' and Soldiers' Deputies at its meeting on June 2 adopted the following appeal to the Socialist parties and central trade union organizations of the whole world:

On the 28th of March the Petrograd Soviet of Workers' and Soldiers' Deputies issued an appeal "To the Peoples of the Whole World," in which it asked "the peoples of Europe to make united, decisive attempts in favor of peace." The Soviet of Workers' and Soldiers' Deputies, and with it the entire Democracy, wrote on their banner: "Peace without annexations and indemnities, on the basis of self-determination for all nations."

The Russian Democracy compelled the first Provisional Government to recognize this platform and, as was proved by events of the 3d and 4th of May, did not allow the first Provisional Government to deviate from it. The second Russian Provisional Government at the insistance of the Soviet of Workers' and Soldiers' Deputies made this platform the first point of its declaration.

On the 9th of May the Executive Committee of the Soviet of Workers' and Soldiers' Deputies resolved to take upon itself the initiative of calling the international Socialist conference and on the 15th of May issued an appeal "To the Socialists of all Countries" asking them to join in a common struggle for peace.

The Soviet of Workers' and Soldiers' Deputies believes that the quickest way of ending the war and establishing peace on conditions demanded by the common interests of the laboring masses and of the entire human race, can be accomplished only by the internationally united efforts of labor parties and trade union organizations of the warring and neutral countries in an energetic and stubborn struggle against the world butchery. The first necessary and decisive step in the cause of the organization of such an international movement is the calling of an international conference. Its principal aim must be an agreement among the representatives of the Socialist proletariat regarding the liquidation of the policy of "national unity" with the imperialistic governments and classes, which excludes the possibility of a struggle for peace, as well as an agreement regarding the means and methods of this struggle. An international agreement for the purpose of putting an end to this policy seems to be essential as a preliminary condition for the organization of the struggle on an international and broad basis. This road has been pointed out to the proletariat by all its international agreements.

The calling of such a conference is also urgently dictated by the common vital interests of the proletariat and of all the peoples.

Parties and organizations of laboring classes which share these views and are ready to unite their efforts for carrying them into effect are invited by the Soviet to participate in the conference which is being called.

At the same time the Soviet expresses its firm conviction that all parties and organizations which accept this invitation will take upon themselves the obligation to carry out firmly all the decisions which may be adopted by the conference.

The meeting place of the conference the Soviet decided should be Stockholm; the time, July 8, 1917.

[14.]

Note from President Wilson to the Russian Government, May 26, 1917.[1]

(*New York Times Current History*, Vol. VI, Part 2, p. 49.)

In view of the approaching visit of the American Delegation to Russia [2] to express the deep friendship of the American people

for the people of Russia, and to discuss the best and most practical means of co-operation between the two peoples in carrying the present struggle for the freedom of all peoples to a successful

---

[1] The Note was published in the United States on the 10th of June.
[2] The American Mission arrived in Petrograd June 13, 1917. It was composed of Elihu Root, John R. Mott, Charles P. Crane, Cyrus H. McCormick, Samuel R. Bertron, James Duncan, Charles Edward Russell, Major-General Hugh L. Scott, and Rear-Admiral James H. Glennon. It left Russia July 10.

consummation, it seems opportune and appropriate that I should state again, in the light of this new partnership, the objects the United States has had in mind in entering the war. Those objects have been very much beclouded during the last few weeks by mistaken and misleading statements, and the issues at stake are too momentous, too tremendous, too significant for the whole human race to permit any misinterpretations or misunderstandings, however slight, to remain uncorrected for a moment.

The war has begun to go against Germany, and in their desperate desire to escape the inevitable ultimate defeat those who are in authority in Germany are using every possible instrumentality, are making use even of the influence of groups and parties among their own subjects to whom they have never been just or fair or even tolerant, to promote a propaganda on both sides of the sea which will preserve for them their influence at home and their power abroad, to the undoing of the very men they are using.

The position of America in this war is so clearly avowed that no man can be excused for mistaking it. She seeks no material profit or aggrandizement of any kind. She is fighting for no advantage or selfish object of her own, but for the liberation of peoples everywhere from the aggressions of autocratic force. The ruling classes in Germany have begun of late to profess a like liberality and justice of purpose, but only to preserve the power they have set up in Germany and the selfish advantages which they have wrongfully gained for themselves and their private projects of power all the way from Berlin to Bagdad and beyond. Government after Government has by their influence, without open conquest of its territory, been linked together in a net of intrigue directed against nothing less than the peace and liberty of the world. The meshes of that intrigue must be broken, but cannot be broken unless wrongs already done are undone: and adequate measures must be taken to prevent it from ever being rewoven or repaired.

Of course, the Imperial German Government and those whom it is using for their own undoing, are seeking to obtain pledges that the war will end in the restoration of the status quo ante. It was the status quo ante out of which this iniquitous war issued forth, the power of the Imperial German Government within the empire and its widespread domination and influence outside of that empire. That status must be altered in such fashion as to prevent any such hideous thing from ever happening again.

We are fighting for the liberty, the self-government, and the undictated development of all peoples, and every feature of the settlement that concludes this war must be conceived and executed for that purpose. Wrongs must first be righted, and then adequate safeguards must be created to prevent their being committed again. We ought not to consider remedies merely because they have a pleasing and sonorous sound. Practical questions can be settled only by practical means. Phrases will not accomplish the result. Effective readjustments will; and whatever readjustments are necessary must be made.

But they must follow a principle, and that principle is plain. No people must be forced under sovereignty under which it does not wish to live. No territory must change hands except for the purpose of securing those who inhabit it a fair chance of life and liberty. No indemnities must be insisted on except those that constitute payment for manifest wrongs done. No readjustments of power must be made except such as will tend to secure the future peace of the world and the future welfare and happiness of its peoples.

And then the free peoples of the world must draw together in some common covenant, some genuine and practical co-operation that will in effect combine their force to secure peace and justice in the dealings of nations with one another. The brotherhood of mankind must no longer be a fair but empty phrase; it must be given a structure of force and reality. The nations must realize their common life and effect a workable partnership to secure that life against the aggressions of autocratic and self-pleasing power.

For these things we can afford to pour out blood and treasure. For these are the things we have always professed to desire, and unless we pour out blood and treasure now and succeed, we may never be able to unite or show conquering force again in the great cause of human liberty. The day has come to conquer or submit. If the forces of autocracy can divide us they will overcome us; if we stand together, victory is certain and the liberty which victory will secure. We can afford, then, to be generous, but we cannot afford, then or now, to be weak or omit any single guaranty of justice and security.

[15.]

Note from the Provisional Government to the Allies, published June 16, 1917.

(*Izvestia*, June 16, 1917.)

The Minister of Foreign Affairs, Tereshchenko, transmitted to the Allied Governments the following note:

The Russian Revolution is not only an upheaval in the internal system of Russia, but also a mighty movement of ideas which expresses the will of the Russian people in their aspiration for equality, freedom, and justice, in the internal life of the State as well as in the realm of international relations. From this will the members of the Russian Revolutionary Government draw their strength, serving this will is their duty and purpose.

Defending in the foreign struggle the great principles of freedom, Russia is aiming to attain a general peace on a basis excluding every kind of violence regardless of its source, as well as all imperialistic intentions, in all their forms. Russia has no designs of conquest whatsoever and emphatically protests against any attempts in this direction. True to these principles, the Russian people firmly decided to struggle against open or secret imperialistic intentions of our enemies in the political, as well as in the financial and economic domains.

Though in regard to the aims of the war there may be differences of views between our Government and Allied Governments, we have no doubt that the close union between Russia and her Allies will insure complete mutual agreement on all questions on the basis of the principles proclaimed by the Russian Revolution.

Remaining unshakably true to the general Allied cause, the Russian democracy welcomes the decision of those of the Allied Powers which expressed readiness to meet the desire of the Russian Provisional Government to subject to reconsideration the agreements concerning the ultimate aims of the war. We suggest that there be called for this purpose a conference of representatives of Allied Powers, which could take place as soon as there are favorable conditions for it. But one of the agreements, the one which was signed in London on September 5, 1914, and which has been published since then, and which excludes the possibility of conclusion by one of the Allied

Powers of a separate peace, must not be a subject of discussion at this conference.

[16.]

Note from Secretary Lansing, explaining the Aims of the American Extraordinary Mission to Russia, published June 19, 1917.

(*New York Times Current History*, Vol. VI, Part 2, p. 58.)

The High Commission now on its way from this country to Russia is sent primarily to manifest to the Russian Governlent and people the deep sympathetic feeling which exists among all classes in America for the adherence of Russia to the principle of democracy, which has been the foundation of the progress and prosperity of this country. The High Commissioners go to convey the greetings of this Republic to the new and powerful member which has joined the great family of democratic nations.

The Commissioners who will bear this fraternal message to the people of Russia have been selected by the President with the special purpose of giving representation to the various elements which make up the American people and to show that among them all there is the same love of country and the same devotion to liberty and justice and loyalty to constituted authority. The Commission is not chosen from one political-group, but from the various groups into which the American electorate is divided. United, they represent the Republic. However much they may differ on public questions, they are one in support of democracy and in hostility to the enemies of democracy throughout the world.

The Commission is prepared, if the Russian Government desires, to confer upon the best ways and means to bring about effective co-operation between the two Governments in the prosecution of the war against the German autocracy, which is to-day the gravest menace to all democratic Governments. It is the view of this Government that it has become the solemn duty of those who love democracy and individual liberty to render harmless this autocratic Government, whose ambition, aggression, and intrigue have been disclosed in the present struggle. Whatever the cost in life and treasure, the supreme object should be and can be attained only by the united strength of the democracies of the world, and only then can come that permanent and universal peace which is the hope of all people.

To the common cause of humanity, which Russia has so courageously and unflinchingly supported for nearly three years, the United States is pledged. To co-operate and aid Russia in the accomplishment of the task, which as a great democracy is more truly hers to-day than ever before, is the desire of the United States. To stand side by side, shoulder to shoulder against autocracy, will unite the American and Russian peoples in a friendship for the ages.

With this spirit, the High Commissioners of the United States will present themselves in the confident hope that the Russian Government and people will realize how sincerely the United States hopes for their welfare and desires to share with them in their future endeavors to bring victory to the cause of democracy and human liberty.

[17.]

Address delivered by the Honorable Elihu Root, to the Russian Provisional Government, June 15, 1917.

(Published in pamphlet by American Consulate, Petrograd, 1917.[1])

Mr. President and Members of the Council of Ministers:

The Mission for which I have the honor to speak is charged by the Government and people of the United States of America with a message to the Government and people of Russia. The Mission comes from a democratic Republic. Its members are commissioned and instructed by a President who holds his high office as Chief Executive of more than 100,000,000 free people by virtue of popular election, in which more than 18,000,000 votes were freely cast, and fairly counted pursuant to law, by universal, equal, direct, and secret suffrage.

For one hundred and forty years our people have been struggling with the hard problems of self-government. With many shortcomings, many mistakes, many imperfections, we still have maintained order and respect for law, individual freedom, and national independence. Under the security of our own laws, we have grown in strength and prosperity. But we

[1] See also *New York Times Current History*, Vol. VI, Part 2, p. 57.

value our freedom more than wealth. We love liberty, and we cherish above all our possessions the ideals for which our fathers fought and suffered and sacrificed that America might be free.

We believe in the competence of the power of democracy, and in our heart of hearts abides faith in the coming of a better world in which the humble and oppressed of all lands may be lifted up by freedom to a heritage of justice and equal opportunity.

The news of Russia's new-found freedom brought to America universal satisfaction and joy. From all the land sympathy and hope went out to the new sister in the circle of democracies. And the Mission is sent to express that feeling.

The American democracy sends to the democracy of Russia a greeting of sympathy, friendship, brotherhood, Godspeed. Distant America knows little of the special conditions of Russian life which must give form to the Government and to the laws which you are about to create. As we have developed our institutions to serve the needs of our national character and life, so we assume that you will develop your institutions to serve the needs of Russian character and life.

As we look across the sea we distinguish no party, no class. We see great Russia as a whole, as one mighty, striving, aspiring democracy. We know the self-control, essential kindliness, strong common sense, courage, and noble idealism of the Russian character. We have faith in you all. We pray for God's blessing upon you all. We believe you will solve your problems, that you will march side by side in the triumphant progress of democracy until the old order everywhere has passed away and the world is free.

One fearful danger threatens the liberty of both nations. The armed forces of a military autocracy are at the gates of Russia and of her Allies. The triumph of German arms will mean the death of liberty in Russia. No enemy is at the gates of America, but America has come to realize that the triumph of German arms means the death of liberty in the world; that we who love liberty and would keep it must fight for it, and fight for it now when the free democracies of the world may be strong in union, and not delay until they may be beaten down separately in succession.

So America sends another message to Russia—that we are going to fight for your freedom equally with our own, and we ask you to fight for our freedom equally with yours. We would make your cause ours, and, with a common purpose and mutual helpfulness of a firm alliance, make sure of victory over our common foe.

You will recognize your own sentiments and purposes in the words of President Wilson to the American Congress, when on the 2nd of April last he advised a declaration of war against Germany. He said:

"We are accepting this challenge of hostile purpose because we know that in such a government (the German Government), following such methods, we can never have a friend; and that in the presence of its organized power, always lying in wait to accomplish we know not what purpose, there can be no assured security for the democratic governments of the world. We are about to accept the gage of battle with this natural foe to liberty and shall, if necessary, spend the whole force of the nation to check and nullify its pretensions and its power. We are glad, now that we see the facts with no veil of false pretense about them, to fight thus for the ultimate peace of the world and for the liberation of its peoples, the German peoples included; for the rights of nations great and small and the privilege of men everywhere to choose their way of life and of obedience. The world must be made safe for democracy. Its peace must be planted upon the tested foundations of political liberty. We have no selfish ends to serve. We desire no conquest, no dominion. We seek no indemnities for ourselves, no material compensation for the sacrifices we shall freely make. We are but one of the champions of the rights of mankind. We shall be satisfied when those rights have been made as secure as the faith and the freedom of nations can make them."

President Wilson further said:

"Does not every American feel that assurance has been added to our hope for the future peace of the world by the wonderful and heartening things that have been happening within the last few weeks in Russia? Russia was known by those who knew it best to have been always in fact democratic at heart, in all the vital habits of her thought, in all the intimate relationships of her people that spoke their natural instinct, their habitual attitude towards life. The autocracy that crowned the summit of her political structure, long as it had stood and terrible as was the reality of its power, was not in fact Russian in origin, character, or purpose, and now it has been shaken off and the great generous Russian people have been added in all their naïve majesty and might to the forces that are fighting for freedom in the world, for justice and for peace. Here is a fit partner for a League of Honor."

That partnership of honor in the great struggle for human freedom, the oldest of the great democracies now seeks in fraternal union with the youngest.

The practical and specific methods and possibilities of our allied co-operation, the members of the Mission would be glad to discuss with the members of the Government of Russia.

[18.]

Address by President Wilson, welcoming Boris A. Bakhmeteff, the new Russian Ambassador to the United States, July 5, 1917.

(*New York Times Current History*, Vol. VI, Part 2, p. 208.)

Mr. Ambassador:

To the keen satisfaction which I derived from the fact that the Government of the United States was the first to welcome, by its official recognition, the new Democracy of Russia to the family of free States is added the exceptional pleasure which I experience in now receiving from your hand the letters whereby the Provisional Government of Russia accredits you as its Ambassador Extraordinary and Plenipotentiary to the United States, and in according to you formal recognition as the first Ambassador of Free Russia to this country.

For the people of Russia the people of the United States have ever entertained friendly feelings, which have now been greatly deepened by the knowledge that, actuated by the same lofty motives, the two Governments and peoples are co-operating to bring to a successful termination the conflict now raging for human liberty and a universal acknowledgment of those principles of right and justice which should direct all Governments. I feel convinced that when this happy day shall come no small share of the credit will be due to the devoted people of Russia, who, overcoming disloyalty from within and intrigue from without, remain steadfast to the cause.

The Mission which it was my pleasure to send to Russia has already assured the Provisional Government that in this momentous struggle and in the problems that confront and will confront the free Government of Russia, that Government may count on the steadfast friendship of the Government of the United States and its constant co-operation in all desired appropriate directions.

It only remains for me to give expression to my admiration of the way in which the Provisional Government of Russia are meeting all requirements, to my entire sympathy with them in their noble object to insure to the people of Russia the blessings of freedom and of equal rights and opportunity, and to my faith that through their efforts Russia will assume her rightful place among the great free nations of the world.

[19.]

Statement by Mr. Root on the Work of the Mission, July 10, 1917.

(*New York Times Current History*, Vol. VI, Part 2, p. 212.)

The Mission has accomplished what it came here to do, and we are greatly encouraged. We found no organic or incurable malady in the Russian Democracy. Democracies are always in trouble, and we have seen days just as dark in the progress of our own.

We must remember that a people in whom all constructive effort has been suppressed for so long cannot immediately develop a genius for quick action. The first stage is necessarily one of debate. The solid, admirable traits in the Russian character will pull the nation through the present crisis. Natural love of law and order and capacity for local self-government have been demonstrated every day since the Revolution. The country's most serious lack is money and adequate transportation. We shall do what we can to help Russia in both.

[20.]

Statement by the Provisional Government to the Allied Powers, August 1, 1917.

(*Izvestia*, August 1, 1917.)

In the hour of the great, new misfortunes which have fallen to Russia's lot,[1] we consider it necessary to tell firmly and decisively to our Allies, who have been sharing with us the hardships of former trials, our view of the future of the war.

The greatness of the problem of the Russian Revolution conditioned a fundamental change in the life of the State, and the rebuilding, while facing the enemy, of the entire system of government could not have passed without serious shocks. Nevertheless, Russia, realizing that there were no other means of salvation for the fatherland, continued, in unison with the Allies, the common effort at the front. Russia took upon herself, while fully realizing the difficulty of the problem, the burden of actively carrying on the war at the same time as she was rebuilding her army and her government. The offensive of our armies, necessary in view of the strategic situation, met with insurmountable obstacles, both in the rear and at the front. The criminal propaganda of irresponsible elements, which was taken advantage of by enemy agents, brought about a rebellion in Petrograd. At the same time, a part of the troops at the front, under the influence of the same agitation, forgot their duty to the fatherland and opened to the enemy a way for a break in our front. The Russian people, shocked by these events, manifested through its Government, created by the revolution, its irresistible will: the rebellion is suppressed and the guilty are brought to trial. At the front measures were taken to re-establish the fighting capacity of the army. The Government intends to accomplish the work of strengthening its power, to resist all dangers and to lead the country to the road of revolutionary regeneration.

In the inflexible decision to continue the war until the com-

[1] July 1. Offensive against the Germans renewed.
July 9. Successful counter-offensive by Germans.
July 15. Resignation of five Constitutional Democrats from the Cabinet because of the Ukranian situation.
July 17-19. Street disorders, with fatalities, in Petrograd. The Provisional Government placed the blame on the leaders of the Bolshevik Party, who denied the charge.
July 20. Kerensky succeeded Prince Lvov as Premier.

plete victory of ideals proclaimed by the Russian Revolution, Russia will not retreat before any difficulties. Replying to the threats of the enemy with renewed courage, the nation and the army will accomplish the great work of reconstruction and, entering upon the fourth year of war, will make all the necessary preparations for a further campaign. We sincerely believe that the sacred cause of the defense of our beloved fatherland will unite all the efforts of Russian citizens, that the great enthusiasm, which has fired their hearts with faith in the triumph of freedom, will direct the entire irresistible force of the Revolution against the enemy who is threatening the fatherland. We know that upon the result of this struggle depends our freedom and the freedom of humanity, and new trials, brought about by treachery and crime, will only strengthen the determination of the Russian people, conscious of the necessity for a great sacrifice, to give all their strength and all their possessions for the salvation of the fatherland.

Strong with this conviction, we are convinced that the temporary retreat of our armies will not prevent them, reorganized and reinforced, from going forward at the given hour in defense of fatherland and freedom, and accomplishing victoriously the great end for which they are forced to fight.

[21.]

Speech by Mr. Root in New York, August 12, 1917.

(*New York Times Current History*, Vol. VI, Part 2, p. 436.)

The extraordinary ease with which the Tsar's Government was removed was due not merely to the fact that it was an autocracy, but also to the fact that it did not govern efficiently; it was not up to the job; it had allowed Russia to drift into a position where there was vast confusion and they were on the verge of bankruptcy, and the Government had become, practically, merely a government of suppression, a government of negatives that ceased to lead the people, so that the Tsar and the bureaucracy were slipped off as easily as a crab sheds its hard shell when the proper time comes.

Now, into that state of affairs there came intervention by that malevolent power which is intermeddling with the affairs of every nation upon earth, stirring up discord, stimulating, feeding, financing all the forces of evil—doing it here among us now—that power which finds its account in alliance with all evil passions, all the sordid impulses of humanity in every nation of the world, entered into Russia. Thousands of agents poured over the border immediately upon the revolution.

Notwithstanding all this, in a country with no Central Government that had power to enforce its decrees, in a country with no police, a country in which the sanction and moral obligation of the laws had disappeared with the disappearance of the Tsar, there reigned order to a higher degree than has existed in the United States of America during this period.

In the first enthusiasm for freedom in the liberation of political prisoners a great many ordinary criminal prisoners were also released, and they went about and committed some depredations, which, of course, all found their way into the newspapers, but even with that the general average of peace and order, of respect for property and life in Russia, was higher than could reasonably be expected from any 180,000,000 people in the world under any Government.

Now, that extraordinary phenomenon called for a study, a careful study, not merely from the newspapers or from talking with government officials, but by countless serious interviews and conversations with men of all grades and stripes, and callings and conditions of life, and those studies satisfied all the members of this mission that the Russian people possessed to a very high degree qualities that are necessary for successful self-government. They have self-control equaled in few countries in the world. They have persistency of purpose; they have a most kindly and ingrained respect—not only respect, regard for the rights of others. They will not willingly do an injustice to any one, and that sense of justice carries with it a broad character. They have a noble idealism which is developed and exhibited in the minds that are enlarged by education, and they have a strong sense of the mission of liberty in the world, and they have an extraordinary capacity for concerted action.

If their character is unequal to the task, all the aid of all the great countries in the world cannot give them their freedom. Freedom must find its foundation, its sure foundation, within the people themselves, and we think the Russians have that sure foundation. . . .

No one can tell what the outcome will be, but this is certain, that Russia, tired of the war, worn and harried by war; Russia, which has lost 7,000,000 of her sons, every village in mourning, every family bereaved, Russia has again taken up the heavy burden; she has restored the discipline of her army; she has put away the bright vision of peace and rest, and returned yet again to the sacrifice and the suffering of war in order that she might continue free.

[22.]

Message from President Wilson to the National Conference in Moscow, August 26, 1917.[1]

(*New York Times Current History*, Vol. VII, Part 1, p. 67.)

President of the National Council Assembly, Moscow:

I take the liberty to send to the members of the great council now meeting in Moscow the cordial greetings of their friends, the people of the United States, to express their confidence in the ultimate triumph of ideals of democracy and self-government against all enemies within and without, and to give their renewed assurance of every material and moral assistance they can extend to the Government of Russia in the promotion of the common cause in which the two nations are unselfishly united.

WOODROW WILSON.

[23.]

Statement by the Provisional Government, October 8, 1917.[2]

(*The Messenger of the Provisional Government*, October 11, 1917.)

Great confusion has once more been brought into the life of our country. In spite of the swift suppression of the revolt

---

[1] The National Conference met in Moscow August 26, 1917. It was composed of representatives of the four Dumas, of the Peasants, of the Soviets of Workers' and Soldiers' Deputies, of the Municipalities, of the Union of Zemstvos and Towns, of Industrial Organizations and Banks, of Co-operative Organizations, and of Trade Unions.

[2] Disasters multiplied during the autumn. Riga fell on September 3. The revolt under General Kornilov (September 9-15) weakened the Provisional Government still further. A Democratic Conference on a widely representative basis called by the Executive Committee of the Soviets of Workers', Soldiers', and Peasants' Deputies met on September 27. The Cabinet was reorganized under Kerensky and attempted to grapple with the difficulties of the situation.

of General Kornilov, the shocks caused by it are threatening the very existence of the Russian Republic.

Waves of anarchy are sweeping over the land, the pressure of the foreign enemy is increasing, counter-revolutionary elements are raising their heads, hoping that the prolonged governmental crisis, coupled with the weariness which has seized the entire nation, will enable them to murder the freedom of the Russian people.

Great, boundless is the responsibility of the Provisional Government, on whom devolves the historic task of bringing Russia to a state where the convocation of the Constituent Assembly will be possible. The burden of this responsibility is alleviated only by the deep conviction that, united by the common desire to save the fatherland and to protect the achievements of the Revolution, the representatives of all classes of the Russian people will understand the necessity for co-operation with the Provisional Government in establishing a firm governmental power, capable of realizing the urgent demands of the country and bringing it, without further upheavals, to the Constituent Assembly, the convocation of which, it is the deep conviction of the Provisional Government, cannot be postponed for one day.

Leaving to the Constituent Assembly, the sovereign master of Russia, the final solution of all great questions on which the welfare of the Russian people depends, the Provisional Government, the personnel of which has now been completed, holds that only by carrying out energetically a series of resolute measures in all spheres of the life of the State, will it be able to fulfill its duty and satisfy the urgent needs of the nation.

In the firm conviction that only a general peace will enable our great fatherland to develop all its creative forces, the Provisional Government will continue incessantly to develop its active foreign policy in the spirit of the democratic principles proclaimed by the Russian Revolution. The Revolution has made these principles a national possession, its aim being to attain a general peace—a peace excluding violence on either side.

Acting in complete accord with the Allies, the Provisional Government will, in the next few days, take part in the conference of the Allied Powers. At this conference the Provisional Government will be represented, among other Delegates, by one who particularly enjoys the confidence of the democratic organizations.

At this conference our representatives, together with the solution of common questions and military problems, will strive towards an agreement with the Allies on the ground of the principles proclaimed by the Russian Revolution.

Striving for peace, the Provisional Government will, however, use all its forces for the protection of the common, Allied cause, for the defense of the country, for resolute resistance to any efforts to wrest national territory from us and impose the will of any foreign power on Russia, and for the repulsion of the enemies' troops from the borders of the fatherland. . . .

For the purpose of securing for the revolutionary authorities close contact with the organized public forces and thus imparting to the Government the necessary stability and power, the Provisional Government will in the next few days work out and publish a decree establishing a Provisional Council of the Republic,[1] which is to function until the Constituent Assembly convenes. This Council, in which all classes of the population will be represented and in which the delegates elected to the Democratic Conference will also participate, will be given the right of addressing questions to the Government and of securing replies to them in a definite period of time, of working out legislative acts and discussing all those questions which will be presented for consideration by the Provisional Government, as well as those which will arise on its own initiative. Resting on the co-operation of such a council, the Government, preserving in accordance with its oath, the unity of the governmental power created by the Revolution, will regard it its duty to consider the great public significance of such a council in all its acts up to the time when the Constituent Assembly will give full and complete representation to all classes of the population of Russia.

Standing firmly on this program, which expresses the hopes of the people, and calling upon all for immediate and active participation in the preparations for the convocation of the Constituent Assembly in the shortest period of time, the Provisional Government presumes that all citizens of Russia will now rally closely to its support for concerted work, in the name of the basic and paramount problems of our time, the defense of the fatherland from the foreign enemy, the restoration of law and

---

[1] This body, better known as the Preliminary Parliament, met on October 20. Its life was ended by the Bolshevik Revolution on November 7, 1917.

order and the leading of the country to the sovereign Constituent Assembly.

[24.]

Kerensky's Interview with The Associated Press, November 1, 1917.[1]

(*New York Times*, November 3, 1917.)

Petrograd, Thursday, November 1.

In view of reports reaching Petrograd that the impression was spreading abroad that Russia was virtually out of the war, Premier Kerensky discussed the present condition of the country frankly to-day with The Associated Press. . . .

"Russia has fought consistently since the beginning," he said. "She saved France and England from disaster early in the war. She is worn out by the strain and claims as her right that the Allies now shoulder the burden."

The correspondent called attention to widely contradictory reports on Russian conditions, and asked the Premier for a frank statement of the facts.

"It has been said by travelers returning from England and elsewhere to America that opinion among the people, not officially but generally, is that Russia is virtually out of the war," was explained.

"Is Russia out of the war?" Premier Kerensky repeated the words and laughed. "That," he answered, "is a ridiculous question. Russia is taking an enormous part in the war. One

[1] The interview first appeared on Nov. 2 in a much shorter form. The startling headlines given it by some papers resulted in the following statement by the State Department (*New York Times*, Nov. 3, 1917):

"There has been absolutely nothing in the dispatches received by the Department of State from Russia nor in information derived from any other sources whatever, to justify the impression created by the *Washington Post* to-day, principally by the headline 'Russia Quits War,' that Russia is out of the conflict. A reading of the full interview with Premier Kerensky, of which the paper published only an abbreviated and preliminary account, itself shows that the headline is entirely unwarranted.

"Our own advices show that the Provisional Government in Petrograd is attacking with great energy the problems confronting it. Reports received from Petrograd by mail and telegraph show that Premier Kerensky and his Government, far from yielding to discouragement, are still animated by a strong determination to organize all Russia's resources in a whole-hearted resistance and carry the war through to a victorious completion. At the same time this Government, like those of the Allies, is rendering all possible assistance."

has only to remember history. Russia began the war for the Allies. While she was already fighting, England was only preparing and America was only observing.

"Russia at the beginning bore the whole brunt of the fighting, thereby saving Great Britain and France. People who say she is out of the war have short memories. We have fought since the beginning and have the right to claim that the Allies now take the heaviest part of the burden on their shoulders.

"At present Russian public opinion is greatly agitated by the question: 'Where is the great British fleet now that the German fleet is out in the Baltic?'

"Russia," the Premier repeated, "is worn out. She has been fighting one and one-half years longer than England."

"Could an American army be of use if sent to Russia?" was asked.

"It would be impossible to send one," said Kerensky. "It is a question of transport. The difficulties are too great."

"If America cannot send troops, what would be the most useful way for her to help Russia?" was the next question.

"Have her send boots, leather, iron, and," the Premier added emphatically, "money."

Premier Kerensky here drew attention to the fact that Russia has fought her battles alone.

"Russia has fought alone—is fighting alone," he said. "France has had England to help her from the start, and now America has come in."

The Premier was asked regarding the morale of the Russian people and army. He answered:

"The masses are worn out economically. The disorganized state of life in general has had a psychological effect on the people. They doubt the possibility of the attainment of their hopes."

"What is the lesson to the democracies of the world of the Russian Revolution?"

"This," Premier Kerensky replied, "is for them to find out. They must not lose faith in the Russian Revolution because it is not a political revolution but an economic one and a revolution of facts. The Russian Revolution is only seven months old. No-one has the right to feel disillusioned about it. It will take years to develop.

"In France, which is only as large as three Russian departments (States) it took five years for their revolution to develop fully."

Asked what he expected from the Constituent Assembly, the Premier said:

"The Constituent Assembly begins a new chapter in the history of the revolution. Its voice certainly will be the most important factor in the future of Russia."

"What future do you picture for Russia after the war?"

"No-one can draw any real picture of the future," Kerensky said. "Naturally a man who really loves his country will hope for all good things, but that is only his viewpoint which may or may not be accepted by others."

[25.]

Decree of Peace.

ADOPTED UNANIMOUSLY AT A MEETING OF THE ALL-RUSSIAN CONVENTION OF SOVIETS OF WORKERS', SOLDIERS', AND PEASANTS' DEPUTIES, ON NOVEMBER 8, 1917.

(*Izvestia*, November 9, 1917.)

The Workers' and Peasants' Government, created by the revolution of the 24th and 25th of October (November 6 and 7), and based on the Soviet of Workers', Soldiers', and Peasants' Deputies, proposes to all warring peoples and their governments to begin immediately negotiations for a just and democratic peace.

An overwhelming majority of the exhausted, wearied, and war-tortured workers and the laboring classes of all the warring countries are longing for a just and democratic peace—a peace which in the most definite and insistent manner was demanded by Russian workers and peasants after the overthrow of the Tsar's monarchy. Such a peace the Government considers to be an immediate peace without annexations (i.e., without seizure of foreign territory, without the forcible annexation of foreign nationalities) and without indemnities.

The Government of Russia proposes to all warring peoples immediately to conclude such a peace. It expresses its readiness to take at once without the slightest delay, all the decisive steps until the final confirmation of all terms of such a peace by the plenipotentiary conventions of the representatives of all countries and all nations.

By annexation or seizure of foreign territory the Government understands, in accordance with the legal consciousness of democracy in general, and of laboring classes in particular, any addition to a large or powerful State of a small or weak nationality, without the definitely, clearly, and voluntarily expressed consent and desire of this nationality, regardless of when this forcible addition took place, regardless also of how developed or how backward is the nation forcibly attached or forcibly retained within the frontiers of a given State, and finally regardless of the fact whether this nation is located in Europe or in distant lands beyond the seas.

If any nation whatsoever is retained within the frontiers of a certain State by force, if it is not given the right of free voting in accordance with its desire, regardless of the fact whether such desire was expressed in the press, in people's assemblies, in decisions of political parties, or rebellions and insurrections against national oppression, such plebiscite to take place under the condition of the complete removal of the armies of the annexing or the more powerful nation; if the weaker nation is not given the opportunity to decide the question of the forms of its national existence, then its adjoining is an annexation, that is, seizure—violence.

The Government considers it to be the greatest crime against humanity to continue the war for the sake of dividing among the powerful and rich nations the weaker nationalities which were seized by them, and the Government solemnly states its readiness to sign immediately the terms of peace which will end this war, on the basis of the above-stated conditions, equally just for all nationalities without exception. At the same time the Government announces that it does not consider the above-stated conditions of peace as in the nature of an ultimatum, that is, it is ready to consider any other terms of peace, insisting, however, that such be proposed as soon as possible by any one of the warring countries and on condition of the most definite clarity and absolute exclusion of any ambiguousness, or any secrecy when proposing the terms of peace.

The Government abolishes secret diplomacy and on its part expresses the firm intention to carry on all negotiations absolutely openly before all the people, and immediately begins to publish in full the secret treaties concluded or confirmed by the Government of land-owners and capitalists from February up to November 7, 1917. The Government abrogates absolutely and immediately all the provisions of these secret treaties in as much as they were intended in the majority of cases for the purpose of securing profits and privileges for Russian landowners and capitalists and retaining or increasing the annexations by the Great-Russians.

While addressing the proposal to the governments and peoples of all countries to start immediately open negotiations for the conclusion of peace, the Government expresses its readiness to carry on these negotiations by written communications, by telegraph, as well as by parleys of the representatives of various countries, or at a conference of such representatives. To facilitate such negotiations the Government appoints a plenipotentiary representative in neutral countries.

The Government proposes to all the governments and peoples of all the warring countries to conclude an armistice immediately; at the same time, it considers desirable that this armistice should be concluded for a period of not less than three months —that is, a period during which it would be fully possible to terminate the negotiations for peace with the participation of the representatives of all peoples and nationalities drawn into the war or compelled to participate in it, as well as to call the plenipotentiary conventions of people's representatives of all countries for the final ratification of the terms of peace.

While addressing this proposal of peace to the governments and peoples of all the warring countries, the Provisional Workers' and Peasants' Government of Russia appeals also in particular to the class conscious workers of the three most forward nations of the world and the largest States participating in the present war—England, France, and Germany. The workers of these countries have been of the greatest service to the cause of progress and socialism. We have the great example of the Chartist movement in England, several revolutions which were of universal historic importance accomplished by the French proletariat, and finally the heroic struggle against the exclusive law in Germany and the prolonged, stubborn, disciplined work—a work setting an example for the workers of the whole world—of creating mass proletarian organizations in Germany. All these examples of proletarian heroism and historic creative work serve as a guarantee that the workers of the above-mentioned countries understand the duties which devolve upon them now in the cause of the liberation of humanity from the horrors of war and its consequences, a cause which these workers by their resolute and energetic activity will help us to bring to a successful end—the cause of peace, and, together with this, the cause of the liberation of the laboring and exploited.

[26.]

Soviet Government's First Note to Allied Ambassadors, November 22, 1917.[1]

(*Izvestia*, November 23, 1917.)

I herewith have the honor to inform you, Mr. Ambassador, that the All-Russian Congress of Soviets of Workers' and Soldiers' Deputies organized on the 8th of November a new Government of the Russian Republic, the Council of People's Commissaries. The chairman of this Government is Vladimir Ilitch Lenin, and the direction of foreign policy is intrusted to me as the People's Commissary of Foreign Affairs.

Calling your attention to the text of the proposed armistice and democratic peace without annexations and indemnities, and on the basis of self-determination of nations which was approved by the All-Russian Congress of Soviets of Workers' and Soldiers' Deputies, I have the honor to request you to consider the above-mentioned document as a formal proposal for an immediate armistice on all fronts and the immediate opening of peace negotiations, with which proposal the plenipotentiary Government of the Russian Republic appeals simultaneously to all the warring peoples and their governments.

Accept assurances, Mr. Ambassador, of the sincere respect of the Soviet Government for the people of the United States, who like all other people are worn out by this unexampled butchery and who cannot but aim for peace.

(signed) People's Commissary of Foreign Affairs,
L. Trotsky,
Managing Secretary of the Council
of People's Commissaries,
Vladimir Bonch-Bruevich.
Witnessed by Secretary N. Gorbunov.

[1] No reply to this is recorded.

[27.]

Note from Soviet Government to Representatives of the following Neutral Countries—Norway, the Netherlands, Spain, Switzerland, Denmark, and Sweden, November 23, 1917.

(*Izvestia,* November 24, 1917.)

On the 8th of November, in accordance with the decision of the convention of the Soviets of Workers' and Soldiers' Deputies, I addressed, in the name of the Council of People's Commissaries, a proposal to the Allied Embassies to begin negotiations regarding an immediate armistice on all fronts and regarding a democratic peace without annexations and indemnities based on self-determination of peoples. At the same time the Council of People's Commissaries instructed the Military Authorities and the delegates of the Republican Army to enter into preliminary pourparlers with the military authorities of the enemy's armies for the purpose of attaining an immediate armistice on our fronts as well as on all fronts.

While informing you of this, Mr. Minister, I have the honor to request you to do all that is possible in order that our proposal for an immediate armistice and a beginning of peace negotiations should in an official manner be brought to the knowledge of the enemy Governments.

At the same time I express the hope that you, Mr. Minister, will do everything possible in order fully to inform the public opinion of the people whose Government you represent about the steps taken by the Soviet Government for peace.

The laboring masses of neutral countries are suffering the greatest misfortunes as the result of that criminal butchery which, if it should not be ended, threatens to draw into its whirlpool the few peoples still outside of the war. The demand for an immediate peace is therefore the demand of the mass of the people of all countries, whether warring or neutral. The Soviet Government firmly hopes, therefore, to find the most whole-hearted support in the struggle for peace from the laboring masses of the neutral countries and requests you, Mr. Minister, to accept our assurances of the readiness of the Russian democracy to strengthen and develop most friendly relations with the democracies of all countries.

(signed) People's Commissary of Foreign Affairs,

L. TROTSKY.

November 23, 1917.

[28.]

Replies to the Soviet Note of November 23.

REPLY OF THE SPANISH AMBASSADOR TO THE SOVIET NOTE OF NOVEMBER 23.

(*Izvestia*, November 27, 1917.)

Petrograd, November 24, 1917.

To the People's Commissary of Foreign Affairs:

I had the honor to receive your note, No. 83, dated November 23, in which you inform me regarding the proposal of the People's Commissaries to the representatives of Allied powers to conclude an immediate armistice and to start negotiations for peace.

Acknowledging the receipt of this note, I hasten to inform you, Mr. Commissary, that in accordance with your just desire, I will not fail this very day to transmit to my government by telegraph the contents of the above-mentioned note in order that my government may be able to make it known to the Spanish people, and also to use all necessary efforts in order to assist in the conclusion of peace which is so desired by all humanity.

Taking the opportunity, Mr. Commissary, to express to you my assurances of most sincere respect,

HARRIDO CIENEROS,
Spanish Ambassador.

REPLIES OF THE NORWEGIAN, SWEDISH, AND SWISS MINISTERS TO THE NOTE OF THE SOVIET GOVERNMENT OF NOVEMBER 23.

(*Izvestia*, November 28, 1917.)

Mr. Commissary:

I had the honor to receive your letter of the 23rd of November and have taken the proper steps.

Accept assurances of respect.

Signature ─────────.

[29.]

Letter from General Judson to the Chief of the Russian General Staff, November 25, 1917.

12/25 November, 1917.

To the
  Chief of the Russian General Staff,
    Petrograd.
Excellency:

There has been brought to my attention the following press communication from the United States:

"The American Government has announced that no shipments of military supplies and provisions to Russia will be effected until the situation of this country will be established. The government before permitting the export of American products wants to know into whose hands they will get in Russia. The exports to Russia will be resumed only after the formation of a steady government which can be recognized by the United States, but if the Bolsheviks will remain in power and will put through their program of making peace with Germany, the present embargo on exports to Russia will remain in force. The credits to the Provisional Russian Government reach to the present day 325 million dollars, of which 191 millions have already been appropriated; the larger part of this money has already been spent for the purchase of supplies, which are ready for loading. The ships allotted by America for the carrying of this freight are ready for sailing, but do not receive permission to leave the ports and they will be refused coal."

It occurs to me that it is but fair to convey to your Excellency the circumstance that neither I nor the American Ambassador has as yet received from the United States of America instructions or information similar to that contained in the press report above quoted. Nevertheless, it seems but fair to express to your Excellency the opinion that the press report correctly states the attitude of the Government of the United States. We are in daily expectation of receiving information similar to that conveyed by the above-mentioned press report.

Before sending you this communication I have submitted it to the American Ambassador who concurs in the expressions contained in it.

I avail myself of this opportunity to renew to your Excellency the assurance of my high consideration.

(signed) W. V. JUDSON,
Brig. Genl. U. S. Army, Amer. Military Attaché,
Chief of American Military Mission to Russia.

[30.]

Statement issued to the Press by Colonel William Boyce Thompson, with regard to American Supplies, November 27, 1917.[1]

I have been shown a statement that implies that America will stop all supplies to Russia and gives an opinion that this is the to-be-expected American attitude.

Since the Revolution of October 23-27th (November 5-9), no suggestion has been made by any one in authority that shipments of American Red Cross supplies for Russia would be discontinued. All our plans are based upon the assurance of shipments to Russia of Red Cross supplies including milk and shoes. No intimation has been received that they will be changed.

WM. B. THOMPSON,
Lieut.Col. Commanding American Red Cross Mission in Russia.

[31.]

Second Letter from General Judson to the Chief of the Russian General Staff, November 28, 1917.

14/28 November, 1917.

To the
Chief of the Russian General Staff,
Petrograd.

Excellency:

Referring to my letter of 12/25th November, 1917, relating to a quotation from American press reports, I desire to say that

[1] Colonel William Boyce Thompson was the second head of the American Red Cross Mission in Russia, having succeeded Colonel Frank Billings. Colonel Thompson left Russia the end of November and Col. Raymond Robins became commander of the Mission. Colonel Robins went to Russia as a Major in the Red Cross in July, 1917, and served in that capacity until he took command.

nothing therein should be construed as indicating that my government has or may be expected to express preference for the success in Russia of any one political party or element over another. Americans have the greatest sympathy for the whole Russian people in the complex situation in which they find themselves and do not wish to interfere except helpfully in the solution of any Russian problem. Their sympathy extends to all sections of the Russian people. Their representatives here are now informed that no important fraction of the Russian people desires an immediate separate peace or armistice. And it is certainly within the rights of Russia, in the position in which she now finds herself, to bring up the question of a general peace.

There is no reason why the attitude of her Allies toward Russia or toward any important elements in Russia should be upon anything but a most friendly foundation.

I desire to avail myself of this occasion to renew to your Excellency the assurance of my high consideration.

(signed) W. V. JUDSON,
Brigadier General, U. S. Army, American Military Attaché, Chief of American Military Mission to Russia.

[32.]

Statement by Allied Military Attachés at the Russian Staff Headquarters, November 23, 1917.

(*Izvestia*, November 27, 1917.)

On the 23rd of November the military agents of the Allied powers addressed a statement to General Dukhonin which in part says:

"The Chiefs of the Missions accredited to the Russian Supreme Command, acting on the basis of definite instructions received from their governments through the plenipotentiary representatives in Petrograd, have the honor to state a most energetic protest to the Russian Supreme Command against the violations of the terms of the treaty of the 5th of September, 1914, made by the Allied powers, by which treaty the Allies, including Russia, solemnly agreed not to make a separate armistice, nor to cease military activities. The undersigned, heads of Military Missions, consider it their duty also to inform your Excellency that any violation of the treaty by Russia will be followed by most serious consequences."

[33.]

Statement by the Chief of the French Military Mission, General Berthelot, addressed to General Dukhonin, Commander-in-Chief of the Russian Armies, November 25, 1917.[1]

(*Izvestia*, November 27, 1917.)

Mr. General:

I have the honor to bring to your knowledge a telegram received by me from the Chairman of the Council of Ministers and the War Minister:

"In the communication from Russian Headquarters of the 21st of November, nothing is said about the situation at the front and instead of that an order of the Council of People's Commissaries is given which tells the Supreme Commander-in-Chief to begin negotiations with the military authorities of the enemy for the immediate cessation of hostilities and to start peace negotiations.

"I request you to inform the Russian Supreme Command to which you are attached that France will not recognize a Government of the Council of People's Commissaries, and fully believing in the patriotism of the Russian Supreme Command, she expects that the latter will categorically repudiate all criminal negotiations, and will hold the Russian Army at the front facing the common enemy.

"Moreover, France considers herself bound to Russia by previous military agreements, and had already stated and now once more definitely states that she will not recognize any government in Russia capable of entering into an agreement with the enemy."

I beg you to accept, Mr. General, assurances of my high regard and consideration.

(signed)   BERTHELOT.

Jassy, November 25, 1917,
No. 01445.

[1] On November 22 Krylenko had been appointed by the Soviet Government Commander-in-Chief of the Russian armies in place of General Dukhonin.

[34.]

Note from the Soviet Government to the Diplomatic Representatives of Allied Countries regarding the Beginning of Armistice Negotiations, November 28, 1917.[1]

(*Izvestia*, November 30, 1917.)

In reply to a formal proposal of the Council of People's Commissaries for the opening of negotiations for an immediate armistice on all fronts for the purpose of concluding a democratic peace without annexations and indemnities, with the right of all nations to self-determination, the German Supreme Command replied affirmatively. All documents and facts concerning this matter were published by me in the bulletins of the Central Executive Committee of the Soviet of Workers' and Soldiers' Deputies.

Hostilities have ceased on the Russian front. Preliminary negotiations will start on the 2nd of December. The Council of People's Commissaries, now as well as formerly, considers it necessary to have simultaneous negotiations together with all the Allies for the purpose of attaining a speedy armistice on all fronts and securing a general democratic peace.

The Allied Governments and their diplomatic representatives in Russia are kindly requested to reply whether they wish to take part in the negotiations which are to begin on the 2nd of December at five o'clock in the afternoon.

(signed) People's Commissary of Foreign Affairs,
L. TROTSKY.

[35.]

Statement by the British Embassy, November 29, 1917.

(*Izvestia*, December 1, 1917.)

In view of various rumors spread throughout the city regarding the attitude of the Allied Embassies to the Council of People's Commissaries, the Embassy of Great Britain, while await-

---

[1] November 28. Russian Commander-in-Chief orders hostilities to cease.
November 30. Preliminary negotiations for a truce with the Germans.
December 1. Truce with the Austrians.

ing final instructions from its Government wishes to state the following:

In an interview with the correspondent of the Reuter Agency, Lord Robert Cecil was alleged to have stated that the Government of Great Britain could not recognize the new Russian Government and had instructed its Ambassador to abstain from any actions which might be considered as recognition by him of the accomplished coup d'état.

Mr. Trotsky's letter to the Ambassador, with the proposal of a general armistice, was received by the Embassy nineteen hours after the receipt by the Russian Supreme Commander-in-Chief of the order to open immediate negotiations for an armistice with the enemy. The Allies therefore were confronted by an accomplished fact, the preliminary discussion of which they had not participated in. Although all communications of Mr. Trotsky were immediately transmitted to London, the Ambassador of Great Britain cannot possibly reply to notes addressed to him by a Government not recognized by his own Government. Further, governments like that of Great Britain whose authority comes directly from the people, have no right to decide problems of such importance until they are definitely informed whether their intended decision will meet with the complete approval and support of their electors.

This is why they cannot get off with ill-considered replies.

Petrograd, November 29, 1917.

[36.]

Reply of the Soviet Government to the Statement of the British Embassy, November 30, 1917.

(*Izvestia*, December 1, 1917.)

Regarding the statement of the British Embassy received by us, we consider it necessary to make the following explanations on the basis of information received by us in the People's Commissariat of Foreign Affairs.

The open proposal of an immediate armistice on all fronts, Allied and enemy, was made by the second All-Russian Congress of Soviets of Workers' and Soldiers' Deputies on November 8. Thus three days before the sending of the note by the People's Commissary of Foreign Affairs, the Allied Governments and

Embassies were fully and correctly informed about the actions of the Soviet Government. It is clear, therefore, that the People's Commissaries had absolutely no interest in making the note known to the German authorities before making it known to the Allied Embassies. The note addressed to the Allies and the radio telegraph order to General Dukhonin were written and sent *simultaneously*. If it is true that the Embassies received the note later than Dukhonin, it is explained entirely and conclusively by secondary technical reasons which have no connection whatsoever with the policy of the Council of People's Commissaries.

There is no doubt, however, that the Council of People's Commissaries made its appeal to the German military authorities independent of the approval or disapproval of the Allied Governments. In this sense the policy of the Soviet Government is absolutely clear. Not considering itself bound by the formal obligations of the old Governments, the Soviet Government in its struggle for peace is guided only by principles of democracy and the interests of the world's working classes. And this is why the Soviet Government is aiming at a general and not a separate peace. It is convinced that by the united efforts of the peoples against the imperialistic governments such a peace will be assured.

[37.]

Statement by Lieutenant-Colonel Kerth to General Dukhonin, November 27, 1917.

(*Izvestia*, December 1, 1917.)

To his Excellency, General Dukhonin, Supreme Commander-in-Chief of the Russian Army:
Your Excellency:
In accordance with definite instructions of my Government transmitted to me by the Ambassador of the United States of America in Petrograd, I have the honor to inform you that in view of the fact that the Republic of the United States is carrying on a war in alliance with Russia, which war has as its basis the struggle of democracy against autocracy, my Government categorically and energetically protests against any separate armistice which may be made by Russia.

I request your Excellency not to refuse to inform me in writing regarding the receipt of this communication, and to accept the expression of my sincere respect.

    (signed) Lieutenant-Colonel M. KERTH,
         Representative of the Army of the
         United States of America with the
         Staff of the Supreme Commander-
         in-Chief.

[38.]

Statement by Trotsky regarding the Note of Lieutenant-Colonel Kerth, December 1, 1917.

(*Izvestia*, December 1, 1917.)

Lieutenant-Colonel M. Kerth, a representative of the Army of the United States of America, with the Staff of the Supreme Commander-in-Chief, and Mr. Lavergne, Chief of the French Mission, considered it possible to address official documents to the former Supreme Commander-in-Chief, General Dukhonin, who was removed by the Council of People's Commissaries for insubordination to the Soviet Government. At the same time the military representatives of the Allied Governments allowed themselves to call upon General Dukhonin to carry out a policy directly contrary to the one carried out by the Council of People's Commissaries in full agreement with the Congress of Soviets of Workers' and Soldiers' and Peasants' Deputies.

Such a state of affairs cannot be tolerated. Nobody demands from the present Allied diplomats the recognition of the Soviet Government. But at the same time the Soviet Government, which is responsible for the fate of the country, cannot allow Allied diplomatic and military agents for any purpose to interfere in the internal life of our country and attempt to fan civil wars. Further steps in the same direction will immediately provoke the most serious complications, the responsibility for which the Council of People's Commissaries refuses beforehand to accept.

  (signed) People's Commissary of Foreign Affairs,
              L. TROTSKY.

[39.]

Statement by the People's Commissariat of Foreign Affairs, regarding the Visit of General Judson to Trotsky, December 1, 1917.

(*Izvestia*, December 2, 1917.)

THE CHIEF OF THE AMERICAN MILITARY MISSION VISITS THE COMMISSARY OF FOREIGN AFFAIRS

Yesterday on the 1st of December General Judson, Chief of the American Mission, visited Comrade Trotsky at Smolny. The General stated that at the present time he had no right to speak in the name of the American Government, as the recognition of the Soviet Government had not yet taken place, but that he had come in order to start relations, and to make clear certain conditions, and to clear up certain misunderstandings. General Judson inquired whether the new Government was aiming to end the war in conjunction with the Allies, who, according to the General, will hardly be able to participate in the negotiations on the 2nd of December. Comrade Trotsky briefly explained to the General the policy of the Soviet Government in the course of the struggle for a general peace. The principal circumstance which was emphasized by the People's Commissary of Foreign Affairs was full publicity of all future negotiations. The Allies can follow every stage in the development of the peace negotiations and therefore may join them during one of the later stages.

General Judson asked for permission to transmit this reply to his Government and in conclusion said:

"The time of protests and threats addressed to the Soviet Government has passed, if that time ever existed."

The General asked whether the People's Commissary insisted on explanations regarding the incidents which took place (protests by the members of the American Military Mission). Comrade Trotsky replied that the formal side of the affair was of no interest and might be considered closed by the statement of the General that "the time of threats and protests addressed to the Soviet Government has passed."

[40.]

Note from Trotsky to the Allied Ambassadors, December 6, 1917.[1]

(*Izvestia*, December 7, 1917.)

The negotiations opened between the delegates of Germany, Austria-Hungary, Turkey, and Bulgaria on the one hand and the delegates of Russia on the other were suspended at the initiative of our delegation for one week in order to give an opportunity during this time to inform the peoples and the Governments of the Allied countries regarding the fact itself of the negotiations and regarding the turn they have taken.

On the Russian side it is proposed:

1. That announcement be made that the proposed armistice has for its aim a peace on a democratic basis on the lines formulated in a manifesto of the All-Russian Congress of Workers' and Soldiers' Deputies;

2. That the condition of the armistice is to be the non-transfer of troops from one front to another;

3. That the Island of Moonzund be evacuated.

With regard to the aims of the war, the delegates of the opposing side evaded a definite reply, stating that their instructions were to deal with the military side of the armistice exclusively. In the same manner regarding the question of a *general* armistice, the delegates of the opposing side claimed that they had no authority for the consideration of the question of an armistice with countries the delegates of which did not participate in the negotiations.

On their part the delegates of the opposing side proposed terms of an armistice on the front from the Baltic to the Black Sea, the length of the armistice to be twenty-eight days. At the same time the delegates of the opposing side agreed to transmit to their Governments the proposal of the Russian delegation for an immediate address to all warring countries, that is to all Allied countries besides Russia, of an offer to participate in the negotiations.

In view of the refusal of our delegation to sign in the present stage of negotiations a formal armistice, it was once more agreed to cease hostilities for a week and to cease for the same period also negotiations for an armistice.

[1] Negotiations for an Armistice began at Brest-Litovsk on December 3.

Thus, between the first decree of the Soviet Government regarding peace (November 8) and the time of the coming renewal of the peace negotiations (December 11), a period of over a month will elapse. This time limit is considered, even with the present disorganized means of international communication, absolutely sufficient to give an opportunity to the Governments of the Allied countries to define their attitude to the peace negotiations:—that is, to express their readiness or their refusal to participate in the negotiations for an armistice and peace, and in the case of a refusal to openly state before the world, clearly, definitely, and correctly, in the name of what purpose must the people of Europe bleed during the fourth year of war.

(signed)   People's Commissary of Foreign Affairs,
L. TROTSKY.

[41.]

Cable from Edgar G. Sisson[1] to George Creel, December 18, 1917.

Creel, Compub: Washington, (District Columbia, U. S. A.)

December eighteenth. News delay is at Washington due apparently to non-receipt of my cable sent from Moscow December ninth in which I reported wireless disability and asked restoration cable service. Westnik[2] waits for it. In same message reported that Russki Slovo had printed two columns President's message sent by us.[3] Paper since suppressed but not for this

[1] Mr. Edgar G. Sisson arrived in Russia about November 25. He was Vice-Chairman of the Committee on Public Information (of which Mr. George Creel was Chairman) and special representative of the Committee in Russia. Mr. Sisson later prepared a report which embodied the so-called "Sisson Documents" published by the Committee on Public Information under the title of the *German-Bolshevik Conspiracy.*

[2] Cable name for the Petrograd Telegraph Agency which was the official Soviet Press Bureau.

[3] In his Message to Congress, December 4, 1917, President Wilson said:
"You catch with me the voices of humanity that are in the air. They grow daily more audible, more articulate, more persuasive, and they come from the hearts of men everywhere. They insist that war shall not end in vindictive action of any kind; that no nation or people shall be robbed or punished because the irresponsible rulers of a single country have themselves done deep and abominable wrong. It is this thought that has been expressed in the formula, No annexations, no contributions, no punitive indemnities.

"Just because this crude formula expresses the instinctive judgment

action. Since then Pravda, government paper Petrograd, also printed large part. First days use of extracts also extensive. All of reading Russia has had parts of message. Got copy from Ambassador and had it translated at once. Million copies in pamphlet form in process.

Brought Bullard from Moscow. Made him head news service. Graham Taylor junior head of Petrograd office. Asked from State Department assignment MacGowan similarly at Moscow. No reply but he is helping. Bullard left free for movement between both offices. Translators hired both places and business headship arranged. Close co-operation with Summers.[1] Before arrival Corse[2] had resigned and is leaving Russia. Hart[3] not here and no word yet of other film party. Love to family. Letters should be arriving. Address me Hotel Europe direct including cable news.

SISSON, COMPUB.

Care The American Red Cross in Russia.
Petrograd, December 5/18th, 1917, Tuesday.

[42.]

Denial by the American Military Mission of the Presence of American Officers with General Kaledin.[4]

(*Izvestia*, December 19, 1917.)

The American Military Mission in Petrograd states:

The Military Mission at the head of which I am, has no representative or agent in the Eastern part of Russia, and has no connection with Kaledin or anybody else. The entire Mission

as to the right of plain men everywhere it has been made diligent use of by the masters of German intrigue to lead the people of Russia astray, and the people of every country their agents could reach, in order that a premature peace might be brought about before autocracy has been taught its final and convincing lesson and the people of the world put in control of their own destinies.

"But the fact that a wrong use has been made of a just idea is no reason why a right use should not be made of it. It ought to be brought under the patronage of its real friends."

[1] Maddin Summers, American Consul General at Moscow.
[2] Frederick Corse, an official of the New York Life Insurance Company in Russia.
[3] Member of Committee on Public Information.
[4] General Kaledin was Cossack commander in the southeast, opposed to the Soviet Government.

is here. At the present time our Lieutenant-Colonel Kerth has been recalled from Mohilev.

[43.]

Communication from Captain Juan of the French Military Mission to the Russian Commander-in-Chief, December 22, 1917.

(*Izvestia*, December 23, 1917.)

Captain Louis Juan of the French Military Mission to the Supreme Commander-in-Chief of the Russian Armies.

In addition to our conversation of the 18th of December, I am ordered by General Niessell, the Chief of the French Military Mission in Russia, to inform you of the following:

1. He had ordered General Lavergne, the Chief of the Mission attached to the Staff, to go to Petrograd a few days ago and to stay temporarily in Petrograd for official duties. General Lavergne left Kiev on the 16th of December.

2. During the absence of General Lavergne I remain attached to the Staff as the representative of the French Mission.

3. I am authorized to enter into official relations with the Russian Supreme Command as soon as the rest of my colleagues receive from their Governments corresponding instructions.

4. I was ordered to return here the archives of the Mission.

Reporting to you the order received from my Chief, I once more ask you to accept the assurances of my devotion to the Russian Army and the Russian nation, and the expression of my hope that the cordial relations which I have had with you and the officers of the Staff will continue in the future.

(signed) L. JUAN.

[44.]

Cable from Colonel Raymond Robins to Henry P. Davison,[1] sent through the American Embassy, Petrograd, December 26, 1917.

PARAPHRASE

Cipher Telegram sent December 27, 1917

American Embassy,
Petrograd,
December 27, 1917.
Counselor's Office.

Sec. State, Washington:
2141 December 27th, 4 p.m. For Davison Red Cross from Robins:
"December 26th, State Department 1920 December 21st. Please urge upon the President the necessity of our continued intercourse with the Bolshevik Government. Otherwise it is impossible for us to arrange for transportation and distribution of supplies, particularly milk. Ambassador approves this statement and has advised the State Department to the same effect. Alleged statement of Trotsky quoted in your message untrue. Statement made by me to Trotsky was from your cables regarding shipment of supplies." Please note my above stated expression of approval.

FRANCIS.

JWP

[45.]

Cable from Henry P. Davison to Colonel Robins, January 6, 1918.

Washington,
January 6, 1918.
Robins, American Red Cross, Hotel Europe, Ptg.: 1512 4.
State Department has cabled approval your unnumbered December 26th.

DAVISON.

---

[1] Henry P. Davison, Director General of the American Red Cross, then in Washington.

[46.]

Note from Trotsky to the Peoples and Governments of Allied Countries regarding Peace Negotiations, December 29, 1917.[1]

(*Izvestia*, December 30, 1917.)

The Peace negotiations which are being carried on at Brest-Litovsk between the delegation of the Russian Republic and the delegations of Germany, Austria-Hungary, Turkey, and Bulgaria have been interrupted for ten days until January 8, 1918, in order to give the last opportunity to the Allied countries to take part in further negotiations, and by doing this to secure themselves from all consequences of a separate peace between Russia and the enemy countries.

At Brest-Litovsk there are represented two programs—one which expresses the point of view of the All-Russian Congress of Soviets of Workers', Soldiers', and Peasants' Deputies, and the other that of the Governments of Germany and her allies.

The program of the Republic of Soviets is the program of a consistent socialistic democracy. This program has for its aim the creation of conditions under which, on the one hand, each nationality regardless of its will and the state of its development would receive complete freedom of national development, and, on the other hand, all peoples could be united in economic and cultural co-operation.

The program of the Governments of the countries at war with us is characterized by their statement that "it is not the intention of the Allied Powers (Germany, Austria-Hungary, Turkey, and Bulgaria) to forcibly annex territories occupied during the war." This means that the enemy countries are ready to evacuate by a peace treaty the occupied territories of Belgium, the Northern Departments of France, Serbia, Montenegro, Rumania, Poland, Lithuania, and Courland, in order that the future fate of disputed territories should be decided by the population concerned in the matter. That step which the enemy Governments under the pressure of conditions, and especially of their own laboring masses, are taking to meet the program of

[1] December 18. Preliminary conference between the delegations of the Central Powers and the Russian delegation at Brest-Litovsk.
December 20. Beginning of negotiations for peace.

democracy, consists in their renunciation of new forcible annexations and indemnities. But while renouncing new forcible annexations, the enemy governments base their conclusion on the idea that old annexations, old violations by the strong of the weak, are hallowed by historic remoteness. This means that the fate of Alsace-Lorraine, Transylvania, Bosnia, Herzegovina, etc., on the one hand, and of Ireland, Egypt, India, Indo-China, etc., on the other hand, is not to be reconsidered. Such a program is highly inconsistent and presents a plan of unprincipled compromise between the aims of imperialism and the resistance of the labor democracy. But the very fact of the proposal of this program is a great step forward.

The Governments of the Allied peoples up to now have not joined in the peace negotiations for reasons which they stubbornly refused to state.

Now it cannot be said again that the war is being carried on for the liberation of Belgium, of the Northern Departments of France, Serbia, etc., because Germany and her allies are expressing their readiness to evacuate these territories in case of a general peace. Now, after the proposal by the opposite side of the terms of peace, general phrases about the necessity of carrying on the war to a finish are not sufficient. It is necessary to clearly and definitely state what is the peace program of France, Italy, Great Britain, and the United States: whether they demand together with us the right of self-determination for the peoples of Alsace-Lorraine, Galicia, Posen, Bohemia, and Jugo-Slav territories. If they do, are they ready on their part to give the right of self-determination to the peoples of Ireland, Egypt, India, Madagascar, Indo-China, etc., in the same way that the Russian revolution gave this right to the peoples of Finland, Ukraine, White Russia, etc.? For it is clear that to demand self-determination for peoples who form part of the enemy states and to deny self-determination to peoples of their own state or their own colonies means the advance of a program of a most open cynical imperialism. If the Governments of the Allied countries would display a readiness, together with the Russian revolution, to build a peace on the basis of complete and unquestionable recognition of the principle of self-determination for all peoples and in all states, if they would begin with the real granting of this right to the oppressed peoples of their own states, it would create international conditions under which the compromising, internally-contradictory program of Germany and especially of Austria-Hungary would appear in all its inconsistency and would be overcome by the pressure of the peoples concerned.

But up to now the Allied Governments did not demonstrate, and owing to their class character could not demonstrate by any move whatever a readiness to make a real democratic peace. They are no less suspicious of and opposed to the principle of national self-determination than the Governments of Germany and Austria-Hungary. But regarding this the class-conscious proletariat of the Allied countries has as few illusions as we.

With the existing Governments it is a case of presenting in opposition to the program of imperialistic compromise which is represented in the peace terms of Germany and her allies, another program of imperialistic compromise from the side of Great Britain, France, Italy, and the United States. What is the program of the latter? In the name of what aims could they demand a continuation of the war? To these questions now, after the two programs of peace have been presented at Brest-Litovsk, it is necessary to give a clear, definite, categorical answer.

Ten days separate us from the renewal of peace negotiations. Russia will not be bound in these negotiations by the consent of the Allied Governments. If the latter continue to sabotage the cause of general peace, the Russian delegation will appear anyhow for the continuation of negotiations. A separate peace signed by Russia would no doubt be a heavy blow to the Allied countries, especially to France and Italy. But the foreseeing of the inevitable consequences of a separate peace must define the policy not only of Russia but also of France, Italy, and the other Allied countries. The Soviet Government until now has struggled by all means for a general peace. Nobody can deny the importance of results attained by us in this direction. But in the future everything depends on the Allied peoples themselves. The question of compelling their own Governments to immediately present their peace programs and to participate on the basis of them in the negotiations now becomes a question of national self-preservation for the Allied peoples.

The Russian revolution opened the door to an immediate general peace by agreement. If the Allied Governments are ready to take advantage of this last opportunity, general negotiations can immediately open in one of the neutral countries. In these negotiations on the indispensable condition of their full publicity, the Russian delegation will as before defend the program of international socialist democracy as a counter-weight to the imperialistic programs of the Governments of the enemy as well as the Allied countries. The success of our program will depend on to what degree the will of imperialistic classes will be paralyzed by the will of the revolutionary proletariat in each country.

If the Allied Governments in the blind stubbornness which characterizes decadent and perishing classes, once more refuse to participate in the negotiations, then the working class will be confronted by the iron necessity of taking the power out of the hands of those who cannot or will not give the people peace.

During these ten days is being decided the fate of hundreds of thousands and millions of human lives. If on the French and Italian fronts an armistice will not be made now, a new offensive just as senseless and merciless and inconclusive as all the previous offensives will swallow innumerable victims on both sides.

The ultimate logic of this butchery let loose by the ruling class leads to the complete annihilation of the flower of the European nations. But the people want to live and have the right to. They have the right and they must throw aside all those who interfere with their living.

Addressing to the Governments the last proposal to participate in the peace negotiations, we at the same time promise full support to the working class of each country which will rise against its national imperialists, against chauvinists, against militarists, under the banner of peace, brotherhood of peoples, and socialistic reconstruction of society.

(signed)   People's Commissary of Foreign Affairs,
L. TROTSKY.

[47.]

Document given by Ambassador Francis to Colonel Robins, January 2, 1918 (No. 1).

(Hearings on Bolshevik Propaganda before a sub-committee of the Committee on the Judiciary, United States Senate, 65th Congress, 1919, p. 1009.)

SUGGESTED COMMUNICATION TO THE COMMISSAIRE FOR FOREIGN AFFAIRS [1]

At the hour the Russian people shall require assistance from the United States to repel the actions of Germany and her allies, you may be assured that I will recommend to the American Government that it render them all aid and assistance within its power. If upon the termination of the present armistice Russia fails to conclude a democratic peace through the fault of the Central Powers and is compelled to continue the war, I shall urge upon my government the fullest assistance to Russia possible, including the shipment of supplies and munitions for the Russian armies, the extension of credits and the giving of such advice and technical assistance as may be welcome to the Russian people in the service of the common purpose to obtain through the defeat of the German autocracy the effective guarantee of a lasting and democratic peace.

I am not authorized to speak for my Government on the question of recognition, but that is a question which will of necessity be decided by actual future events. I may add, however, that if the Russian armies now under the command of the people's commissaires commence and seriously conduct hostilities against the forces of Germany and her allies, I will recommend to my Government the formal recognition of the de facto government of the people's commissaires.

Respectfully,

(Note in lead-pencil at bottom: O.K.D.R.F. Subject to change by Dept. of which Colonel Robins will be promptly informed 1/2/18.)

(In the margin: "To Colonel Robins.")

[1] This was never sent.

[48.]

Document given by Ambassador Francis to Colonel Robins, January 2, 1918 (No. II).[1]

(Hearings on Bolshevik Propaganda before a sub-committee of the Committee on the Judiciary, United States Senate, 65th Congress, 1919, p. 1009.)

(Note in lead-pencil in margin: "To Colonel Robins: This is substance of cable I shall send to Dept. on being advised by you that peace negotiations terminated and Soviet government decided to prosecute war against Germany and Austria-Hungary. D.R.F. 1/2/18.")

From sources which I regard as reliable I have received information to the effect that Bolshevik leaders fear complete failure of peace negotiations because of probable demands by Germany of impossible terms.

Desire for peace is so fundamental and widespread that it is impossible to foretell the results of the abrupt termination of these negotiations with only alternatives a disgraceful peace or continuance of war.

Bolshevik leaders will welcome information as to what assistance may be expected from our government if continuance of war is decided upon. Assurances of American support in such event may decidedly influence their decision.

Under these circumstances and notwithstanding previous cables, I have considered it my duty to instruct General Judson to informally communicate to the Bolshevik leaders the assurance that in case the present armistice is terminated and Russia continues the war against the Central Powers, I will recommend to the American government that it render all aid and assistance possible. Have also told Robins of Red Cross to continue his relations with Bolshevik government, which are necessary for the present.

Present situation is so uncertain and liable to sudden change that immediate action upon my own responsibility is necessary; otherwise the opportunity for all action may be lost.

Nothing that I shall do will in any event give formal recognition to the Bolshevik government until I have explicit instructions, but the necessity for informal intercourse in the present

[1] This was never sent.

hour is so vital that I should be remiss if I failed to take the responsibility of action.

[49.]

Cable from Edgar G. Sisson to George Creel, January 3, 1918.

Creel, Compub: Washington (District Columbia, U. S. A.)

January third. If President will restate anti-imperialistic war aims and democratic peace requisites of America thousand words or less, short almost placard paragraphs, short sentences, I can get it fed into Germany in great quantities in German translation and can utilize Russian version potently in army and everywhere. Excerpts from previous statements will not serve. Need is for internal evidence that President is thinking of the Russian and German common folk in their situation of this moment and that he is talking to them. Can handle German translating and printing here.

Obvious of course to you that disclosure German trickery against Russia in peace negotiations promises to immensely open up our opportunities for publicity and helpfulness. With film expedition send supplies of transformers, rheostats, carbons, cement rewinders, number four cable. Gaumont or Pathé machines preferable account convenience local repairs. Intersperce thousand foot comedies with educational reels. Soon as possible themes of some educational films should be built into emotional dramas five to eight thousand feet. Choose film leader carefully. No American not kindly and democratic must come into Russia. Smith is competent, can handle advertising if necessary and attached him to my staff December first. First film has gone admirably.

Presently may be desirable to start our own newspaper. It is mechanically feasible. What is your view? Would need desk man as capable as Rochester to get out paper. Would Sam Adams come to swing writing end, devoting himself solely to this work? Put some general news in cable. Several short items better than one long one. Could you utilize few paragraphs return service? Cable tolls low outgoing. Have you seen Thompson?

SISSON, COMPUB.

Care American Red Cross in Russia, Hotel d'Europe.
Petrograd, Thursday, December 21/January 3, 1918.

[50.]

President Wilson's Address to Congress, January 8, 1918.

(*President Wilson's Foreign Policy.* Edited by James Brown Scott. P. 354.)

Gentlemen of the Congress:
Once more, as repeatedly before, the spokesmen of the Central Empires have indicated their desire to discuss the objects of the war and the possible bases of a general peace. Parleys have been in progress at Brest-Litovsk between Russian representatives of the Central Powers to which the attention of all the belligerents has been invited for the purpose of ascertaining whether it may be possible to extend these parleys into a general conference with regard to terms of peace and settlement. The Russian representatives presented not only a perfectly definite statement of the principles upon which they would be willing to conclude peace, but also an equally definite program of the concrete application of those principles. The representatives of the Central Powers on their part, presented an outline of settlement which, if much less definite, seemed susceptible of liberal interpretation until their specific program of practical terms was added. That program proposed no concessions at all either to the sovereignty of Russia, or to the preferences of the populations with whose fortunes it dealt, but meant, in a word, that the Central Empires were to keep every foot of territory their armed forces had occupied,—every province, every city, every point of vantage,—as a permanent addition to their territories and their power. It is a reasonable conjecture that the general principles of settlement which they at first suggested originated with the more liberal statesmen of Germany and Austria, the men who have begun to feel the force of their own peoples' thought and purpose, while the concrete terms of actual settlement came from the military leaders who have no thought but to keep what they have got. The negotiations have been broken off. The Russian representatives were sincere and in earnest. They cannot entertain such proposals of conquest and domination.

The whole incident is full of significance. It is also full of perplexity. With whom are the Russian representatives dealing? For whom are the representatives of the Central Empires speaking? Are they speaking for the majorities of their respective parliaments or for the minority parties, that military and imperialistic minority which has so far dominated their whole policy and controlled the affairs of Turkey and of the Balkan states which have felt obliged to become their associates in this war? The Russian representatives have insisted, very justly, very wisely, and in the true spirit of modern democracy, that the conferences they have been holding with Teutonic and Turkish statesmen should be held within open, not closed, doors, and all the world has been audience, as was desired. To whom have we been listening, then? To those who speak the spirit and intention of the Resolutions of the German Reichstag of the ninth of July last, the spirit and intention of the liberal leaders and parties of Germany, or to those who resist and defy that spirit and intention and insist upon conquest and subjugation? Or are we listening, in fact, to both, unreconciled and in open and hopeless contradiction? These are very serious and pregnant questions. Upon the answer to them depends the peace of the world.

But, whatever the results of the parleys at Brest-Litovsk, whatever the confusions of counsel and of purpose in the utterances of the spokesmen of the Central Empires, they have again attempted to acquaint the world with their objects in the war and have again challenged their adversaries to say what their objects are and what sort of settlement they would deem just and satisfactory. There is no good reason why that challenge should not be responded to, and responded to with the utmost candor. We did not wait for it. Not once, but again and again, we have laid our whole thought and purpose before the world, not in general terms only, but each time with sufficient definition to make it clear what sort of definitive terms of settlement must necessarily spring out of them. Within the last week Mr. Lloyd George has spoken with admirable candor and in admirable spirit for the people and Government of Great Britain. There is no confusion of counsel among the adversaries of the Central Powers, no uncertainty of principle, no vagueness of detail. The only secrecy of counsel, the only lack of fearless frankness, the only failure to make definite statement of the objects of the war, lies with Germany and her Allies. The issues of life and death hang upon these definitions. No statesman who has had the least conception of his responsibility ought for a moment to permit himself to continue this tragical and appalling outpouring of blood and treasure unless he is sure beyond a peradventure that the objects of the vital sacrifice are part and parcel of the very life of Society, and that the people for whom he speaks think them right and imperative as he does.

There is, moreover, a voice calling for these definitions of principle and of purpose which is, it seems to me, more thrilling and more compelling than any of the many moving voices with which the troubled air of the world is filled. It is the voice of the Russian people. They are prostrate and all but helpless, it would seem, before the grim power of Germany, which has hitherto known no relenting and no pity. Their power, apparently, is shattered. And yet their soul is not subservient. They will not yield either in principle or in action. Their conception of what is right, of what it is humane and honorable for them to accept, has been stated with a frankness, a largeness of view, a generosity of spirit, and a universal human sympathy which must challenge the admiration of every friend of mankind; and they have refused to compound their ideas or desert others that they themselves may be safe. They call to us to say what it is that we desire, in what, if in anything, our purpose and our spirit differ from theirs; and I believe that the people of the United States would wish me to respond, with utter simplicity and frankness. Whether their present leaders believe it or not, it is our heartfelt desire and hope that some way may be opened whereby we may be privileged to assist the people of Russia to attain their utmost hope of liberty and ordered peace.

It will be our wish and purpose that the processes of peace, when they are begun, shall be absolutely open and that they shall involve and permit henceforth no secret understandings of any kind. The day of conquest and aggrandizement is gone by; so is also the day of secret covenants entered into in the interest of particular governments and likely at some unlooked-for moment to upset the peace of the world. It is this happy fact, now clear to the view of every public man whose thoughts do not still linger in an age that is dead and gone, which makes it possible for every nation whose purposes are consistent with justice and the peace of the world to avow now or at any other time the objects it has in view.

We entered this war because violations of right had occurred which touched us to the quick and made the life of our own people impossible, unless they were corrected and the world secured once for all against their recurrence. What we demand in this war, therefore, is nothing peculiar to ourselves. It is that the world be made fit and safe to live in; and particularly that it be made safe for every peace-loving nation which, like our own, wishes to live its own life, determine its own institutions, be assured of justice and fair dealing by the other peoples of the world as against force and selfish aggression. All the peoples of the world are in effect partners in this interest, and for our own part we see very clearly that unless justice be done to others it will not be done to us. The program of the world's peace, therefore, is our program; and that program, the only possible program, as we see it, is this:

I. Open covenants of peace, openly arrived at, after which there shall be no private international understandings of any kind but diplomacy shall proceed always frankly and in the public view.

II. Absolute freedom of navigation upon the seas, outside territorial waters, alike in peace and in war, except as the seas may be closed in whole or in part by international action for the enforcement of international covenants.

III. The removal, so far as possible, of all economic barriers and the establishment of an equality of trade conditions among all the nations consenting to the peace and associating themselves for its maintenance.

IV. Adequate guarantees given and taken that national armaments will be reduced to the lowest point consistent with domestic safety.

V. A free, open-minded, and absolutely impartial adjustment of all colonial claims, based upon a strict observance of the principle that in determining all such questions of sovereignty the interests of the populations concerned must have equal weight with the equitable claims of the government whose title is to be determined.

VI. The evacuation of all Russian territory and such a settlement of all questions affecting Russia as will secure the best and freest co-operation of the other nations of the world in obtaining for her an unhampered and unembarrassed opportunity for the independent determination of her own political development and national policy and assure her of a sincere welcome into the society of free nations under institutions of her own choosing; and, more than a welcome, assistance also of every kind that she may need and may herself desire. The treatment accorded Russia by her sister nations in the months to come will be the acid test of their good will, of their comprehension of her needs as distinguished from their own interests, and of their intelligent and unselfish sympathy.

VII. Belgium, the whole world will agree, must be evacuated and restored, without any attempt to limit the sovereignty which she enjoys in common with all other free nations. No other single act will serve as this will serve to restore confidence among the nations in the laws which they have themselves set and determined for the government of their relations with one another. Without this healing act the whole structure and validity of international law is forever impaired.

VIII. All French territory should be freed and the invaded portions restored, and the wrong done to France by Prussia in 1871 in the matter of Alsace-Lorraine, which has unsettled the peace of the world for nearly fifty years, should be righted, in order that peace may be once more made secure in the interest of all.

IX. A readjustment of the frontiers of Italy should be effected along clearly recognizable lines of nationality.

X. The peoples of Austria-Hungary, whose place among the nations we wish to see safeguarded and assured, should be accorded the freest opportunity of autonomous development.

XI. Rumania, Serbia, and Montenegro should be evacuated; occupied territories restored; Serbia accorded free and secure access to the sea; and the relations of the several Balkan states to one another determined by friendly counsel along historically established lines of allegiance and nationality; and international guarantees of the political and economic independence and territorial integrity of the several Balkan states should be entered into.

XII. The Turkish portions of the present Ottoman Empire should be assured a secure sovereignty, but the other nationalities which are now under Turkish rule should be assured an undoubted security of life and an absolutely unmolested opportunity of autonomous development, and the Dardanelles should be permanently opened as a free passage to the ships and commerce of all nations under international guarantees.

XIII. An independent Polish state should be erected which should include the territories inhabited by indisputably Polish populations, which should be assured a free and secure access to the sea, and whose political and economic independence and territorial integrity should be guaranteed by international covenant.

XIV. A general association of nations must be formed under specific covenants for the purpose of affording mutual guarantees of political independence and territorial integrity to great and small states alike.

In regard to these essential rectifications of wrong and assertions of right we feel ourselves to be intimate partners of all the governments and peoples associated together against the Imperialists. We cannot be separated in interest or divided in purpose. We stand together until the end.

For such arrangements and covenants we are willing to fight and to continue to fight until they are achieved; but only because we wish the right to prevail and desire a just and stable peace such as can be secured only by removing the chief provocations to war, which this program does remove. We have no jealousy of German greatness, and there is nothing in this program that impairs it. We grudge her no achievement or distinction of learning or of pacific enterprise such as have made her record very bright and very enviable. We do not wish to injure her or to block in any way her legitimate influence or power. We do not wish to fight her either with arms or with hostile arrangements of trade if she is willing to associate herself with us and the other peace-loving nations of the world in covenants of justice and law and fair dealing. We wish her only to accept a place of equality among the peoples of the world,—the new world in which we now live,—instead of a place of mastery.

Neither do we presume to suggest to her any alteration or modification of her institutions. But it is necessary, we must frankly say, and necessary as a preliminary to any intelligent dealings with her on our part, that we should know whom her spokesmen speak for when they speak to us, whether for the Reichstag majority or for the military party and the men whose creed is imperial domination.

We have spoken now, surely, in terms too concrete to admit of any further doubt or question. An evident principle runs through the whole program I have outlined. It is the principle of justice to all peoples and nationalities, and their right to live on equal terms of liberty and safety with one another, whether they be strong or weak. Unless this principle be made its foundation, no part of the structure of international justice can stand. The people of the United States could act upon no other principle; and to the vindication of this principle they are ready to devote their lives, their honor, and everything that they possess. The moral climax of this, the culminating and final war for human liberty, has come, and they are ready to put their own strength, their own highest purpose, their own integrity and devotion to the test.

[51.]

Cable from Edgar G. Sisson to George Creel, January 13, 1918.

(District Columbia, U.S.A.)
Creel, Compub, Washington:
January thirteenth. President's speech placarded on walls Petrograd this morning. One hundred thousand copies will have this display within three days. Three hundred thousand handbills will be distributed here within five days. Proportionate display Moscow by end of week. YMCA agreed distribute million Russian and million German copies along line. Other channels into Germany being opened. Izvestia, official government newspaper nearly million circulation throughout Russia, printed speech in full Saturday morning with comment welcoming it as sincere and hopeful. Much of other newspaper comment still cynical but shifting rapidly as speech makes its own mighty appeal. German version in hands printer now. Call's[1] editorial useful, also Thompson's interview. What was comment Nova Mir, New York Bolshevik paper? Place third allotment my credit New York. Will hold balance second allotment in New York as moving picture reserve. Will have to transfer third to Russia. Before I send bank instructions as to method cable rate of rouble exchange. First transfer was unfavorable as purchasing value of rouble is only ten cents. In this case all right to deposit with National Bank Commerce.

SISSON, COMPUB.

Petrograd, January 13, 1918.
Care American Red Cross, Hotel d'Europe.

[1] The *New York Call.*

[52.]

Protest of the Diplomatic Corps in Petrograd regarding the Arrest of the Rumanian Minister in Petrograd, January 14, 1918.[1]

(*Pravda*,[2] January 16, 1918.)

The following memorandum was presented by the American Ambassador, Mr. Francis, to Lenin:

"We, the undersigned chiefs of the diplomatic missions of all nations represented in Russia: United States of America, Japan, France, Sweden, Norway, Switzerland, Denmark, Siam, China, Serbia, Portugal, the Republic of Argentine, Greece, Belgium, Brazil, Persia, Spain, Netherlands, Italy, and Great Britain, are profoundly insulted by the arrest of the Rumanian Minister, and in confirmation of our solidarity regarding this violation of diplomatic immunity recognized for centuries by all governments, state the necessity of immediately liberating Mr. Diamandi and the members of his legation."

Petrograd, January 14, 1918.

[53.]

Resolution Adopted by Constituent Assembly, January 18, 1918.[3]

(*Dielo, Narvda*,[4] January 20, 1918.)

In the name of the peoples of the Russian Republic, the All-Russian Constituent Assembly, expressing the firm will of the

[1] The Rumanian Minister was arrested with his staff on January 13, 1918. The Soviet Government in a statement issued with regard to this arrest declared that it had been done in order to call the attention of the entire world to the unjustifiable treatment of the Russian troops in Rumania, who had been surrounded by the Rumanians and cut off from food supplies without a declaration of war.

[2] Official organ of the Communist (Bolshevik) Party.

[3] Elections to the Constituent Assembly took place on November 25. After several unsuccessful attempts the Assembly was finally allowed to convene on January 18. The Palace was filled with Soviet troops. After the supremacy of the Soviets had been demanded and refused, the Bolsheviks left in a body. Several resolutions were hurriedly passed. The following day the Soviet Government issued a decree abolishing the Constituent Assembly.

[4] Organ of the Central Committee of the Party of Social Revolutionists.

people to immediately discontinue the war and conclude a just and general peace, appeals to the Allied countries, proposing to define jointly the exact terms of a democratic peace acceptable to all the belligerent nations, in order to present these terms, on behalf of the entire Allied coalition, to the Governments fighting against the Russian Republic and her Allies.

The Constituent Assembly firmly believes that the attempts of the peoples of Russia to end the disastrous war will meet with a unanimous response on the part of the peoples and Governments of the Allied countries, and that by common efforts a speedy peace will be attained, which will safeguard the wellbeing and dignity of all the belligerent countries.

The Constituent Assembly resolves to elect from its midst an authorized delegation which will carry on negotiations with the representatives of the Allied countries and which will present the appeal to jointly formulate terms upon which a speedy termination of the war will be possible, as well as for the purpose of carrying out the decisions of the Constituent Assembly regarding the question of peace negotiations with the countries fighting against us.

This delegation is to start immediately under the guidance of the Constituent Assembly to carry out the duties imposed upon it.

Expressing, in the name of the peoples of Russia, its regret that the negotiations with Germany, which were started without a preliminary agreement with the Allied democracies, have assumed the character of negotiations for a separate peace, the Constituent Assembly in the name of the peoples of the Russian Democratic Federative Republic takes upon itself the further carying on of negotiations with the countries warring with us, in order to work towards a general democratic peace, at the same time protecting the interests of Russia.

[54.]

Cable from Colonel Robins to Colonel William Boyce Thompson, January 23, 1918.

(U.S.A.)

William Boyce Thompson, 14 Wall, New York City:

Ten. January twenty-third. Soviet Government stronger to-day than ever before. Its authority and power greatly consolidated by dissolution of Constituent Assembly which was led and controlled by Chernoff as permanent president. Acceptance of dissolution as final without important protest general throughout Russia. Chernoff's program not essentially different from Bolshevik industrial and social program but criticized Bolsheviks as unable to conclude peace. Had control finally rested with this assembly under such leadership chances are that separate peace would have been concluded without regard to principles controlling Bolshevik leaders. It becomes increasingly evident that present leaders without regard to consequences will refuse to abandon principles adopted in negotiations with Central Powers. Cannot too strongly urge importance of prompt recognition of Bolshevik authority and immediate establishment of modus vivendi making possible generous and sympathetic co-operation. Sisson approves this text and requests you show this cable to Creel. Thacher and Wardwell concur.[1]

ROBINS.

Petrograd, Wednesday, January 23, 1918.

[55.]

Text of Decree repudiating Russia's Debts, February 8, 1918.

(*New York Times Current History*, Vol. VIII, Part 1, p. 75.)

1. All loans contracted by former Russian Governments which are specified in a special list are canceled as from December 1, 1917. The December coupons of these loans will not be paid.

2. All the guarantees for these loans are canceled.

3. All loans made from abroad are canceled without exception and unconditionally.

4. The short-term series of State Treasury bonds retain their validity. The interest on them will not be payable, but they will circulate on a par with paper money.

5. Indigent persons who hold stock not exceeding 10,000 rubles in internal loans will receive in exchange, according to the nominal value of their holdings, certificates in their own

---

[1] Major Thomas D. Thacher, secretary to the American Red Cross Mission in Russia.

Major Allen D. Wardwell, member American Red Cross Mission in Russia.

name for a new loan of the Russian Socialist Federal Republic of Soviets for an amount not exceeding that of their previous holding. The conditions of this loan are specially defined.

6. Deposits in the State savings banks and the interest upon them are not to be touched. All holdings in the canceled loans belonging to these banks will be replaced by debt entered to their credit in the Great Book of the Russian Socialist Republic.

7. Co-operative and other institutions of general or democratic utility, and possessing holdings in the canceled loans, will be indemnified in accordance with the special regulations laid down by the Supreme Council of Political Economy, in agreement with their representatives, if it is proved that the holdings were acquired before the publication of the present decree.

8. The State Bank is charged with the complete liquidation of loans and the immediate registration of all holders of bonds in the State loans and other funds, whether annulled or not.

9. The Soviet of the Workmen's, Soldiers', and Peasants' Deputies, in accord with the local economic councils, will form committees for the purpose of deciding whether a citizen is to be classed as "indigent." These committees will be competent to cancel entirely all savings acquired without working for them, even in the case of sums below 5,000 rubles.

[56.]

Protest by the Diplomatic Corps in Russia against the Repudiation of State Debts.

(*Izvestia*, February 15, 1918.)

All Allied and neutral ambassadors and ministers accredited to Petrograd, herewith inform the Commissariat of Foreign Affairs that they consider all decrees of the Workers' and Peasants' Government regarding the repudiation of state debts, confiscation of property, etc., in so far as they concern the interests of foreign subjects, as non-existent. At the same time the ambassadors and ministers state that their Governments reserve to themselves the right at any time when they consider it necessary, to insistently demand the satisfaction and replacement of all damage and all losses, which may be caused by the operation of these decrees to foreign states in general and to their subjects who live in Russia in particular.

[57.]

Cable from Colonel Robins to Colonel William B. Thompson, February 15, 1918.

(Hearings on Bolshevik Propaganda before a sub-committee of the Committee on the Judiciary, United States Senate, 65th Congress, 1919, p. 808.)

Am convinced by daily consideration and reconsideration of facts and events as they have occurred since you left Russia that Trotsky's astounding answer to Germany at Brest-Litovsk [1] was uninfluenced by any consideration other than the purpose of international Socialism striving for world revolution. Every act of Bolshevik government is consistent with and supports this theory. Contrary theory of German control and influence no longer tenable. Great values for Allied cause in resulting situation depend on continuance of Bolshevik authority as long as possible. No other party will refrain from accepting German peace or so deeply stir internal forces opposed to German government. Questions put to Trotsky by Kuhlman after his statement indicate Germany's disinclination to continue military operations if satisfactory trade relations can be re-established. Re-establishment of such relations vastly more valuable to Central Empires than conquest of disorganized revolutionary Russian territory. Soviet organizations throughout all Russia representing entire laboring and peasant class will not readily submit to domination of German troops. This class may in time change leadership and policies, but will not relinquish power without a struggle and certainly not to an invading imperialistic force. Germany, therefore, cannot control extensive resources by conquest. Any effort to force her terms of peace by hostilities will be an attack on Russian revolution and will be met vigorously. Greatest danger to Allied cause is re-establishment of German commercial relations which may result if Germany abandons hostilities and Russia cannot obtain American supplies and assistance. Revolutionary Russia having

[1] A separate peace between the Central Powers and the Ukraine was signed at Brest-Litovsk on February 9, 1918. The following day Russia formally withdrew from the war, while refusing to sign an annexationist peace. The Russian delegation, feeling further negotiations hopeless, sent out a statement by wireless declaring the war with Germany and Austria-Hungary, Turkey and Bulgaria at an end, and ordering complete demobilization on all fronts.

broken with German Imperialism and regarding other Allied governments as imperialistic will naturally turn to United States for commodities and supplies of non-military character for which she is willing to exchange surplus metals, oil and other raw material vitally necessary to Germany's continued prosecution of the war. Conferences now being held with Bolshevik authorities who have expressed willingness to deal on this basis with United States and desire American assistance and co-operation in railway reorganization. Commercial attaché at Embassy is conducting negotiations and Ambassador will strongly urge vigorous action by government. Danger of some American supplies ultimately reaching Germany unworthy of consideration because supplies Russia needs from America less valuable to Germany than supplies America will receive from Russia which otherwise would go to Germany. By generous assistance and technical advice in re-organizing commerce and industry American may entirely exclude German commerce during balance of war. Commercial attaché should immediately be authorized and ample funds placed at his disposal to enter into contracts which will assure control of Russia's surplus products most needed by Germany. This should be followed by prompt action along lines of our eight and nine.

[58.]

Telegram from Colonel Robins to Lenin and Lenin's Reply, February 28, 1918.

Vologda, February 28, 1918.
2:45 p/m.

From Colonel Robins to
  President Council People's Commissaires Lenin:
Train of American Ambassador Francis arrived Vologda.[1] All well. Express gratitude Council People's Commissaires for co-operation. What is the situation in Petrograd? What is the last news of German offensive? Was peace signed? Did the French and British Embassies leave? When and by which route? Tell about our arrival Lockhart,[2] British Embassy.

[1] In consequence of the German advance the American Embassy left Petrograd on February 26, 1918, for Vologda. Several of the Allied Embassies tried to leave Russia through Finland but, being unsuccessful in the attempt, joined the American Embassy at Vologda a few weeks later.
[2] R. H. Bruce Lockhart, British High Commissioner.

TELEGRAM FROM LENIN TO COLONEL ROBINS.

(Received February 28th—3:10 p.m.)

Peace not signed. Situation without change. Rest will be answered by Petroff, Department of Foreign Affairs.

(signed) LENIN.

[59.]

Note from the Soviet Government, given by Trotsky to Colonel Robins for transmission to the American Government, March 5, 1918.

(*Congressional Record*, January 29, 1919, p. 2336.)

In case (a) the all-Russian congress of the Soviets will refuse to ratify the peace treaty with Germany, or (b) if the German government, breaking the peace treaty, will renew the offensive in order to continue its robbers' raid, or (c) if the Soviet government will be forced by the actions of Germany to renounce the peace treaty—before or after its ratification—and to renew hostilities—

In all these cases it is very important for the military and political plans of the Soviet power for replies to be given to the following questions:

1. Can the Soviet government rely on the support of the United States of North America, Great Britain, and France in its struggle against Germany?
2. What kind of support could be furnished in the nearest future, and on what conditions—military equipment, transportation supplies, living necessities?
3. What kind of support would be furnished particularly and especially by the United States?

Should Japan—in consequence of an open or tacit understanding with Germany or without such an understanding—attempt to seize Vladivostok and the Eastern-Siberian Railway, which would threaten to cut off Russia from the Pacific Ocean and would greatly impede the concentration of Soviet troops toward the East about the Urals—in such case what steps would be taken by the other allies, particularly and especially by the

United States, to prevent a Japanese landing on our Far East, and to insure uninterrupted communications with Russia through the Siberian route?

In the opinion of the Government of the United States, to what extent—under the above-mentioned circumstances—would aid be assured from Great Britain through Murmansk and Archangel? What steps could the Government of Great Britain undertake in order to assure this aid and thereby to undermine the foundation of the rumors of the hostile plans against Russia on the part of Great Britain in the nearest future?

All these questions are conditioned with the self-understood assumption that the internal and foreign policies of the Soviet government will continue to be directed in accord with the principles of international socialism and that the Soviet government retains its complete independence of all non-socialist governments.

[60.]

Cable from R. H. Bruce Lockhart to the British Foreign Office, March 5, 1918.

Secret and Confidential

Copy of Telegram to Foreign Office

Despatched March 5, 1918 (written by hand).

I had a long interview with Trotsky this morning. He informed me that in a few days the Government will go to Moscow to prepare for the Congress on the 12th. At the Congress holy war will probably be declared or rather such action will be taken as will make a declaration of war on Germany's part inevitable.

For the success of this policy, however, it is necessary that there should be at least some semblance of support from the Allies. He could not say friendly relations, because that would be hypocritical on both sides, but suggested some working arrangement such as he has already outlined to me in previous conversations. If, however, the Allies are to allow Japan to enter Siberia, the whole position is hopeless. Every class of Russian will prefer the Germans to the Japanese, and he considered that the settlement of this question would have the most decisive influence at the Congress.

I need not repeat his numerous arguments against this action as I have already reported them in my immediately preceding telegram. I would only add that in my opinion and in the opinion of such Englishmen as Mr. Harold Williams [1] this action is quite unnecessary at the present moment as far as safeguarding supplies from Siberia is concerned, and secondly that Japanese intervention in Siberia is likely to do us the most serious and lasting harm after the war, with every class of Russian.

I must make the same remarks about our own action if the rumors are true that we are about to occupy Archangel and Murmansk. The position here is certainly not yet hopeless. The revulsion of feeling against Germany is so strong that some form of resistance is almost certain to ensue out of the present chaos. If events turn out as I think they will and if you will only have some confidence in my judgment, I do not think it will be impossible to obtain subsequently a direct invitation from the Russian Government to the English and American Governments to co-operate in the organization of Vladivostok, Archangel, etc. The action, however, which the Allies are said to be contemplating does not consider the feelings of the Russian Government in the slightest and naturally arouses the greatest resentment. I fear its only result will be to strengthen the German position in Russia both during the war and afterwards, and at the same time to destroy all hopes of resistance on the part of the Russians themselves.'

I feel sure that you can have no idea of the feeling which Japanese intervention will arouse. Even the Cadet Press which cannot be accused of Bolshevik sympathies is loud in its denunciation of this crime against Russia, and is now preaching support of any party that will oppose Germany and save the revolution.

If ever the Allies have had a chance in Russia since the revolution, the Germans have given it to them by the exorbitant peace terms they have imposed on Russia. And now when Germany's aims have been unmasked to the whole world, the Allies are to nullify the benefits of this by allowing the Japanese to enter Siberia.

If H.M.G.[2] does not wish to see Germany paramount in Russia, then I would most earnestly implore you not to neglect this opportunity.

[1] Correspondent of important London newspapers.
[2] His Majesty's Government.

The Congress meets on March 12th. Empower me to inform Lenin that the question of Japanese intervention has been shelved, that we will persuade the Chinese to remove the embargo on foodstuffs, that we are prepared to support the Bolsheviks in so far as they will oppose Germany and that we invite his suggestions as to the best way in which this help can be given. In return for this, there is every chance that war will be declared (in fact, war between the Bolsheviks and Germany is in any case inevitable) and that it will arouse a certain amount of enthusiasm. Further, I think I can obtain assurances that R.G.[1] will at any rate for the present refrain from revolutionary propaganda in England.

I cannot help feeling that this is our last chance. If we accept it, we stand to gain considerably, and in any case we can lose nothing more than we lost already.

I leave in a few days for Moscow. Please telegraph your answer in duplicate both to Moscow and Petrograd.

Please show my telegram to the Prime Minister and Lord Milner.

(signed)   LOCKHART.

[61.]

Cable from the American Ambassador to the State Department, March 9, 1918 (1).

SPECIAL CIPHER MESSAGE

March 9, 1918

Sec. State, Washington:

Colonel Robins arrived at midnight. He returned from Petrograd after an important conference with Trotsky on the fifth.[2] The result of that conference he wired to me in the code of the Military Mission but as the Mission had left for Petrograd of which fact you were advised, with the code, I did not learn of the conference until the arrival of Robins an hour ago. Since R. left Petrograd, Moscow and Petrograd Soviets have both instructed their delegates to the Conference of March 12th to support the ratification of the peace terms. I fear that such

[1] The Russian Government.
[2] See Document 59.

action is the result of a threatened Japanese invasion of Siberia which I have anticipated by sending Wright[1] eastward. Trotsky told Robins that he had heard that such invasion was countenanced by the Allies and especially by America, and it would not only force the Government to advocate the ratification of the humiliating peace but would so completely estrange all factions in Russia that further resistance to Germany would be absolutely impossible. Trotsky furthermore asserted that neither his government nor the Russian people would object to the supervision by America of all shipments from Vladivostok into Russia and a virtual control of the operations of the Siberian railway, but a Japanese invasion would result in non-resistance and eventually make Russia a German province. In my judgment a Japanese advance now would be exceedingly unwise and this midnight cable is sent for the purpose of asking that our influence may be exerted to prevent same. Please reply immediately. More to-morrow.

FRANCIS.

[62.]

Cable from the American Ambassador to the State Department, March 9, 1918 (II).

PARAPHRASE OF SPECIAL CIPHER

March 9, 1918

Sec. State, Washington:

I have seen the Bolshevik and anti-Bolshevik press since sending my cable at 12 o'clock last night. Both lay great stress upon the threatened Japanese invasion and all harmoniously express violent opposition to the same. I am just in receipt of a confidential message from Ruggles[2] and he reports that in accordance with his instructions he has interviewed Trotsky besides the Chief of Staff and the French Military Mission; he states that as yet it is too early to judge what the Bolshevik leaders can do but thinks their intention is to fight the Germans even if peace is ratified by the Moscow All-Russian Soviet Con-

---

[1] J. Butler Wright, Counsellor of Embassy.
[2] Col. James A. Ruggles, Chief of American Military Mission and Military Attaché.

gress; he personally urges avoidance of reprisals and occupations and states that there is time therefor if the situation becomes hopeless later on; that he will accompany the Russian, French, Italian staffs to Moscow March 11th.

I cannot too strongly urge the folly of an invasion by the Japanese now. It is possible that the Congress at Moscow may ratify the peace, but if I receive assurance from you that the Japanese peril is baseless I am of the opinion that the Congress will reject this humiliating peace. The Soviet Government is the only power which is able to offer resistance to the German advance and consequently should be assisted if it is sincerely antagonistic to Germany. In any case the peace ratification only gives Russia a breathing spell as the terms thereof are fatal to Bolshevikism as well as to the integrity of Russia.

[63.]

Telegram from Colonel Robins to Trotsky, March 9, 1918.

TELEGRAM TRANSMITTED FROM VOLOGDA TO PEOPLE'S COMMISSARY, TROTSKY—MARCH 9—1 P.M.

Colonel Robins at the apparatus. The Ambassador and his entire staff have settled in Vologda. His stay in Vologda is approved by the American Government at Washington by a telegram sent from Washington on the fourth of March and received in Vologda on the sixth. The Ambassador telegraphed to Washington an energetic protest against all Japanese plans in Siberia. Also telegraphed recommendation of support by the United States in case of a conflict with the Central Powers. The Ambassador officially states that he will remain in Russia and that the American Embassy will remain in Russia even if it should be necessary for the Embassy to maintain itself on wheels. Your note [1] has been transmitted. Are leaving for Moscow to-morrow. Inform the last important news.

[1] Note of March 5, Document 59.

[64.]

Telegram from Tchicherin to Colonel Robins, received March 9, 1918.

American Embassy, for Colonel Robins:

The People's Commissariat of Foreign Affairs warmly thanks the American Embassy for the friendly attitude which is being shown by it at the present critical time and for assistance being given by it in the complications which are arising now in the Far East. The People's Commissariat hopes that the American Government will act against this unpermissible interference in our internal affairs and in the very organization of the Soviet Republic which recently took place in Vladivostok by all the Allied consuls, including the American. According to information received by us from Khabarovsk, the consuls in Vladivostok presented an ultimatum protesting against the reorganization of local institutions on Soviet lines and the creation of a local Red Guard. At the same time the Allied consuls stated that they withheld final decision until the following day, after which local manufacturers came out with the statement of non-recognition of the Council of People's Commissaries and of the recognition by them only of the Constituent Assembly. The action of the Allied consuls is a step directed against the Soviet Government itself. The American Embassy will no doubt realize the adverse influence which this action will have. The People's Commissariat feels certain that the American Embassy will use all means to solve at its earliest convenience this new complication.

Assistant People's Commissary of Foreign Affairs,
TCHICHERIN.

[65.]

Cable sent by President Wilson to the All-Russian Congress of Soviets at Moscow, March 14-16, 1918.

(*New York Times Current History*, Vol. VIII, Part 1, p. 49).

May I not take advantage of the meeting of the Congress of the Soviets to express the sincere sympathy which the people of the United States feel for the Russian people at this moment when the German power has been thrust in to interrupt and turn back the whole struggle for freedom and substitute the wishes of Germany for the purpose of the people of Russia?

Although the government of the United States is, unhappily, not now in a position to render the direct and effective aid it would wish to render, I beg to assure the people of Russia through the congress that it will avail itself of every opportunity to secure for Russia once more complete sovereignty and independence in her own affairs, and full restoration to her great rôle in the life of Europe and the modern world.

The whole heart of the people of the United States is with the people of Russia in the attempt to free themselves forever from autocratic government and become the masters of their own life.

WOODROW WILSON.

Washington, March 11, 1918.

[66.]

Cable sent by Samuel Gompers, President of the American Federation of Labor, to the All-Russian Congress of Soviets, March 14-16, 1918.

(*New York Times Current History*, Vol. VIII, Part 1, p. 49).

To the All-Russian Soviet, Moscow:

We address you in the name of world liberty. We assure you that the people of the United States are pained by every blow at Russian freedom, as they would be by a blow at their own. The American people desire to be of service to the Russian people in their struggle to safeguard freedom and realize its opportunities. We desire to be informed as to how we may help.

We speak for a great organized movement of working people who are devoted to the cause of freedom and the ideals of democracy. We assure you also that the whole American Nation ardently desires to be helpful to Russia and awaits with eagerness an indication from Russia as to how help may most effectively be extended.

To all those who strive for freedom we say: Courage! Justice must triumph if all free people stand united against autocracy! We await your suggestions.

American Alliance for Labor and Democracy,

SAMUEL GOMPERS, President.

[67.]

Resolution adopted by the All-Russian Congress of Soviets in reply to President Wilson, March 14-16, 1918.

(*New York Times Current History*, Vol. VIII, Part 1, p. 49).

The congress expresses its gratitude to the American people, above all to the laboring and exploited classes of the United States, for the sympathy expressed to the Russian people by President Wilson through the Congress of Soviets in the days of severe trials.

The Russian Socialistic Federative Republic of Soviets takes advantage of President Wilson's communication to express to all peoples perishing and suffering from the horrors of imperialistic war its warm sympathy and firm belief that the happy time is not far distant when the laboring masses of all countries will throw off the yoke of capitalism and will establish a socialistic state of society, which alone is capable of securing just and lasting peace, as well as the culture and well-being of all laboring people.

[68.]

Speech by Mr. Balfour, British Secretary of State for Foreign Affairs, in Parliament, March 14, 1918.

(*New York Times Current History*, Vol. VIII, Part 1, p. 273.)

(The speaker took up an inquiry regarding a suggestion of Japanese intervention in Siberia. He said the hypothesis that whenever one country sends troops into another country those troops invariably stay where they are sent, and annexation is the result, was false; if such were the case there would be a bad outlook for the north of France. He argued that if the Japanese did intervene it would be as friends of Russia and enemies of Germany, to preserve the country from German domination, and he proceeded thus):

Russia lies absolutely derelict upon the waters, and now it has no power of resistance at all; there can be a German penetration from end to end of Russia, which, I think, will be absolutely disastrous for Russia itself, and certainly will be very injurious to the future of the Allies. I suspect that at this moment a German officer is much safer traveling at large through Russia than an allied officer. Why? Not because the Russians love the Germans, but because, as a matter of fact, the German penetration has really struck at the root of Russian power. I was informed the other day that only one bank was allowed at Moscow. That bank is a German bank.

The Bolshevist government, I believe, sincerely desire—I hope not too late, though I fear it may be so—to resist this German penetration. How can they resist it when they themselves or their predecessors have destroyed every instrument which makes resistance possible?

Inevitably Russia's allies have to ask themselves whether, if Russia herself has destroyed every instrument of self-protection which she once possessed, they cannot themselves among themselves supply that which she now lacks. We do that in Russia's own interests and for Russia's own sake, if it is done. It is not done to satisfy the greed of this or that power. That is the Allies' point of view. May I ask the House to consider the question from the Russian point of view? It is impossible to penetrate the future. Russia has always been a country of surprises, and that she remains at the present moment. What are the things which most of us fear for Russia when we look to the future? Frankly, I tell the House what I myself fear for Russia is that: Under the impulse, under the shadow of the great revolution, the cataclysm of social order has been shaken to its foundations, and many disasters, and I fear many crimes, have been committed.

It is Germany's interest, I believe, to foster and continue and promote that condition of disorder. Those who watch her methods throughout the world know that she always wishes to encourage disorder in every other country but her own. If the country is a republic she wishes to introduce absolutism; if it is an absolutist Government then she seeks to encourage republicanism. She counts it her gain that other Governments should be weak, and she knows that there is no better way of making other countries weak than by making them divided—a house divided against itself. Therefore, I believe that Germany unchecked will do her best to continue those disorders which have unhappily stained the path of the Russian revolution.

What must be the result? The result must be—especially in a country where the sense of national unity appears, at all events, for the moment to be singularly weak compared with that which prevails in other civilized countries—that men will at last look around and say to themselves, "This disorder is intolerable; it makes life impossible; human effort cannot go on; something must be done, good or bad, to put an end to mere chaos." There will therefore be classes in Russia, some with patriotic motives, but some with personal and selfish motives, who will welcome anything in the world which gives them the semblance of a stable, orderly, and civilized Government.

When that time comes, then I can see Germany will say, Now we will step in; we will, by both the open and subterranean methods which we have developed and cultivated, now exercise our power in the country. We will re-establish, possibly in the same form, possibly in some new form, the autocracy which we in this House hoped had gone forever; and you will have in a Russia shorn of some of its fairest provinces set up again an autocracy far worse than the old autocracy, because it will lean upon a foreign power to continue its existence. Then, indeed, if that prophecy came to pass—and I most earnestly hope I am in this a false prophet—all our dreams of Russian development and Russian liberty would be gone. Russia under this Government would be a mere echo of the Central Powers; she would cease to be a make-weight in any sense to German militarism. She would have lost all that initiative, all that power for self-development that we so earnestly hoped the revolution had given her.

I admit that this picture is dark and somber. Will anybody have the courage to say he can draw a horoscope for the future more likely to be fulfilled, if Russia remains, as I fear she is at this moment, absolutely helpless in face of the German penetration? It all turns upon that. If Russia could only rouse herself now and offer effective resistance to the German invader, that might give her a national spirit and sense of unity, and make her future far more splendid than her past. Therefore, the question will inevitably be asked: Can any of the Allies give to Russia in her extremity that help and that sympathy of which she so sorely stands in need? It is help and sympathy which the Allies desire to give, and not invasion and plunder. I agree that there may be circumstances, prejudices, and feelings which render assistance in the East by the only country which can give it in the East a question of difficulty and doubt—a question which must be weighed in every balance and looked at from every point of view; but that the Allies—America, Britain,

France, Italy, and Japan—should do what they can at this moment to help Russia, if she fails to help herself, through the great crisis of her destiny appears to me to be beyond doubt, and I will not reject, a priori, any suggestion which seems to offer the slightest solution of our doing any good in that direction.

I do not think this debate should finish without repudiating the suggestion made that Japan is moved by selfish and dishonorable motives in any course which may have been discussed in Japan, either among her own statesmen or the Allies. Japan has maintained perfect loyalty. She has kept all the promises made to the Allies. I hope I have said enough to indicate the general problems as they present themselves to this Government, and at the same time also to show that we recognize to the full how difficult this problem is, how hard it is to help a nation which is utterly incapable for the moment of helping itself. The House will feel, I think, that the decisions which the Allies may have to give are not without difficulty, and the principles upon which those decisions will be come to are neither ungenerous, unfair, nor hostile to Russia or the Russian revolution; but on the contrary that our one object is to see Russia strong, intact, secure, and free. If these objects can be attained, then, indeed, and then only, will the Russian revolution bring forth all the fruits which Russia's best friends desire to see.

[69.]

Statement by the Prime Ministers and Foreign Ministers of the Entente, March 19, 1918.

(*New York Times Current History*, Vol. VIII, Part 1, p. 56.)

The Prime Ministers and Foreign Ministers of the Entente, assembled in London, feel it to be their bounden duty to take note of the political crimes which, under the name of a German peace, have been committed against the Russian people.

Russia was unarmed. Forgetting that for four years Germany had been fighting against the independence of nations and the rights of mankind, the Russian Government in a mood of singular credulity expected to obtain by persuasion that "democratic peace" which it had failed to obtain by war.

The results were that the intermediate armistice had not

expired before the German command, though pledged not to alter the disposition of its troops, transferred them en masse to the western front, and so weak did Russia find herself that she dared to raise no protest against this flagrant violation of Germany's plighted word.

What followed was of like character, when "the German peace" was translated into action. It was found to involve the invasion of Russian territory, the destruction or capture of all Russia's means of defense, and the organization of Russian lands for Germany's profit—a proceeding which did not differ from "annexation" because the word itself was carefully avoided.

Meanwhile, those very Russians who had made military operations impossible found diplomacy impotent. Their representatives were compelled to proclaim that while they refused to read the treaty presented to them, they had no choice but to sign it; so they signed it, not knowing whether in its true significance it meant peace or war, nor measuring the degree to which Russian national life was reduced by it to a shadow.

For us of the Entente Governments the judgment which the free peoples of the world will pass on these transactions would never be in doubt. Why waste time over Germany's pledges, when we see that at no period in her history of conquest—not when she overran Silesia nor when she partitioned Poland—has she exhibited herself so cynically as a destroyer of national independence, the implacable enemy of the rights of man and the dignity of civilized nations.

Poland, whose heroic spirit has survived the most cruel of national tragedies, is threatened with a fourth partition, and to aggravate her wrongs, devices by which the last trace of her independence is to be crushed, are based on fraudulent promises of freedom.

What is true of Russia and Poland is no less true of Rumania, overwhelmed like them in a flood of merciless passion for domination.

Peace is loudly advertised, but under the disguise of verbal professions lurk the brutal realities of war and the untempered rule of a lawless force.

Peace treaties such as these we do not and cannot acknowledge. Our own ends are very different. We are fighting, and mean to continue fighting, in order to finish once for all with this policy of plunder and to establish in its place the peaceful reign of organized justice.

As incidents of this long war unroll themselves before our eyes, more and more clearly do we perceive that the battles for freedom are everywhere interdependent; that no separate enumeration of them is needed, and that in every case the single but all-sufficient appeal is to justice and right.

Are justice and right going to win? In so far as the issue depends on battles yet to come the nations whose fate is in the balance may surely put their trust in the armies, which, even under conditions more difficult than the present, have shown themselves more than equal to the great cause intrusted to their valor.

[70.]

Interview with Mr. Francis, the American Ambassador, March 15, 1918.

(Published in the American Bulletins issued by the Committee on Public Information of the United States in Moscow, No. 10, March 22, 1918.)

Vologda, March 15. American Ambassador Francis in reply to questions whether he will now leave Russia after peace with Germany has been ratified by the Moscow convention and what will be the attitude of the American government toward Russia, made the following statement:

I will not leave Russia until I am compelled to do so by force. My government and the American people are too deeply interested in the welfare of the Russian people to leave Russia —to leave the Russian people to the mercy of Germany. America is sincerely interested in Russia and in the freedom of the Russian people. We will do everything possible in order to secure the real interests of Russia and to defend and preserve the integrity of this great country. Friendship between Russia and the United States, which has lasted for a century or longer will rather be strengthened than weakened by the fact that Russia became a republic; and all Americans sincerely wish that Russians should be given the opportunity to remain free and independent and that they should not become subject to Germany. I have not yet seen a true copy of the peace treaty; but I am sufficiently acquainted with its contents to know that if the Russian people will submit to it, then Russia will not only be robbed and will lose large sections of its rich territory, but eventually it will become a German province, and the Russian people will lose all liberties for which former generations have struggled and died.

My government still considers America an ally of the Russian people, and they of course will not refuse the proffered aid when we will be ready to give such aid to any government in Russia which will show serious and organized resistance to German invasion. If the Russian people, who are brave and patriotic, will lay aside for the time being their political differences and will act decisively, firmly, and unitedly, they will succeed in driving out the enemy from their country and will secure before the end of 1918 a firm peace for themselves and for the whole world.

[71.]

Certificate given by the American Ambassador to Colonel Robins, March 10, 1918.

> Embassy of the United States of America,
> Vologda, Russia,
> March 10, 1918.

CERTIFICATE

The Holder of this Document, is Colonel Raymond Robins, an American Citizen, and Chief of the American Red Cross Mission to Russia. I commend him to the courtesies of all to whom this Certificate may be presented. Colonel Robins is traveling in the Special Car No. 447 and is accompanied by eight or ten men engaged in Red Cross work. Colonel Robins will name these men if required to do so. I specially request that he be permitted to enter Moscow and any other city in Russia he may desire to visit.

> (signed)   DAVID R. FRANCIS,
> American Ambassador.

Seal of the Embassy of the
United States of America,
    Petrograd.

[72.]

Correspondence between the American Ambassador, David R. Francis, and Colonel Robins, March 11-May 14, 1918.

(The following correspondence consists partly of direct wire telegraphic communications between Mr. Francis in Vologda and Colonel Robins in Moscow, partly of ordinary telegraphic communications between the two, and partly of letters sent by courier. Apart from necessary punctuation the correspondence is presented as nearly as possible in its original form.)

1. FROM AMBASSADOR FRANCIS

(Received March 11, 1918.)

For Robins:

Ruggles returned after satisfactory interview with Trotsky and chief of staff but no definite program adopted. Ruggles talked to him on same lines as you in accordance with my instructions, consequently interview had good effect. Cable from Davison requests you cable Wardwell's report concerning accumulation of supplies, railroad transportation and political conditions Murmansk.

Thacher telegraphed remaining Murmansk several days thence London and requests you cable his father.

FRANCIS.

2. FROM COLONEL ROBINS

(Sent March 14, 1918.)

American Ambassador, Vologda:

Telegraphed you last night. To-day presented President's message to Soviet Congress to Mr. Lenin, who will advise me of action of organization committee on same.

Mr. Lenin discussed two resolutions to be presented by Bolsheviks to the congress. One for ratification of Brest treaty which is expected to pass by three fourths of congress. Other a call to all people of Russia for defense and organization of an army which is expected to pass unanimously. Opposition to German domination increasing steadily. Strong support of Soviet government from peasant districts heretofore indifferent. Mr. Lenin desires to express to you his appreciation.

Send important messages direct wire. Open telegrams should be addressed Robins, American Red Cross, Hotel Elite. Code messages care consulate.

ROBINS.

3. FROM COLONEL ROBINS

(Sent March 14, 1918.)

The fourth All-Russian Soviet congress opened this evening in the Hall of the Nobles in Moscow at eight o'clock. After the greetings of the chairman of the Executive Committee of the All-Russian Soviets and the chairman of the Moscow Soviet the message of President Wilson was read amid great applause. The following resolution was then unanimously adopted: "The congress expresses its appreciation to the American people and first of all to the laboring and exploited classes of the United States in reply to the message of sympathy sent to the Russian people by President Wilson through the congress of soviets, in this time when the Russian Socialist Soviet Republic is living through the most difficult trials. The Russian Socialist Federated Republic of Soviets uses the occasion of this message from President Wilson to express to all peoples who are dying and suffering from the horrors of this imperialistic war, its warm sympathy and firm conviction that the happy time is not far off when the laboring masses of all bourgeois countries will overthrow the yoke of capital and will establish the socialist state of society, which is the only one that is capable of assuring permanent and just peace, as well as the culture and welfare of all who toil."

In the convention are seated 1,164 delegates from all parts of Russia: 732 Bolsheviks, 238 Left Social Revolutionists and the rest scattered among six minor parties. Lenin made the principal speech and was greeted with prolonged applause, the entire convention standing. Chicherin read the peace terms. Trotzki not present. More to-morrow. Convention still in session; order of business ratification of peace treaty, moving the capital to Moscow and the election of a new executive committee.

Sent March 14, 1918.
Midnight.

4. FROM AMBASSADOR FRANCIS

(Received March 15, 1918.)

The following confidential message for my information received late last night and I am imparting same to you for like purpose. You will of course not impart any of its contents without obtaining my consent thereto. If these interrogatories do not indicate Japan's designs, the reply clearly defines the position of our government in considering Russia an ally still. Observe it does not state the Soviet government will not be recognized. "Japanese chargé d'affaires read to the Department on March seventh an inquiry from his government to the following effect—provided it is correctly reported: That the Bolshevik government of Russia signed the provisions of the convention at Brest-Litovsk; shall the allied powers regard Russia as a neutral or as an enemy, or shall they consider that the treaty was the invalid act of a self-instituted government not recognized by any of the Allies, and the relations between the Allies and Russia remain unaltered?

Department to-day read to the Japanese chargé d'affaires an answer to that inquiry as follows: 'In the view of the Government of the United States recent events have in no way altered the relations and obligation of this government toward Russia. It does not feel justified in regarding Russia either as a neutral or as an enemy but continues to regard her as an ally. There is in fact no Russian government to deal with. The so-called Soviet government upon which Germany has just forced or tried to force peace was never recognized by the Government of the United States as even a government de facto. None of its acts therefore need be officially recognized by this Government, and the Government feels that it is of the utmost importance as affecting the whole public opinion of the world and giving proof of the utter good faith of all the Governments associated against Germany, that we should continue to treat the Russians as in all respects our friends and allies against the common enemy.' Polk, acting." FRANCIS.

Robins for Summers:[1] "Please give Robins substance of MacGowan's[2] reports as wired me.[3] Francis."

[1] American Consul General at Moscow.
[2] American Consul at Irkutsk, Siberia.
[3] See Document 73.

Ambassador asks what report from executive committee [1] to-day. Message partially deciphered continues message just sent you. Have you any questions?

No further information on Eastern question. See Cecil's statement in House of Commons. Apparently J.[2] was preparing move and if stopped was by our intervention. MacGowan's reports to Summers indicate Germans preparing to take Siberian railway. Up to what hour did the conference adjourn? Thanks for your message received two A.M. What other business transacted, and when did conference adjourn and to when? Niessel [3] sent message by French officer en route Moscow last night, that was satisfied no material resistance be offered and no effort made, and Niessel would leave Russia if peace ratified, but that Lavergne and twenty of mission would remain. I replied tell Niessel I purpose remaining and should like to see him here.

The following confidential message received by me from the Department with some words unintelligible. Cannot definitely determine where or to whom Polk delivered this carefully framed message but nevertheless it outlines our policy on Japanese invasion. You should, if appears advisable, discreetly impart the substance of same to the proper parties. Polk's preface states message was sent on March third to be read in some place and that he had read same at a dinner to the Ambassadors of France, England, and Italy. The message follows: "The most careful and anxious consideration has been given by the American Government to the prevailing conditions in Siberia and a possible remedy therefor. It is cognizant of the peril of anarchy which surrounds the Siberian Provinces and also the overshadowing risk of German invasion. It shares with the Governments of Blank and Blank the view that if intervention is deemed advisable, the Government of Japan is in complete touch with the situation and could accomplish it most efficiently. It has moreover the utmost confidence in the Japanese Government and would be entirely willing so far as its own feelings towards that Government are concerned to entrust the enterprise to it. But it is bound in frankness to say that the wisdom

[1] Central Executive Committee of Soviets.
[2] Japan.
[3] General Niessel, Chief of French Military Mission in Russia.

of intervention seems to it most questionable if it were undertaken emphasizing the assumption that the most explicit assurances would be given that it was undertaken by Japan as an Ally of Russia in Russia's interest and with the sole view of holding it safe against Germany and at the absolute disposition of the final peace conference. Otherwise the Central Powers could and would make it appear that Japan was doing in the East exactly what Germany is doing in the West, and so seek to counter the condemnation which all the world must pronounce against Germany's invasions of Russia which she attempts to justify on the pretext of restoring order; and it is the judgment of the United States, uttered with the utmost respect, that even with such assurances they could in the same way be discredited by those whose interest it was to discredit them, and that a hot resentment would be generated in Russia, and particularly of the enemies of the Russian Revolution for which the Government of the United States entertains the greatest sympathy, in spite of all the unhappiness and misery which has for the time being sprung out of it. The Government of the United States begs once more to express to the Government of Japan its warmest friendship and confidence and once more begs it to accept these expressions of . . . judgment as uttered only in the frankness of friendship"[1] . . . This message sent to Ambassador for his confidential information and guidance and of course will be very discreetly used by you. . . .

2889—2890, both were requesting you to come . . . to direct wire. Sent 10:30 P.M. to-day . . . received your report delivery President's message.

Other important message on same subject not completely deciphered at what hour to-morrow do you wish to receive same on this wire?

5. FROM COLONEL ROBINS

(Sent March 15, 1918.)

American Ambassador:
Your call to direct wire did not reach me until one this morning. Have arranged for immediate delivery of such calls in future. To avoid duplication and confusion, please send

[1] This message appeared in the New York *Nation*, February 21, 1920.

such communications as you wish me to use or transmit addressed to me personally. Wide divergence of opinion and recommendation between yourself and American officials here.

Careful use confidential message received last night will be made. Have you deciphered second part message?

Fully advised. Have you anything further to ask?

Five P.M.

Engaged for entire day unless matter of importance to transmit. Suggest eleven A.M. to-morrow.

Will report later on interview. Soviet government actively engaged organization army for defense. German control Petrograd and Moscow not provided for in treaty. Rumor baseless. I remain in Moscow for the present.

Will communicate daily at eleven A.M. Vologda time. Please have your daily communication written out. Good-bye for to-day.

6. FROM AMBASSADOR FRANCIS

(Received March 16, 1918.)

Colonel Ruggles asks whether Riggs [1] is in Moscow. Japanese, Chinese [2] going direct Vladivostok. Unable proceed Harbin because that road cut at Manchurian border by Bolsheviks. No further eastern news. Call us when conference adjourned. Good-bye.

Has conference adjourned finally? What was vote on ratification? What your plans? Bullard here yesterday. In Moscow this evening. Only British Embassy got through Finland to Sweden. Others returning for exit via Murmansk. . . . Am inclined to announce our policy of alliance with Russian people regardless of separate peace by Soviet government.

Think can insert in Petrograd papers from here. What was vote against—two hundred fifty-one? Ambassador has not seen Balfour's statement.[3]

[1] Captain Riggs, Military Attaché American Military Mission in Russia.
[2] Japanese Embassy and Chinese Legation.
[3] See Document 68.

Following cable received to-day for you from New York. Message begins—Eleven. March thirteenth. Following cable sent you March eighth from Washington signed Thompson-Davison [1] "15155. Course you urge in special number one already adopted in strong note that will undoubtedly halt proposed action. More positive policy waits on decision of Soviet. Feel strongly that repudiation of Germany by Russian people will assure remarkable results and an appeal from Soviet to America will bring desired aid."

7. FROM COLONEL ROBINS

(Sent March 16, 1918.)

Colonel Robins to Ambassador Francis:
Final vote on ratification of treaty not yet taken. Preliminary vote shows substantial majority for ratification. Bolshevik party supports ratification, all of seven other parties represented in the convention are against ratification. Full and fair discussion by leaders of all parties permitted. President Lenin in easy and complete control of convention. Consul Summers yesterday morning received telegram stating that Roumanian Red Cross Mission, thirty-three in number, were in Kharkoff on way to Moscow bound for America. Please advise Davison from Vologda as I have done from here. Complete copy of treaty terms published by government, eighteen printed pamphlet pages, now being translated by consulate and Compub here. Convention expected to reach final vote on ratification this afternoon. Have you any further information regarding the Far East? Have you any further instructions? Have important engagement now overdue.

8. FROM COLONEL ROBINS

(Sent March 17, 1918.)

American Ambassador, Vologda:
Congress finally adjourned. Moving of Government to Moscow approved. Permanent executive committee of two hundred elected. Conference on national defense now sitting. Public review to-day of first regiment volunteer army with three

---

[1] The explanation of two signatures is that the cable was sent by Colonel Thompson, and transmitted through Mr. Davison.

other regiments in review. Addresses made by representative government leaders declaring revolution saved only by organization large revolutionary army. Shall remain here until further developments. Colonel Anderson [1] delayed transportation difficulties. Hopes leave to-night. Your interview received too late for translation and delivery in time morning papers. Will appear in full next issue Moscow press. Compub handling publicity.[2] Statement made to-day by Karahan of department foreign affairs that Japanese advance in Siberia stopped. Stated this due to American intervention. Trotzki arrived Moscow to-day. Opens his office as war minister here to-morrow. Lockhart and staff arrived to-day. They expect to remain. Captain Riggs has secured quarters for military mission.

ROBINS.

Moscow, Sunday, March 17, 1918.

9. FROM COLONEL ROBINS

(Sent March 18, 1918.)

American Ambassador, Vologda:

Please keep us advised up to minute in Far Eastern situation. Eight hundred word cable was message for you containing inquiry by Soviet government upon possible co-operation of United States, which upon failure to get deciphered in Vologda was transmitted direct to war department from Petrograd. Colonel Anderson left last night for Vologda. He sent me message to ask you by wire to secure two first class wagons for further transport of mission from Vologda regardless of expense. For Ruggles from Riggs: "Eighteenth, twelve. Have found quarters and office in large house of friends just opposite Kremlin. Sadoul [3] in same house. Question of lodging here extremely difficult but now settled definitely. Could use Wardell or Calder here. Advise your being ready to come to Moscow soon, leaving Bukovski [4] in Vologda; have quarters for seven, if necessary. Am seeing Chicherin and Trotzki to-day with Sadoul. French and Italian missions apparently settling down here."

ROBINS.

[1] Chief of American Red Cross Mission in Rumania, 1917-18.
[2] See Document 70.
[3] Captain J. Sadoul, Military Attaché, French Military Mission in Russia.
[4] Lieutenant attached to American Mission.

11. FROM COLONEL ROBINS

(Sent March 19, 1918.)

For Ambassador Francis,—Robins at the wire:
Conference with Trotzki yesterday most satisfactory. He asks for five American army officers to act as inspectors of the organization, drill and equipment of the Soviet Army. Have told Riggs of this request and he is to see Trotzki to-day. Trotzki asks further for railroad operating men and equipment. Has Ruggles advised you of Riggs' suggestion that the first contingent of railroad men [1] now waiting in the east be ordered by you to Vologda, and has any action been taken by you? Trotzki in response to claims and reports that war prisoners are armed in great numbers in Siberia requests that we send responsible investigator at once to Irkutsk with Soviet official and under full authority of government to make report. Am sending Webster, American Red Cross with Captain Hicks of British Mission for this purpose.[2]

11. FROM AMBASSADOR FRANCIS

(Received March 19, 1918.)

Far Eastern advices through YMCA [3] and Harbin indicate prisoners being organized and armed. Cable from department likewise and probably from same source. Your message just received. MacGowan also thinks prisoners organizing. Huntington [4] also at Irkutsk with clerk and interpreter. Is it necessary send another man there? Ruggles did not tell me Riggs suggested that contingent of railway men now waiting in East be ordered to Vologda. What for? Pleased that Trotsky investigating reports concerning war prisoners. If such reports confirmed, would be excuse for sending Japanese troops into Siberia, who apparently estopped from invasion by America. Nothing from Japanese Ambassador who left Irkutsk 12th for Vladivostok

---

[1] The men referred to belonged to the American Railway Mission, headed by John F. Stevens. At that time its members were stationed in Japan and at Harbin.

[2] See Documents 74 and 75.

[3] This refers to representatives of the Young Men's Christian Association in Siberia.

[4] Commercial attaché to American Embassy in Russia.

instead of Harbin as planned. Do you know why? Chinese Minister same train wired of safe arrival Manchuria station. Hear that Emerson [1] with hundred men operating on Chinese Eastern, but no direct information from him or Stevens. What is effect of my interview? Is Soviet Army being organized to fight Central Empires? Petrograd reported under German control in accordance with provisions of peace treaty authorizing Germany to see its provisions observed. Moscow likely be treated same way. Possibly Vologda. What are your plans? Should like to hear result of Riggs' conference with Trotsky as soon as possible. Anything more?

12. FROM COLONEL ROBINS

(Sent March 20, 1918.)

For Ambassador Francis, Robins at Wire:
Japanese representative here says that ambassador passed Manchuria safely Sunday, March seventeenth. Your interview appeared in evening papers and this morning in full on first page. It has excited great interest and very favorable comment. It was cabled in full to the British foreign office with an appreciative note from Lockhart. Smith of the AP [2] tells me that it was cabled in full to the American press and will appear in the London papers as well. For Ruggles from Riggs: "Have appointment Trotzki to-day—will wire results. Still think advisable have American railway engineers Vologda for present, Moscow later. Their activities—consultation on operation and evacuation if necessary."

Webster and Captain Hicks left last night by special train for Vologda to take Siberian Express for Irkutsk. Webster has letter for you from me. Please have ready for him a copy of MacGowan's telegrams and such other material as you deem helpful for his investigation. Still regard Vologda as the safest and most desirable point in European Russia for temporary Embassy. Have Webster advise me if he has received from the Commissair who accompanies him the proper papers from the Soviet government. Have you been advised by our government of any move of allies for general peace conference?

[1] Colonel Emerson, member American Railway Mission.
[2] The Associated Press.

Confidently believe war prisoner reports and Petrograd under German control rumors are skillful German propaganda to discredit Soviet government with Allies. All for to-day. Good-bye.

13. FROM AMBASSADOR FRANCIS

(Received March 20, 1918, Noon.)

Johnston on the wire. The Ambassador composed the following:::: Colonel Robins are you ready? The Ambassador composed the following for you—the Ambassador is not here, having been detained by Colonel Anderson whose train is about to leave. No further advice from the East concerning Japanese. Reported through sources considered reliable that war prisoners being armed by German officers on orders from Soviet Government. Have wired Huntington and MacGowan in Irkutsk to make report. Suppose Riggs will report about interview. Nothing more. Have you anything? Shall return at eleven to-morrow unless called sooner and have messages prepared, if desire ask anything. Thought called to wire yesterday by you; consequently had no message prepared.

From Johnston: If there is such, I have not heard of same.

14. FROM COLONEL ROBINS

(Sent March 21, 1918.)

To the American Ambassador from Colonel Robins:
The Chairman of the Central Siberian Government, Yanson, and the Military Commissair, Strenberg, by direct wire from Irkutsk to Moscow, issued official statement in which they say that all rumors about occupation of Siberian RR by war prisoners are pure inventions and laughable. War prisoners are not armed and are guarded.

The Rustel Telegraph Agency informs that according neutral embassies, American Ambassador Francis is returning from Vologda to Petrograd in connection with ratification. This statement printed Moscow morning papers.

In speech in Moscow Soviet Trotsky said, among other things, we must have an army. We must become strong in the present world situation. We must re-establish our railroads, feed our people, and organize the defense of the country. Re-establish discipline within the country. We do not plan to organize partisan army. We need army organized according to the latest word of military technique. We must use experienced officers and generals regardless of their politics but have our commissairs control them politically. We may have to establish ten hour day. Everybody must strain and obey military discipline in order save our fatherland. We expect to start with army 300 to 500 thousand, maximum three quarters million.

Organization for the enrollment and training of the Soviet army progressing rapidly. For Ruggles from Riggs: "Sadoul and I had interview Trotzki to-day and yesterday. Soviet government asks French military mission for inspector instructors for new army. Also following message Ambassador through you: Riggs to remain as military link here. Am anxious for co-operation railway mission and want part of them in European Russia, headquarters Moscow. My strong impression Soviet government making sincere effort for serious reconstruction of forces and I cannot too strongly recommend that they be encouraged by prompt support. Request information movements railway mission. Riggs."

From Prince [1] for Ruggles: "Please send my suitcase, pouch with clothes and raincoat at first opportunity. Prince."

Your wire on platinum came too late to get information for this communication. Wire from Murmansk states that English and French are co-operating with Soviet government in the protection of the port and railroad, under express instructions for such co-operation from Trotzki. English and French promise everything necessary for civil and military population and agree not to interfere in local government.
Nothing further to-day. Good-bye.

15. FROM AMBASSADOR FRANCIS

(Received March 21, 1918.)

Johnston on the wire, instructed by the Ambassador. No further news from the East. Webster caught express on which

[1] Captain Prince, attached to the American Military Mission in Russia.

Todobush and two other Embassy clerks also left, also Japanese general. Treadwell,[1] Stevens[2] arrived last night, leaving bank in charge Dutch clerk only, and say German commission headed by Baltic Baron Fredericks issuing exit permits which difficult procure. Callahan and Casey[3] not succeeding and only Americans remaining Petrograd. Emery and number English captured on Danish ice breaker in Finnish waters and sent Danzig for internment, and reported American and England protested to Finland.

Webster has paper from Russian Federated Republic with seal, stating that he is going Siberia on behalf of this Government and asking full aid and protection. They are on private car number fifty-seven. Please convey to Summers, and this also for your information, Treadwell and Stevens coming Moscow to-night. If there is anything needed that they can bring and word can be gotten to Embassy, shall send same.

16. FROM COLONEL ROBINS

(Sent March 22, 1918, 11:00 A.M.)

For Ambassador Francis, Robins at Wire:

Direct and specific denial by both Trotzki and Chicherin of Baron Fredericks German Commission Petrograd tale. French mission here has accepted Trotzki offer and is making assignment of officers for inspection work for Soviet army. Specific request by Soviet government that I ask you to inquire of American government if Commission for economic and business purposes sent by Economic Commission of Soviet government will be received in United States. It is guaranteed by Soviet government that this commission will have no political purpose and will not engage in any propaganda work of any description en route or in America. Please get reply to this inquiry at earliest moment. Have just received from Chicherin signed statement to the effect that German commission control at Petrograd is fantastic and false tale. Authorizes the statement that if Callahan and Casey wish to leave Petrograd and only difficulty is permit, peremptory order will be given from

---

[1] American Consul at Petrograd.
[2] R. R. Stevens, Manager Petrograd branch of National City Bank of New York.
[3] American business men.

here to grant them permits. For Ruggles from Riggs: "Important you send me word of numbers and movements of railway men when received. Please send a clerk and cipher and blank forms. Am sending you cipher message to-day."

Nothing further to-day. Good-bye.

Know of no definite treaty violations by Germany. Platinum can be secured. Terms to-morrow. Have you any instructions re platinum?[1]

17. FROM AMBASSADOR FRANCIS

(Received March 22, 1918.)

Johnston on the wire, instructed by the Ambassador. *From the Ambassador to Colonel Robins:*

My advices from MacGowan and other reliable sources charge Strenberg,[2] who is pro-German Swede, with aiding and directing organization and arming of prisoners. Recently MacGowan wires that uniforms of German officers only partly concealed by Russian overcoats.

Summers wires Germans advancing from south with practically no resistance and that Trotsky efforts organize army for defense unpromising. Are Germans openly violating peace treaty?

Railroad force and equipment under Willard's order, although have waited three months in Japanese waters on my recommendation through Department. I have made no recommendation for operation because as you know have been endeavoring to arrange with Government for safety of men and equipment. Department in badly garbled cable replying to my inquiry concerning conditions and railroad commission stated understood Emerson has hundred operating on Chinese Eastern, which surprises me as have asked Willard many times keep me advised. State Department doubtless overwhelmed and probably thinks I pay too much attention to non-diplomatic matters. Nevertheless I am cabling Felton to-day asking him to remind Willard that I have been devoting much time and thought to improving Russian transportation facilities and am not badly qualified therefore, and to urge Willard to be prepared to send

[1] The American Government wished to buy this platinum from the Soviet Government.
[2] Military Commissary of the Central Executive Committee of the Soviets of Siberia.

at least one unit from Chinese Eastern to Moscow or Vladivostok when I so recommend, which will be immediately upon being satisfied that same will not be used to promote German interests or be captured by Germans. Summers wires paper says British French and Persian chargés engaging quarters. Is it true? Ruggles advised that Yates and military and civil officers under him ordered to report to Ruggles.

Treadwell and Stevens left last night for Moscow, also Graham Taylor.

For Captain Riggs: "Consul left midnight bringing Prince suitcase and raincoat and letter for you. We have no information concerning American railway detachments. Ruggles."

Everything understood. Do you wish to wait re platinum while I telephone Ambassador regarding terms? Nothing more.

18. FROM COLONEL ROBINS

(Sent March 23, 1918.)

For Ambassador Francis, Robins at wire:
Regarding Consul Summers' reports it must be remembered that he considers all work of and co-operation with the Soviet government as unpromising. He favored support of the Ukranian Rada [1] and the Don [2] enterprise. While he is an able business man and delightful gentleman perhaps the opinion of the American, French, English, and Italian officers who are now co-operating with Trotzki is of more value as to the merit of his plans for a Soviet army. Regard report of quarters being engaged by British, French, and Persian chargés as unfounded rumor. In the case of the British and French I know it to be untrue. For the present, responsible chiefs and valuable records should be in Vologda with trustworthy agents here and elsewhere as needed. Entirely possible that Moscow may be evacuated hurriedly if German advance begins. Yesterday's *Izvestia* contains two column editorial favorable to America. Speaks appreciatively of your statement. International Harvester offi-

[1] The Ukranian Rada was in close relations with some of the Allies at the time when it concluded a separate peace with the Central Powers. It was claimed by Trotsky that the Rada's action at Brest-Litovsk fatally weakened the position of the Soviet Government.
[2] The revolt against the Soviet Government in the Don region, led by General Kaladin, who later committed suicide.

cials called for help yesterday and through Gumberg secured desired aid.[1] For Ruggles from Riggs: "Crementchug reported taken. Germans in force estimated four corps advancing together with Ukranians and Austrians in Ukraine. Absolutely necessary now in our negotiations to have prompt information that railway men have been put en route. Can't urge too strongly that Ambassador set them in motion on his own responsibility and at once. Half should come to Moscow for European Russia. News here very valuable. Will wire you this afternoon. Riggs."

Promised details upon platinum from government to-day. Nothing further to-day. Good-bye.

19. FROM AMBASSADOR FRANCIS

(Received March 23, 1918.)

Johnston on the wire instructed by the Ambassador.
To Colonel Robins:
President Zinovief's speech to the Petrograd Soviet on return from Moscow conference and Trotsky's interview in Russcoe Slovo seem quite inopportune to say the least when Soviet is asking that economic commission be received by President whom the former boasts of the convention of Soviets having slapped in the face and by bourgeoisie republic with whom latter says Soviet Russia can never make an alliance. Ruggles now deciphering message from Riggs. Please get definite information about platinum price for delivery Vladivostok also quantity obtainable. Nothing further on Far Eastern situation. Have wired MacGowan give all possible assistance Webster.

For Captain Riggs:
"Advise number of war warrant for ten thousand dollars and held by you. Have again requested Prince be made quartermaster. Send ten thousand roubles first opportunity for telegrams. Ask consul general get in touch with Stevens due Moscow to-night regarding purchasing committee. Ruggles."

[1] Alexander Gumberg, Colonel Robins' Russian secretary and interpreter. The help desired by the International Harvester Company was exemption from workers' control which had been laid down by a decree of the Soviet Government. The exemption was granted by Lenin.

20. FROM COLONEL ROBINS

(Sent March 24, 1918.)

For Ambassador Francis, Robins at wire:
Have conferred with Stevens, Treadwell and Browne; net result is to discredit utterly the Baron Fredericks German commission control tale. It is not the first time that persons desiring to act in a certain way have used imagination for facts as justification. German war prisoner commission has asked officially that Siberian prisoners be given preference in exchange because of danger of their capture by allies in Siberian advance. Our German friends seem disposed to aid in the Siberian scare. Why should we help their game? Callahan and Casey both here. Secured permits without any difficulty. State that they asked for Baron Fredericks as advised by consul and that no one at the evacuation headquarters knew who he was nor could he be found. Both expect to return in a few days to Petrograd for business. Reported on good authority that French embassy will return to Russia with temporary headquarters at Vologda. Regarding platinum there are eighteen poods immediately available and more that can be secured. Bronski [1] suggests that purchase be made through the National City Bank. Have seen Stevens and he prefers not to undertake the purchase but says that he would consider it if you can give the National City Bank authority to buy this platinum for the account of the government at the best price obtainable with official guarantee of repayment by the U.S. Government to the National City Bank. Nothing further. Good-bye.

21. FROM AMBASSADOR FRANCIS

(Received March 24, 1918.)

Johnston on the wire, instructed by the Ambassador.
To Colonel Robins:
Wired Stevens [2] through consuls and Vladivostok to send immediately hundred railroad men to Vologda if has authority, and cabled Department had done so and requested order be given

[1] Commissary of Commerce in Soviet Government.
[2] John F. Stevens.

by Willard if power so vested. No news from East. Neither Wright nor Huntington yet wired. Are Germans advancing towards Moscow?

Following telegram received yesterday evening for you from Murmansk: "Four. March twenty-second. Suggest Ransome [1] request his people show me his cables since February. Hope to receive your full advices on arrival, possibly as early as twenty-eighth. All your wires including number six received. Thacher."

Have nothing more. Am awaiting your reply over the same route.

22. FROM AMBASSADOR FRANCIS

(Received March 25, 1918.)

Johnston on the wire, instructed by the Ambassador. *To Colonel Robins:*

Is German advance checked? By Germans or by resistance? Tone of garbled cable received last night makes me fear my request of Department and order to Stevens for hundred railroad men may be delayed, possibly ignored, as cable which is in my private code insinuates Department has heard that Soviet leaders acting under direction German General Staff. Do you think this possible? Of course don't tell this. Think Motono present Minister Foreign Affairs and former Ambassador to Russia favors intervention but Ishii opposed without America's approval.

Reports Chinese troops guarding Manchurian border. Siberian railroad between Chita, Irkutsk and Manchuria now repaired and bearing traffic. Reports Uchida reached Harbin and issued statement but message so garbled unintelligible—indicates has made public statement concerning my help but may mean American help.

Where is Roumanian military mission?

Who wrote "Letters from an American Friend," issued by Compub reflecting on American policy in Russia?

Following message for you dated Paris March twenty-one, repeat March twenty-fourth from Tokio. From Davison: "Arrived in Paris recently. As to your movements am not informed. Assuming no personal risk involved, it is important that you remain in Russia in the interest of the Red Cross work

[1] Arthur Ransome, correspondent London *Daily News.*

which is to be done there. Please telegraph in care of the American Ambassador Paris all possible information of interest. Also acknowledge receipt of this telegram." This message was received in cipher yesterday evening. The Ambassador asks why Davison in Paris. Nothing further. Have you anything? Good-bye.

23. FROM COLONEL ROBINS

(Sent March 25, 1918.)

For Ambassador Francis, Robins at wire:
Bronski agrees that price for platinum shall be quoted price in New York and London on date of sale. Delivery will be made in one of the three places suggested by you. Location of platinum held secret for the time but is definite and certain.

From Riggs for Ambassador: "No news from Yates."

For Ruggles from Riggs: "Repeating thirteen also ciphering to-day."

News direct from Petrograd reports all quiet there.

Russian resistance checking Germans at some points in south; at others Germans slowly advance.

Regard suggestion of German control Soviet government as absurd and impossible. If Washington credits this contention why are we wasting time here? Bullard did.[1]

Do not know why Davison in Paris.

Nothing further. Good-bye.

24. FROM AMBASSADOR FRANCIS

(Received March 26, 1918.)

Johnston on the wire, instructed by the Ambassador. Yes, received your message about four PM yesterday afternoon.

For Colonel Robins:
Have cabled asking authority for Stevens to purchase platinum. Can you get government to fix price either delivered to Stevens or to me here or F.O.B. Vladivostok or Archangel? Where is it? Government need have no fear of getting paid in

---

[1] This is a reply to the Ambassador's question in No. 22 with regard to the authorship of "Letters from an American Friend."

money. Suppose desires to sell to bank because fears we might credit on indebtedness. Did Treadwell deny he had given me Baron Fredericks episode? What progress in formation new army? Have British and other allies than French been asked to assist? Are Germans advancing? Have you heard anything concerning American military mission to Roumania which ordered to report to my military attaché?

For Riggs: "You have probably received our telegram regarding Stevens the railroad man but if not for your information Ambassador has telegraphed Stevens that they be put en route at once. Please repeat your thirteen.

For Prince: "Packer requests that kodak films be purchased and sent here. Keep in daily communication with me. Ruggles."

Please instruct Webster to communicate direct with me and inform me of Huntington's movements as I have not heard from latter for two weeks. Information you report from Webster and Hicks very gratifying. American ambassador Tokio with whom have direct cipher communication cables twenty-third Japanese government has no present intention of intervening in Siberia; don't think Japanese desirous to intervene especially without approval of allies who seem to differ on the subject. Impending changes in Japanese government caused by differences concerning interfering.

25. FROM COLONEL ROBINS

(Sent March 26, 1918.)

For Ambassador Francis, Robins at wire:
Did you receive my direct wire message yesterday? Yours reached me at three P.M. German advance seems checked in the south for the present. No threat against Moscow for the moment. Your order for railroad engineers greatly appreciated by government. Following from Webster at Ekaterinburg: "Military prisoners in no way active in this district. Food trains moving west without delay. Returning soldiers disarmed at Perm. Politically all quiet. Should arrive Irkutsk Wednesday." Do you hear from Webster direct? Following from Captain Hicks, Ekaterinburg: "Bridges all carefully guarded by Soviet troops. No concern here by informed persons over war prisoner scare."

For Ruggles from Riggs: "Number warrant ten thousand dollars four thousand ninety one. Will send money. Stevens in touch with Summers. Sending other message to-day. Brennenridge wired Keith arrived and departed. Send Prince's trunk and small baggage."

Treadwell denies authorizing statement you wired me re Baron Fredericks. Army is reorganizing. Italians, Americans, British and French co-operating to date.

Nothing further. Good-bye.

26. FROM COLONEL ROBINS

(Send March 27, 1918.)

For Ambassador Francis, Robins at wire:

Hope you are sending Washington the facts of almost complete change of Bolshevik press which now prints daily war bulletins and gives allied reports activities on Western Front while Cadet press prints reports exaggerating German success. Just as we begin to get co-operation, all the military missions working with Soviet power, is Washington to credit discarded forgeries of German control? Lockhart has shown me government cables showing change in England and France favorable to our position. England has ordered admiral at Murmansk to co-operate fully with Soviet power. France ditto. Vladivostok ultimatum has been liquidated creditably for Soviet power. Shall we lose our hold throwing away American advantages just when support in London and Paris won? Please send following cable in cipher to Thomas D. Thacher, American Embassy, London: "Special number one. March twenty-seventh. Am convinced Soviet government hostile to Germany: will help us to control raw materials and use our help to organize economic power. American, English, French, Italian missions now co-operating in organizing Soviet revolutionary army which can become effective against German aggression. Ambassador has recommended railroad engineers come European Russia organize transportation. Plan for economic co-operation recommended should be adopted now and men and money sent into Russia at once. Soviet government only Russian power that can organize against German domination. After four months twenty days still in undisputed control of all effective power. Ransome and Lockhart have cabled for you. Davison is in Paris. Robins." Will inquire re commission.

27. FROM AMBASSADOR FRANCIS

(Received March 27, 1918.)

Johnston on the wire, instructed by the Ambassador.

Yesterday two Russian technical men Senez and Gruzit called at embassy as members of the "commission for liquidating Russian purchases in America." Upon inquiry they stated there was no head of this commission at the present time but General Schwartz had been the head. Commission consists of twenty members—seven from military, five naval, four ways and communications, one artillery, one agricultural, one foreign affairs, one finance. Is this the same commission which you requested me to inquire of our government whether it would be received in America? How can purchases be "liquidated?" When obligations therefor repudiated?

Nevertheless just received cable reporting shipment of two hundred forty-five thousand pairs of shoes April for railway union and families when cost of same debited to Russian obligation which present government repudiated. This done on my urgent recommendation as think told you.

Have authorized Ruggles to instruct Riggs to render active assistance in organizing Soviet army. Nothing more from East.

Do you hear of any organized opposition to Soviet government in Russia? I have not. Where are Milyukoff, Kerensky, Rodzianko, Prokopovitch, Goutchkoff, and other leaders?

Lieut. Madgearu of "Roumanian Military Mission" called at embassy Petrograd requesting Miss Sante to ask me whether knew anything concerning supplies purchased by Roumanian mission and American Red Cross and stored in warehouse 2 Kievskaya Petrograd. Who is Lieut. Madgearu? Have you such supplies? Papers state allies severed diplomatic relations with Roumania: Message is garbled beginning with "Ultimatum has been . . ." Please repeat four or five words following same.

28. FROM COLONEL ROBINS

(Sent March 28, 1918.)

For Ambassador Francis, Robins at wire:
Received from Chicherin, commissair foreign affairs following: "In view of liquidation of the conflict which took place between Russian Soviet republic and Roumanian government the people's commissariat of foreign affairs offered to the Roumanian government through the Roumanian consul general in Moscow to begin negotiations for settlement of the issues involved in accordance with the agreement made in Odessa by the mixed commission. In the above mentioned commission it was arranged to have the representatives of England, France, and the United States." The note was handed to me without instructions and I forward it to you and await your orders.

There seems to be some confusion in the matter of the commission be sent to the U.S. and I suggest waiting further word from here before transmitting answer from Washington or taking action with any individuals whatever. Know of no organized opposition to Soviet government internally. Whereabouts of persons named matter of mere rumor. Do not know Roumanian Lieut. named. We had the goods referred to in our warehouse and they were commandeered by Soviet government when war against Roumania was begun. The German government has made a formal protest to the Soviet government against your statement. I have not been officially informed.

For Ruggles from Riggs: "Please have Yankiewicz prepare memorandum receipt all property. Packer knows how. Have you received ten thousand City Bank? Yesterday cable was eighteen. Nothing new."

Send no more cipher messages by direct wire.
Nothing further. Good-bye.

29. FROM AMBASSADOR FRANCIS

(Received March 28, 1918.)

Johnston on the wire, instructed by the Ambassador.
To Colonel Robins:
Siamese minister asks at what rate can sell thousand pound

draft on Credit Lyonnais London, proceeds doubtless to be used for legation expenses as he has been advised by his government to leave Russia. Nothing more from East. What became of Siberian convention called for some date in March to organize independent Siberian republic? Department did not say it believed leaders influenced by Germans but that such suggestion been made to Department. This elicited by my statement that Trotsky had requested allied military missions to assist in organizing army. Did not ask for authority to comply with such suggestion but instructed Ruggles to render all assistance possible. Ruggles asked War Department for governmental policy here and received reply that same would be given by State Department through Ambassador. Through American Ambassador. Whence started rumor that I planning to go Moscow? Have no such intention at present. Where is Sisson? Japanese and Chinese have chargés here who see me daily. What is Compub doing? Received nothing from them. Just learned from French officer that special train bearing French and other allied missions left Petrograd this morning for Vologda. I suppose to locate here. Nothing further. Have you anything?

30. FROM COLONEL ROBINS

(Sent March 29, 1918.)

For Ambassador Francis, Robins at wire:
Have asked Summers regarding draft for Siamese. He will answer direct. Siberian convention reported abandoned. Taylor says Sisson in Finland. Chicherin asks formally for the appointment by the American government of one representative in each of six commissions to settle Roumanian-Russian affairs—said commissions sitting in Petrograd, Moscow, Odessa, Kief, Jassy, and Golatz respectively. Please advise me. Are you advised of the policy or desire of U.S. in the matter of Slovak troops en route U.S. for service in France?[1] It would seem a foolish waste of time, money, and tonnage to send these troops around world to get to French front. Major Wardwell has left Murmansk for Petrograd. Can he serve you there? Latest word from Petrograd, Radek[2] just arrived says all quiet there.

[1] This refers to the Czechoslovak troops in Russia who were later engaged in hostilities with the Soviet Government.
[2] Karl Radek, official in Commissariat of Foreign Affairs in Soviet Government.

He says over eight thousand red guards in barracks with machine guns and armored cars will fight for Soviet government. No word for the last two days from Webster or Hicks. Have checked on train and am advised it delayed by freight wreck. French ambassador's statement at Petrograd commented on unfavorably. Your position is specially strong under the circumstances. Moscow papers print to-day, "American consul informed supreme economic council that the American government agrees to resume commercial and industrial relations with Russia regardless of the repudiation of debts." Should not such statements of policy come through you?

For Ruggles from Riggs: "No change here in general situation."

Please be on time.

Nothing further. Good-bye.

31. FROM AMBASSADOR FRANCIS

(Received March 29, 1918.)

Johnston on the wire, instructed by the Ambassador. *To Colonel Robins:*

Making effort to have wire and operator established in embassy which very desirable. Government pays annually million incoming outgoing. Understand telegraph manager of district lives Archangel has authority, but if general commissaire would instruct by wire would greatly facilitate, otherwise material delay. Please assist.

Will follow. Department replying my request for railway men asks what "men are to do and on what railroad they will work. Their efforts must not result in facilitating communications with Germans. Recall also that original agreement provided that Russian ministry ways and communications should maintain railway men after work commenced." Of course such arrangement would obtain now but regardless thereof I shall urge men be sent immediately to report here. Starting is first step and urgently requesting Department and commission that start immediately. Of course shall guarantee government men shall not be used to aid Germans, consequently I must be advised generally concerning their work. Is Chicherin or Joffe commissaire of foreign affairs? Is our government requested to appoint representative for Roumanian peace negotiations? By whom?

Should be by both parties, but Balfour announced in House of Commons that allies had severed diplomatic relations with Roumania.

Papers state Kuhlmann protested against my utterance concerning separate peace to Soviet government. If I had known it would displease Herr K. would probably not have uttered it, but seriously, government if replying at all will not assume responsibility for my expressions or acts.

French, Italian, and Servian missions arrived here few minutes ago. Nothing further. Good-bye.

32. FROM COLONEL ROBINS

(Sent March 30, 1918.)

For Ambassador Francis, Robins at wire:
Direct wire for embassy under consideration; will wire answer when received. From Hicks and Webster direct wire Irkutsk: "Major Walter Drysdale American military attaché Peking here after inspection of all prisoner camps along Amur line and related district. He returns to Peking to-night after full conference with us. No armed prisoners in district from Vladivostok to Chita. All well guarded. Some prisoners here armed: all Hungarian social revolutionists and being enlisted in Red army to fight against Semenoff in Manchuria. Full discussion with Soviet officials to-morrow. Drysdale wants American advisory commission working on Siberian railway. Report in full to-morrow." Moscow press prints statement of Cossack Ataman Bogaevsky chief leader in Kaledin movement as follows: "Struggle against Bolsheviks political mistake and merely harmful to Russia. Popular masses with Bolsheviks. This written at moment of life when no purpose in pretense and lies, Now appeal to Cossacks to cease useless slaughter in interest of privileged classes using brave and honest men as tools for unscrupulous politicians." Am sending my car to Petrograd with Hardy and Magnusen [1] to-day. Illowaisky [2] has arrived from Murmansk via Petrograd, reports all quiet there. For Ruggles from Riggs: "In my opinion first work of railroad men is problem of evacuation of material and rolling stock to points beyond limit of probable German advance. Headquarters

[1] Captains in American Red Cross Mission in Russia.
[2] Cossack officer, interpreter for American Red Cross Mission in Russia.

Moscow with men at important points in European Russia making telegraphic reports. Permanent work as situation clears. When are you coming here? Is Yates detachment coming here? There are tasks intelligence, technical advice, etc."

Chicherin is national commissar of F.A. Joffe is local for Petrograd. Nothing further. Good-bye.

33. FROM AMBASSADOR FRANCIS

(Received March 30, 1918.)

Johnston on the wire, instructed by the Ambassador. *To Colonel Robins:*
Understand diplomatic relations between allies and Roumania severed. Can you confirm? When do commissions begin work?

French, Italian, Serbian missions here. Serbian minister says no troops going America, but two hundred fifty thousand formerly on Russian front going Salonika, some via Archangel, others eastern route, and that Soviet government responding promptly to all requests in this connection. Why send such troops out of Russia if army forming to resist Germans? Please answer. Will Wardwell remain in Petrograd? And when will he arrive? Shall read French ambassador's interview when comes.

Don't think consul made such statement but if did thought so authorized by Department. We have had no commercial treaty with Russia since 1912, but that not interfering with commercial transactions which all consuls doubtless trying to promote and Soviet government should encourage. Of course you are doing nothing to impair Summers' efficiency as consul. He is consul general of Russia. Has extended experience, possesses confidence of Department which has recently warmly commended his services.

Authoritatively informed that large shipments being made to interior from Archangel where immense accumulations of munitions and other supplies furnished by allies on credits represented by loans since repudiated, but Russian government claims ownership notwithstanding. Such position untenable and not recognized by local Soviet at Archangel but liquidating commission sent from Petrograd is defiantly and hurriedly shipping such supplies. Please discreetly investigate and report governmental policy. Also what destination of supplies. Nothing further. Good-bye.

34. FROM COLONEL ROBINS

(Sent March 31, 1918.)

For Ambassador Francis, Robins at wire:
Unable to reach Chicherin yesterday; cannot answer Roumanian questions until to-morrow. Sending of Slavic troops from Russia seems mistaken policy but French and Bohemians insist. Wardwell should reach Petrograd Tuesday. Will remain until milk is all distributed unless conditions force departure. Shipments from Archangel investigated by Riggs, will report direct. From Hicks and Webster direct wire Irkutsk: "We are more than ever convinced that the Soviet here does not mean to extend the practice of arming war prisoners and they have begun to withdraw arms because of local trouble from some of the armed prisoners. Battle between Bolsheviks and white guard at Blagovieshchensk ended in complete victory for Bolsheviks. In that district no war prisoners used. Japanese subjects who aided white guard were killed. Semenoff beaten and retreating into Manchuria. His forces Russian officers, cadets, Hunhuzas, and Mongols. It is claimed by Soviet that allies have aided Semenoff, which we denied. More to-morrow." Have just learned that Major Drysdale's report has been made public. Believe conditions here warrant your coming to Moscow if you desire. Your coming would strengthen co-operation and again set pace for allied embassies. Can arrange special train when desired.
Nothing further. Good-bye.

35. FROM AMBASSADOR FRANCIS

(Received March 31, 1918.)

Johnston on the wire, instructed by the Ambassador.
To Colonel Robins:
Have instructed Webster to wire me direct as you suggested. Suppose will continue wiring you. Have ordered Huntington and Thomas to Moscow immediately to assist Summers who says

overwhelmed. Bailey [1] wires from Harbin stating unsafe for me leave Russia via Siberia and that Japanese ambassador and Chinese minister concur and state their people when leaving European Russia will be ordered out east. Having no intention of leaving Russia myself I give you this for information. Long garbled message just received from Wright Vladivostok which he reached twenty-two days after leaving here. Message garbled and being deciphered.

Appears Trotsky after telling Ruggles was organizing new [2] under last word of military science and under iron discipline, and purposed recalling Russian officers to assume command, now says Russian officers be employed as instructors only and given no authority, that general officers be appointed by government and lower officers elected.

36. FROM COLONEL ROBINS

(Sent April 1, 1918.)

For Ambassador Francis, Robins at wire:
From Irkutsk Webster and Hicks speaking: "Have had long conference with Irkutsk Soviet including Yanson, Yakovleff, and Strenberg to-day, all very friendly. Facts in full confirmed by independent testimony which we believe to be true. There are in all Siberia not over twelve hundred armed prisoners most from Omsk. These selected with great care as social revolutionists who gave up old allegiance and became citizens of the Russian republic. They are guarding prisoners and specially German officers whom Soviet fears. Not intended to use them in any military operations. Soviet states absurd to think they will arm aliens to take away their own land. Soviet gave official guarantee to be communicated to our governments that a maximum of fifteen hundred prisoners will be armed in all Siberia and kept under strict control of Bolshevik officers and never allowed to act as independent force. Soviet states no objection to right free investigation at all times for senior allied consuls in Siberia to check the integrity of these limitations. We assured Soviet that allies anxious to help Russia and asked best way. They replied first manufactured materials from England and America

---

[1] Former Secretary to American Embassy.
[2] Word Army omitted.

through Vladivostok and Archangel, specially agricultural machinery exchanged for Siberian products. We asked for list of available products. Second, to help in transport of supplies beginning by opening the Chinese Eastern Railway from Harbin to Manchuria station which is now broken with approval of allied consulates at Harbin, they claim. Third, allies could help prevent China giving protection to Semenoff forces that now assemble men and supplies on Chinese territory to raid Siberia. Soviet claims it could follow and defeat Semenoff forces but will not invade, unless forced to do so. Soviet said that people were enthusiastic against Germany and if invaded would fight to the last man. We were very favorably impressed by the sincerity and energy of the officials we met to-day. They are fully alive to the danger of broadcast arming of war prisoners and gave us the guarantees above stated without reserve. We feel it may be necessary to proceed eastward as far as Darien which is the center of the Semenoff trouble and site of large prisoner camps. Soviet encourages us to investigate this territory and it is the only place where armed prisoners are active."

Riggs sent code message to Ruggles last night with important information and recommendation. Seriousness of proposed action is only equalled by its stupidity. President's acid test message and generous word to Soviet congress, together with your wise action and recommendations, will be falsified if this proposed action is adopted. It will not help the Western front and it will lose Russia permanently. Callahan leaves for Petrograd to-night with Smith of A.P.

Riggs making inquiries re Archangel shipments. Did you sent Thacher message forwarded by direct wire to be enciphered?

Nothing further. Good-bye.

37. FROM AMBASSADOR FRANCIS

(Received April 1, 1918.)

Johnston on the wire, instructed by the Ambassador.
To Colonel Robins:

French, Serbian chiefs and wives lunched with me yesterday. When asked troops leaving country, replied had not done so, but no alternative from departure remained after Serbian generals asked Russian authorities if Russian troops would stand by them in offensive or defensive warfare and received reply that would not. Am anxiously awaiting information as to destination supplies shipped from Archangel and government's theory concerning ownership. Furthermore, peace treaty requires peaceful remaining in Russian ports or disarming of all Russian war vessels, and requires Russia to treat likewise all foreign war craft in Russian waters. British, French war vessels are in harbors Archangel and Murmansk and Japanese, British, and American in Russian Pacific ports. Goes without saying such cannot be dismantled; how can Soviet recognize peace terms and permit such to remain? Can you send copy of Drysdale's report or substance? Huntington wires Drysdale returned to China. I am not considering going Moscow.

Following message received last night for you from London: "Five. March thirty-first. Arrived to-day. Your seven last received. Thacher."

Re Riggs message, will you see if Moscow operator still has it unsent?

38. FROM COLONEL ROBINS

(Sent April 2, 1918.)

For Ambassador Francis, Robins at wire:
Riggs left for Vologda late last evening. Please advise me of any developments in the Eastern situation. Four Red Cross men and Smith of A.P. with Callahan now in Petrograd. Two men of Compub planning to go Siberia to-morrow. Compub has had no word from Sisson since March fourteenth. Did Morris [1] succeed in getting him across line in Finland? Nothing further here from Far Eastern situation from British sources. For Ruggles from Prince: "Has cipher message number twenty been received? Telegram just received from Petrograd April first signed Hardy: "Everything quiet. Have wired Wardwell to come direct."
Give Stevens' exact address.
Smith expects remain three days.
Nothing further. Good-bye.

[1] American Minister to Sweden.

39. FROM AMBASSADOR FRANCIS

(Received April 2, 1918.)

Johnston on the wire, instructed by the Ambassador. *To Colonel Robins:*

Riggs message received. Am cabling Washington; think be exceedingly unwise to follow recommendation now; think highly improbable our government will comply with request. Meantime colleagues here and myself anxiously awaiting information concerning organization of army and disposition of supplies shipped from Archangel.

Message from Stevens, Harbin received three days ago acknowledged receipt my telegram but think garbled message stated would await positive orders from Washington before sending railway men to European Russia; telegram received late yesterday also badly garbled indicated men were starting for Vologda. As men are sent on urgent request of government, steps should be promptly taken for their protection, maintenance and for expediting their movements. Suggest your sending following for me to Stevens: "Vologda April second. Your unnumbered, undated message received; garbled but think it states units under Colonel Emerson representing yourself starting for European Russia. Have asked government to expedite and protect train conveying Emerson party and have assurance same will be done. Please give professions and number of men. Also date of departure from Harbin and from Manchuria station. Francis."

Am sending like message from here, but think you can probably get it through quicker from there. Suggest you arrange to have experienced transportation official unconnected, unidentified with politics to come here to arrange disposition of Emerson force before it arrives. Following received signed Davison but not through Department nor addressed to embassy —who is acting in Davison's place? "Washington 15156 March 30. Your special Red Cross: glad do any relief and hospital work that is feasible and practicable. Keep us advised all you do and make recommendations. All well. For Robins: 'Met Bessie Beatty New York. Doing our utmost here for Russia. Thank God your staying. Mizpah. Signed Margaret.'[1] Davison."

[1] Mrs. Raymond Robins.

How long will Smith remain in Petrograd? Wish inform Rennick. Stevens, care American consul Harbin.

40. FROM COLONEL ROBINS

(Sent April 3, 1918.)

For Ambassador Francis, Robins at wire:
    Telegrams have been sent by government here to All-Siberian Soviet, local Soviets, and railroad authorities to protect, expedite and aid in every way the transport of American railroad engineers under command of Colonel Emerson to Vologda. As soon as possible the railroad official desired will report at Vologda for the purposes named. I sent telegram to Stevens as instructed noon yesterday. Eliot Wadsworth acts for Davison in his absence. Letter sent by messenger from Petrograd signed Hardy gives details of milk distribution and condition of city, all very satisfactory.
From Webster and Hicks direct wire Irkutsk:
    "Have visited large prison camp here; eleven thousand, mostly Austrians. Given every facility to see management and talk with prisoners. Camp discipline excellent; Russian sentries on guard; rigid permit system to leave camp; only about score of prisoners armed and used as guards. Have been asked to visit Chita and Manchurian border and report upon Semenoff raids. Latest information Semenoff gathering supplies and men for new raid into Siberia. He has ample money, is paying high price for soldiers and has fourteen pieces of artillery. Source of money and guns claimed to be Russian monarchists and allies. Soviet states if allies wish orderly Siberia, only necessary to withdraw protection from Semenoff ventures and prevent use allied territory for preparation of his raids. China seems troubled over Russian troops on her border. If she will outlaw Semenoff and similar ventures, all Russian troops in that area will be withdrawn. We feel difficult to convince of our sincerity, if we cannot stop this unfair protection on allied soil of those who invade her territory and seek to overthrow her government."
    Later from same persons: "Yacovleff president all Siberian Soviet and Yanson president of Irkutsk Soviet just visited us making urgent request we proceed to-morrow to Chita for the following reasons. Some twenty days ago the Chinese and Rus-

sian governments came to an agreement that Semenoff should not be allowed Chinese territory for a certain period. This period expires April fifth. Chinese delegates will be at Chita and Yacovleff and Yanson go for conference. Soviet urge us to accompany them and have sent telegram to Trotzki asking his aid for us in accompanying them. We think it ill advised to refuse this offer, and if we miss this opportunity for unbiased report upon actual conditions, Soviet can always claim it made offer and we refused to get the facts. Especially will this be unfortunate if the fighting continues and the allied cause in Siberia suffers thereby." Lockhart joins in ordering Hicks and Webster to accept offer and accompany Soviet officials to Chita simply for the purpose of making report. Let me know that this action has your approval. Elections here have kept all government officials busy in factory meetings and other gatherings. Conference with Chicherin yesterday satisfactory, but delay report until confirmation by Lenin who I expect to see six this evening.

For Ruggles from Prince: "Repeat yesterday's message."
Nothing further. Good-bye.

41. FROM AMBASSADOR FRANCIS

(Received April 3, 1918.)

Johnston on the wire, instructed by the Ambassador.
Heard nothing from Sisson since I left Petrograd. Stockholm cabled Crosley and twelve Americans expected arrive Stockholm twenty-ninth. Gave no names. No advice since.

Department cables authorizing purchase of platinum through any agency, and shipment by whatever route I may select but says "For your guidance, material highly desirable but not absolutely necessary. Market here about one hundred dollars per ounce." I suppose Russian government not so disturbed about the price as fears we may wish to credit value on indebtedness of Russian government to us. Please confer with Stevens and Bronsky, and give price for delivery American consul Vladivostok, or me here, or consul Archangel. Suppose Bronsky would prefer Stevens draft on National City, New York to mine on State Department; tell Stevens I will give him draft on Department or cable for payment if he prefers. If shipment made via Atlantic insurance would be important factor, and much less via Pacific. Understand quantity in question is eighteen poods. Would government demand payment in roubles here? If so tell Stevens must know rate exchange. If government desires, credit in America or London or Paris might be arranged, but probably no other city.

Riggs arrived. Have most pathetic letter from Kalpachnikoff's [1] sister saying he has been placed in solitary confinement and is eking out a horrible existence. As he was a Red Cross worker, I feel it my duty to ascertain charges against him. Can you assist? Nothing further. Have you? Good-bye.

42. FROM COLONEL ROBINS

(Sent April 4, 1918.)

For Ambassador Francis, Robins at wire:

Munitions that are being evacuated from Archangel are sent to Moscow, the Urals and Siberian towns. Soviet government desires to take up the matter of payment for these munitions, and expects to pay for them in raw materials, but asks for time to organize the economic resources of the country. Soviet government is evacuating all war materials from Petrograd into the interior, and asks who can seriously think that a government, whose best soldiers have fought against German control in Ukraine and Finland, can now be planning to furnish to Germany the power to enslave their own land. Nothing short of Japanese invasion can change the deep resentment all Russians feel against Germany's robber raid and shameful peace forced upon Russia at the point of the bayonet. Soviet government is eager to satisfy America of good faith and secure economic organization through American supervising skill, but, if every evil rumor becomes foundation for suspicion, co-operation will be impossible. Is not five months of control undisputed by any effective internal force, and which has survived armed conflict in the Don, Ukraine, Caucasus, Siberia, and Great Russia, together with the signing of a shameful peace and the abandonment of the capital, and still maintains control of undisputed power, sufficient evidence of the foundation in Russian life and

---

[1] Colonel Kalpachnikoff, a Russian previously connected with the American Red Cross Mission to Rumania. He was charged by the Soviet authorities with an attempt to ship American Red Cross automobiles to General Kaledin on the Don.

will of the Soviet government? This was the substance of conference yesterday evening with Lenin. Will take up Kalpachnikoff release at first opportunity. Unable to get copy of Drysdale's report, simply saw extracts and comment upon same, both limited and insufficient. Your message platinum reached Stevens too late for him to see Bronski yesterday. Stevens wants payment his bank in New York ordered by you by cable. Purchase of this platinum more important to prevent falling into other hands than for use in U.S. Expect definite result from negotiations to-day. Reliable report from Petrograd just received assures control there of effective force by Soviet power for all domestic needs. Commander of Red Guard, Waskoff, personal friend of mine, fearless and resourceful. He went to Finland, personally led three assaults on the White Guards, in which five of his staff command were killed. So long as he commands Petrograd Red Guard, I am entirely satisfied with local situation.

Instruct Wardwell advise fully with you—then go to Petrograd at once.

Nothing further. Good-bye.

43. FROM AMBASSADOR FRANCIS

(Received April 4, 1918.)

Johnston on the wire, instructed by the Ambassador.
To Colonel Robins:
After two sessions of two hours each with military attachés and Garston,[1] allied ambassadors agreed to cable their respective governments, advising against Japanese interference or intervention for present. I had done so day or two before.

44. FROM COLONEL ROBINS

(Sent April 5, 1918.)

For Ambassador Francis, Robins at wire:
Have not received your approval of order authorizing Webster to continue investigation eastern Siberia. Prince[2] formally put in undisputed possession of palace in which American

[1] Captain attached to British Mission.
[2] Captain Prince.

military mission are occupying two rooms, by Muralloff, commander Moscow district, six yesterday evening. Anarchists entered on formal order of Soviet committee without violence and left ditto. Whole matter tempest in teapot, growing out of effort to protect large palace and wine cellar occupied by Russian Prince, by what I consider misuse of American flag. Effort made by some here to create an international issue against Soviet authority entirely unwarranted by the facts. Anarchists here as in Petrograd are being financed under questionable circumstances. Charge that Soviet power fears them is simply another false tale. Am making this statement to you confidentially and with no desire to make trouble for anyone, but will not allow stupid incident to be used against co-operation either here or in America, if I can help it, and am prepared to prove the above statement of facts if necessary. Stevens conferred with Bronski regarding platinum purchase yesterday. Stevens asks that you cable Washington and find out if the price they gave was per ounce troy or avoirdupois, also for what percentage fineness. From Webster, Hicks en route Matzievskaya: "Conference takes place April sixth. We are with Soviet officials and are fully advised of their position. Will get the other side upon arrival."

Nothing further. Good-bye.

45. FROM AMBASSADOR FRANCIS

(Received April 5, 1918.)

Johnston on the wire, instructed by the Ambassador. I note what you say concerning removal of supplies from Archangel, but that is the first information I have had from any source as to plan of Soviet to compensate allies for supplies removed from Archangel, in face of protest from allied representatives. Pleased to learn of evacuation of Petrograd war munitions. Military attachés left yesterday afternoon six o'clock; Garston requests Lockhart be informed. French and Italian generals lunched with me yesterday and expressed themselves as pleased with the result of the conference which I proposed, and which satisfactory from every viewpoint. Riggs and Garston will give you results. Wardwell arrived one PM yesterday; dined with me, left for Petrograd about ten PM; made interesting report concerning situation and occurrences Murmansk.

46. FROM AMBASSADOR FRANCIS

(Received April 6, 1918.)

Johnston on the wire, instructed by the Ambassador. *To Colonel Robins:*

Of course don't object to Webster proceeding Chita—in fact think he should, as consider him admirably qualified for such investigation. You will recall, however, that when you first advised that Webster and Hicks were going and suggested they be accompanied by American military officer, I replied that Huntington and MacGowan were already at Irkutsk and that was sufficient, my impression being that Webster and Hicks were going on request of Trotsky accompanied by Soviet representative as their testimony would carry weight. Furthermore, was pleased that they were going, as was provoked at Huntington for delaying to report, and MacGowan's cipher telegrams were unintelligible. Hope you understand and don't think I am criticising, as sincerely pleased that Webster and Hicks investigating.

The following is strictly confidential for the present. Wired the second that Stevens advised railroad men were starting, and asked you to forward message to him in which I gave him instructions, sending the same telegram from Vologda. Was surprised yesterday to receive cable from Department, stating were withholding decision about railroad men coming here until learned specifically for what needs and what duties. This notwithstanding I had requested them to come to Vologda for conference with me, and natural inference was that would be assigned no work without my approval.

Immediately cabled Department giving reasons for railway men; also wired Stevens asking when Emerson party started and how composed. My impression was that government would employ Emerson party in advisory capacity, which would result in American railway mission reorganizing and virtually directing entire Russian railway system, especially Trans-Siberian, whose efficiency was augmented by adopting American railway commission methods.

Think platinum sold by troy ounce, one hundred per cent fineness, but have cabled for confirmation and have asked New York value. Understand Stevens wishes purchase money deposited with his bank New York when transaction closed, and so cabled. Is Bronsky receiving credit in New York or roubles in Russia? And if latter at what rate? Embassy staff salary checks for March not yet sold. What rate could be realized at Moscow?

Following message received from Martin, Murmansk, for Wardwell, dated fourth: "British admiralty states Red Cross and YMCA supplies are not included in shipment now en route from England." Following from Thacher, London: "One. Arrived March thirty first. Your one received." Following from Helene Wardwell: "Easter greetings, well." For Riggs from Ruggles: "Orders relative Yates temporarily suspended." From Johnston: "Since receiving yours attempted to communicate with Ambassador but failed."

Nothing further. Good-bye.

47. FROM COLONEL ROBINS

(Sent April 6, 1918.)

For Ambassador Francis, Robins at wire:
Riggs, Garston et al returned last evening. Congratulations upon your diplomacy both in purpose and method. Yesterday evening I was called by Chicherin to foreign office where Japanese landing at Vladivostok [1] was discussed. Spoke guardedly of your efforts to prevent hostile intervention and your success with foreign representatives at Vologda, and what seemed to be the friendly purpose of allies. Urged that Vladivostok incident be treated as local and to be settled by friendly diplomacy. Later urged this same policy upon other leaders of government here. Evident that Soviet government fears hostile intervention and will, if this purpose develops within next days, declare war on Japan. In that event the latent hostility of all Russian people to Mongolian domination will transform present resentment against Germany into far more bitter resentment against allies. Already complete mobilization of all Soviet forces in Siberia has been ordered by All-Siberian Soviet. We are now at most dangerous crisis in Russian situation, and if colossal blunder of hostile Japanese intervention

[1] On April 5 Japanese and British marines were landed at Vladivostok. Protests were made by the Vladivostok Soviet. The Japanese representative stated that the incident was only a local one and that Admiral Kato had acted on his own initiative. See Document 82.

takes place all American advantages are confiscated. Important that I should be able to make some statement from you to Soviet government to-day. Have you any instructions? Soviet government believes America can prevent hostile intervention, and if Japanese advance, it means America has consented. From *Izvestia:* "The imperialists of Japan want to choke the Russian revolution and cut off Russia from the Pacific. They want to grab the rich territory of Siberia and enslave Siberian workmen and peasants. What do the other allied countries intend to do? Until now their policy was evidently uncertain. The United States was, it seemed, against Japanese invasion, but now the situation cannot any longer remain uncertain. The British have landed a descent right after the Japanese. Does this mean that England intends to go hand in hand with Japan in strangling Russia? This question must be put to the British government most categorically. Such a question must be put to the diplomatic representative of the United States and also to the other allied governments. One or another answer, and mainly the action of the allies, will have an important meaning for the nearest international policy of the Soviet government."

From statement issued by Vladivostok Soviet: "We have taken measures through the city militia and others to find the criminals who attacked and killed the Japanese storekeeper. The unusual circumstances of the murder without robbery makes it evident that it was political. The lie of Japanese Admiral Kato is evident and shows that it was an excuse."
The All-Russian Central Committee of Soviet government has issued an order to show resistance to any invasion of Russian territory.

For Ruggles from Riggs: "All well. Please send Bukovsky to relieve Prince."

Nothing further. Good-bye.

48. FROM AMBASSADOR FRANCIS

(Received April 7, 1918.)

Johnston on the wire, instructed by the Ambassador.
To Colonel Robins:
Soviet government attaching undue weight to landing of Japanese, which American consul confirms, but says nothing about landing of British. There is thorough understanding

among the allies concerning their intervention in Russia, including Japanese intervention, and that understanding is to the effect that there is no intention or desire on the part of any of Russia's allies to attach any of Russia's territory or to make an invasion of conquest. On the other hand the allies desire to see the integrity of Russia preserved and are willing and desirous to aid the Russian people to that end.

Nothing further.

49. FROM COLONEL ROBINS

(Sent April 7, 1918.)

For Ambassador Francis, Robins at wire:
Right to use direct wires was abolished for all except Soviet officials. Secured renewal only on direct government order. Direct wires greatly overburdened, government requests communications brief as possible and cipher messages excluded. Andrews, Hardy returned Moscow yesterday; Wardwell Petrograd safely; all quiet there. Riggs sent cipher recommendations allied military missions Far East situation. Tone government press indicates preparedness to resist Japanese invasion. Both instruments held for us since eleven o'clock. Please be on time.

Nothing further. Good-bye.

50. FROM COLONEL ROBINS

(Sent April 8, 1918.)

For Ambassador Francis, Robins at wire:
Gave substance of your yesterday's wire to Chicherin. Soviet government waits for definite answer from America and other allied governments upon questions arising from Japanese landing at Vladivostok. While urging accommodation steadily, there is, in my judgment, little hope agreement with Soviet government for intervention under present circumstances. German menace is much more immediate, and if Soviet forced to choose between Japanese bayonets five thousand miles away and German bayonets two hundred miles away, the choice is not difficult to guess. Fear of Mongolian domination is now rallying support for Soviet, and may well give them longer lease of life than

possible otherwise. Tokoi of Finnish Soviet government, whom you met, here to-day, and tells of German landing ten thousand troops in southern Finland and their co-operation with White Guard. States that treaty makes Finland German Ukraine, and unless help from England or America comes, Murmansk Red Guard slowly starved out. Answered would send you information.

For Ruggles from Riggs: "Believe written reply to letter brought you advisable."

From Chita signed Jenking: "Webster, Hicks passed, returning from Manchuria. Will report from Irkutsk after conference there."

Nothing further. Good-bye.

51. FROM AMBASSADOR FRANCIS

(Received April 8, 1918.)

Johnston on the wire, instructed by the Ambassador. *To Colonel Robins:*
Nothing from Department concerning Japanese policy. Statement sent you yesterday morning was based on status before landing of Japanese and British, and, if same is given out, should be changed, omitting "but says nothing about landing of British" and should say "previous to this incident, and when I last received advices from Washington and from Tokio, there was thorough understanding, etc. etc."

Stevens delivered Chicherin's letter on arrival last evening and same cabled immediately to Department with your explanation as made to Stevens. Why addressed to you? Situation difficult, delicate, requiring adroit handling to prevent Japanese-German alliance. Russo-German alliance not impossible, but would mean inevitable overthrow of Soviet government.

Nothing further. Good-bye.

52. FROM COLONEL ROBINS

(Sent April 9, 1918.)

For the Ambassador, Robins at wire:
Chicherin letter addressed me, unauthorized, unofficial representative, to avoid necessity of direct reply by you, avoiding

complication involved non recognition status. Chicherin wise, well informed, wishing co-operation for help Soviet government. Desires avoid conflict, if possible. Substance of your revised statement given foreign office, but no publication authorized. Cannot prevent unauthorized statements, but so far have seen nothing hurtful. Cable from Thompson April third: "Believe all relief you may ask for will be furnished Russian government, to prevent German interference Russian freedom." Conservative paper here prints alleged despatch from Vologda, stating that American embassy has received cable from Washington, saying Japanese landing was with approval of allied governments. Government press bitterly anti-Japanese.

For Ruggles from Riggs: "Assume you get data Stevens, City Bank. Cabling you to-day. For Packer: Please send military information books and maps for compiling weekly cable."

Nothing further. Good-bye.

53. FROM AMBASSADOR FRANCIS

(Received April 9, 1918.)

Johnston on the wire, instructed by the Ambassador.
To Colonel Robins:

Had thorough talk with Stevens about platinum which he is looking after. Garbled message from Department through Vladivostok, indicates had heard of landing, about which apparently unconcerned. My diplomatic colleagues, including Japanese chargé, think landing merely police precaution and not beginning of general intervention scheme, which is view I endeavored to indicate in statement wired you, which was cabled to American press. Of course allies will not openly disagree.

Johnston says telegraph manager told him could not permit him to remain in operating room or use direct wire without special order from national commissaire. Johnston will file this for you at usual place promptly at eleven and will wait fifteen minutes only. Commissaire been exceedingly accommodating for four weeks, and I appreciate same highly, being not the least offended by withdrawal of privilege, which expect to pay therefore. Can send Johnston to wire or go myself any time on fifteen minutes notice, which telegraph manager can transmit to embassy. Otherwise must respect wishes of local manager. Nothing further. Good-bye.

54. FROM AMBASSADOR FRANCIS

(Received April 10, 1918.)

Colonel Robins, Hotel Elite, Moscow:
Ninth. Department cables Kato solely responsible for landing troops, and immediately advised British and American admirals and consuls had done so purely for protection Japanese life and property.

FRANCIS.

55. FROM COLONEL ROBINS

(Sent April 10, 1918.)

For Ambassador Francis, Robins at wire:
Hope to have your direct wire service resumed shortly. From Webster, Hicks, direct wire Irkutsk: "Had final meeting with Soviet, who reaffirmed limitation of armed prisoners, with reservation in case of uninvited intervention, liberty arming all resources necessary. Re Manchurian front, obliged to state without in any way taking sides, that Soviet very moderate and reasonable. Chinese constrained against settlement as agreed at first conference, refusing to negotiate with government unrecognized by allies, stating Semenoff might be regarded as power favored by allies. Chief aim negotiations by Soviet, opening railway for transport, which desirable, but handicapped by allied non-recognition. Soviet desires recognition: First, assure them central Russian government; second, would make foreign troops unnecessary preserve domestic order; third, if Germany attacks enable them invite allies co-operate; fourth, assure exchange of raw materials for manufactured supplies with allies. We heartily agree these statements and urge utmost effort to secure such recognition. We fully convinced mutual advantage such co-operation after investigation along entire Siberian line. Impressed with sincerity and strength of authorities Siberian Soviets. Soviets regard peace agreement same Moscow leaders. Soviet fears Vladivostok incident prejudice allies, notwithstanding Soviet doing utmost to protect foreigners. Some three hun-

dred Red Guards passed on way Manchurian front. We speak of this forestall rumors. Will investigate Krasnoyarsk and Omsk, returning to-night Moscow.''

Two more long telegrams same source, assume you have contents direct. Your telegram of ninth, beginning department ending property, received. Will give substance of contents to foreign office at once. Confusion here over press reports of alleged statement from embassy published in Vologda: "Rustel agency wires from Vologda April seventh: American embassy received from its government cable, stating Japanese landing in Vladivostok took place with general approval allied powers. Purpose of landing assistance Russian interests in struggle with German invasion.''

I have denied that this statement was authorized by you. Nothing further.

56. FROM COLONEL ROBINS

(Sent April 11, 1918.)

For Ambassador Francis, Robins at wire:
Did not receive direct wire message from you yesterday. Have sent you daily message; have all been received? Have you been notified of the renewal of right to use direct wire from Vologda? Far Eastern situation better, but still greatly embarrasses understanding and co-operation. Am asked about coming of railroad men. What shall I answer? Ditto economic commission. Telegram just received Wardwell, Petrograd, states evacuation all supplies from warehouse rapid and satisfactory. City quiet.

Nothing further. Good-bye.

57. FROM COLONEL ROBINS

(Sent April 12, 1918.)

For Ambassador Francis, Robins at wire:
Ransome returned from Petrograd yesterday. Reports city quiet, Red Guard control absolute. No difficulty entering or leaving city. Some concern over German and White Guard advance in Finland. Brought letter from Wardwell. He reports everything satisfactory. British cables Lockhart support view of your last telegram to me April ninth. General Man-

nerheim, commander White Guards Finland, Russian general of old Tsar's Staff issued an order: "The German victorious and mighty army landed Finland to help against infamous Bolsheviks, and to help the friendship the Finnish people have always had for the noble Kaiser and mighty German people. Fighting shoulder to shoulder with the great German army, the Finnish army should be imbued with the discipline that has brought that army from victory to victory. He greets the brave German troops and hopes that every Finn will realize the great sacrifice of the noble German people, who are helping them in an hour when every man is needed on the Western front."

Have had nothing from you since message April ninth. Nothing further.

58. FROM AMBASSADOR FRANCIS

(Received April 12, 1918.)

Vologda.

Robins, Hotel Elite, Moscow:

Tenth. If see no objection embassy requests following be wired Webster: "If possible purchase and bring for embassy and military mission following provisions, reimbursement to be made you on arrival Vologda: 2,000 pounds white flour, 600 pounds potatoes, 600 pounds rice, six cases eggs, three poods butter and 1,000 pounds meat, 1,000 pounds sugar."

FRANCIS.

59. FROM AMBASSADOR FRANCIS

(Received April 12, 1918.)

Colonel Robins, Hotel Elite, Moscow:

Twelfth. Following message received to-day from London for you, partly badly garbled, from Thacher: "Six. April ninth. Your special number one and eight received. Leaving to-morrow, doing everything possible. No telegrams from Lockhart or Ransome. Saw Graham, his attitude general situation encouraging. Tell Lockhart, Phelan says he has seen everyone who matters and is much encouraged with progress made. Send future cables America. Your sister delighted to hear of your splendid work. Sends love. Davison in Italy."

Answering your inquiry, not notified resumption direct wire.

Cabled inquiry concerning admission economic commission, no reply. Meantime wired you of arrival here some technical members of a proposed commission to America and you replied. As appeared some confusion, do nothing more for present.

Also wired you that Department asked more definite information concerning work of railroad men after apparently ordering Stevens to come, and Stevens having advised was sending Emerson. Subsequently received telegram from Stevens saying no men be sent, and also cable from the Department stating had instructed Stevens to await further advice. Sending of railroad men complicated if not prevented by excitement over Japanese, British landing, and probably nothing will eventuate until excitement allayed. Meantime might get more detail from government concerning use of railroad men. You thought government might assign operation of Siberian to American railway commission; if would do so and commission would be protected in operation I would so recommend; confidentially, however, Stevens been frightened since October and would recommend his remaining on Chinese Eastern or returning America. Trotsky letter to Riggs of March twenty-first, giving assignments of railway units, was brought by Riggs to Vologda April third, and did not come to my notice until several days later, two weeks after I had cabled Department and wired Stevens to send railroad men to Vologda for conference with me, and I again cabled such plan when asked by Department for what purpose men required.

FRANCIS.

60. FROM AMBASSADOR FRANCIS

(Telegram sent April 12, 1918, by courier.)

Colonel Robins, Hotel Elite, Moscow:

Twelfth. American consul Vladivostok wires eleventh: orders received there from Soviet to ship immediately to European Russia all machinery, machine tools, explosives, shells, metals now there, and that other freight and if necessary passenger traffic be suspended for such purposes. This confidential but am advising you because if true may possibly cause concerted allied action. Am also advising Summers by same courier. The situation is delicate and requires consideration before making any move.

FRANCIS.

61. FROM COLONEL ROBINS

(Sent April 13, 1918.)

For Ambassador Francis, Robins at wire:
Your telegrams tenth re Webster purchasing supplies for embassy, and twelfth general daily message three hundred forty words, received together noon yesterday. Message for Webster too late for transmission. Suggest you send courier Petrograd to bring you such butter, flour, and sugar as remains Red Cross supplies warehouse there. On instructions from you will so advise Wardwell. April ninth, eleven o'clock morning, AmRedCross automobile stolen ten armed anarchists. Placed event before leaders of Soviet government without resentment, demanding final demonstration power government against armed bandits and fortress centers calling themselves anarchists. Yesterday morning at two o'clock Soviet forces appeared simultaneously before twenty-six different bandit headquarters, demanded surrender all weapons five minutes. Some cases immediate surrender, others offered strong resistance machine guns from windows, bombs and small cannon. Soviet used four inch cannon where resistance lasted beyond ten minutes. One big house blown pieces anarchists fighting from cellar until dislodged by smoke bombs. Five hundred twenty-two arrests, forty killed wounded anarchists. Soviet, three killed, fourteen wounded. Large rooms found packed with stolen goods, some great value. Some German machine guns new make, not elsewhere found in Russia. Number of ex officers Russian army among prisoners. Soviet government has now destroyed bandit organization born in first days first revolution March, which Kerensky government and Duma dared not attack. Moscow quiet to-day. Soviet action commended by all press except Menshivik, which denounces Soviet for violence. National commissar post and telegraphs had wired order to Vologda office to let you use direct wire as before.

Nothing further.

62. FROM AMBASSADOR FRANCIS

(Received April 13, 1918.)

Robins, Hotel Elite, Moscow:
Thirteenth. Serbian minister Spalaikovitch in Moscow to see government concerning Serbian refugees and soldiers. Legation secretary brought to embassy yesterday telegram from Serbian professor Moscovlevitch, who appears to have arrived at Samara after departure of large number Serbian refugees, who were at Samara when last heard from. Moscovlevitch wires from Tchelabinsk, where he has 100 school children, and appeals through American embassy to American Red Cross, which, telegram says, has already extended amount forty-five thousand roubles. This aid may have been extended by Roumanian mission, but don't you think relief now proper Red Cross work? If not, cannot see how American aid can be extended. Understand 1800 refugees Serbians, when driven from own country, settled in Roumania, but thence by German advance into Russia where have been since; received seventy-five thousand roubles monthly from empire and provisional government, but Soviet extended forty-five thousand only and stopped. Please inquire of government and Serbian minister now in Moscow and tell me how to answer Serbian legation here.

FRANCIS.

63. FROM COLONEL ROBINS

(Sent April 14, 1918.)

For Ambassador Francis, Robins at wire:
Saw Summers regarding Serbian relief; found you had wired him and he had acted without conference with me. Accepted his action and leave matter in his hands. Kindly advise me in future when same matters are referred to both. This will save confusion, duplication, and regrets. Talked with Wardwell over telephone yesterday regarding food supplies for embassy; found nearly all our supplies already distributed. Ordered him to hold all possible until your wishes were known. There seems to be some check on our co-operation here. Confidently expect prompt notification from you direct, when policy altered or changed. British co-operation increasing steadily.

Did you see Ambassador Buchanan's[1] interview? Lockhart seems winning, both here and at home, increasing support British help Soviet government. Wire connections Finland broken. Please send via Archangel following message clear: "Davison, American Red Cross, Washington: Wardwell, Magnusen—Petrograd, finishing milk distribution. Hardy, Andrews—Moscow. Webster returning war prisoner investigation Siberia, admirably done. Sec. State has substance reports. "For Thompson: 'Have seen Hoffman family. All well, send love. Our old friend still unwilling help here. All recommendations further work wait upon large co-operation between governments.' All well. April fourteen, Moscow. Robins."

64. FROM AMBASSADOR FRANCIS

(Received April 15, 1918.)

Robins, Hotel Elite, Moscow:
Fourteenth. Unconfirmed report here that Murman line cut. Is it true? Please answer immediately. Martin wires eleventh, severe fighting on line between White Guards and Russians, and reported White Guard advance on Kemm repulsed; says armored train eight cars equipped with three inch pieces and machine guns with French gunners and train load of Russian, French, and British gunners and engineers left Murmansk Wednesday night in defense of line. Please answer immediately. Nothing further from Department or East. Following received yesterday for you from London: "Seven. April tenth. Telegram from Davison in Rome necessitates change of plans. He wishes me go Paris for conferences matters covered by your cables. Probably here few days, then Paris. Will write dates when settled. Suggest you cable fully through embassies here and Paris, progress made along lines indicated special number one and effect of recent events on these plans. Scare tales referred to your eighth still persist. Thacher."

Vologda office not received necessary order for use of apparatus.

FRANCIS.

[1] Sir George Buchanan, British Ambassador, who was then in England.

65. FROM AMBASSADOR FRANCIS

(Received April 15, 1918.)

Colonel Robins, Hotel Elite, Moscow:
Fifteenth. Am awaiting explanation from Summers concerning Serbian relief.

What are relations between Soviet and Finland? How near are White Guards to Petrograd? Where is cable cut? Few? Why are White Guards attacking Murman line? New map Finland seen by Kliefoth when returning from Torneo February comprised Russian territory to Murman line, showing Finns endeavoring to recover territory lost to Peter the Great. This movement against Russia evidently encouraged and assisted by Germany, and is hostile to Russia, while Soviet is receiving Mirbach [1] and sending Joffe to Berlin. What is explanation?

When will Webster arrive Vologda? Note you advise Davison Sec. State has substance Webster reports. Have you sent same other than through me? Please answer.

FRANCIS.

66. FROM COLONEL ROBINS

(Sent April 15, 1918.)

For Ambassador Francis, Robins at wire:
Received your telegram by courier yesterday. Nothing by direct wire. Your fourteenth just received. Unable secure confirmation Murmansk line cut. Will advise first authentic information. American citizen, engineer named Barry, arrested Saturday night and quarters searched. Authorities claim incriminating papers found. Consul general has protested. Above substance of statement made me by Chicherin. Told Chicherin must decline investigate incident until authorized by you or interests of AmRedCross involved. Please send following cipher: "Davison, AmRedCross, American Embassy, Paris. Extra three, Moscow April fifteenth. Thacher's seven, April tenth, received. Recent events emphasize recommendations for economic constructive program co-operation between Soviet government and America. Complete wiping out anarchist organized force Moscow final vindication Soviet internal control. Simply repeat

[1] Count von Mirbach, German Ambassador to Russia.

cumulative conclusions for five months. Unless such co-operation between governments, useful work ended May first. Wardwell finishing milk distribution Petrograd. Webster returning from Siberian war prisoner investigation, admirably done. Substance reports Sec. State, Washington. Complete refutation armed war prisoner scare. Hardy, Andrews here. All well."
Nothing further.

67. FROM AMBASSADOR FRANCIS

(Received April 16, 1918.)

Colonel Robins, Hotel Elite, Moscow:
Sixteenth. Your fourteenth, fifteenth. Did Summers say he had been working on the Serbian relief before receipt of my telegram, which did not instruct or request his work thereon, but only suggested that he direct Serbian minister then in Moscow to you on the subject? This is proper Red Cross work, and you acted very discreetly in refusing participation in Barry case, which proper consular work at all times. What business relations has Summers with Soviet? Your messages forwarded. Following received this morning from London for you: "Leaving for Paris to-night. Probably there ten days. If possible will then return home to co-operate with Thompson. Thacher."
FRANCIS.

68. FROM COLONEL ROBINS

(Sent April 16, 1918.)

For Ambassador Francis, Robins at wire:
Yesterday Tokoi, with four members of the revolutionary Finnish government, submitted the following for transmission to America through you: "Considering that representatives from foreign states from time to time have drawn the attention of the Finnish republican commissioners to the fact that the present fight still raging everywhere in Finland ought to be considered as a regular war, and consequently the prisoners taken ought to be treated as usual prisoners of war, in accordance with everywhere accepted national law, and further considering that the Finnish republican commissioners have always shown themselves ready to take due notice of the complaints and remarks

of the said foreign representatives, and in many instances even have acted in accordance with their appeals, the commissioners of the Finnish republic now venture to approach the governments of all the allied nations with an appeal of a similar kind in favor of the soldiers belonging to the Finnish Red Guard. In doing this we beg to draw your attention to the fact that the troops of General Mannerheim have repeatedly shot or maltreated not only their prisoners but also the civil population, men as well as women and children, and even persons belonging to the Finnish Red Cross, which, especially the last indictment, by the whole civilized world must be and will be classed among the vilest crimes. Now that the troops of General Mannerheim assisted by Germans during the last days of battle have taken several thousands of our soldiers prisoners, we feel it our duty to apply for assistance in the name and in the service of humanity. Consequently we appeal to all the powers belonging to the entente, that they might first demand that the troops of General Mannerheim and his German confederates shall treat the armed prisoners they have taken in Finland as prisoners of war; second, demand the immediate release of all persons belonging to the Red Cross service in Finland as well as of all aged people, women, and children that have been imprisoned or interned by the above mentioned forces. Third, grant the right of emigration to all political refugees from Finland, and finally, fourth, give an official declaration to the fact that the forces of the Finnish Socialist Republic have not acted as terrorists or lawbreakers but as revolutionary soldiers in regular armed conflict.''

Your two telegrams dated fifteenth received this morning. Soviet government friendly, Finnish socialist revolutionary government carefully avoiding violation openly treaty terms. Cable connections Helsingfors cut. Murmansk line still open seven last night. Webster instructed confer fully with you Vologda, should arrive about Sunday. Have sent nothing Sec. State direct except through you. Report in full Red Cross of course. Recent elections Moscow Soviet, total to date four hundred sixty-nine: Bolsheviks four hundred fifteen, Mensheviks forty-two, Right Soc. Rev. twelve. Previous Soviet contained one hundred eighteen Mensheviks. Again advised direct wire service for you Vologda renewed.

Nothing further.

69. FROM COLONEL ROBINS

(Sent April 17, 1918.)

For Ambassador Francis, Robins at wire:
Re Serbian relief, first came to my attention telegram from Colton, YMCA Samara, asking for money help. Took matter up with Summers, reached agreement. Summers said Crane would give forty thousand dollars his request, consul's policy against Colton proposal AmRedCross help. Your telegram reopened closed subject consul preferred dealing with without advising me, this is the long and short of it. Summers' business relations wholly with Moscow Soviet. He unknown national leaders. Unable secure correct copy treaty until furnished by me, now seeking map which I will have to get for him. Business relations not usually strengthened through policy kicking people in the face. Constant desire and expectation overthrow Soviet power poor foundation business co-operation. Unable help Harvester people. I saw Lenin and help secured. German foreign office to Soviet government: "Information from authentic sources that German and Austrian voluntary fugitives menacing Moscow, intending capture Swedish, Danish general consulates, same way have captured war prisoner camps, forced prisoners enlist Red Guards. Civil and military authorities Moscow show utter helplessness, even favor these activities. German government expects Russian government immediate energetic steps, and insists first disbanding all war prisoner committees voluntary fugitives under direction Austrian Ebenholtz; second, demands arresting members above committees." Study language this official communication, suggests origin war prisoner scare stories. Boobing allies Russia, special sport German secret service. Period playing second trailing rumor mongers about over. When German direct action commercial organization begins, our opportunity gone. What your wish regarding my longer stay Moscow?

Please answer. Nothing further.

70. From Colonel Robins

(Sent April 18, 1918.)

For Ambassador Francis, Robins at wire:
Conference Finnish revolutionary leaders. They promise keep fighting, while retreat southeast, holding permanent strip eastern Finland. Want Arne Orjalsalo, orator, writer, and wife Helen, go America agitate among Finns anti-German pro-war help Finland. Orjalsalo speaks English, able speaker, inspired patriot, hates Germany, believe desirable admit him America, Finnish passports. Will you inquire? Please send cipher following: "Davison, AmRedCross, Washington. 10095. Moscow, April eighteenth. For Thompson: Cabled you direct March twenty-second: 'After departure Creel's agent, all financial resources for special work from funds under his control stopped. Now using your personal funds, work continues same character, should not be charged your personal account.' Again cabled you direct April fourth: 'Unless US will create commission with power for economic co-operation, supporting constructive program, all useful work finished May first. Nothing short Japanese invasion can change resentment against Germany's robbers raid and shameful peace forced upon Russia bayonets point. Soviet government eager satisfy America good faith, secure economic organization through American supervising skill, but when every evil rumor skillful German propaganda becomes foundation for distrust, co-operation impossible. Is not five months control all effective internal force, that has survived armed conflict Don, Ukraine, Siberia, that has signed shameful peace, abandoned capital, and still maintains undisputed control internal power, sufficient evidence foundation in Russian life and will of Soviet government?' Robins."

From Webster, Hicks direct wire Omsk: "Leaving eighteenth for Moscow. Investigations Krasnoyarsk, Omsk give entirely satisfactory results confirming impressions communicated previous telegrams. No armed prisoners Krasnoyarsk, discipline strict. Omsk chief center arming prisoners, total number, including those sent against Semenoff, eleven hundred. Omsk provincial Soviet and general staff directly controlling arming prisoners, confirmed guarantees obtained All-Siberian Soviet.

All armed prisoners violently socialistic, present conditions without menace except against Central Empires or Japanese invasion." Nothing further.

71. FROM COLONEL ROBINS

(Sent April 19, 1918.)

For Ambassador Francis, Robins at wire:

Following submitted council Finnish leaders, requesting you give copy each allied embassy Vologda and cable same America: "On behalf Republican Socialist Government Finland, Kulleroo and Tokoi, both former speakers Finnish diet, formally protest against German Imperial Government. First, leaders anti-revolutionary White Guard publicly admitted themselves unable crush workers government unaided German imperialism which secured by selling Finland to Germany. Second, German military occupation Finland begun. German militarism, proved enemy popular government and international labor movement, unites with White Guard for destruction Finnish labor. Third, German occupation specially demonstrated Tammerfors, results systematic murder defenseless prisoners, wounded leaders in hospitals and non-combatant laborers. Fourth, revealing before whole world these crimes against civilization in name Finnish workers and their government, we solemnly protest and denounce German imperialism as common enemy freedom and humanity everywhere, and declare Finnish workers prepared continue defend with their blood freedom already won, and further proclaim hatred and contempt for German imperialism as arch enemy of democracy and labor in all lands." The quality this manifesto seemed justify sending you. Hope you will get large publicity Finnish communities America, Canada. What your wish re food supplies from AmRedCross stores Petrograd? No reply received April thirteenth inquiry. Re White Guard and other German inspired advances into agreed Russian territory, three formal protests made Soviet government. Germany responded after third, saying other two not received, that advances forced by bandit bands retreating into Russia. Promised trespass cease, when order restored. Nothing further.

72. FROM AMBASSADOR FRANCIS

(Received April 19, 1918.)

Johnston on the wire, instructed by the Ambassador. *For Colonel Robins:*

Forwarded request for permit for Oratos, also cable for Thompson. Cable just received states Senator Stone died Sunday. Stevens still in Petrograd, but apparently received no reply from government concerning platinum. Department not replied to inquiry concerning reception of commercial commission, nor have I received more from you since you wired to do nothing with two technical men here, as appeared be confusion. Am endeavoring foster commercial relations between Russians and Americans through Archangel and Vladivostok. Did Lockhart make reply to London concerning conditions to be observed before two shiploads provisions could land Archangel—understand ships now at Murmansk awaiting advices? Am awaiting return Serbian minister from Petrograd before again considering relief for refugees including children. Nothing further.

73. FROM COLONEL ROBINS

(Sent April 20, 1918.)

Ambassador Francis, Vologda:

Your direct wire message yesterday first word received from you since sixteenth. Question message seventeenth "What your wish my longer stay Moscow?" Unanswered. Please answer. Death Korniloff verified, this final blow organized internal force against Soviet government. Your coming Moscow would greatly advantage American interests Russian economic development. Allies remaining Vologda, while Central Powers open embassies Moscow, places former great disadvantage. Unless organized opposition planned, organized co-operation only alternative intelligent action. Micawber policy becoming daily more impossible. Government asks daily regarding railroad men, army instructors, economic commission, agricultural machinery, other technical experts and manufactures. Russian economic conditions force general reorganization internal economy under either German or American supervision and support. Largest economic and cultural enterprise remaining world. Your position, influence most powerful factor final consequence. Replying your question yesterday Lockhart answers, "I am carrying on negotiations here with Central authorities to reach agreement on lines laid down by HMG.[1] Favorable progress here, and British consul Archangel wires local committee now taking up favorable attitude regarding this question."

ROBINS.

74. FROM AMBASSADOR FRANCIS

(Received April 20, 1918.)

Colonel Robins, Johnston on the wire, from the Ambassador:
Cabling Finnish protest. Have received through Washington following statement from American Legation, Copenhagen: "Learned from reliable source that commission of 115 members will soon arrive Petrograd from Germany for exchange prisoners, and such commission will not negotiate, but will deliver following ultimatum to Soviet government. Able-bodied prisoners of war in Russia to be sent home immediately, but invalids retained under neutral physician; only invalid Russian prisoners in German camps will be permitted to return to Russia, able-bodied men being retained in Germany." Statement further says, if demand not immediately complied with, Germany will take Petrograd and some other city as hostages. Italian ambassador received the same from Italian Legation, Copenhagen. Please inquire discreetly and advise.

Department says Stevens requesting permission to send home hundred railroad men, as can't use them west of Manchuria station until order restored, which he thinks unlikely.

75. FROM COLONEL ROBINS

(Sent April 20, 1918.)

Urgent

Ambassador Francis, American Embassy, Vologda:
Careful conference with Chicherin regarding war prisoner treaty provisions discovers no idea German ultimatum upon

[1] His Majesty's Government.

point covered your telegram to-day. Treaty terms clear. Parity treatment specified. Probably another fantastic rumor. Nothing in any message from me suggesting that government had taken any of our provisions. Soviet government has taken nothing claimed by American Red Cross Mission in Russia, but has granted many valuable favors. Cannot give items supplies now held Petrograd, but you should send courier or arrange for one to bring such supplies remaining Petrograd you desire Vologda. Wire direct Wardwell, who instructed reserve distribution further until word from you, giving your desires preference. Matter of payment arranged suit you afterward. Special decree reserving direct wires government service only; notice will reach you day or so, until which daily communication as before.

ROBINS.

76. FROM COLONEL ROBINS
(Sent April 21, 1918.)

Ambassador Francis, Vologda:

Regarding shipments from Vladivostok Chicherin gives definite assurance destination supplies safely east possible German advance. Material used for defense Russian republic ready arrange payment raw materials. Robert Minor radical American journalist here, represents *Philadelphia Public Ledger*, states great desire American business interests commercial co-operation Russia. Left America March ninth. Came via Stockholm Murmansk. John Reed Christiania, refused passport America.

ROBINS.

77. FROM COLONEL ROBINS
(Sent April 22, 1918.)

For Ambassador Francis, Robins at wire:

Unsealed envelope addressed me, containing sixteen sheets typewritten copies telegrams to and from embassy Vologda, found under my room door Elite Hotel this morning. Nothing indicating by whom or why sent. Careless saying least. Mirbach expected Wednesday with full staff. Last word received from you direct wire message Saturday. Sent you direct wire also paid message Saturday. Also direct wire yesterday. Nothing further.

To-day concludes direct wire communications. Part our telegrams, part other communications to embassy. Telegrams Elite Hotel delivered promptly.

78. FROM COLONEL ROBINS

Moscow, 22nd April, 1918.

Dear Governor:

I am taking advantage of the opportunity through Mr. Bailey's going to Vologda to send you this letter by him.

My direct wire message to you of the 14th April contained the following regarding the Red Cross supplies at Petrograd. "Talked with Wardwell over telephone yesterday regarding food supplies for Embassy found nearly all our supplies already distributed. Ordered him to hold all possible until your wishes were known." Immediately upon the receipt of your telegram for Webster, which was then too late for transmission to him before his leaving Siberia, I sought to hold what food you might desire at Petrograd. Wardwell has been under instructions to meet your desires as far as possible upon receipt of your list from that date. I hope this matter is now arranged so that you get some needed supplies.

Mr. Lockhart has cabled regarding the landing of the Dora's cargo at Archangel. Thank you for the information.

I regard this hotel as quite safe for messages sent to me by wire. There has been no question regarding delivery since the first days.

It is possible that I shall leave in a few days for Petrograd and shortly thereafter be in Vologda. It will be a great pleasure to see you and give you at first hand the last impressions of the general situation from this outlook.

Wardwell reports all well at Petrograd and that our Red Cross work will be finished by the first of May in that city. This is as I wish it to be. We have already evacuated all our medical supplies and they are being distributed here and in cities further east for hospitals and general public relief.

I have not heard from Webster since I last wired you his message from Omsk. I suppose ere this he has arrived at Vologda and you have been enabled to get the last word on the Siberian situation from his standpoint.

With appreciation and kindest regards,

Faithfully yours,
(signed) RAYMOND ROBINS.

Hon. David R. Francis,
  American Ambassador to Russia,
    Vologda.

79. FROM AMBASSADOR FRANCIS

(Received April 22, 1918.)

Johnston on the wire to Colonel Robins from the Ambassador:
Do not feel I should be justified in asking you to remain longer in Moscow to neglect of the prosecution of your Red Cross work, but this does not imply any want of appreciation of the service you have rendered me in keeping me advised concerning matters important for me to know, and giving suggestions and advice, as well as being a channel of unofficial communication with the Soviet government. When will Webster and Hicks return? Will they stop at Vologda or go direct Moscow from Omsk? Following message received from Thompson, American consul Omsk, yesterday: "Please inform Webster and Hicks on their arrival that Turen's figures exceed theirs eight times. Tell Webster copy telegram not found at Jordans. Will mail staffs letter Monday Moscow?" Also following from Halsey, Murmansk: "Forward to Robins and Wardwell latest indications that Dora's Red Cross cargo coming here early May. Advise you urge London to send it directly to Archangel, as it must eventually go there. Murman railway now suffering from first washout of season."

Have not forwarded Wardwell. Re food supplies, yours fourteenth says "Talked with Wardwell over telephone yesterday regarding food supplies for embassy, found nearly all our supplies already government."

MacClelland, embassy clerk, is in Petrograd and I have wired him to see Wardwell. Were telegrams our direct wire conversations? If not what was subject matter or to whom addressed in Moscow? Do you receive promptly messages sent Elite Hotel? Reported suspicious characters hotel and I have hesitated sending you messages lest same be intercepted in hotel. Nothing further. Good-bye.

80. FROM AMBASSADOR FRANCIS

(Received April 23, 1918, 8 P.M.)

Colonel Robins, Hotel Elite, Moscow:
Twenty-third. Please inform Chicherin his telegram my first knowledge that China prohibited any exportations to

Russia, and have instituted inquiries to ascertain facts. Why does he think such is result of allied agreement, and, if so, why does he think same based on misunderstanding?

FRANCIS.

81. FROM COLONEL ROBINS

(Sent April 24, 1918.)

Ambassador Francis, American embassy, Vologda:
Your telegram twenty-third received. Soviet government claims papers found search Koloboff lodgings April twenty-first, Vladivostok, disclose allied negotiations supporting conspiracy against Siberian Soviet government; these named Admiral Knight and American consul Vladivostok. Further claimed Chinese embargo furtherance such conspiracy. Soviet government believes allied support these plans secured through misunderstanding actual situation. Chicherin promises further information to-morrow.[1]

ROBINS.

82. FROM AMBASSADOR FRANCIS

(Received April 26, 1918.)

Robins, Hotel Elite, Moscow:
Twenty-sixth. What disposition if any have you made of Chicherin communication of this date other than transmitting to me? Is he endeavoring to transmit to our government other than through myself? What reply if any have you made Chicherin?

FRANCIS.

83. FROM COLONEL ROBINS

(Sent April 26, 1918.)

American Ambassador Francis, Vologda:
Moscow press this morning carries several stupid stories, evidently prepared produce dissension, suspicion among American representatives Russia. Confidently expect your understanding give untroubled mastery situation. Your proved strength sufficient guarantee against absurd stories both Washington, Russia.

ROBINS.

[1] See Document 85.

84. FROM COLONEL ROBINS

Moscow, 26th April, 1918.

Dear Governor:

Yesterday I sent you by wire a communication received from the Foreign Office that seemed of sufficient importance to justify telegraphing its contents.

To-day I have another communication that I am sending you by Courier.

This morning I wired you as follows: "Moscow press this morning carries several stupid stories evidently prepared produce dissension and suspicion among American representatives in Russia. Confidently expect your understanding to give you untroubled mastery of the situation. Your proved strength sufficient guarantee against absurd stories both Washington and Russia."

This wire was occasioned by several stories in unofficial papers to the effect that you had resigned or been recalled and that I was to be appointed in your stead upon some new principle of economic diplomacy. Evidently your management of the situation troubles our enemies and they would have you out of the way or get me out of the way or both if possible.

I have given no interviews and of course will not give any. I have seen no Russian newspaper men and will not see any.

These small matters I would not bring up at so critical a time were it not for the fact that they are sought to be used to confuse a delicate situation.

The papers here received by the foreign office seem to justify complaint against the Vladivostok Consul as being at least indiscreet. Investigation will discover the truth of the matter. The foreign office asked me to-day if I had an answer upon yesterday's communication. I said no and asked for time as you would need to consider the entire matter with due care.

Please let me have some word at your earliest convenience upon yesterday's and to-day's communications.

With regards to all,

    Faithfully yours,
     (signed) RAYMOND ROBINS.

Hon. David R. Francis,
 American Ambassador Russia.

DOCUMENTS AND PAPERS

85. FROM COLONEL ROBINS
(Sent April 26, 1918.)

American Ambassador Francis, Vologda:
 Moscow, twenty-sixth April. Webster with interpreter Stephen arrives Vologda Sunday next with report; conference with you. Please arrange lodgings for both.

ROBINS.

86. FROM COLONEL ROBINS
(Sent April 27, 1918.)

American Ambassador Francis, Vologda:
 Moscow, April twenty-seventh. Answering your twenty-sixth: First question, answer none. Second question, answer not to my knowledge. Third question, answer none whatever.

ROBINS.

87. FROM COLONEL ROBINS

Moscow, 27th April, 1918.

Dear Governor:
 Yesterday I sent you by Mr. Shiller of the International Harvester Corporation a second communication received from the Foreign Office here relative to the Vladivostok—Autonomous Siberian Government affair.

Late last evening I received the note enclosed with this letter answering more fully your telegram of the twenty-third. It was sent from the Foreign Office here.

Your telegram of the twenty-sixth received this morning. I replied to by telegraph as follows "First question answer none. Second question answer not to my knowledge. Third question answer none whatever."

Captain Webster plans to leave for Vologda to-night and I shall send this letter with him.

My present plans contemplate my leaving Moscow about May 3rd for Vologda en route America. I shall wire you twenty-four hours before leaving and at the time of leaving if possible.

With appreciation and kindest regards,
    Faithfully yours,
        (signed)   RAYMOND ROBINS.

Hon. David R. Francis,
 American Ambassador, Russia,
  Vologda.

88. FROM AMBASSADOR FRANCIS

(Received April 29, 1918.)

Colonel Robins, Hotel Elite, Moscow:

Twenty-ninth. Note from Chicherin in Russian enclosed in your letter April twenty-seventh by Webster, concerning the Chinese embargo, about which I received urgent telegram in Russian April twenty-second from Chicherin, addressed American Ambassador Vologda. Immediately cabled Department, also Peking and Harbin, mainly for information. Received prompt reply from Moser, Harbin expressing regret, could not request annullment of prohibition, to which I as promptly replied had made no such request, but only inquiry as to facts which again demanded reply concerning, and added that if should decide to request annullment, would do so through legation Peking. Nothing further from Harbin and nothing from Peking. Just received however cable from Department giving detailed history of embargo, which clearly shows government never consented thereto; quite contrary, stated specifically to China thought such prohibition inadvisable. February nineteenth American legation Peking advised Department that foodstuffs permitted to go to Irkutsk and points east under consular control—latter to prevent such shipments reaching enemy, war prisoners at that time not being factor in situation. This agreement influenced by my conferring with Chinese minister Petrograd and latter's cooperation. Obtaining this information within seven days is quick work and demonstrates disposition of Department and embassy toward embargo on foodstuffs to relieve distress. Cannot account for renewed operation of embargo, but expecting further information as Department cable says repeated to American Legation Peking my cable on subject and its reply thereto. Might discreetly inform Chicherin of facts above mentioned, but take care that no friction produced between China and America or Japan and America. If you fear imparting such information likely result in further complication, better withhold for present and only state I am energetically investigating embargo.

FRANCIS.

89. FROM AMBASSADOR FRANCIS

(Received May 3, 1918.)

Colonel Robins, Hotel Elite, Moscow:
Third. Don't understand your message thoroughly. What kind co-operation? Embassy's enciphered messages refused at office last night on government order prohibiting reception and transmission of enciphered messages from any source other than government. French cables also refused. Advised Department by enclaire message of this highhanded, unprecedented action, which am unable to account for if true. Does prohibition include German, Austrian, Turkish representatives?

FRANCIS.

90. FROM COLONEL ROBINS

(Sent May 2, 1918.)

American Ambassador Francis, Vologda:
Moscow, May second. Your twenty-ninth and May first received. Chicherin carefully advised following your instructions. British co-operation stronger daily. They now hold first place with Soviet government. Demonstration yesterday great success. Complete order without single casualty. Center all publicity labor discipline. Telegrams Paris, Washington require my remaining here some days longer. Please tell Webster return Moscow earliest convenience.

ROBINS.

91. FROM AMBASSADOR FRANCIS

The Embassy of the United States of America.
Vologda, May 3, 1918.

Colonel Raymond Robins, Commanding
American Red Cross Mission to Russia,
Moscow, Russia.

My dear Colonel:
Your telegram of May second received this morning but it says nothing about the unprecedented order of the Soviet Government prohibiting the reception and transmission of cipher

telegrams from any source other than the Government. I thought until the receipt of your telegram that you were en route to Vologda; suppose you have learned of this order to-day—did you know of it before it was issued? In my judgment this means the withdrawal of privileges heretofore enjoyed by all diplomatic representatives and it may possibly be the beginning of the withdrawal of all diplomatic immunities; in that event all Embassies and Legations will be subject to indignities and pilfering and regardless of personal comfort or safety of their members, would through consideration of the dignity of the Governments they represent be compelled to withdraw from Russia.

Do you think the Soviet Government would oppose Allied intervention if they knew it was inevitable? I can understand the difficulty of the position of Lenin and Trotsky and their colleagues and know that they are compelled to profess when organizing an army or preparing any kind of resistance, that such is for the promotion of a world-wide social revolution; at the same time you I know have always felt that it was necessary to encourage such professions in order to organize any resistance whatever to the Central Empires and were confident that such an organization would never be used against existing governments including our own but it is difficult to induce our government to accept that view. You are acquainted with my efforts to bring railroad men to the assistance of the Soviet Government and you are also aware of my action in bringing about the aid of the military missions toward organizing an army and you are likewise familiar with the result of such efforts.

But Webster has just come in to tell me good-bye and I have not the time to write at greater length.

If this prohibition of cipher telegrams is applicable to neutrals as well as Allies, I shall as Dean of the Diplomatic Corps recommend that united protest be made and it will doubtless be made through the Consuls of all the Missions that have Consuls in Moscow or in Petrograd. My opinion is that the Soviet Government has made a great mistake in issuing this decree or order.

There are many things which I would like to talk to you about and cannot write even if I had the time. You are correct in thinking that I was not at all disturbed by the newspaper surmise that I was to be succeeded by yourself, not that I think such suggestion absurd but I did not for a moment feel that you were a party to any such move.

It is possible I may write you again to-morrow after learning more about this prohibition of cipher telegrams.

The food has arrived from Petrograd but has not yet been unloaded I am told.

Must close now in haste,

Yours sincerely,

DAVID R. FRANCIS,
By direction.
(signed)   E. W. JOHNSTON,
Secretary.

92. FROM COLONEL ROBINS

(Sent May 4, 1918.)

American Ambassador Francis, Vologda:

May fourth. Answering your May third. Prohibition your cipher rights result misunderstanding order prohibiting cipher rights Siberian consuls. Orders issued restoring cipher rights allied embassies.   ROBINS.

93. FROM COLONEL ROBINS

(Sent May 5, 1918.)

American Ambassador Francis, Vologda:

Your letter received. Leaving for Vologda to-night. Please secure lodgings for self and interpreter. Wardwell leaves Petrograd for Vologda Tuesday.   ROBINS.

94. FROM COLONEL ROBINS

(Sent May 13, 1918.)

American Ambassador Francis, Vologda:
May thirteenth. Leaving to-morrow Siberian express. Please send cipher following "10097. Moscow, May fourteenth. Leaving to-day for America with Hardy and Andrews. Wardwell, Webster, Magnuson remaining here. Wardwell commands mission Russia. More men unnecessary now. Wardwell fully informed, admirably fitted command situation. All well."

ROBINS.

Moscow, Monday, May 13, 1918.

95. FROM COLONEL ROBINS

(Sent May 14, 1918.)

American Ambassador Francis, Vologda:
May fourteenth. Leaving to-night Siberian express, due Vologda about ten to-morrow morning. Hope to see you.

ROBINS.

Moscow, Tuesday, May 14, 1918.

[73.]

Paraphrase of Cipher Message received from Mr. MacGowan at Irkutsk by Ambassador Francis, March 15, 1918.

7. Fourteenth. Special train Bailey, Japanese, Chinese—arrived thirteenth, proceeded ostensibly Amuralsk (?) Dr. Huntington, his assistant Edward Thomas, with me by direction Ambassador and their presence is appreciated highly as work was crushing. Have wired Pekin for the Secretary of State substance of following, also duplicated to Vologda. Siberian Bolsheviks are outspoken in opposition to ratification peace and their local organ tentatively suggests immediate declaration independence and conclusion commercial treaties with America, Japan, and China. Careful preparations making to check expected advance allied forces east Baikal, concentrating Verkhne-Udinsk and Sretensk. Trainload prisoners passed eastward twelfth with dozen machine guns, is stated, and two thousand stopped here. There is concurrent testimony that 3 and 6-inch guns are arriving, two of latter already commanding railway bridge and station. Is daily machine gun practice cadet school. Informant hitherto reliable states German major generals, even other officers (omission?) over thirty pioneers arrived, and general staff expected from Petrograd to direct destruction bridges, tunnels, and execute plan defense. German, Turkish, and Austrian officers at times throng station and streets with insignia of rank visible beneath Russian military overcoat. Every prisoner whether at large or in camp has rifle. American Consul Irkutsk sufficient address.

MACGOWAN.

[74.]

1.

Armed War Prisoner Investigation Siberia: Record of Captain Webster's [1] and Captain Hicks' [2] Special Mission.

(Telegrams and direct wire communications.)

Robins, American Red Cross, Hotel Elite, Moscow:

Number one, March twenty-one. We were at Vologda only forty minutes. Unable find Ambassador or Armour at Embassy or station but saw Johnston and Ruggles. Taylor last night just from Petrograd gave me certain information which Embassy will transmit to you. I will determine truth same in Irkutsk and will inform you immediately. Express thirteen hours late here Viatka. We have special car number fifty-seven which we will retain. We have each paper signed by Muraloff, Chief Moscow military district, stating we go to Siberia on behalf Russian Federated Republic and asking officials give us aid. It would seem desirable that Trotsky send telegram to Irkutsk officials informing them concerning us.

2.

Robins, American Red Cross, Hotel Elite, Moscow:

Number 2, March 22. All is well. Everything is quiet along the way. Express will arrive Perm late twenty hours.

WEBSTER.

3.

Colonel Robins, American Red Cross, Hotel Elite, Moscow:

Number three. March twenty-four. Express about forty hours late at Omsk. Line taken up with a few troop trains moving east and many goods trains moving west destined for Moscow and Petrograd. At Perm large bridge well guarded and here exists a soldiers' committee which is disarming all soldiers from the front and demanding that all food trains move west without delay. Railway officials state this is having very good effect upon movement of congested freight. Military prisoners

---

[1] Captain William B. Webster, Attaché American Red Cross Mission in Russia.

[2] Captain W. L. Hicks of the British Mission in Moscow.

in no way active in Perm or Ekaterinburg districts. A few prisoners have joined the Red Army these two places but well guarded and in no way control its operations. Exact figures not now obtainable. Life along line very normal and exceptionally quiet from a political standpoint. Telegrams we are sending seem not to be going due to carelessness our commissar who is not an exceptional man. Due Irkutsk now about Wednesday.

WEBSTER,
5348.

4.

Number four, following for Colonel Robins, Moscow:

Webster and Hicks speaking—arrived this morning sixty hours late—troop trains delayed us. Found Major Walter Drysdale, American Military attaché Peking, had been here for three days alone, having made trip over Amur line stopping at all camps —and making full investigation. He returns Peking to-night after full conference with us. Semenoff trouble in Manchuria but Amur line still working. No prisoners in district from Vladivostok to Chita are armed and all well guarded. In Irkutsk district some Hungarian prisoners who are social-revolutionists are being enlisted in Red Army to fight against Semenoff. Exact figures later but number not large at present. There preceded us by one day from Omsk train load five hundred Hungarian military prisoners armed with machine guns and rifles going for above object. These men according to good authority are from those who deserted at the beginning of the war into Russian lines and are thoroughly instilled with Bolshevik ideas. They would not dare to return Hungary under any conditions and have cast in their lot with Russian revolutionists. They seized Swedish Red Cross office at Omsk including funds and supplies and have sent ultimatum to Austro-Hungarian government that unless they are given permission to carry on socialistic propaganda and full amnesty they will prevent all Austrian prisoners from returning. With this object —failing reply from their government—they are intercepting all trains at Omsk. Relations between these prisoners and their officers are very bad of which more later. The arming of these men might possibly be considered a danger to the allies and this is the attitude which will be pressed by Major Drysdale on his return. Exception might also be taken to the freedom of movement maintained by these prisoners. We think this suggestion would be supported by Drysdale who would also like to see an American advisory commission working on the Siberian railway. We think that American soldiers acting in this capacity would be well received and might furnish best solution of problem. This rather than full allied intervention would no doubt be much less opposed by all parties. If allies should find further guarantee of prisoners' behavior necessary could not arrangement be come at for certain small number American soldiers to be attached to the guard of each camp to see the conditions? Full discussion promised with Soviet officials to-morrow. There is no immediate danger of armed prisoners seizing Siberian railway.

WEBSTER-HICKS.

5.
Desp. March 30, 1918.
Recd. March 30.

Number five.
Lockhart, British Mission, Moscow, from Hicks and Webster:

Your telegram of to-day received. In our telegram of last night we stated facts as we had found them, feeling sure that the authorities here would have no objection to our doing so. In actual fact we have been given every facility. Although we have not many additional facts we think we can help to interpret motives and indicate possible course of events. We are more than ever convinced that the Soviet here does not mean to extend the practice of arming war-prisoners as it is not part of their program and indeed there is a distinct tendency to commence to withdraw arms in the near future for the reasons: first, that they are not considered reliable, and, second, that the party of 500 which passed through Irkutsk recently caused trouble. As had a long conversation to-day with Yanson, President of the Irkutsk Soviet, who appreciated our point that the Allies could not help feeling uneasy on account of possible action to their detriment of armed prisoners at a later date. We asked whether the complete disarmament of all prisoners and their immediate internment would not be the best way to allay Allies' apprehensions. This question will again be raised at our conference to-morrow with Yanson and Yakovleff, President of All-Siberian Soviet, and Strenberg, Military Commander of Irkutsk District. Will you telegraph at five o'clock to-morrow, Sunday, afternoon by Petrograd time. Fight between White Guard and Bolsheviks three weeks ago at Blagovieshchensk resulted in complete victory for the latter, who numbered about four thousand. No use was made of the three thousand prisoners in that district, who remained in strict internment. Some Japanese subjects who sided with the White Guard were killed. Order now completely restored. As regards Semenoff affair, his force after hasty retreat from Chita during which he lost two hundred men, is now in Manchuria. He has about nine hundred officers as well as hired Hunhuzas, and his forces appear to be increasing somewhat. Opposing him are about four thousand Red Guards, who drove him over frontier but have hesitated to follow him into foreign territory. It is generally stated here that Allies have recognized Semenoff faction as a real political factor and are supporting it. We denied this. End of message of Hicks and Webster.

6.

Following Colonel Robins, Moscow, Webster and Hicks speaking:
Telegram number six. March 31st.

Had a long interview Irkutsk Soviet to-day including Yanson and Yakovleff, Strenberg, and others, all of whom were very friendly. They gave us full facts which confirmed our information and which we believe to be true. There are in all Siberia not over twelve hundred armed prisoners, most of whom are from Omsk. These men were selected with great care as being social-revolutionaries and internationalists who have given up their old allegiance and have become citizens of the Russian Republic and not intending to return home. They are being used for guarding other prisoners and especially German officers in whom Soviet places no confidence. It is not intended to use them in the future for any military operations. The Soviet states that they would not think of placing arms at the disposal of prisoners who would take up cause against them, when their cause is so categorically opposite to their own. The Soviet further gave us their official guarantee to be communicated to our Governments through this channel that no more than a maximum of fifteen hundred prisoners will be armed in the whole of Siberia, and that these would always be kept under strict control and surveillance of Bolshevik officers and will never be allowed to act as an independent force. They also stated that they would have no objections to the senior consuls of the Allies in Siberia having the right of free investigation and at all times to check the maintenance and integrity of the limitations. We stated that the Allies were very anxious to help Russia and asked how this could be done best. They replied, *first*, by supplying manufactured materials from America and England through Vladivostok and Archangel. They were especially anxious about agricultural machinery. In exchange would be given any products of Siberia. We asked them to draw up a list of such products available. *Second*, in order to facilitate the rapid transport of supplies from East would the Allies open up the line of the Chinese Eastern Railway from Harbin to Manchuria Station which is at present partially broken with the approval seemingly of Allied Consulates at Harbin. *Third*, we were informed that if the Allies were sincere in their desire to help they might prevent China from giving protection to Semenoff's forces. The latter's tactics appear to consist in the assembling of men and supplies on Chinese territory, followed by raids into Siberia. The Soviet claims that its troops would follow and annihilate force if they cared to invade Chinese territory. That they do not wish to do. We asked how the Siberian Soviet would look upon Allied intervention in case Germany advanced through Russia. They replied that the Soviet is convinced of its power to meet such an advance successfully with its own troops, now that the people are enthusiastically against Germany. We might say that we were very favorably impressed with the sincerity and energy of the officials whom we met to-day, who were so fully alive to the danger of the broadcast arming of indiscriminately selected prisoners that they readily gave us their guarantees noted above. We feel it may be necessary to proceed eastward as far Dairien near Manchuria Station. Major Drysdale did not visit this center of the Semenoff trouble and site of large prisoners' camp. The Soviet encourage us to investigate this matter which is of extraordinary importance, and it is the only case in which armed prisoners are active. This will not greatly delay our return. End of message.

7.

For Lockhart, British Mission, Moscow:
Number seven. April first. We have just visited the large war prisoners' camp outside Irkutsk where we were given every

facility to see everything and talk with the prisoners. The officer prisoners are Austrians only, while the soldiers consist of Austrians, Magyars, Slovaks, etc., and a few dozen Germans. Although there are over eleven thousand prisoners on the books, the greater portion are employed in work in the town and district and only two thousand remain in confinement. We saw the senior officer prisoner and several leading soldiers with all of whom we had long conversations. We in all cases asked the following questions: first, Is there any pressure put on you to join the Red Guard or the Socialists. Answer, None at all. Second, How do you regard any of your comrades who express Bolshevik sympathies? Answer, With very strong disapproval. Third, Have you any committees in the camp consisting of prisoners and dealing with questions of control and discipline? Answer, None—the only committees are for amusements, etc. Fourth, Are any of your fellow prisoners armed? Answer, About a score who help to guard the prison supply depot. They stated that a small explosive depot was in the same block and therefore being partially guarded by the prisoners. We are taking up this point with the Soviet. A sergeant stated that some of the Hungarians were anxious to return to spread socialistic ideas in their country and these men were, he knew, convinced Bolsheviks. The prison commandant said that officers only could leave camp after obtaining a permit from his office, but that the men could dispense with the permit provided they were in camp by seven o'clock. These statements were confirmed by the prisoners and the leading soldier prisoner added that men were encouraged to stay in camp because of danger in town. Yesterday an officer was killed in the town and the case is under investigation. We found the camp discipline to be excellent and Russian sentries on duty. The latest information about Semenoff is that he is on the point of making another raid into Siberia, after having gathered his supplies and forces on Chinese territory. He has considerable sums of money with which he pays his hired soldiers and he has collected fourteen pieces of artillery. The source of both money and guns is as yet unknown. The All-Siberian Soviet states that if the Allies wish disorder in Siberia to cease they have only to withdraw all protection to ventures such as Semenoff's and prevent him from using Allied territory for his preparations, then order will be established with promptitude. It is said that China is anxious about the collection of Russian troops in that area including the armed Hungarian Russians mentioned in our telegram number four on her frontier. The Soviet wishes to point out if China will outlaw Semenoff, there will be no further need of Russian troops in that area and they will be withdrawn. We have gone into this question at length because we feel it to be most urgent and it will be difficult to convince Siberia of our sincerity if we cannot procure for her a cessation of this unfair protection of those who are attempting to invade her territory and overthrow her government. We start for Moscow to-morrow night, provided that the river is passable as the ice is moving and there is no bridge. End of message. Webster and Hicks speaking.

8.

Moscow, April 2, 1918.

By direct wire.
Webster and Hicks speaking:—Number eight. April 2nd.
Colonel Robins from Webster and Hicks:
Yakovleff, President of the All-Siberian Soviet and Yanson, President of the Irkutsk Soviet, visited us to-day in order to make us a very urgent request, namely, that we should proceed to-morrow to Chita or Dauria. The facts are as follows: Some twenty days ago the Chinese and Russian Governments came to an agreement that Semenoff should not be allowed to leave Chinese territory for a certain period. This period expires on April 5th, and another conference is to be held on April 4th before the expiration of the treaty. Chinese delegates will be at Chita or Dauria on that day and Yakovleff and Yanson and others are leaving Irkutsk on a special train to-morrow morning to meet and confer with them. The above-mentioned treaty had the following among other terms: first, that none of Semenoff's troops should enter Russian territory during the period agreed upon. This term was broken by Semenoff's scouts being continually working over the frontier. Second, that trains should be allowed to pass in both directions. This has been broken, as no trains have arrived from the East. The Soviet permitted some trains to go East at the beginning, but as none were returned, they were obliged to discontinue their dispatch. At this conference the Soviet has hopes of coming to some agreement which will end the fighting and enable the Soviet to withdraw their troops. It is evident that the Chinese are very uncertain as to what their action should be. They seem not altogether

unsympathetic with the Russian point of view, but are influenced by strong and perhaps ill-advised pressure from the East. This is clear from a telegram just received by the Soviet from its Commissar, its representative in the Trans-Baikal district. A full translation of the telegram will be sent to you a little later to-day. The Soviet urgently requested us to accompany them, knowing that as Allied representatives who fully appreciate the Russian situation, our help would be invaluable in explaining the Russian point of view to the Allied delegates from the East, and proving to them that it is to the benefit of Russia and the Allies that this guerilla fighting should cease. The Soviet were dismayed to learn that we had received instructions to return to Moscow at once, and implored us to forward their request which they are supporting by a direct wire to Trotsky. Unless you have extremely urgent reasons for our immediate return, we think you will be well advised to sanction this expedition, because although we do not think that our influence is so important, yet on the spot where the situation seems to be hanging in the balance between war and peace, we may be just those factors which will bring about a satisfactory settlement. In our opinion it would be ill-advised to refuse the request of the All-Siberian Soviet, who stated that they were anxious that a report of the whole affair should be presented to the Allies through unbiassed channels. Also they seem anxious to have moral support from the Allies in their very difficult situation. If you miss the opportunity of hearing the facts first-hand, the Soviet can always report in case of dispute that they gave you all facilities and that you refused to take them. Especially will this be unfortunate if the fighting continues and the Allied cause suffers thereby. End of message.

9.

Number nine. From Webster and Hicks.
To Mr. Lockhart, British Mission, Moscow:
   Translation of telegram from Commissar Yako (Yazo?) to Soviet.
   ''On the 31st March at 16 o'clock there arrived at Dauria Chinese delegates consisting of an interpreter and Colonel Pal Jiju in command. The reason for the delegation's arrival was the approaching termination of the period during which Semenoff was not to be allowed to leave Chinese territory, namely,

April 5th. It has been arranged that the Chinese delegation will arrive on the morning of the fifth of April at Dauria and negotiations will be opened at Dauria or possibly at Chita in order to suit the convenience of the Russian delegates. The Chinese will inform us on April 3rd which place has been decided on, and I request that plenipotentiaries from the Siberian republican Soviet should be sent. The Chinese themselves request this and it is evident that they will be represented by a large delegation. We gathered the following information in private conversation. Chinese explained the breaking of some of the terms of the March 18th conference at Matzievskaya as follows: When the treaty was made no one except the Chinese were in Manchuria, but immediately after the ratification English, French, and Japanese representatives from Pekin arrived and the Chinese Central (?) could not keep his promises in face of their influence. The Chinese say that Semenoff is in such a mood that they cannot answer for our safety as far as Junction 86, and in private asked me not to go so far as Semenoff gave an order that I was to be killed wherever found, even on neutral territory."

10.

From Irkutsk.
Colonel Robins, Hotel Elite, Moscow:
Number twelve. April eighth. The following is the report of the conference at Matzievskaya on April sixth as given by the Soviet: "Chinese delegates General Huan Luan Ling and Colonel Pae Jeju. (?) Soviet delegates Yanson, Siberian Commissar for Foreign Affairs and Commissar Lazo, (?) commander Soviet forces on Manchurian front. Soviet delegates arrived at Matzievskaya ten o'clock in morning on special train from Dauria under guard. Chinese delegates arrived eleven-thirty on special train from Manchuria station. Soviet set forth two propositions to Chinese—first, will Chinese government either surrender up Semenoff or deny him sanctuary within their territory? Second, or will they take active measures with Chinese troops against Semenoff's forces? Chinese answered China could comply with neither, that China intended to remain neutral in this affair and that they would act toward Semenoff the same as they would toward the Soviet. The Soviet asked how can China allow armed men of another nation in her territory? Chinese answered China has always permitted Russian armed forces in

their territory to guard Chinese Eastern Railway. Soviet stated these were always sent there under the direction and control of the Russian Government, but Semenoff was not, and he was really stopping traffic on the railway and was the enemy of the present government in Russia. Chinese answered Semenoff came first and now they cannot permit any other Russian troops in China. If the Soviet forces had come first they would not have let Semenoff in. Soviet asked if China is really neutral and still allows Semenoff's forces upon their territory, they must then permit the Soviets forces to also go onto Chinese territory. Chinese answered if the Soviet forces came there would be a fight and this the Chinese would not like. They stated however if the Soviet Government had been officially recognized by the Allies as the true Russian government, then China could act with the Soviet to prevent such trouble as this. Soviet replied Semenoff affair purely local, and it was to the mutual benefit of China and Russia to open up the railway, and this could only be done by liquidation of Semenoff affair. Soviet further stated that the Chinese were very unneutral in allowing Semenoff's forces to remain in China and make raids into Russia, especially when the Soviet had stated that they would never break international law by sending forces after him. Chinese delegates explained that in regard to this question they had no power to answer, but would have to confer with their government on the point. Chinese delegates then admitted that they could not possibly act against Semenoff without consent of the Allies. Soviet advised them that this was a matter for China to act independent of their Allies as only their territory was involved. As to their future action the Chinese would give no promise and could not guarantee that Semenoff would longer be held in Chinese territory and admitted that Semenoff had practically taken over the railway and was handling it for his purposes, although China was supposed to be guarding the railway in the territory of Manchuria. The Chinese delegates then departed. As soon as their train was out of sight Semenoff's scouts were seen to be coming toward Matzievskaya in the distance, indicating his immediate advance into Russia. Soviets conclusion was that Chinese were allowing Semenoff to act freely but not allowing Soviet to do so. Felt that Chinese delegates were subject to an undue pressure and that they could not have come to any other decision—in fact had been instructed to act as they had and were powerless to have reached any other conclusion. A train of Red Guards was immediately sent from Matzievskaya to meet the advancing Semenoff forces."

11.

Colonel Robins, Hotel Elite, Moscow:
Number thirteen. April eighth. Just reached Irkutsk and hope to continue journey to-morrow evening after final conference with All-Siberian Soviet. Manchurian conference very unsatisfactory, hazy, and indefinite and no conclusion was arrived at. We think Soviet's official account as given in our telegram number twelve correct but for obvious reasons we do not care to comment on it. This expedition has only confirmed our views on this question as expressed in our previous telegrams. The railway will remain closed, which is very regrettable, and the necessity of keeping armed forces on the Manchurian frontier but lessens Russia's chances of opposing Germany on the west. You will notice that China makes a point that the Soviet Government is not recognized by the Allies, which puts Russia at serious disadvantage in such negotiations. In regard to the five hundred armed Hungarian prisoners mentioned as being on that frontier in previous telegrams we are more than ever convinced of the entire lack of danger from this source. We had conversation with several of the Hungarian leaders who appeared well behaved and well disciplined. They were without doubt Socialists and looked upon Russia as their future home. We are sure that anyone after talking with and seeing these men would get the impression that it was absurd to think that they would act against Russia. End of message.

WEBSTER and HICKS.

12.

(Direct wire communication from Irkutsk to Moscow.)

For Robins and Lockhart, Moscow, Webster and Hicks speaking:
Number fourteen. April ninth. We have called you to the apparatus in order to insure secrecy. Just had final meeting with Soviet who reaffirmed their resolve to keep the terms of their letter re. limitation of armed prisoners. They made the reservation however that in case of uninvited intervention on part of Japan they would feel themselves at liberty to arm any resources they might think fit. With regard to the Manchurian front we feel obliged to state without in any way taking sides

in this affair that the Soviet has behaved in a very moderate and reasonable way. We cannot possibly know what is happening on the other side but it is clear that the Chinese are so constrained as to be unable to settle the question in the way decided upon at the first conference. The Chinese further stated that they could not negotiate with a Russian government which was not recognized by the Allies and that for all they knew Semenoff might be regarded as the official Russian government and the one favored by the Allies, while the Soviet were nothing more than revolutionaries without standing. The chief aim of negotiations with the Chinese from the Soviet point of view is to open up the railway for transport, and if (?) they are to be handicapped in this entirely praiseworthy object by lack of recognition. The Soviet stated that they strongly desired Allied recognition for several reasons—first, it would strengthen their position as the central government of Russia, which would also be to the interest of the Allies. Second, it would tend to make foreign intervention unnecessary. Third, should it appear from Germany's activities that foreign help was necessary, they would then be in a position to invite the Allies to help them. Fourth, it would make it possible to co-operate with the Allies, both in facilitating requests for definite supplies from our side and arranging for exchange of materials from theirs. We agree most heartily with these statements and implore you to do your utmost to———— without delay as we are more than ever convinced that it would be to our mutual———after having had personal————along the lines we are impressed with the sincerity, strength, and stability of the authorities. The All-Siberian Soviet looks upon the peace agreement in the way which you are already familiar in Moscow. The Soviet fears that the finding of two Japanese subjects dead in Vladivostok may prejudice the Allies against them to the extent of preventing recognition, notwithstanding the fact that Soviet deeply deplores such incidents which appear to them as highly mysterious. It is doing its utmost to investigate the case and is taking every step to protect the safety of foreign subjects. We assured them that in our opinion this incident coupled with the landing of Japanese marines need not be interpreted in this way. Within the last two days about three hundred Red Guards passed through Irkutsk on the way to the Manchurian front. The majority of these were Lettish subjects returned from France and England during the Kerensky régime but among them were about fifty Hungarian prisoners. We inform you of this as exaggerated rumors are sure to arise. Up to the present no decisive action on the Manchurian front. We shall examine conditions at Krasnoyarsk and Omsk on our return journey. Did you get our telegrams number twelve and thirteen sent last night? End of message.

13.

For Robins and Lockhart, Moscow, Hotel Elite:
Number fifteen. April seventeenth. Leaving Omsk early to-morrow for Moscow without further delay. Our investigations at Krasnoyarsk and Omsk have given entirely satisfactory results and confirmed the impressions communicated to you in previous telegrams. In Krasnoyarsk there are no armed prisoners and the discipline is strict. Omsk has always been as you know the chief center of this arming but the total numbers of prisoners armed here including those sent against Semenoff do not exceed a thousand. The Omsk provincial Soviet and also the general staff which directly controls the arming of prisoners confirmed the guarantees obtained from the All-Siberian Soviet as to limitation of numbers and agree to the other clauses. All armed prisoners are violently Socialistic and as things are at present there is not the least cause of anxiety. For Robins from Webster: "Harold Alpin and Wilfred Humphries of the YMCA arrived Omsk this morning with two special trains of nine hundred Serbian refugees from Samara. They are looking for place in this district to house these people. As all dwellings here are overflowing I sent them to the staff to secure the use of army barracks in some food center this district. This they will attempt to do and report their results direct to you from time to time." End of message.

WEBSTER and HICKS.

[75.]

Report of English and American Officers in regard to arming of Prisoners of War in Siberia, April 26, 1918.

Moscow, April 26 (13), 1918.
On the 19th of March last, the undersigned officers left Moscow for the purpose of investigating the conditions in Siberia relative to the many rumors concerning the extensive

arming of German and Austrian prisoners of war, and the danger of their seizing the Trans-Siberian Railway in the interests of the German cause. The journey to Irkutsk was uneventful, and the railway seemed to be running smoothly and without special difficulty in all its branches. Many transports of prisoners were seen, but they were men being transferred from one locality to another either on account of food conditions or change of work. They all appeared very meek and subdued, and were far from threatening.

Upon our arrival in Siberia we used every means possible in making investigations. We consulted with the various Allied consuls, with the Swedish and Danish Red Cross representatives, with the Russian Secret Service, with the Y.M.C.A. men working the prison camps, with the Soviets in charge of prisoners, and finally, with prisoners of war, both civil and military, many of whom were personally known to Captain Webster in his work as American Embassy Delegate in Central Siberia during 1916-17.

Our investigations carried us to Irkutsk, Chita, Dauria, Krasnoyarsk, and Omsk where we also visited the prison camps or the Red Guard training barracks when we found such to be necessary.

We did not deem it necessary to go further east than Chita on the Amur line, inasmuch as Major Walter Drysdale, the American Military Attaché in Peking, whom we met in Irkutsk, had just made this trip, stopping at all places where prisoners of war were interned, and reported that none of them had been armed and that they were all well guarded.

It became apparent from the first that the only place where prisoners of war were armed to any significant extent was at Omsk. At Irkutsk not more than a dependable score were given arms for the purpose of protecting their own warehouses against thieves. In Chita, Dauria, and Krasnoyarsk no prisoners have been given arms nor is it the intention of the Soviets, as stated to us, to arm men in those places. At Novo-Nikolaevsk and Tomsk, the Soviet authorities at Omsk and Krasnoyarsk informed us, about 100 Hungarian Internationalists were being used to restore order in the prison camps and to help guard the German and Austrian officers to prevent any possible use being made of them by Cadets [1] and counter-revolutionists to overthrow the

[1] The Party of Constitutional Democrats, commonly called "Cadets" from its initials.

Bolshevik rule. At Tomsk the Hungarians raided the German Officers' camp and seized two machine guns supposedly given them by the White Guard.

We found at Omsk that three sets of prisoners consisting of Hungarians, Czechs, and Slavs had been incorporated into the Revolutionary Red Army and were being used in conjunction with the latter to fight the enemies of Russia. The first party, consisting of 434 men, was sent to the Manchurian Front and here we were able to see and talk with them. A second unit, consisting of about 300 men, was later sent to this same front, and while we were in Omsk we interviewed the third set, consisting of 197 men. This made a total of 931 prisoners who have been officially armed for military purposes. In no other place in Siberia was this being done so far as we were able to determine, and if there is an arming of prisoners of war on a large scale it is a mystery where the arming is taking place and where the prisoners are being kept.

The Soviets stated that before any prisoners could join the Revolutionary Red Guard they must be Socialists of standing, vouched for personally by three responsible Russians, and after a period of six months, having renounced their old allegiance, become citizens of the Federated Russian Republic. The Central All-Siberian Soviet, at Irkutsk, stated that naturally such a number was limited and that they would guarantee that not more than fifteen hundred prisoners of war would be armed in all Siberia; also that they would never be allowed to act as an independent military command, would always be under the control and command of Russian Socialists, and that to satisfy any feeling of security which the Allies might deem necessary they would be glad to permit any American and English Mission to make investigations to see that such guarantee was fulfilled, or in their absence to permit the American and English Consuls in Siberia to do the work. They submitted this guarantee to writing and a translation thereof is enclosed herewith for reference (April 2, 1918, No. 253, Irkutsk). The Omsk Soviet affirmed this guarantee and stated that they did not intend to arm more than one thousand men from their district, including those already armed, which affirmation they also submitted to writing.

At Omsk the Hungarian Red Guards sent an ultimatum to their former country demanding that they be given full amnesty and be permitted to return or they would arrest all prisoners of war at Omsk, forbidding them to continue their journey homeward. The reply of the German and Austrian Governments to this ultimatum came through the Swedish Red Cross, in which it was stated that all such Internationalists would be hung. The prisoner-soldiers with whom we talked stated that they felt this to be too true, and that it was not their intention to return to Germany or Austria until at least there had been a Social Revolution in those countries. Many stated that they intended to remain permanently in Siberia. They said that they had cast their lot with the Russian Revolutionists, would fight with them against all enemies of Socialism and felt that they were far better off, both financially and socially, by taking such action. The sincerity and devotion of these men to their chosen cause is not to be doubted, and when asked whether it was not possible for friends of Germany and enemies of Socialism to join their ranks they were quite scornful, and stated that although they considered such impossible, still if any of their colleagues were found to be unfaithful, "they would surely meet with sudden death."

There are various reasons why our report concerning the arming of prisoners of war in Siberia has differed materially from those set forth by Allied consular reports and other sources of information in Siberia. We found, first, that the Allied consuls in Irkutsk were unanimously anti-Bolshevik in sympathy, had had nothing to do with the Soviet authorities personally, and had not even met Mr. Yakovleff, the President of the All-Siberian Soviet, a very intelligent and sincere man who could have given them a satisfactory explanation to many doubtful questions.

Second, their sources of information were, in all cases, pre-revolutionary—as coming from property-holders, officers, Cadets, White Guards, etc., who were strong enemies of the present régime and were naturally desirous of strengthening their own position and damning those now in power; while

Third, the Consuls seemed to have no time to make proper investigation on account of their staffs being so small that, as one consul said to us, he was so busy coding the information he received that he did not have time to confirm it. If they heard a story concerning great intrigues or secret movements of unseen German activities, especially in regard to armed prisoners, they did not get to the bottom of the particular rumor but reported the statements as they had received them. Even those things which were at hand and which could have been checked easily by proper care on their part did not receive the attention necessary to draw out the real truth. For instance, when the first party of 434 armed prisoners passed through Irkutsk going from Omsk to the Manchurian front the report sent to Paris was that the number of such prisoners was one thousand. While we were in the American Consulate talking with Major Drysdale at Irkutsk, one of his interpreters brought in the information that ten armed prisoners and three Russians seized the Government telegraph office every night, driving out the regular operators, and after placing sound-proof hoods upon the machines, would operate them for two hours and then retire. However, we found this rumor to be false, as we were in the telegraph office every night for nearly a week, sometimes until three in the morning, upon our own business, and no official there with whom we talked knew anything about such seizure and all regarded the idea as "mad."

We can well say that we found all the Soviet authorities with whom we came in contact as sincere and bright men, good leaders, thorough partisans of their party, and seeming in all cases to well represent the cause for which the Soviet Government stands. We feel, therefore, that their assurances to us concerning the limitation in regard to the arming of prisoners is a statement upon which faith and confidence can be based. The Soviets have both the power and the inclination to carry out this guarantee.

The Soviet power is growing stronger instead of weaker in Siberia, and the activities of the White Guards and counter-revolutionaries at Vladivostok, Blagovieshchensk, Chita, Tomsk, and Irkutsk met with overwhelming defeat. In the case of Irkutsk considerable blood was shed and considerable property destroyed as there were three cadet schools at this place and they were able to offer a formidable resistance for ten days, after which they completely capitulated. The Soviet leaders are mild-mannered and vengeance for past wrongs does not seem to be part of their programs.

We can but add after seeing the armed prisoners and the type of men which they are, that we feel there is no danger to the Allied cause through them. On the contrary, we feel that there would seem to be a large social danger to the cause of the Central Empires, as the Socialist activity among the prisoners of war is very far reaching. For instance, at Krasnoyarsk 1,500 prisoners of war have subscribed their names to the socialistic principles, while 5,000 have done so at Omsk. The German officers as a whole, and the Austrian officers, with the exception of the Slavs, are very bitter against this response on the part of the men and are making lists of those whom they deem dangerous to be given to their governments at the first opportunity. Much friction between the prisoner officers and men has arisen on this account and all officers with whom we talked were not only angry concerning the matter but considerably worried as to the outcome. They stated that the large number of men were not only becoming demoralized from disciplinary standpoints, but were being made dangerous subjects to their Fatherlands. Of course, they regarded those who had taken up arms on behalf of Russia as nothing short of traitors.

The Central All-Siberian Soviet was naturally interested in the question of intervention in Siberia either by Japan or the Allies. They stated in their final interview with us on April 9th that they were only too glad to reassure us on the question of the limitation regarding the arming of prisoner Socialists, but that in the case of uninvited intervention they would feel free to arm such resources as they saw fit to defend their territory. They intimated that they intended to oppose to the best of their ability the march of uninvited foreign armies into Siberia even though such resistance amounted merely to destroying bridges and tunnels. They stated that the Japanese peace terms, as printed in the Siberian papers, although probably not official, were undoubtedly officially inspired; and that they reflected what Japan would desire in Siberia were she able to demand it. They stated that Russia had been in severe competition with Japan ever since the ascendency of that Empire and that the Soviet could not but feel the safety of its power or the integrity of their country would be jeopardized in case Japanese troops were spread over it. However, the Soviet did state that in case the Allies recognized the Soviet Government as the Central Government of Russia, then in case of renewed military activities between Germany and Russia and the military help of the Allies seemed both practical and necessary, they thought that it might be arranged to have Allied troops brought in to assist the Russian soldiers in repelling the Germans.

At Krasnoyarsk, where 3,600 prisoner-officers are interned (3,000 Austrian and about 600 German), we secured confidential information from Germans personally known to Captain Webster that these officers were being counted upon to be used to command a nucleus consisting of German, Austrian, and Russian troops to oppose Japanese intervention. It was stated that without doubt the South end of Lake Baikal would be used as the point of defense.

At the request of the All-Siberian Soviet we attended the conference on April 6th at Matzievskaya between the Soviet representatives and the Chinese delegates to take up the matter of the Semenoff trouble. It appeared very quickly here that the Chinese delegates had no power or discretion in the matter except to break off all negotiations with the Soviet and to state that they could no longer be responsible for Semenoff's activities. The matter in so far as the Soviet is concerned was of no great significance to them as a counter-revolutionary movement; but the closing of the Manchurian Railway between Chita and Harbin was of the utmost importance. The Chinese stated that they would not permit the Soviet forces to pursue Semenoff into Chinese territory. The Soviet stated that they did not wish to invade foreign soil which might be deemed an act of war upon China. They did desire, however, that sanctuary be refused Semenoff in as much as he was blocking the railway and making raids from his place of security into Russian territory. As the Chinese delegates retired without making satisfactory replies, they asked us to take up with our respective governments the question of having pressure brought upon China to refuse to longer give sanctuary to these robber bands, and, second, to bring all pressure to bear to have the Chinese Eastern Railway again open to traffic.

The All-Siberian Soviet and the Provincial Soviets at Krasnoyarsk, Chita, and Omsk asked us to take up with our governments three economic points of interest to Siberia: First, they desired to have sent as soon as possible manufactured articles of all kinds, especially agricultural machinery. The demand for repair parts and binder twine was especially critical. It was stated at Omsk by the International Harvester Company representatives that unless these things were forthcoming very soon there would be a tremendous loss in the usual high yield of wheat in the monster plain 1,500 versts long and 1,000 versts wide, comprising that district. Second, the Soviets would be glad to arrange in exchange for these things, such raw products as Siberia was able to furnish, including wool, hemp, hides, furs, flax, lumber, sunflower seed oil, minerals, etc. Third, it was stated by the All-Siberian Soviet especially, that Siberia was in need of expert aid of all kinds, not only for her railways but for every branch of industry,—if possible to the extent of 10,000 men.

We feel that co-operation on a commercial basis would not only tend to prevent Germany securing the Siberian raw products but would be the best point of contact we could secure, and the best influence we could use from a political standpoint.

(signed) W. L. HICKS,
Captain of the British Mission in Moscow.

(signed) WILLIAM B. WEBSTER,
Captain and Attaché, American Red Cross Mission in Russia.

(ENCLOSURE.)

MEMORANDUM GIVEN BY THE CENTRAL EXECUTIVE COMMITTEE OF SOVIETS IN SIBERIA TO CAPTAIN WEBSTER AND CAPTAIN HICKS, APRIL 2, 1918.

April 2, 1918, No. 253,
Irkutsk.
Russian Federated Republic of Soviets.

Central Executive Committee of Soviets of Workers', Soldiers', Peasants' and Cossacks' Deputies of Siberia.

Memorandum

To the interrogations of Captain Hicks, a member of the British Mission in Moscow, and Captain William Webster of the American Red Cross Mission in Russia, who arrived in Siberia for the special purpose of investigating the rumors which have appeared in the foreign press regarding mass arming of German war prisoners in Siberia, the Presidium of the Central Executive Committee of Soviets of Workers', Soldiers', Peasants', and Cossacks' Deputies of Siberia, in conference assembled replies:

I. Arming of war prisoners in Eastern Siberia is not practiced; in Western Siberia there are being armed exclusively Socialists, Internationalists, enemies of Imperialism. The arming started during the beginning of the German invasion of Russia after the Russian Republic refused to sign the annexationist peace, with the purpose of sending the companies that were formed to the German front. The cessation of hostilities with Germany which exists at present, prompted the use of these strong Socialist companies for the defense of the Workers' Republic against the attempts of the counter-revolutionaries within the country. One of these companies consists of five hundred Hungarian Socialists, who, because they were accepted citizens of the Russian Soviet Republic, were sent under the command of a Russian officer for action against armed robber bands of Esaul Semenoff, who is hiding on Chinese territory, in case he should again attack the Baikal district. The majority of the armed Socialists who were former war prisoners are of Hungarian nationality or belong to the Slavonic nationalities of Austria-Hungary. The relations between them and the former officers are extremely acute. At the present time there are armed in the whole of Siberia a little over one thousand former war prisoners, and this number will not be increased to more than fifteen hundred men, because the number of absolutely reliable party Socialists, who are ready to come out openly in the defense of labor revolution against the Imperialism of any country, is naturally limited.

II. As commanders of companies formed from former war prisoners Russian Socialists are appointed; these companies never act as an independent force, and are subject to absolute orders of the general command of the Workers' and Peasants' Red Army.

III. The Central Executive Committee of Soviets of Siberia willingly expresses its readiness to always give the representatives of the British and American Missions, and upon their departure to British and American Consuls, all information that interests them relating to the above-mentioned facts concerning war prisoners.

IV. The Central Executive Committee in repudiation of the stupid rumors about mass arming of war prisoners in Siberia informs the honorable representatives of the American and English Missions that long before these rumors appeared, in consideration of the food problem, a plan was on foot to evacuate the war prisoners from districts and provinces which lie east of Irkutsk to the western and central Siberian provinces, where the food supply is secure. At the present time the War Commissariat of Siberia is engaged in preparatory work for carrying out of this plan.

(signed) Chairman Central Executive Committee of Soviets of Siberia,

N. YAKOVLEFF,
Commissary of Foreign Affairs of Siberia,

YANSON,
Acting War Commissary of Siberia,
(Signature)

Seal of the Central Siberian Committee of Soviets of Workers', Soldiers', and Peasants' Deputies.

[76.]

Communication from Tchicherin to Colonel Robins with Two Enclosures, March 21, 1918.

21 March, 1918, Moscow.

THE PEOPLE'S COMMISSARIAT OF FOREIGN AFFAIRS

Dear Colonel Robins:

I am sending you here both the text of a communication given out through the Press Bureau and of a radiogram sent out abroad. We shall be very glad if you make of it the use you think most proper.

Yours most faithfully,
(signed) G. TCHICHERIN.

(ENCLOSURE 1.)

March 21, 1918, Moscow.

PEOPLE'S COMMISSARIAT OF FOREIGN AFFAIRS

In spite of the repudiation of newspaper rumors about German control, about occupation of Petrograd, etc., lately a new rumor was started regarding some kind of a German commission headed by Fredericks, which is alleged to exist in Petrograd, to control entry and exit to and from the city, and in particular is alleged not to issue passes to leave Petrograd to American, English, and French subjects.[1]

[1] See Document 72: Nos. 11, 15, 16, 20.

In view of the fact that all these fantastic and provocative rumors receive undeserved confidence in certain circles of America, England, and France, the People's Commissariat of Foreign Affairs once more affirms the absolute falsity and improbability of these rumors.

(signed) GEORGE TCHICHERIN,
Acting People's Commissary of Foreign Affairs.

(ENCLOSURE 2.)

Radiogram, Moscow, March 21, 1918.

Lately through unknown sources rumors are being spread systematically which say that Germany intends and has the right according to the treaty to create controlling commissions in various cities of Russia or only in Petrograd. The People's Commissariat of Foreign Affairs stated previously that this evidently provocative rumor which is being spread for the purpose of sowing panic is absolutely unfounded on any fact. By the treaty it was arranged to create Germano-Russian commissions for the regulation of the exchange of war prisoners, the mutual compensation of losses, for mutual return of captured ships, for reconsideration of treaties, and for the establishment of local frontier lines. There is absolutely no hint of the creation of any such controlling commissions in the treaty, and the Soviet Government would never agree to such an invasion of its internal life and independence.

In spite of the denials of the People's Commissariat of Foreign Affairs, such rumors continue to be spread. A rumor is going round that in Petrograd there already exists a controlling commission under the chairmanship of Baron Fredericks, and it is alleged that without permission of this commission it is not possible to leave Petrograd.

The People's Commissariat of Foreign Affairs announces that this rumor is absolutely fantastic and stupid, and that it clearly comes from some sources which are engaged in dark purposes.

(signed) PEOPLE'S COMMISSARIAT OF FOREIGN AFFAIRS.

[77.]

Cable from Colonel Robins to Henry P. Davison, March 26, 1918.

Davison, Care American Embassy, Paris:
  Number extra one. March twenty-sixth, acknowledging yours March twenty-first via Tokio.[1] Following sent you Washington: "Special five. March twentieth. Soviet government organizing army for defense Russian socialist republic. Government asks co-operation American Red Cross units for hospital service. Have sent Captain Webster Irkutsk for report on war prisoner conditions. Milk distribution Petrograd continues satisfactorily. Organizing for distribution of medical supplies in warehouse here. Co-operation of government continues satisfactory. Hardy, Andrews, Magnuson here. All well. Please notify our families. Have you any instructions?" American, British, French, and Italian military missions co-operating with Soviet government here. Riggs wired Ambassador Francis March twenty-first: "My strong impression Soviet government making sincere effort for serious reconstruction of forces and I cannot too strongly recommend that they be encouraged by prompt support." Washington seems confused by Siberian army war prisoner scare and German control Petrograd and Moscow rumors. Regard all this as skilful propaganda to prevent allied co-operation with Soviet government.

ROBINS.

Moscow, Tuesday, March 26, 1918.

[78.]

Statement given by Soviet Government to Colonel Robins, regarding Red Cross Activities in Russia.

PEOPLE'S COMMISSARIAT OF FOREIGN AFFAIRS.

29 March, 1918, Moscow.
  The work of the American Red Cross of medical-sanitary assistance to the civilian population, as well as to the sick and wounded soldiers, as well as in the supplying of our medical

[1] Embodied in Document 72, No. 22.

institutions with necessary medicines, proved to be of great value to the Russian medical sanitary institutions.

Considering that this useful and valuable work of the American Red Cross cannot be considered as ended, we call your attention, Colonel Robins, to the fact that the further work of the American Red Cross, and together with this the further stay of the Mission with you at the head of it, in Russia we consider absolutely essential.

(signed) Chairman of the Council of People's Commissaries,
V. ULIANOV (LENIN.)
Acting People's Commissary of Foreign Affaires,
GEORGE TCHICHERIN.

[79.]

Telegram from Henry P. Davison to Colonel Robins, sent through the American Ambassador in Paris, April 4, 1918.

(Telegram received April 5, 1918.)

American Consul, Moscow,
Paris 21844 56 4/4 0 40.

Third for Robins:

"Am thinking of sending you two or three assistants from France and would like to know what route you advise them to use in going from France to Petrograd. Have left for Rome but would like all messages sent to me care American Embassy Paris. Davison." SHARP.

April 5, 1918.

[80.]

Telegram from Colonel Robins to Henry P. Davison, April 5, 1918.

Davison, American Embassy, Paris:

Number extra two. April fifth. Your number three received. Murmansk best route for speed, Vladivostok for safety. No need now for more Red Cross men here. Unless U.S. supports economic co-operation and constructive program all useful work finished May first. If administration Red Cross here unsatisfactory kindly recall me.

ROBINS.

Moscow, Friday, 5th April, 1918.

[81.]

Address by President Wilson at Baltimore, April 6, 1918.

(*President Wilson's Foreign Policy.* Edited by James Brown Scott, p. 374.)

Fellow-Citizens:

This is the anniversary of our acceptance of Germany's challenge to fight for our right to live and be free, and for the sacred rights of freemen everywhere. The nation is awake. There is no need to call to it. We know what the war must cost, our utmost sacrifice, the lives of our fittest men, and, if need be, all that we possess.

The loan we are met to discuss is one of the least parts of what we are called upon to give and to do, though in itself imperative. The people of the whole country are alive to the necessity of it and are ready to lend to the utmost, even where it involves a sharp skimping and daily sacrifice to lend out of meager earnings. They will look with reprobation and contempt upon those who can and will not, upon those who demand a higher rate of interest, upon those who think of it as a mere commercial transaction. I have not come, therefore, to urge the loan. I have come only to give you, if I can, a more vivid conception of what it is for.

The reasons for this great war, the reason why it had to come, the need to fight it through, and the issues that hang upon its outcome, are more clearly disclosed now than ever before. It is easy to see just what this particular loan means, because the cause we are fighting for stands more sharply revealed than at any previous crisis of the momentous struggle. The man who knows least can now see plainly how the cause of justice stands, and what the imperishable thing he is asked to invest in. Men in America may be more sure than they ever were before that the cause is their own, and that, if it should be lost, their own great nation's place and mission in the world would be lost with it.

I call you to witness, my fellow-countrymen, that at no stage of this terrible business have I judged the purposes of Germany intemperately. I should be ashamed in the presence of affairs so grave, so fraught with the destinies of mankind throughout all the world, to speak with truculence, to use the weak language of hatred or vindictive purpose. We must judge as we would be judged. I have sought to learn the objects Germany has in this war from the mouths of her own spokesmen, and to deal as frankly with them as I wished them to deal with me. I have laid bare our own ideals, our own purposes, without reserve or doubtful phrase, and have asked them to say as plainly what it is that they seek.

We have ourselves proposed no injustice, no aggression. We are ready, whenever the final reckoning is made, to be just to the German people, deal fairly with the German power, as with all others. There can be no difference between peoples in the final judgment, if it is indeed to be a righteous judgment. To propose anything but justice, even-handed and dispassionate justice, to Germany at any time, whatever the outcome of the war, would be to renounce and dishonor our own cause, for we ask nothing that we are not willing to accord.

It has been with this thought that I have sought to learn from those who spoke for Germany whether it was justice or dominion and the execution of their own will upon the other nations of the world that the German leaders were seeking. They have answered—answered in unmistakable terms. They have avowed that it was not justice, but dominion and the unhindered execution of their own will.

The avowal has not come from Germany's statesmen. It has come from her military leaders, who are her real rulers. Her statesmen have said that they wished peace, and were ready to discuss its terms whenever their opponents were willing to sit down at the conference table with them. Her present Chancellor has said—in indefinite and uncertain terms, indeed, and in phrases that often seem to deny their own meaning, but with as much plainness as he thought prudent—that he believed that peace should be based upon the principles which we had declared would be our own in the final settlement.

At Brest-Litovsk her civilian delegates spoke in similar terms; professed their desire to conclude a fair peace and accord to the peoples with whose fortunes they were dealing the right to choose their own allegiances. But action accompanied and followed the profession. Their military masters, the men who act for Germany and exhibit her purpose in execution, proclaimed a very different conclusion. We cannot mistake what they have done—in Russia, in Finland, in the Ukraine, in

Rumania. The real test of their justice and fair play has come. From this we may judge the rest.

They are enjoying in Russia a cheap triumph in which no brave or gallant nation can long take pride. A great people, helpless by their own act, lies for the time at their mercy. Their fair professions are forgotten. They nowhere set up justice, but everywhere impose their power and exploit everything for their own use and aggrandizement, and the peoples of conquered provinces are invited to be free under their dominion!

Are we not justified in believing that they would do the same things at their western front if they were not there face to face with armies whom even their countless divisions cannot overcome? If, when they have felt their check to be final, they should propose favorable and equitable terms with regard to Belgium and France and Italy, could they blame us if we concluded that they did so only to assure themselves of a free hand in Russia and the East?

Their purpose is, undoubtedly, to make all the Slavic peoples, all the free and ambitious nations of the Baltic Peninsula, all the lands that Turkey has dominated and misruled, subject to their will and ambition, and build upon that dominion an empire of force upon which they fancy that they can then erect an empire of gain and commercial supremacy—an empire as hostile to the Americas as to the Europe which it will overawe—an empire which will ultimately master Persia, India, and the peoples of the Far East.

In such a program our ideals, the ideals of justice and humanity and liberty, the principle of the free self-determination of nations, upon which all the modern world insists, can play no part. They are rejected for the ideals of power, for the principle that the strong must rule the weak, that trade must follow the flag, whether those to whom it is taken welcome it or not, that the peoples of the world are to be made subject to the patronage and overlordship of those who have the power to enforce it.

That program once carried out, America and all who care or dare to stand with her must arm and prepare themselves to contest the mastery of the world—a mastery in which the rights of common men, the rights of women and of all who are weak, must for the time being be trodden underfoot and disregarded and the old, age-long struggle for freedom and right begin again at its beginning. Everything that America has lived for and loved and grown great to vindicate and bring to a glorious realization will have fallen in utter ruin and the gates of mercy once more pitilessly shut upon mankind!

The thing is preposterous and impossible; and yet is not that what the whole course and action of the German armies have meant wherever they have moved? I do not wish, even in this moment of utter disillusionment, to judge harshly or unrighteously. I judge only what the German arms have accomplished with unpitying thoroughness throughout every fair region they have touched.

What, then, are we to do? For myself, I am ready, ready still, ready even now, to discuss a fair and just and honest peace at any time that it is sincerely purposed—a peace in which the strong and the weak shall fare alike. But the answer, when I proposed such a peace, came from the German commanders in Russia, and I cannot mistake the meaning of the answer.

I accept the challenge. I know that you accept it. All the world shall know that you accept it. It shall appear in the utter sacrifice and self-forgetfulness with which we shall give all that we love and all that we have to redeem the world and make it fit for free men like ourselves to live in. This now is the meaning of all that we do. Let everything that we say, my fellow-countrymen, everything that we henceforth plan and accomplish, ring true to this response till the majesty and might of our concerted power shall fill the thought and utterly defeat the force of those who flout and misprize what we honor and hold dear.

Germany has once more said that force, and force alone, shall decide whether justice and peace shall reign in the affairs of men, whether right as America conceives it or dominion as she conceives it shall determine the destinies of mankind. There is, therefore, but one response possible from us: Force, force to the utmost, force without stint or limit, the righteous and triumphant force which shall make right the law of the world and cast every selfish dominion down in the dust.

[82.]

Soviet Government Statement regarding the Attack on Russia from the East.

(*Izvestia*, April 6, 1918.)

JAPAN BEGINS HER CAMPAIGN AGAINST THE SOVIET REPUBLIC BY LANDING TROOPS IN VLADIVOSTOK

ENGLAND EVIDENTLY FOLLOWS IN THE FOOTSTEPS OF JAPAN

A statement has been received from Siberia from the Soviet authorities in Vladivostok and Irkutsk to the effect that Admiral Kato, the commander of the Japanese fleet, has landed troops in Vladivostok and issued an appeal to the local population, informing them of the fact that Japan takes upon itself the preservation of order. As a pretext for the landing, the murder of two Japanese by unknown people, which took place in Vladivostok, is used.

Regarding this murder, its causes, circumstances, and the culprits, the Soviet Government at the present moment has no information whatsoever. But it knows, as does the whole world, that the Japanese Imperialists for several months were preparing a landing in Vladivostok. The official Japanese press wrote that Japan was called upon to re-establish order in Siberia up to Irkutsk, and even up to the Urals. The Japanese authorities were looking for an appropriate pretext for their robbers' raid into Russian territory. In the General Staff of Tokio monstrous statements were being invented about conditions in Siberia, about German war prisoners, etc., etc. The Japanese Ambassador in Rome stated a few weeks ago that the German war prisoners were armed and ready to seize the Siberian railroad. This statement has made the round of the world's press. The military authorities of the Soviet Republic sent a British and an American officer along the Siberian line, and gave them a complete opportunity to convince themselves of the falsity of the official Japanese statement. With this excuse removed, the Japanese Imperialists have to look for other excuses. The murder of two Japanese, from this point of view, was very opportune. On the 4th of April the murder took place, and on the 5th the Japanese Admiral, without awaiting any investigation, has accomplished his landing.

The course of events leaves no doubt whatsoever that all this was pre-arranged and that the provocative murder of two Japanese was a necessary part of this preparation. In this way the Imperialistic blow from the East, which has been contemplated for a long time, has fallen. The Imperialists of Japan wish to strangle the Soviet revolution, wish to cut off Russia from the Pacific Ocean, wish to seize the rich territories of Siberia and to enslave Siberian workers and peasants. Bourgeois Japan acts as the deadly enemy of the Soviet Republic. What is the plan of action of the other Governments of the Entente: America, England, France, and Italy? Up to the present moment their policy in regard to the predatory intentions of Japan was evidently undecided. The American Government, it seems, was against the Japanese invasion. But at present the situation cannot remain indefinite any longer. England intends to go hand in hand with Japan in working Russia's ruin.

This question must be put to the British Government categorically. The same question must be put to the diplomatic representatives of the United States and the other countries of the Entente. The answer given, and even more, the action taken by the Allied countries will have inevitably a great influence on the future international policy of the Soviet Government.

While undertaking the proper diplomatic steps, the Soviet Government at the same time issues an order to the Soviets in Siberia to offer resistance to any forcible invasion of Russian territory.

WORKERS AND PEASANTS! HONEST CITIZENS!

A new horrible trial is coming from the East. Within the country the dark forces are raising their heads. The bourgeoisie of Siberia is stretching out its hand to foreign invaders. The City Duma of Vladivostok, which consists of Mensheviks and Right Social Revolutionists passed a resolution welcoming the armed invasion by Japan. In its desire to strangle the Russian revolution, to take away from the workers and peasants political power, the land, the control of industry—the Russian bourgeoisie and its lackeys—Mensheviks and S-R—are acting in concert with the Japanese plunderers. Resistance to Japanese invasion and merciless struggle with Japan's agents and assistants within the country is a matter of life and death for the Soviet Republic, for the laboring masses of all Russia.

April 5, 1918.

[83.]

Statement by Ambassador Francis, April 16, 1918.

(*New York Times Current History*, Vol. VIII, Part 1, p. 239.)

The Soviet Government and the Soviet press are giving too much importance to the landing of these marines, which has no political significance, but merely was a police precaution taken by the Japanese Admiral on his own responsibility for the protection of Japanese life and property at Vladivostok, and the Japanese Admiral, Kato, so informed the American Admiral, Knight, and the American Consul, Caldwell, in Vladivostok. My impression is that the landing of the British marines was pursuant to the request of the British Consul for the protection of the British Consulate and British subjects in Vladivostok, which he anticipated would possibly be jeopardized by the unrest which might arise from the Japanese landing.

The American Consul did not ask protection from the American cruiser in Vladivostok Harbor, and consequently no American marines were landed. This, together with the fact that the French Consul at Vladivostok made no request for protection from the British, American, or Japanese cruisers in the harbor, unquestionably demonstrates that the landing of allied troops is not a concerted action between the Allies.

[84.]

Cable from Henry P. Davison to Colonel Robins, sent through the American Ambassador in Paris.

(Received April 18, 1918.)

Consul American, Moscow, Russia:

Sixteenth. For Robins. "Be assured your services to Red Cross of extraordinary value and highly appreciated inside and outside Red Cross organization. Distressed you should have misconstrued cable regarding assistance. You will be advised by cable later relative this point. Assume you will not contemplate leaving Russia except for personal safety without advising me in plenty of time. Seems to all here that it would be misfortune to have Red Cross withdrawn from Russia and certainly as you have made such signal success. Give no further consideration question assistant until further advised. Perkins."

SHARP.

[85.]

Letter from Tchicherin to Colonel Robins with Enclosure, April 25, 1918.

RUSSIAN FEDERATED SOVIET REPUBLIC

ACTING PEOPLE'S COMMISSARY OF FOREIGN AFFAIRS

No. 136, Moscow.

April 25, 1918.

Mr. Colonel:

The People's Commissary of Foreign Affairs is herewith enclosing documents regarding the disclosure of a conspiracy against the Government of Soviets in Siberia and has the honor to ask you to bring to the knowledge of the Government of the United States the following:[1]

The documents that have been published establish beyond doubt that in this conspiracy were involved the consular representatives of America, Great Britain, and France in Vladivostok, and that the diplomatic representatives of the same powers in Pekin were in communication with the counter-revolutionary organization which calls itself "The Siberian Government."[2]

On the basis of the above stated, the Government of the Russian Federated Soviet Republic requests of the Government of the United States:

1. To recall the American consular representative in Vladivostok as soon as it is possible.

2. As soon as it is possible to arrange a public investigation into the activities of the above mentioned agent as well as into the connection of the American Mission in Pekin with the counter-revolutionary conspiracy.

[1] Mr. Francis notified the Soviet Government informally that, in his opinion, the documents failed to involve the American officials. An official report of the demand for the removal of the American Consul, John K. Caldwell, was received by the State Department May 6. On May 9, Mr. Lansing instructed Mr. Francis to present informally a denial of the charge.

[2] On April 20 the diplomatic representatives of the Allies were formally notified of the formation of the Government of Autonomous Siberia.

3. To define in a definite and straightforward manner the attitude of the Government of the United States to the Government of the Russian Federated Soviet Republic and to all attempts of the various representatives of America to interfere in the internal affairs of Russia.

Accept, Mr. Colonel, assurances of my sincere respect.

(signed) GEORGE TCHICHERIN,
Acting People's Commissary of Foreign Affairs.

To Colonel Robins,
Chief of the American Red Cross Mission in Russia.

(ENCLOSURE.)

(*Izvestia*, April 25, 1918.)

THE DISCOVERY OF A COUNTER-REVOLUTIONARY CONSPIRACY IN THE FAR EAST

The People's Commissariat of Foreign Affairs received by direct wire the following information: The Commissary of Foreign Affairs of Eastern Siberia, Comrade Yanson, transmits from Vladivostok that on the 21st of April a search was made in the apartment of Citizen M. A. Kolobov by members of the Executive Committee. As a result of the search it was disclosed that Kolobov is a member of the Government of Autonomous Siberia. From the papers we found it is evident that the Siberian Government is taking steps for the accomplishment of its adventure with the aid of the Allies. We present the documents in full.

FIRST DOCUMENT

"The interview with the British Consul must have the effect of bringing to his knowledge the real circumstances of the intended practical measures, and in particular must cover the bringing into Vladivostok of military units and the organization of forces in Vladivostok. It is necessary to ask the Consul the following questions:

Can one depend upon the assistance of the military forces of the Allies in preventing the Bolshevik forces from entering Vladivostok after it is occupied by the forces of the Government of Siberia?

Can one depend upon the assistance of the military forces of the Allies in preventing the movement of the forces of the

Bolsheviks on Nikolsk-Ussuriisk from Khabarovsk so that the territory within the district east of the railroad line Vladivostok-Harbin, and the railroad line itself, shall remain in the hands of the Government of Siberia?

As a preliminary, the Consuls must be informed about the state of affairs in the West.

As information has been received that arms could be obtained only through Japan, could not questions to that effect be asked of Japan? Would it not be necessary to visit the Japanese and French Consuls as well as the others?

Regarding the interview with Knight, it is necessary to say that the interview was preceded by a statement about the situation in Western Siberia, as he is interested in our affairs. Then it is necessary to point out to him that the uncertainty of the situation favors extremely the strengthening of the influence of Japan at the expense of the other Allies. The position maintained by the representatives of Japan regarding the recognition of the Siberian Government gives room for a thought that Japan holds entirely in her hands the possibility of recognition, she makes definite terms of recognition, among which it is necessary to point out the condition that Vladivostok remain unfortified.

Such predominance of Japanese influence worries the Government of Siberia extremely, as there are public groups who are, it seems, ready to use the separate assistance of Japan, which she is ready to give. The aim of Japan is to obtain complete control over certain economic factors, such as for instance the fisheries in Kamchatka. The non-recognition of the Siberian Government makes this struggle for influence in the Far East very difficult and compels us to think that the uncertainty of the situation in the future will lead to an extremely unfortunate increase of the influence of Japan at the expense of all other powers.

Therefore we considered it necessary to bring to the knowledge of America that further uncertainty in the Far East will lead to a concrete victory of Japanese influence and that certain circles may go the limit, inclusive of a separate agreement with Japan. As to the Government of Siberia, the uncertainty of the position may compel it to act prematurely from the point of view of work of organization and, by doing so, to risk everything. We consider that America must define her attitude to the Government of Siberia if she is well-disposed to us.''

SECOND DOCUMENT

"The practical work of the Siberian Government is characterized in the correspondence of Ustrugov and Kolobov. In view of the complicated international situation and diplomatic relations, we formally request in the interest of the cause that all actions of international significance should be previously agreed upon with us. Discounting all other conversations, I consider that until the final construction of the Government, or at least until an agreement with the Allied Ministers in Pekin: (1) Derber must remain in Harbin, (2) members of the Siberian Government who are in Vladivostok must remain quiet, (3) you must send an urgent telegram to Vladivostok that neither a declaration nor a decree regarding the volunteer army should be published. Besides this we find it necessary that until the establishment of official representation in Japan the members of the Siberian Government who are in Vladivostok should be the connecting link through Admiral Knight or the American Consul with the embassies of the Allied powers. In case of necessity of communications of the Allied powers with the members of the Siberian Government who are at Vladivostok we shall telegraph to them in your cipher, addressing the communication to the American Consul through the American Ambassador in Pekin."

THIRD DOCUMENT

"Ustrugov and Stal to-day visited the French Minister. Immediate recognition of the Siberian Government cannot be expected. It is his opinion that at this moment the Siberian Government must not act, but the military organization must act; in case of the least success of the latter, he cannot imagine any other government than the Siberian Government which is the real representative of the population. We disagreed with this opinion, but believe that a concession to our point of view is a personal question for the creators of the Manchurian detachments, and therefore we must act very gradually.

If Horvat agrees with the scheme of the organization or in general will co-operate, a point which must be attained, we ask Horvat to telegraph to Shanghai through the Consul to Kolchak.

Inform of Derber's departure."

FOURTH DOCUMENT

"Ustrugov and Stal, in accordance with your telegram of the 8th of April, had interviews with the American and French Ministers. They consider that the publication of the declaration, and the decree of the volunteer army and the appeal to the Allies is premature for it will place them in a difficult situation.

The reports of the Ambassadors to the Governments are still on the way and the most important problems of organization are in Harbin. Information of considerable support by various groups became known to the Ministers of the Allies in Pekin only after you had transmitted them to us, and must be supplementarily transmitted to the Governments of the Allies.

We are advised to suggest to the Government, in order to avoid an undesirable attitude of the Pekin Ministers and an unfavorable reply to you from their Governments, or simply leaving your appeal without a reply, to send urgently to the Allied Governments a supplementary telegram in which it must be pointed out: (1) that there are in Pekin two representatives authorized by you to make a more detailed explanation to the Ministers of the Allied powers of the program of work of the Siberian Government; (2) that in case the Allied Governments for the convenience of negotiations will find it advisable that your representatives should move to Japan, you request the Allied Governments to give corresponding instructions to the Ministers in Japan. Besides this, Pichon, after negotiations with his minister, finds that if an agreement should finally be reached between Horvat and the propertied element, then the Allies would no longer apprehend that they might be charged with intervening in the internal affairs of Russia by a one-sided support of a Government which represents one group to the detriment of others."

We are transmitting only part of the documents in connection with the investigation. Further documents will be telegraphed.

Vice-Chairman of the Vladivostok Soviet.

NIKOFOROV.

[86.]

Cable from Colonel Robins to Henry P. Davison, April 25, 1918.

Davison, American Red Cross, Care American Embassy, Paris:
Extra four. April twenty-fifth. Perkins cable regarding assistants last received. Liquidation American Red Cross supplies relief work Russia practically complete. Recommend return all members mission America. Planing departure about May fifteenth. All well. Original to Washington.

ROBINS.

Moscow, Thursday, April 25, 1918.

[87.]

Cable from Henry P. Davison to Colonel Robins, sent through the American Ambassador in Paris.

(Received April 27, 1918.)

American Consul General, Moscow:
7198/-Paris 52334 8 PM 27 TH 16 30
Twenty-sixth. For Robins:
"Your extra three. From your various cables and my conferences with Thacher believe thoroughly understand situation. Obviously can accomplish nothing here relative attitude own people. Leaving Paris to-day. Should arrive Washington about two weeks where address me. Will upon arrival immediately take up with proper persons subject and cable you. Meantime hope you will remain unless for personal reasons you deem inexpedient. Davison."

SHARP.

[88.]

Letter from R. H. Bruce Lockhart to Colonel Robins, May 5, 1918.

Moscow, 5th May, 1918.

Dear Colonel:
I am afraid you will have left for Vologda before I have a chance of seeing you. Do let me, in support of my view of

things here, put before you the following definite instances in which Trotsky has shown his willingness to work with the Allies.

(1) He has invited Allied officers to co-operate in the reorganization of the New Army.

(2) He invited us to send a commission of British Naval officers to sáve the Black Sea Fleet.

(3) On every occasion when we have asked him for papers and assistance for our naval officers and our evacuation officers at Petrograd he has always given us exactly what we wanted.

(4) He has given every facility so far for Allied Co-operation at Murmansk.

(5) He has agreed to send the Czech Corps to Murmansk and Archangel.

(6) Finally, he has to-day come to a full agreement with us regarding the Allied stores at Archangel whereby we shall be allowed to retain those stores which we require for ourselves.

You will agree that this does not look like the action of a pro-German agent, and that a policy of Allied intervention, with the co-operation and consent of the Bolshevik Government, is feasible and possible.

Yours very sincerely,
(signed)   R. H. BRUCE LOCKHART.

[89.]

Cable from the Secretary of State to Colonel Robins, May 9, 1918.

American Consul General, Moscow:

128. Ninth. Washington. For Robins, Moscow. Twenty-two. Seventh. 15158, 10095. Under all circumstances consider desirable that you come home for consultation. We are very reluctant however to withdraw entire Red Cross commission anticipating that there will be many opportunities to help distribution food and other Red Cross relief measures next two months. Must leave decision in your hands, for you alone can judge possibilities of personal welfare members commission, also likelihood continuing service, but all here feel that Red Cross will find much valuable relief work to do, and hope you before leaving will find possible arrange for sufficient personnel to remain, and if you desire we will endeavor send other Red Cross

representatives to help in maintaining Red Cross efforts, position in Russia, founded on fine basis already established. Cable promptly care Davison.

LANSING.

[90.]

Cable from Colonel Robins to Henry P. Davison, May 9, 1918.

Davison, American Red Cross, Washington:
May ninth. Your seventh 15158 received. Cables Serbian relief and answering Davison's last Paris advices unanswered. Leaving about May fifteenth unless otherwise ordered. Details final arrangements mission later.

ROBINS.

[91.]

Plan for Russian-American Commercial Relations, sent by Lenin to Colonel Robins, May 14, 1918.

CHAIRMAN OF PEOPLE'S COMMISSARIES, MOSCOW, KREMLIN

14 May, 1918.

To Colonel Robins.
Dear Mr. Robins:
I enclose the preliminary plan of our economic relations with America. This preliminary plan was elaborated in the Council of Export Trade in our highest Council of National Economy.

I hope this preliminary can be useful for you in your conversation with the American Foreign Office and American Export Specialists.

With best thanks,
Yours truly,
(signed)   LENIN.

RUSSIAN-AMERICAN COMMERCIAL RELATIONS [1]

I.

The fourth year of war greatly exhausted the economic might of Russia. The productive forces of the country being

---

[1] This plan was prepared shortly after the conclusion of the Brest-Litovsk treaty and under the duress of the conditions imposed on Russia by that treaty.

by necessity directed first of all to military needs were far from satisfying the needs of the population.

It is sufficient to quote the following example:

The internal production of agricultural machinery in 1915 was half of the internal production of 1913, in 1916 it was one-fifth, and in 1917 it was one-tenth.

At the same time the importation of tools of production was diminished; in 1913 the importation from foreign countries of agricultural machinery and implements was equal in value to the internal production; in 1914 this importation was reduced to one-fourth of that of 1913; and in 1916 it was equal to one-fifth.

Therefore the internal production of agricultural machinery and implements in comparison with the figures of 1913 was 2.25 times less than necessary. The real shortage of agricultural supplies was much greater than shown by figures.

The same thing is evident in the production of coal, pig iron, etc., and in all branches of mining and manufacturing.

We must consider the reason for the decline of the productive forces of the country to be not so much the falling off in the productivity of *labor* as the decline of production in foreign countries, and consequently the reduction of imports from foreign countries of tools of production.

II.

Russia's exit from a state of war makes it possible at once to adopt the necessary measures for the re-establishment of the apparatus of production. With the demobilization of the army millions of working men became available. Shops and factories which were engaged in production of munitions are returning to the production of articles of everyday use. One of the principal problems of the present time is the immediate renewal and increase of the tools of production for manufacturing as well as for agricultural purposes.

At the same time it is urgently necessary to put transportation in order for the re-establishment of proper exchange of commodities, which would render it possible to transfer the supplies of bread which have accumulated in some districts into consuming districts, and to transport the surplus to foreign countries, and to unload the accumulation of foreign freight in Vladivostok and Archangel.

Without the assistance of countries, which are producing a

large quantity of the tools of production for agricultural purposes as well as parts of railroad stock, it will not be easy for Russia, and she will not be able with any degree of speed to overcome all the difficulties of re-establishing the economic life of the country. Even before the war, Russia imported three hundred and fifty millions of roubles worth of these materials, Germany being the principal source of supply of them. In 1913 Germany exported to Russia metals and all kinds of products of metals amounting to about two hundred thirty-six million roubles worth, which makes 17.2% of the entire imports of merchandise of this category. Great Britain exported during that year only 48.2 million roubles, or 3.5% of the entire imports, and the United States of America only 18.4 million roubles, or 1.3%. It is true that during the war the situation changed so much that the first place in exports for this group of products was transferred to the United States of America. In 1914 Germany brought in 15.1% of the entire imports, amounting to 166 million roubles, Great Britain 6%, amounting to 66 million roubles, and the United States 1.19%, or equal to 21 million roubles. In 1915 exports from England and America greatly increased; from England they increased to 104 million roubles, and from America to 137 million roubles, which is seven times the previous amount. Changes in the same direction and to the same degree took place in the exports to Russia from America and England in 1916 and 1917.

The same thing is evident in other articles of import and export. In general, the war changed the entire picture of Russian-American commerce. While before the war America occupied the sixth place in commerce, now she occupies the second.

The increase of exports from America to Russia took place in the following manner:

Years	Total amount of imports to Russia (In millions of roubles)	Exports from the U. S. to Russia	Percentage of imports from the U. S. in comparison with total imports
1912	1,171.8	87.4	7.5
1913	1,374.0	79.1	5.8
1914	1,098.0	82.2	7.3
1915	956.7	256.4	26.8
1916	2,414.9	801.7	33.2

The exports from Russia to the United States are as follows:

Years	Exports from Russia (in millions of roubles)	Exports to U. S. from Russia (in millions of roubles)	Percentage of exports to U. S. as compared with total exports
1912	1,518.8	18.0	1.2
1913	1,320.1	14.2	0.9
1914	956.1	8.8	0.9
1915	320.5	3.3	0.9
1916	500.3	14.0	2.8

In 1917 the exports from America to Russia made a collosal jump, even in comparison with 1916. According to statistics during the first eight months of 1917 exports from the United States to Russia are as follows:

(In thousands of roubles)

1913	1914	1915	1916	1917
45,186	71,429	48,151	239,142	336,454

Although one of the causes for the increase of the cost of imported merchandise is the increase of prices, it is true without a doubt that the amount of imported merchandise has greatly increased.

III.

While considering the problem of what commerce is possible at the present time with the Central Powers which were furnishing to us the necessary merchandise before the war and with those countries which have served us during the war, it is necessary to consider the terms of the Brest treaty, which introduces the principle of a favored nation. Legally no country can have better conditions of foreign commerce than the countries of the Central Powers, but the real situation of the internal production of the warring countries has changed to such an extent during the war that the position now occupied by America in commercial relations with Russia will hardly suffer a loss within the next few years. With the present drain on the economic life of Germany, there is no reason to expect that she will be in a position to export to Russia merchandise needed by the latter.

The following merchandise was exported from the United States of America to Russia during 1916:

(In thousands of roubles)

Dressed skins	15,289
Shoes	28,874
Twine	8,764
Machinery made from pig iron, iron, and steel	92,116
Agricultural machinery	5,847
Cotton ($570,595) about	30,000
Total	150,840

Above are mentioned only the most important group of articles of import into Russia, while sugar, paper, and many articles of food are not mentioned.

If we compare the export of merchandise from Germany into Russia before the war with the probabilities of what Germany, together with Austria-Hungary, can now furnish for the economic life of Russia, it will be evident that the prospects of commerce between America and Russia are very good.

Germany exported the following merchandise to Russia:

Name of Merchandise	1911	1912	1913
	(In millions of German marks)		
Yarn	20.6	12.2	17.6
Hides of horned cattle	18.2	15.7	27.6
Coal	16.6	19.9	29.2
Cotton (raw)	15.3	9.9	11.7
Leather for lasts	14.9	16.2	23.9
Merino wool, washed	13.0	15.9	14.8
Hides	11.8	17.5	20.6
Hides of lambs, goats, and horned cattle—lacquered (patent leather)	9.3	8.9	11.8
Internal combustion motors	8.9	9.0	10.2
Metal working machinery	8.0	9.0	15.5
Passenger automobiles	7.7	10.7	17.8
Sewing machines and parts	7.0	6.7	7.9
Household and kitchen ware made of brass	7.0	7.2	9.8
Goats' hides, finished	7.0	5.2	6.4
Electric lamps	6.8	9.5	8.1
Zinc	6.5	6.3	8.9
Woolen goods	6.2	6.2	6.6
Iron plows	6.2	6.7	8.7
Metalloids—acids, salts, etc.	6.2	6.1	8.3
Super-phosphates	5.8	6.6	7.5
Coke	5.8	7.7	10.6
Horse hides	5.6	5.4	5.5
Books	4.9	5.2	5.3
Chemical products for medicinal purposes	4.5	4.4	6.0
Remnants, silk and woolen	4.4	5.3	7.8
Locomobiles (besides automobiles for plows)	4.3	3.8	3.8
Furs	4.2	3.2	2.6
Pianos	4.0	4.8	5.1
Typographical machinery	3.8	3.1	3.7
Electrical supplies—transmitters and parts	3.8	5.4	9.0
Brass and copper merchandise, polished and lacquered	3.6	4.2	5.0
Rubber	3.3	4.7	2.7
Tar Products	3.3		

There is no doubt that during the next few years, Russia could not expect to receive from Germany many of the above mentioned articles of merchandise. The exhaustion of the economic apparatus of Germany will not allow her to furnish to other countries tools of production even under the most advantageous commercial and political conditions. By force of events Germany will be compelled to surrender her leading place as a source for the economic life of Russia for the next few years to a country which has not been disorganized as much as Germany by the war. Only America can become that country. With the inability of Germany to exploit the Russian market for German industry during the next few years, it will be very difficult for her in the future to regain the leading part, if during that time America succeeds in taking advantage of the favorable circumstances created for her by events and establishes a working apparatus of commerce between the two countries.

How did Russia pay for merchandise which was received from other countries, and how can she pay for it now? We used to pay by raw materials—by exporting grain, meat and poultry, lumber materials, extracts of cotton seed, hides, wool, ore, oil and its products, flaxen and hempen products, bristles, calves hides, furs, animal intestines, stomachs and bloaters, caviar, etc.

During the war we have exported of the most important products not prohibited for export, the following:

	1914			1915			1916		
	Total export (In thousands of roubles)	To U. S.	%	Total export	To U. S.	%	Total export	To U. S.	%
Flax	64,256	154	.03	31,057	249	.08	98,261	2,506	.03
Unfinished skins	16,346	3,034	.19	7,057	—	—	5,641	1,460	.26
Persian lamb	6,857	2,535	.37	875	734	.82	1,934	576	.30
Hides (other kinds)	6,265	10	.02	2,739	691	.26	10,768	3,608	.33
Bristles	5,620	20	.04	4,986	90	.02	10,100	635	.06
Wool	4,635	686	.15	853	87	.10	2,659	—	—
Flax	1,637	—	—	7,545	379	.05	12,688	953	.08
Licorice root	705	617	.88	426	25	.06	194	183	.92
Sugar beet	654	—	—	238	—	—	9,603	2,282	.25

Besides these products directly exported to America, Russia could pay for merchandise bought in America also with other products of its agricultural and mining industry, but there is no doubt that in the near future, it will be hardly possible to bring our greatly depressed commercial balance to a normal state, because to do this, we must have tools of production, in order to increase the amount of production of merchandise which could be exported to foreign countries. Therefore the country which is interested in receiving payment as soon as possible for merchandise brought into Russia should naturally be also interested in the quickest and increased delivery to Russia of all those articles of industry—machinery, locomotives, etc., which would increase the productivity of the agricultural and mining industries of Russia.

What do we need and on what conditions can we receive what we need from America? It is not easy to answer the first question, because in each branch of the mining and manufacturing industries it is necessary to investigate the need for essential products, to ascertain the possibilities of internal production and its capacity to satisfy the requirements of internal consumption. Some time is necessary to accomplish this. This will be one of the first problems of the various departments of the Council of Foreign Trade, in which all important branches of the mining and manufacturing industries will be represented. At the present time the following categories of merchandise of foreign origin are urgently needed in Russia: railroad supplies, agricultural machinery, electric machinery for obtaining cheap power, mining machinery—in view of a' necessity of transferring the mining industry from the Donetz basin to the Ural, machines for improving transportation on highways and building of narrow gauge electric railroads, cotton and machinery for needs of the cotton textile industries, certain articles of food such as sugar, wheat, etc.

The conditions under which the United States could furnish the economic life of Russia with the necessary products must be a subject of special negotiations. As an economic basis for these negotiations, the following approximate export plan for 1918 could serve:

The following could be exported from Russia:

	In millions of roubles
Lumber	800
Flax and hemp	220
Oil	250
Manganese ore	400
Platinum	200
Bristles, horses' hair and hoofs	25
Raw hides	400
Furs	200
Tobacco	200
Other products	150

A total of approximately three billions of roubles.

The Brest treaty made it inconvenient and undesirable for us to give to any country exclusive concessions for the exploitation of the natural resources of Russia. But by carrying out the nationalization of foreign trade the Government of Russia has the right to buy merchandise wherever it finds it necessary and to sell it wherever it finds it most profitable for itself. On this basis it is possible to make commercial agreements and bargains in every separate concrete case regardless of the amount involved. Not on the basis of some written concessions but on the basis of business arrangements, could America participate actively in the exploitation of the marine riches of Eastern Siberia, of coal and other mines, as well as in the railroad and marine transportation construction in Siberia and northern European Russia. Especially in the connection of the Northern Sea route with the Enisei River, the improvement of water routes, building of ports and using of the water power, there is great need.

As security of payment for products brought into Russia, America could be given the privilege of participating in certain construction enterprises, such as: the building of electric power stations on the Volkhov and Sir, the digging of a canal from Soretskoe to Petrograd, the development of the water routes of the Donetz basin and the Volga-Don canal, the development of coal mines, the exploitation of the seal industry in the Commandor Islands, the lumber industry in Southern Kamchatka, the construction of railroads from Irkutsk to Bodaibo on the river Rion, Nikolaevsk-Amur-Grafskaya, the Bay of Olga, Verkhneudinsk-Urga, etc. The United States could also participate on a large scale in the development of certain well-known extensive agricultural tracts, by introducing modern methods, receiving in return a large proportion of the products.

Further, Russia guarantees that the military stores which are on hand in Russia will not be sold to Germany, and that all war materials which were manufactured in England and America for Russia will be transferred to the United States.

[92.]

Report presented by Colonel Raymond Robins to the Secretary of State, July 1, 1918.

AMERICAN ECONOMIC CO-OPERATION WITH RUSSIA.

I.

Russia Will Welcome American Assistance in Economic Reconstruction.

America's democratic war aims are such as to make allied intervention by force in Russia inconceivable unless desired by the great mass of the Russian people. Thus far there has been no expression of any such desire, but there is now presented in the invitation coming from the responsible head of the Soviet Government for America's co-operation in economic reconstruction, the opportunity for taking a vitally important preliminary step toward complete economic and military co-operation in the creation of an effective Eastern front. This suggestion should be considered solely as a war measure, uninfluenced by altruistic concern for the Russian people.

The Russian people and their leaders are learning by bitter daily experience the necessity of organizing resistance to German power. When the peace written by Germany at Brest-Litovsk was signed the condition of the old army was such that it was utterly incapable of resisting any organized force. Demobilization was the first indispensable prerequisite for the creation of an effective force with which German power could be opposed. The next step is the reconstruction of the economic situation. Modern armies cannot survive unsupported by economic and industrial organization.

It was upon the plea of the necessity for economic reconstruction that the peace, frankly described as shameful, was accepted. The leaders of the Soviet Government realize that their social-economic revolution must fail, and that Russia will inevitably fall under the complete domination of autocratic Germany unless immediate and effective assistance in the reconstruction of economic life can be obtained. Their faith in the formulas of International Socialism naturally repels the suggestion of friendly co-operation with so-called Imperialistic and Capitalistic Governments, but the compelling realities and necessities of life have led in this case, as in many others, to readjustment and compromise. Hence the present suggestion coming from the responsible head of the Soviet Government which is an earnest request for America's co-operation in the internal reconstruction of economic life.

It is my sincere conviction, if this suggestion is acted upon and such economic reorganization is accomplished as is needed to equip and support a revolutionary army, that such an army can and will be formed and that in such event the assistance of armed forces of the Allies will be gladly accepted by the Soviet Power. This Power cannot be expected to countenance Allied intervention until convinced that the intervening force will not be used to destroy it.

II.

General Purposes of an Economic Commission

The aims of an Economic Commission sent to Russia to co-operate in the problem of economic reconstruction will be—

First. To so reconstruct commercial distribution as to assure the consumption of Russian resources in Russia where they are vitally needed, thus preventing such resources from being used for the support of the German people and the German armies.

Second. To control the use and disposition of surplus resources and through such control to prevent such use in the service of Germany.

Third. If possible to re-establish trade with Russia upon a basis which, while facilitating economic reconstruction in Russia, will at the same time furnish to the Allies for use in England and France necessary products shipped from Russia via Archangel, which otherwise would necessarily be brought to England from more distant ports requiring longer voyages and consequently a greater use of tonnage.

Fourth. To convince the Russian people that the interests of Russia and the Allies in overthrowing German autocracy are identical, and that American assistance is given solely with a view to hastening the day when Russia will be able to aid the destruction of the German menace.

Fifth. To encourage and assist in the organization of a

voluntary revolutionary army, creating behind such an army the necessary organization for its economic support.

Sixth. To convince the leaders of Revolutionary Russia, whoever they may be, that the Allied Governments have no imperialistic purposes in Russia and will gladly send forces to assist the Russian people in opposing the aggression of German force; and through co-operation with these leaders, to obtain their consent to sending Allied troops which in co-operation with Russian forces may be sufficient to re-establish the Russian front.

Seventh. To obtain an accurate understanding of the fundamental social forces at work in Russia and to keep the American and other Allied Governments advised of the actual facts controlling the development of the Russian, social, economic, and political revolution.

III.

The Economic Problem

Russia is not suffering so much from a lack of resources as from the break-down of the ordinary processes of distribution. The Russian peasant finds himself with a large quantity of grain and a large amount of depreciated paper currency. If he takes his grain to the local center of trade he finds none of the necessities of his life for sale, and cannot exchange his grain except for more depreciated paper money. Consequently the grain is not brought to market. In several instances where shipments of manufactured articles needed by the peasants have been sent to villages, theretofore suffering from the lack of grain, abundant supplies of grain have at once been brought from the surrounding country by the peasants to be exchanged for the manufactured articles.

While this is typical of the situation in many provinces, other neighboring provinces are facing famine conditions because of crop failures or other reasons, and have no grain with which to sow their fields or to feed their people. In a district near Samara, the handling of such a situation was attempted by the local peasant's co-operative society. Going to the peasants who lacked the seed wheat with which to sow their fields, this organization proposed to procure the necessary seed-wheat, provided the peasants would advance the price of the grain which the society promised to deliver within a fixed period of time. Many of the peasants, ignorant of all methods of business involving even the simplest form of credit, refused this offer made solely in their own interest. A unit of the American Friends Society, which has been doing excellent work in that district, determined to bridge the gap; and sending a man to Omsk found no difficulty in purchasing the necessary seed-wheat, and after procuring the same transported and sold it to the peasants without loss in a majority of cases.

Meanwhile, the factories in the industrial centers have in many cases continued their operations and have produced manufactured articles that are lacking in the country districts. In illustration: The J. M. Coates Company, which produces 60 per cent of all the cotton thread produced in Russia, and which has large factories in Petrograd, continued its operations up to the end of February, 1918, and at that time had on hand the largest stock of manufactured products its books had ever shown. Owing to difficulties of communication, transport, and hauling, the distributing branch of the business had not been functioning. That efficient production is possible under Soviet rule has been demonstrated by the experience of the International Harvester Company which has largely increased its producing efficiency during the past six months under Soviet rule. This experience was made possible through tactful handling of a very difficult situation which resulted in effective co-operation from the Soviet authorities who in order to get results were willing when faced with the practical necessities of the situation, to modify the rigid formulas of their economic theory. No doubt the experience of this company is exceptional, but the tactful handling of daily problems as they arise through a competent American Economic Commission will be the most effective method of accomplishing similar results in like cases.

IV.

Government Co-operation

Obviously nothing can be accomplished without the co-operation of governmental power. The commission must, therefore, go if it goes at all, willing to deal with the leaders of Revolutionary Russia actually in power, without regard to their principles or formulas of economic, social, or political life, so long as such leaders sincerely desire to recreate forces in Russia which will be used in resisting the force of German arms. Seeking such co-operation, the members of this commission will be asked to advise regarding problems of a most practical and controlling nature. They will be able to exert powerful influence to prevent large commercial transactions with Germany. All of this work will from necessity be done under Government control and protection. Their advice reinforced by the uncompromising facts of life will lead inevitably to the modification, adjustment, and softening of the hard and impossible formulas of radical socialism; and because of the necessity of finding it, a practical basis for progress will be found. The Russian Revolution has now reached the stage where it is to be controlled, not by theory, but by the unyielding necessities of life. This fact is becoming each day more clear to the radical socialistic group now in control of the Soviet Government.

It is apparent from the informality of the suggestion inviting American co-operation that formal recognition of the Soviet Government is not a necessary prerequisite to co-operation. Acting upon this informal invitation, a commission can proceed to Russia and be placed in direct touch with the entire situation without further formality.

American co-operation will give the Allies effective and controlling influence upon the internal situation. Such co-operation will be able to direct the forces supporting the Soviet Power against Germany. If effective, co-operation will ultimately compel the continued utilization against the Russian people of tyrannical German force, thus preventing German co-operation and increasing the bitter resentment against Germany which is steadily gaining ground in Russia. If the economic life of Russia can be sufficiently organized to make possible the support of an effective army, this growing resentment will surely crystallize in the organization of an army which will effectively oppose the German menace in Russia.

V

Organization of Commission

Through co-operation with the Government the work of such a Commission will be concerned with:—

(1) Railway control, management and operation;
(2) Reorganization of credit and finance, governmental and commercial;

(3) Commercial distribution of grain and manufactured articles in exchange for grain;

(4) Food administration and control;

(5) Shipping and foreign trade, with particular reference to Allied war needs;

(6) Industrial management and control in co-operation with labor;

(7) Reorganization of manufacturing and coal mining industries;

(8) Development of agriculture;

(9) Prevention, or utilization, of speculative markets;

(10) Education;

(11) Propaganda.

To accomplish substantial results the most competent organizing and technical ability will be required. Members of the Commission must be men of liberal views and sympathetic understanding, capable of meeting fact conditions with practical ability to achieve results under difficult and complex circumstances.

Under the control of the Commission it will be necessary to create an extensive organization with representatives in all important centers of Russian life. For this purpose the distributing and sales organizations of large business concerns, both American and English, which have heretofore been organized in Russia and which are now in danger of being disorganized should be utilized and reorganized to meet the actual demands of the situation. There are many such organizations in Russia as, for instance, the New York Life Insurance Company, the J. M. Coates Company, and the International Harvester Company.

The organization thus created by the Commission will co-operate in the various local centers with various Russian agencies, including the local Soviets, the Peasants' Co-operative Societies and the local Zemstvos where they are functioning. Thus the commercial and industrial needs necessary for recreation of commercial life may be effectively ascertained. Through co-operation in railway management the opportunity will be created of transporting manufactured goods from the place of production to the place of consumption. The Commission will be able to control the disposition of manufactured goods by the use of American credit and upon transportation of such goods to the local centers will, with them, be able to control the disposition of large food products.

These products should of course be primarily used for consumption in Russia and will be transported to the centers where food products are lacking. Any surplus will be available for export.

If export trade with the Allies can be re-established upon such a basis as to result in economic use of tonnage in bringing from Archangel products required in England and France it should be possible in exchange for these products to ship to Russia agricultural and other tools and machinery and manufactured products. This trade should be in the absolute control of the Commission, so that the distribution of the goods sent to Russia will be, in so far as possible, under the control of the Commission. With American credit and American goods the Commission will be able to control the disposition of Russian resources, vitally needed by Germany. In this connection it is encouraging to note that there are authentic reports to the effect that Germany has been endeavoring to make large purchases of American bank notes for the purchase of grain from the Ukraine peasants. This fact indicates that Germany has not at her disposal the goods required by the Ukrainian peasants for which they would be willing to exchange their grain. Effective organization combined with the use of American credit and the control of American goods should effectively prevent the commercial exploitation of Russia by Germany during the balance of the war.

The work of this Commission will be so extensive that the burden of responsible supervision should not be placed upon any of the departments of the Government already so greatly overburdened with work. In order to meet this situation and at the same time to obtain proper co-ordination it is suggested that a separate and independent department of the Government be created under the Overman Act; that at the head of this department there should be a man enjoying the absolute confidence of the President, who shall be responsible only to the President; that there be associated with him representatives of the various Government departments having vital interests connected with the prosecution of the war which may be related to the work of the Commission.

The Commission should be responsible only to this independent department and, through it, responsible to the President. This department should be granted an appropriation by Congress adequate to effectively carry on its work. The very large amount of money which will be required is indicated by the character of the work to be done.

Independent facilities of communication in cipher should be established between the Commission and the department to which it is to be responsible.

Time is of the utmost importance. The Commission should be organized as quickly as possible and should proceed to Russia via Archangel so as to reach the center of European Russia without unnecessary delay.

RAYMOND ROBINS.

July 1, 1918.

(37895)

[93.]

Statement by Ambassador Francis, given out by the Committee on Public Information, May 31, 1918.

(*Izvestia*, May 31, 1918.)

The policy of my Government is not to intervene in the internal affairs of Russia—and this policy has never been violated.

America has entered the present war to fight for peace, and not for the sake of territorial acquisitions or commercial advantages and she will not lay down arms until all people receive the right of self-determination and until humanity is assured a permanent peace.

President Wilson, in his address of the 18th of May, speaking of the attempt of the Central Powers to make peace at Russia's expense, made the following statement concerning that country:

"I intend to stand by Russia as well as France. The helpless and the friendless are the very ones that need friends and succor, and if any men in Germany think we are going to sacrifice anybody for our own sake, I tell them now they are mistaken."

The Allied Missions in Russia have been subjected to many inconveniences, and perhaps have suffered undignified treatment, but they intend to tolerate such further, in order not to miss any available opportunity for assisting the Russians, in order to prevent the possibility of turning Russia into a German province.

In the name of the American Embassy I state that I have not considered for a minute the thought of leaving Russia, and now reiterate my statement, made two months ago, at the time of the ratification of the Brest-Litovsk treaty, that I will not leave Russia until I am forced to do so.

In spite of the attempt to repudiate the loans which were made by my Government to Russia I insistently encouraged delivery from America to Russia of clothing, agricultural machinery, etc., and now, at the time of writing these lines, I am trying to obtain delivery in Russia of 750,000 pairs of footwear which are ready in one of the Pacific ports and are intended for the members of the Railway Workers' Union and their families.

I am also using every effort in order to lift the embargo on the export of tea from China into Russia. A certain number of experienced American railroad builders and engineers are at present on their way to Vologda for a conference with myself and representatives of the Department of Ways of Communication, for the purpose of improving the disorganized railroad traffic of Russia.

This Railroad Commission, consisting of several hundred Americans, arrived at Vladivostok in December, and has been awaiting further instructions here. Some of them are helping with their advice in the management of the Chinese Eastern Railway, from Vladivostok to the station Manchuria. Some were invited to assist in the transportation of troops and supplies intended for Semenov, but my Government refused to give its sanction, and gave me instructions accordingly—such precautions we maintain in order not to interfere in the internal affairs of Russia.

There is no need for me to state that the American Railroad Commission, carrying out the purpose for which it was sent—and that is improving the railroad traffic in Russia—will receive instructions to abstain completely from any actions which would increase the possibility of exporting Russian bread and products to the Central Empires, as such a result would be contradictory to the purpose in question and would not be for the good of the Russian people themselves.

All Americans, with the exception of those who are training

for the battlefield, are diligently engaged in the production of supplies for America's Allies, and without boasting I may state that America can satisfy not only all Russia's need of manufactured products but also all the demands of the Allies for products which they themselves cannot produce.

[94.]

Statement cabled by Mr. Lansing to Ambassador Francis, and given out by the Committee on Public Information, May 31, 1918.

(*Izvestia*, May 31, 1918.)

The Department received yours 127 and 128 as well as cables from Vologda, Vladivostok and Moscow, which informed regarding the prohibition of use of cipher in telegraphic communications. In reply to this report you are herewith informed that the representatives of the United States of America have not assisted any of the internal movements in Russia, which is confirmed in statements issued by you.

The friendly intentions of the United States towards Russia were clearly defined by the President in his speech to Congress of January 8th and his message to the Russian people through the Soviets.

They will not be changed under the influence of accusations like those that have reached us nor through any denials of diplomatic privileges accepted in international relations throughout the whole world.

At the present time several groups are appealing to us for assistance in their attempts to establish a new government in Siberia. Our Government did not reply to any of these appeals, as you were informed by cable of the 2nd of May, when it was reported that Colonel Semenov asked for assistance to the Russian Railroad Corps by American engineers who were organized for the purpose of assisting the Russian Railroad Administration. Orders were issued that the work of these engineers must not be used in favor of any single movement participating in civil war, and must not assist the military operations of Semenov, and if this could be prevented only by their departure, they must leave.

At the same time you were informed that Colonel Emerson

and some of his assistants were going to Vologda to organize, together with you, a conference regarding the way these engineers could be used for assisting people in European Russia, as well as for the purpose of increasing the resistance of the Russian people to the Central Powers. Colonel Emerson, together with three assistants, left Harbin for Vologda May 3rd.

The aims of the United States are evident, and are not covered by any secret diplomacy. The United States is at war with the Central Powers for the purpose of the overthrow of German militarism, and is aiming, as far as possible, that the people of the whole world should live in peace, liberated from the threat of autocratic powers.

The Government of the United States understands perfectly the desire for rest of the Russian people, exhausted by heroic sacrifice made in the war, and shares its hopes for a permanent peace based on principles of liberty and justice.

The United States sees now how Russia is violated by German and Austrian troops. The Soviets' Communiqúes show that where the Russians in peaceful centers do not immediately acquiesce in the orders of the German Commanders, they are subjected to the cruelest persecutions or court martialed, and that the German military chariot is riding over, with its wheels, the prostrate body of the Russian people.

In spite of the fact that in many districts of Russia the population is starving, and that North Russia is threatened with a general hunger, the Central Powers insist on the exact carrying out of the terms of the contract, and are taking out of the Ukraine food supplies which are necessary for the other part of Russia and without which it cannot exist.

The Department cannot understand how such a state of affairs can continue without awakening the attention of the Russian people to the dangers threatening their liberty, which they have won, thanks to the revolution. The Department, however, desires that you should make clear the friendly intentions of the United States towards Russia, which will remain unchanged until the time when Russia voluntarily submits to the autocratic rule of the Central Powers.

[95.]

Statement by the American Ambassador—supplied to the Press by, the Committee on Public Information, June 1, 1918.

(*Izvestia*, June 1, 1918.)

In reply to a question whether his Government or any other of the Allied Governments made any offers to the Soviet Government the American Ambassador states as follows:

It seems that there exists a misunderstanding or a not sufficiently clear understanding regarding the question of the attitude of the Allied Governments to the present Soviet Government.

In the name of the American Government I may state that no authoritative offer, official or even semi-official, was made to the Soviet Government.

Soon after my arrival in Vologda or at the time of the ratification of the Brest-Litovsk peace treaty by the All-Russian Congress of Soviets in Moscow, I made the statement that my Government did not recognize this separate peace, and that the American people continued to consider themselves Allies of the Russian people in the struggle against the Central Empires, and that my Government was ready and willing to give moral and material support to any organization which would be willing to resist the German offensive. The same points were reiterated by me in further statements regarding preparations made by America as a result of the resoluteness and enthusiasm which inspired all the American people.

American representatives all over Russia attempted to preserve as *modus vivendi* with the Governments of the localities where they were stationed.

These representatives have received various requests for assistance or moral support from organizations already existing or attempting to organize an opposition to the existing Government, but such requests were unequivocally declined or ignored. In other words, the policy of my Government consists in nonintervention in the internal affairs of Russia and in giving the opportunity to the people of this great country to select their own form of government, make their own laws and elect their own officials.

President Wilson in all those points of his speeches which concerned Russia expressed the firm decision of the American Government and the American people to assist the Russian people and not allow any injustice or injury to be inflicted upon Russia or the Russians.[1]

[96.]

Note from the Soviet Government regarding the Czechoslovaks, June 13, 1918.

(*Izvestia*, June 13, 1918.)

The following note was delivered to the British representative, French Consul General, American Consul General and Italian Consul General:

On the 4th of June representatives of four powers, England, France, Italy, and the United States of America, furnished us with a statement regarding the Czechoslovaks in which they pointed out that if the disarming of the Czechoslovaks should be carried out the above-mentioned Governments would consider it as a hostile act, directed against them, as the Czechoslovak troops are Allied troops and are under the protection and care of the powers of the Entente.

The People's Commissariat of Foreign Affairs has the honor to make the following explanation regarding this letter:

The disarming of the Czechoslovaks cannot be considered in any way as an act of hostility to the powers of the Entente.

It was due first of all to the fact that Russia as a neutral country cannot tolerate on its territory armed troops that do not belong to the army of the Soviet Republic.

The direct reason for the taking of decisive and severe measures for the disarming of the Czechoslovaks is their own actions.

[1] *Izvestia*, June 22, 1918 contained the following:
"Vologda newspapers publish an interview with the representatives of the American, Japanese, and Italian Embassies. The American representative expressed the readiness of that country to give Russia economic and food assistance on condition that these supplies would not reach Germany. The Japanese representative denied any possibility of intervention and said that the troops in Vladivostok would be withdrawn as soon as order should be re-established in that city. . . . The American representative, among other things, said: 'The existing Russian Central Government of Soviets is recognized by us to be much more stable than it could be supposed in the beginning.'"

Long before the present armed counter-revolutionary rebellion in Siberia, which is not as yet put down, the Czechoslovak troops by refusing to obey the railroad regulations and the local Soviet authorities, brought about disorganization in the railroad communications and especially in the organization of the food supply. By force of arms they have seized stores of food supplies and in several places committed acts of violence against Socialist Internationalists. The Soviet Government was seeking a peaceful solution of the increasingly threatening situation but in view of the defiant attitude of the Czechoslovaks and in consequence of the danger created by their armed movements, it was decided to hasten the necessary measures for their disarming.

However, only the direct counter-revolutionary armed rebellion of the Czechoslovak troops against the Soviets compelled the Soviet Government to adopt the severe method of suppression of the rebels by force of arms.

The Czechoslovak rebellion started in Tcheliabinsk on the 26th of May, where the Czechoslovaks occupied the railroad station and the city; stole arms, arrested and removed the local authorities, and, in reply to a demand to discontinue their disorders and to disarm, fired on our forces.

The further development of the rebellion led to the occupation by the Czechoslovaks of Penza, Samara, Novo-Nicholaevsk, Omsk, and other cities.

The Czechoslovak rebellion everywhere was followed by arrest of the Soviet authorities and shootings, as well as by the creation of counter-revolutionary organizations which called themselves local governments. The Czechoslovaks everywhere are acting in conjunction with White Guards and counter-revolutionary Russian officers.

In some places there are among them French officers. At all points of the counter-revolutionary Czechoslovak rebellion, institutions are being restored which were abolished by the Workmen's and Peasants' Soviet Republic.

The incidents that took place prove to us that in this case we have before us a rebellion of White Guards, reactionary officers, and other counter-revolutionary elements against the Soviet Republic, supported by the armed force of the Czechoslovak troops and basing itself on this force.

The Soviet Government took the most decided measures for the suppression by armed force of the Czechoslovaks and their complete disarming. There is no other solution possible for the Soviet Government.

The People's Commissariat of Foreign Affairs expresses its belief that after the above statement the representatives of the four powers of the Entente will not consider the disarming of the Czechoslovak troops who were characterized by them as Allies and who are under their protection as an act of hostility, but on the contrary, will recognize the necessity and propriety of the action undertaken by the Soviet Government against the rebels.

The People's Commissariat furthermore expresses the hope that the representatives of the four powers of the Entente will not hesitate to express censure of the Czechoslovak troops who are considered to be under their protection for their counter-revolutionary armed rebellion, which is a most brazen and unmistakable interference in the internal affairs of Russia.

(signed) TCHICHERIN,
People's Commissary of Foreign Affairs.

[97.]

Note handed by Tchicherin to R. H. Bruce Lockhart, British Representative, June 28, 1918.

(*Izvestia*, June 28, 1918.)

By the will of laboring people who are conscious of the unity of their interests and their solidarity with the laboring masses of the whole world, the Russian Socialist Federative Republic left the ranks of the warring powers and discontinued the state of war, the further continuation of which the internal conditions of Russia made impossible.

The laboring people of Russia and the Workmen's and Peasants' Government, doing its will, are concerned only to live in peace and friendship with all other nations.

The laboring people of Russia do not threaten war against any nation, and no danger can menace Great Britain from the Russian people.

The Workmen's and Peasants' Government of Russia cannot but most emphatically protest against the invasion, unprovoked by any aggressive measures on the part of Russia, by British armed troops that have just arrived in Murmansk.[1]

Upon the armed forces of the Russian Republic rests the duty of protecting the Murmansk District against any foreign invasion, and this duty the Soviet troops will unrelentingly fulfill, carrying out to the very end their revolutionary duty of guarding Soviet Russia.

The People's Commissariat of Foreign Affairs most emphatically insists that no armed forces of Great Britain, or any other foreign power, should be present in Murmansk, which is a city of neutral Russia. At the same time, it repeats once more the protest which we have made several times, against the presence in the port of Murmansk of British warships, and it expresses our firm expectation that the British Government will revoke this measure which is inconsistent with the international position of Russia, and that the laboring people of Russia, who warmly desire to remain in unbroken friendly relations with Great Britain, will not be placed, against their will, in a position out of keeping with their most sincere aims.

(signed)   TCHICHERIN,
People's Commissary of Foreign Affairs.

[98.]

Note sent by Tchicherin to R. H. Bruce Lockhart, June 30, 1918.[2]

(*Izvestia*, June 30, 1918.)

The People's Commissariat of Foreign Affairs has sent the following note to the British diplomatic representative, Mr. Lockhart:

[1] The original operations of French and British troops on the Murman coast in April, 1918, were undertaken in co-operation with the Soviet authorities. The troops landed now included a small number of American marines who guarded supplies at Kola. By the middle of July the Allied forces had occupied the whole of the Murman coast and held the northern end of the railway.

[2] Similar notes, with slight changes, were delivered to the representatives of the United States, France, Japan, and Italy. According to later issues of *Izvestia*, the Italian, French, British, and American Consuls General visited the Commissariat of Foreign Affairs in succession and each denied any connection with or responsibility for the statements in *Nashe Slovo*.

In view of the published statements in the newspaper, *Nashe Slovo* of several foreign diplomats in Moscow, which statements defined the conditions under which, according to the opinion of these diplomats, the intervention of Great Britain and her Allies in Russian affairs will be possible, the People's Commissariat of Foreign Affairs will be very grateful to the British diplomatic representative for an explanation as to whether or not these statements are to be construed as an expression of the true opinions of the Government of Great Britain.

Such an explanation, in the opinion of the People's Commissariat, is still more necessary, because in the above-mentioned statements there is no evidence that the intended intervention will not be directed against the Soviet Government in Russia, and will not bear the character of an armed foreign invasion.

This explanation will have a special meaning now, when British military forces have already landed on the northern coast of Russia and when the Czechoslovak troops, whom the representatives of Great Britain and her Allies declared to be under the protection of the Allied troops, continue their armed rebellion against the Soviet Government, and replace the Soviets, everywhere that they can do so, by counter-revolutionary institutions, and commit all kinds of acts of violence against the active defenders and officials of the Soviet Government. We also state that the representatives of Great Britain and the Allies have not expressed a single word of condemnation of the actions of the troops under their protection.

The People's Commissariat expresses the firm belief that the representative of Great Britain will repudiate all complicity in the plans of armed intervention, on the territory of the Russian Soviet Republic.

In the name of the friendly relations, which Russia hopes to preserve and establish firmly between the peoples of Russia and Great Britain, the People's Commissariat of Foreign Affairs fully expects that the representative of Great Britain will anounce the disagreement of his Government with the plans which are leading to the break of friendly relations, in view of the fact that absence of such repudiation cannot but be considered by the laboring people as tacit agreement with the views referred to.

(signed) TCHICHERIN,
People's Commissary of Foreign Affairs.

[99.]
Protest by Tchicherin against the Movement of British Troops.

(*Izvestia*, July 13, 1918.)

The People's Commissariat of Foreign Affairs delivered the following note to the British diplomatic representative, Mr. Lockhart:

In spite of repeated assurances by the British Government that the landing of the British troops in Murmansk is not a hostile act against the Russian Soviet Republic, the British Government has not fulfilled our elementary demand for the removal of troops from Soviet territory, but together with French and Serbian auxiliary forces, its detachments are moving south to the interior. Soviet officials are being arrested and even sometimes shot. Railroad guards are being disarmed. Railroads and telegraph are taken under control. After occupying Kem and Soroki, the British troops moved further east and occupied Sumski-Posad, on the road to Onega. Such actions of the British troops can be considered only as an occupation of territory of the Russian Soviet Republic. No other explanation can be given for the moving of the British troops eastward.

The People's Commissariat of Foreign Affairs declares its most solemn protest against this unjustified violation in regard to Soviet Russia. We have stated, and we are stating once more, that Soviet troops will do everything possible in order to protect Russian territory, and will offer the most determined resistance to the foreign armed invasion. We point especially to the feeling that is being developed among the wide masses of Russia by the unprovoked British invasion, and to the results which this feeling will have upon the masses in the future.

(signed) TCHICHERIN,
People's Commissary of Foreign Affairs.

[100.]
Note from Tchicherin to the United States.

(*Izvestia*, July 13, 1918.)

The People's Commissariat of Foreign Affairs has sent the following note to the Consul General of the United States:

The People's Commissariat of Foreign Affairs cannot but express its great surprise regarding the action of the representative of the United States of America, the friendly attitude of which to the Russian Republic is so highly valued, in concluding the so-called treaty with the Murmansk Soviet, which has failed in its civic duty to Soviet Russia, in the matter of an agreement to an armed invasion by troops of the Allies of the territory of Soviet Russia, against the latter's will. The Russian Government hopes that the friendly American Government will not continue to follow the road of violating the territorial integrity and elementary rights of the Soviet Russian Republic, but, on the contrary, will assist in removing everything that leads to such violation.

(signed)   Tchicherin,

[101.]

Statement by the Allied Consuls.

(*Izvestia*, July 26, 1918.)

Regarding the departure of the Allied Ambassadors from Vologda on the 25th of July,[1] the American Consul General, Mr. Poole, who is in charge of maintaining diplomatic relations with the Soviet Government, visited the People's Commissariat of Foreign Affairs, and stated in the name of the British diplomatic representative, Mr. Lockhart, and the French, Italian, and Japanese Consuls General, that they confirmed the statements made previously by Mr. Poole, the substance of which is as follows:

According to the personal opinion of the Allied Consuls, there is no need to suppose that the political situation has been affected seriously by the departure of the Ambassadors from Vologda.

The above-mentioned representatives of the Allies intend to remain in Moscow as long as conditions warrant it, and as long as they receive the proper privileges in accordance with their positions and, especially, as long as they can, without interfer-

[1] The Soviet Government had made repeated requests that the Allied Ambassadors should move to Moscow on the ground that Vologda was no longer safe and would soon be a center of counter-revolutionary fighting. This the Ambassadors refused to do, and went to Archangel instead.

ence, communicate with their Governments or, until they receive different instructions from their Governments.

[102.]

Message sent to Tchicherin by Ambassador Francis, July 25, 1918.

(*New York Times*, August 13, 1918.)

This reviewed the correspondence that had led to the removal to Archangel and continued:

Your message expressing friendly feelings for the people I represent and the desire on your part to maintain relations with them is appreciated, but you will permit me to say that your treatment of me as their representative does not accord with such expressions. While I have refrained from interfering in the internal affairs of Russia, I have considered the Russian people were still our allies and have more than once appealed to them to unite with us in resisting the common enemy. I have, furthermore, recommended to my Government many times to send food to relieve the sufferings of the Russian people and to ship agricultural implements.

A wireless message sent from Washington on July 10 and received at Moscow was delivered to me after last midnight —July 24. It stated that no message had been received from me of later date than June 24 except one sent through Archangel on July 7 advising of the killing of the German Ambassador;[1] it furthermore stated the Department had cabled me often and fully. I have received no cable from my Government that was sent after July 3, except two wireless messages inquiring why they did not hear from me. I had cabled fully every day.

Moreover, the press of Vologda, and doubtless the entire press of Russia, had received an order to print nothing from any Allied Ambassador or representative without first submitting the same to the Soviet Government. Some journals in Vologda and some in Petrograd did print your first telegram, inviting and ordering the Diplomatic Corps to come to Moscow, and our reply thereto; these were given to the press by myself

[1] Count von Mirbach was murdered on July 6, by members of the Social Revolutionary Party.

and for the information of the Russian people, and because I thought secret diplomacy had been abolished in Russia.

Upon hearing that the press was forbidden to publish further correspondence concerning our removal to Moscow, the Diplomatic Corps decided to have printed in pamphlet form in Russian the entire correspondence on the subject, together with some excerpts from the stenographic report of an interview between your representative, Radek, and myself. These pamphlets have been ready for delivery for two days past, but we are informed that the Central Soviet Committee or the extraordinary revolutionary staff of Vologda has prohibited the delivery of the same to us.

Ambassador Francis then informed Tchicherin that all the Allied Ambassadors were acting in harmony and shared the same views. He continued: Your document states that Archangel is not a fit residence for Ambassadors in the event of a "siege." Do you expect a German siege of Archangel? Certainly you do not anticipate an Allied siege of that city.

I can only repeat what I have said to you and to the Russian people many times, and that is, the Allies have nothing to fear from the Russian people, with whom they consider themselves still in alliance against the common enemy. Speaking for myself, I have no desire or intention of leaving Russia unless forced to do so and in such event my absence would be but temporary. I would not properly represent my Government or the sentiment of the American people if I should leave Russia at this time.

The Allies have never recognized the Brest-Litovsk peace and it is becoming so burdensome to the Russian people that in my judgment the time is not far distant when they will turn upon Germany, and the repulsion of the enemy from the Russian borders will demonstrate what I have continuously believed, and that is the national spirit of great Russia is not dead, but has only been sleeping.

[103.]

Agreement between the Allies and the Murmansk Soviet, concluded July 17, 1918.

(British *Daily Review of the Foreign Press*.)

The following is transmitted through the wireless stations of the Russian Government (July 29):

The General Assembly of the Murman Regional Soviet has sanctioned without opposition the following agreement, which is temporary in character and made necessary by special circumstances, between the representatives of Great Britain, the United States of North America and France, and the Presidium of the Murman Regional Council.

Item 1. The present agreement, which has to be sanctioned by the Governments of the Allies, is concluded between the representatives of Great Britain, the United States of North America and France on the one side, and the representative of the Murman Regional Council on the other side, with the object of securing co-ordinated action on the part of those who have signed this agreement for the defense of the Murman region against the Powers of the German Coalition. For the purpose of obtaining this aim, both the signing parties take upon themselves the obligation to support each other mutually.

Item 2. The Murman region is composed of the former Alexandrovsk district of the Province of Archangelsk.

Item 3. All detachments of Russian armed forces of the Murman region, alike those which already exist and those which will be formed, will be under the direction of the Russian Military Command appointed by the Murman Regional Soviet. (Remark: It is recognized as very desirable that an independent Russian Army should be created, but with the object of obtaining more speedily the principal aim of this agreement, the admission of Russian volunteers into the Allied forces is permitted. In the case of such admissions, it is to be taken as recognized that of these volunteers no independent Russian detachments shall be formed, but that, as far as circumstances permit, the detachments should be composed only of an equal number of foreigners and Russians.)

Item 4. The representatives of Great Britain, the United States of North America, and France will give to the Russian Command necessary help in equipments, supplies, and transports and for the instruction of the Russian armed forces which are formed.

Item 5. The whole authority in the internal administration of the region belongs without qualification to the Murman Regional Soviet.

Item 6. The representatives of Great Britain, the United States of North America, and France, and their agents will not interfere in the home affairs of the region. In all matters in which it may be found necessary to have the support of the local population, the representatives of Great Britain, the United States of North America and France, and their agents will address themselves to the respective Russian authorities and not directly to the population, excepting in the belt along the front, in which the orders of the military command, justified by the conditions of field service, must be obeyed unconditionally by all. The conditions for entrance into and departure from the Murman region will be determined by the Murman Regional Soviet, which will take into consideration the state of war in which the region is involved and the necessity for most energetic precaution against espionage. Salaries and the standard of labor productivity will be established by the Murman Regional Soviet.

Item 7. In view of the impossibility of importing the necessary food from Russia, the representatives of Great Britain, the United States of North America, and France promise, as far as it shall be possible, to secure food to the Murman Regional Soviet for the whole population of the region, including all immigrant workmen with their families, the rations to equal in food value the rations which the privates of the Allied armed forces in Murman are receiving.

Item 8. The distribution of food among the population is to be carried out by trustworthy Russian troops.

Item 9. The representatives of Great Britain, the United States of North America, and France promise to secure, as far as may be possible, the importation of manufactured goods and other articles of the first necessity.

Item 10. The representatives of Great Britain, the United States of North America, and France promise as far as it may be possible to secure to the Murman Regional Soviet all necessary materials and implements for technical equipment and supplies so that it may carry out its program of construction which has been elaborated by mutual agreement. In this agreement first, the requirements of wartime are taken into consideration; secondly, the development of international trade intercourse; and thirdly, the local fisheries.

Item 11. All expenses which may be incurred by the Governments of Great Britain, the United States of North America and France as the result of this agreement are to be set down to the account of the respective Powers.

Item 12. The representatives of Great Britain, the United

States of North America and France recognize that their Governments must give the necessary financial assistance to the Murman Regional Soviet.

Item 13. The present agreement comes into force from the moment of its ratification by the Murman Regional Soviet, and will remain in force as long as normal relations between the Russian Central Authority on the one side and the Murman Regional Soviet and the Governments of Great Britain, the United States of North America and France on the other side are not re-established.

Item 14. Before signing this agreement, the representatives of Great Britain, the United States of North America and France in the name of their Governments again affirm the absence of any purpose of conquest in respect to the Murman region as a whole or in regard to any of its parts. The Presidium of the Murman Regional Soviet before the Russian people, and the Governments of Great Britain, the United States of North America, and France declares that the only object of this agreement is to guard the integrity of the Murman Region for a Great United Russia.

The original of this agreement has been signed by the Presidium of the Murman Regional Soviet and by the representatives of the above-named Powers.

The agreement was sanctioned by the Murman Regional Soviet on July 17th.

[104.]

Statement issued by the Czechoslovak National Council at Washington, July 27, 1918.

(*New York Times Current History*, Vol. VIII, Part 2, p. 468.)

There have been so many promising campaigns started in Russia during the last year of which nothing more is heard, that the people in this country watch with a certain lack of confidence the successes of the Czechoslovak forces in Siberia and Eastern European Russia.

Will they be permanent or will they come to nothing, as did the ill-fated campaigns of Korniloff, the Don Cossacks, the various Siberian governments and many others? Can the Czechoslovaks stand their ground, a hundred thousand men among a hundred million, and are they not themselves talking about withdrawing from Russia?

It is, of course, well known that the Czechoslovaks are not Russians; that they are a well organized and thoroughly disciplined force recruited from former Austrian soldiers of the Bohemian and Slovak races, who surrendered to the Russians. The Czechoslovak Army in Russia was created in order to fight the Germans and the Austrians, and when Russia deserted the cause of the Allies arrangements were made by Professor T. G. Masaryk, President of the Czechoslovak National Council, and by virtue of that Commander-in-Chief of the Czechoslovak forces, with the allied representatives in Russia and also with the Bolsheviks to march the Czechoslovaks out of Russia and take them to the western front.

It should be kept clearly in mind that occupation of Russian territory or the restoration of an eastern front was not thought of when these arrangements were made, in February, 1918. It was due to one of those German blunders, like the one that brought America into the war, that the Czechoslovaks, instead of withdrawing from Russia, are now in control of Siberia and of considerable territory west of the Urals.

Under pressure of Austrian and German demands Trotsky tried to disarm the Czechoslovaks and put them in prison camps, with a view of turning them over to the Austrian authorities. The Czechoslovaks, being attacked, had to defend themselves, and as a result found themselves in control of the greatest portion of the Trans-Siberian Railroad and the Volga River. They were like Saul, who went to seek his father's asses and found a kingdom.

Professor Masaryk was by this time in America, and the Czechoslovak leaders, under the changed conditions, hesitated as to their own course of action. The only orders they had were to take their forces to the Pacific. They had no desire to play policemen in Russia, and they realized that their position could not be indefinitely sustained unless they were assured of a steady flow of supplies. And yet the unparalleled strategic opportunities which their position gave them made a strong appeal to their imagination. This seems evident from the fact that, instead of withdrawing from European Russia, they occupied more cities on the Volga, stretching out their detachments in the direction of the Murman Coast.

A week ago Professor Masaryk received a lengthy cable report from the leader of the Czechoslovak forces in which the following words are found indicative of the present desires of these men:

"In our opinion it is most desirable and also possible to reconstruct a, Russia-Germany front in the east. We ask for instructions as to whether we should leave for France or whether we should stay here to fight in Russia by the side of the Allies and of Russia. The health and spirit of our troops are excellent."

Professor Masaryk has since then instructed the forces in Siberia to remain there for the present. The question, however, of staying in Russia or getting out does not depend on the Czechoslovaks alone. That is something which must be decided by the Allies. The Czechoslovak Army is one of the allied armies, and it is as much under the orders of the Versailles War Council as the French or American Army. No doubt the Czechoslovak boys in Russia are anxious to avoid participation in a possible civil war in Russia, but they realize at the same time that by staying where they are they may be able to render far greater services, both to Russia and the allied cause, than if they were transported to France. They are at the orders of the Supreme War Council of the Allies.

[105.]

Official Announcement issued at Washington, August 3, 1918.

(*New York Times Current History,* Vol. VIII, Part 2, p. 465.)

In the judgment of the Government of the United States— a judgment arrived at after repeated and very searching consideration of the whole situation—military intervention in Russia would be more likely to add to the present sad confusion there than to cure it, and would injure Russia, rather than help her out of her distresses. Such military intervention as has been most frequently proposed, even supposing it to be efficacious in its immediate object of delivering an attack upon Germany from the east, would, in its judgment, be more likely to turn out to be merely a method of making use of Russia than to be a method of serving her. Her people, if they profited by it at all, could not profit by it in time to deliver them from their present desperate difficulties, and their substance would meantime be used to maintain foreign armies, not to reconstitute their own or to feed their own men, women, and children. We are bending all our energies now to the purpose, the resolute and confident purpose, of winning on the western front, and it would, in the judgment of the Government of the United States, be most unwise to divide or dissipate our forces.

As the Government of the United States sees the present circumstances, therefore, military action is admissible in Russia now only to render such protection and help as is possible to the Czechoslovaks against the armed Austrian and German prisoners who are attacking them, and to steady any efforts at self-government or self-defense in which the Russians themselves may be willing to accept assistance. Whether from Vladivostok or from Murmansk and Archangel, the only present object for which American troops will be employed will be to guard military stores which may subsequently be needed by Russian forces and to render such aid as may be acceptable to the Russians in the organization of their own self-defense.

With such objects in view, the Government of the United States is now co-operating with the Governments of France and Great Britain in the neighborhood of Murmansk and Archangel. The United States and Japan are the only powers which are just now in a position to act in Siberia in sufficient force to accomplish even such modest objects as those that have been outlined. The Government of the United States has, therefore, proposed to the Government of Japan that each of the two Governments send a force of a few thousand men to Vladivostok, with the purpose of co-operating as a single force in the occupation of Vladivostok and in safeguarding, as far as it may be, the country to the rear of the westward-moving Czechoslovaks, and the Japanese Government has consented.

In taking this action the Government of the United States wishes to announce to the people of Russia in the most public and solemn manner that it contemplates no interference with the political sovereignty of Russia, no intervention in her internal affairs—not even in the local affairs of the limited areas which her military force may be obliged to occupy—and no impairment of her territorial integrity, either now or hereafter, but that what we are about to do has as its single and only object the rendering of such aid as shall be acceptable to the Russian people themselves in their endeavors to regain control of their own affairs, their own territory, and their own destiny. The Japanese Government, it is understood, will issue a similar assurance.

These plans and purposes of the Government of the United States have been communicated to the Governments of Great Britain, France, and Italy, and those Governments have advised the Department of State that they assent to them in principle. No conclusion that the Government of the United States has arrived at in this important matter is intended, however, as an effort to restrict the actions or interfere with the independent judgment of the Governments with which we are now associated in the war.

It is also the hope and purpose of the Government of the United States to take advantage of the earliest opportunity to send to Siberia a commission of merchants, agricultural experts, labor advisers, Red Cross representatives, and agents of the Young Men's Christian Association accustomed to organizing the best methods of spreading useful information and rendering educational help of a modest kind in order in some systematic way to relieve the immediate economic necessities of the people there in every way for which an opportunity may open. The execution of this plan will follow and will not be permitted to embarrass the military assistance rendered to the Czechoslovaks.

It is the hope and expectation of the Government of the United States that the Governments with which it is associated will, wherever necessary or possible, lend their active aid in the execution of these military and economic plans.

[106.]

Declaration by the Japanese Government, August 3, 1918.

(*New York Times Current History*, Vol. VIII, Part 2, p. 466.)

The Japanese Government, actuated by sentiments of sincere friendship toward the Russian people, have always entertained most sanguine hopes of the speedy re-establishment of order in Russia and of the healthy, untrammeled development of her national life.

Abundant proof, however, is now afforded that the Central European Empires, taking advantage of the defenseless and chaotic condition in which Russia has momentarily been placed, are consolidating their hold on that country and are steadily extending their activities to Russia's eastern possessions. They have persistently interfered with the passage of Czechoslovak troops through Siberia. In the forces now opposing these valiant troops German and Austro-Hungarian prisoners are freely enlisted, and they practically assume a position of command.

The Czechoslovak troops, aspiring to secure a free and independent existence for their race and loyally espousing the common cause of the Allies, justly command every sympathy and consideration from the co-belligerents, to whom their destiny is a matter of deep and abiding concern.

In the presence of the danger to which the Czechoslovak troops actually are exposed in Siberia at the hands of the Germans and Austro-Hungarians, the Allies have naturally felt themselves unable to view with indifference the untoward course of events, and a certain number of their troops already have been ordered to proceed to Vladivostok.

The Government of the United States, equally sensible of the gravity of the situation, recently approached the Japanese Government with proposals for the early dispatch of troops to relieve the pressure weighing upon the Czechoslovak forces. The Japanese Government, being anxious to fall in with the desire of the American Government, have decided to proceed at once to make disposition of suitable forces for the proposed mission, and a certain number of these troops will be sent forthwith to Vladivostok.

In adopting this course, the Japanese Government remain constant in their desire to promote relations of enduring friendship, and they reaffirm their avowed policy of respecting the territorial integrity of Russia, and of abstaining from all interference in her internal politics. They further declare that upon the realization of the objects above indicated they will immediately withdraw all Japanese troops from Russian territory, and will leave wholly unimpaired the sovereignty of Russia in all its phases, whether political or military.

[107.]

Statement issued by the Russian Embassy at Washington, August 5, 1918.

(*New York Times Current History*, Vol. VIII, Part 2, p. 467.)

Direct and authoritative information has been received by the Russian Embassy concerning the program and intentions of the groups which have newly revealed themselves in Siberia, and which without bloodshed or violence have succeeded the Soviets, the latter having disappeared naturally by the very fact of the valiant Czechoslovak troops liberating different cities and regions of Russia. It appears at present that the group in Vladivostok, known under the title of "The Siberian Temporary Government," is closely united and, in fact, does not differ in any way from the authorities established in Omsk, which seem to be but a part of the same Government.

The United Siberian Government states that it was elected on the 26th of January, 1916, by the members of a regional Siberian Duma—representative assembly. The point where this Government has temporarily transferred its center is Vladivostok, the other members of it remaining at Omsk. A message from those at Omsk has just been received, stating that owing to combined efforts of the Czechoslovaks and the military organizations of the Siberian Government itself, the following cities have been liberated from the Bolsheviki: Marlinsk, Novo Nicolaievsk, Tomsk, Narime, Tobolsk, Barnaoul, Camipalatinsk, Carcaralinsk, Atchinski, and Crasnoiarsk.

Everywhere the people belonging to different classes and political groups have manifested vivid interest and sympathy with the organization of their army, which is intended to reestablish, together with the Allies, a battlefront against Germany, and the formation of which is proceeding very successfully. Their relations with the Czechoslovaks are brotherly.

To that most valuable information the "Temporary Government of Siberia" adds a public statement of its political aims, which are: The creation of a Russian Army, well disciplined, in

[1] Mr. Bakhmeteff still claimed to be the authorized diplomatic representative of Russia by virtue of credentials received from the Provisional Government, and the Embassy throughout this period was the center of activity in the United States for all the elements opposed to the Soviet Government.

order to re-establish, in co-operation with the Allies, a battle-front against Germany. Siberia being an inseparable part of United Russia, the Temporary Government of Siberia believes it to be its first duty to safeguard, in the territory of Siberia, the interests of the whole of Russia, to recognize all the international treaties and agreements of Russia with friendly nations which were in force until October 25, 1917, the moment of the Bolshevist uprising.

The Siberian Government is tending to re-establish government and order in Siberia and to start the reconstruction of a unified Russia and the creation of a central all-Russian authority which would be generally recognized.

[108.]

Proclamation by the Provisional Government of the Country of the North, August 7, 1918.[1]

(*New York Times Current History*, Vol. VIII, Part 2, p. 471.)

The power of the Bolsheviki is ended. Because of the treason to the country committed at Brest-Litovsk; because of famine, the failure to recognize the rights and liberties of the country; because of pillaging, illegal shootings and constant arrests, the power of the so-called Soviet of traitors and criminals, is past. The representatives of the so-called people's Government have fled.

At the present moment, in the interests of all Russia, we take upon ourselves the duty of governing the Country of the North.

By this proclamation we inform the inhabitants that from to-day the power of government is confided to the Government of the Country of the North, which is composed of members of the Constituent Assembly and representatives of the Zemstvos of this district, which considers itself as the supreme authority from now on to hand over power immediately after Russia has chosen her government and as soon as there is a possibility of

[1] On August 3 an uprising in Archangel resulted in the overthrow of the Soviet. Under the protection of Allied troops, the Provisional Government of the Country of the North was organized, having its headquarters at Archangel. The new Government was composed of nine persons—all members of the Russian Constituent Assembly—and had Nicholas Tchaikovsky at its head. Early in September Tchaikovsky was temporarily overthrown by an attempted coup d'état, but the Allied representatives insisted on his immediate restoration to power.

freely communicating with her. The aims of the Government are:

1. Regeneration of Russia, the resumption of relations between Russia and other Governments, and the organization of local power with the Government of the North.
2. Defense of the region of the north and the whole nation against all territorial violation by Germany, Finland, and other enemies.
3. Re-union with Russia of the peoples taken from her.
4. Re-establishment of the two organs of the people, the Constituent Assembly, Municipal Dumas, and Zemstvos.
5. Re-establishing legal order by the expressing of the will of the citizens and re-establishing political and religious liberty.
6. The security of the rights of agricultural workers.
7. Defense of the interests of labor in accordance with the political and economic interests of the north and the rest of Russia.
8. Suppression of famine.

The Government counts upon the Russian, American, and British peoples, as well as those of other nations, for aid in combating famine and relieving the financial situation. It is recognized that intervention by the Allies in Russia's internal affairs is not directed against the interests of the people, and that the people will welcome the allied troops who have come to fight against the common enemy.

The Government in making the present declaration, calls upon all the people to preserve calm and order.

[109.]

Declaration of the British Government to the Peoples of Russia, August 8, 1918.[1]

(*New York Times Current History*, Vol. VIII, Part 2, p. 472.)

Your allies have not forgotten you. We remember all the services your heroic army rendered us in the early years of the war. We are coming as friends to help you save yourselves from dismemberment and destruction at the hands of Germany,

[1] Issued by British representatives at Vladivostok, Murmansk, and Archangel.

which is trying to enslave your people and use the great resources of your country to its own ends.

We wish to solemnly assure you that while our troops are entering Russia to assist you in your struggle against Germany, we shall not retain one foot of your territory. We deplore the civil war that divides you and the internal dissensions that facilitate Germany's plans of conquest.

The destinies of Russia are in the hands of the Russian peoples. It is for them, and for them alone, to decide their form of government and to find a solution for their social problems.

Peoples of Russia, your very existence as an independent nation are at stake. The liberties you have won in the revolution are threatened with extinction by the iron hand of Germany. Rally around the banner of freedom and independence that we, who are still your allies, are raising in your midst, and secure the triumphs of those two great principles without which there can be no lasting peace or real liberty for the world. . . .

We wish to aid in the development of the industrial and natural resources of your country, not with a view to exploiting them for our own benefit. We desire, too, to restore the exchange of commodities, to stimulate agriculture, and to enable you to take your rightful place among the free nations of the world. Our one desire is to see Russia strong and free, and then to retire to watch the Russian people work out their own destinies.

[110.]

Address by Ambassador Francis to the Russian People, August 9, 1918.

(Approved and Signed by the Diplomatic Corps.)

As stated above, it was never our intention or desire to quit Russia and we have not done so. On our return to Archangel we find the city and the surrounding country under the new Government which had already explained to you its organization and its plan for the future. While considering you as allies against a common enemy of the Governments and the peoples whom we represent, we have no intention of interfering in your internal affairs. We hold to the belief that all civilized peoples have the right themselves to determine their own form of Government. We have never recognized the Brest-Litovsk peace and so stated to you when it was signed and again when it was ratified by the Soviet Congress at Moscow, March seventeenth, and that position has been reported time and again, by your Government as well as by ourselves. We will never recommend to our Government the recognition of any Russian Government which has not a national character, which disregards Russia's solemn bonds of alliance and which observes the Brest-Litovsk treaty.

We feel confident that the Allied Countries we represent could make our own peace terms with Germany at any time we would agree to leave Russia to the tender mercies of the Central Empires. Such a peace, however, if effected, would be temporary, as Germany after strengthening herself with the immeasurable resources and immense man power of Russia, prompted by her insatiable ambition to rule the world, would threaten the liberties of the peoples whose trust we hold. Moreover, we not only sympathize with Russia in the difficulties she has encountered but we feel really grateful to her for her heroic struggle and the sacrifices she made and the timely assistance she gave the Allied cause in the beginning of this world struggle. If you have any doubt in your minds and hearts concerning the dominating spirit or the grasping selfishness of Germany you need only read the expressions of her rulers, of her military party, of her political leaders, of her clergy, and even of her socialists, to dispel such doubt. The Germans profess to believe that they are God's chosen agents not only for the subjugation of Russia but for all of the peoples of the entire world. When Germany brought on this world war her people were so imbued with their potentialities for success that they assumed a haughty and overbearing attitude toward all opponents. Within a few months a Minister of Foreign Affairs who dared to question the strength of Germany to settle this conquest by force of arms was compelled to resign.

Surely you will not accept peace which had already dismembered your great country in whose record and achievement every Russian with National spirit cherished a pardonable pride. Indifference or luke-warmness or inaction on your part at this time will result in additional and still greater curtailments of your liberties and still greater encroachment on your territories by the Central Empires and will bring down on your memories the anathemas of your descendants. The defense of their country is nevertheless a question between every Russian and his own conscience. The Allies leave it there with every confidence and have no intention of forcing any one to fight against their will.

There can be no doubt about the outcome of this war. It will result in the absolute defeat of the Central Empires. The German dream of world power will be dissipated and even the Germans themselves will look back with humiliation upon the time when they indulged in such vanity and folly. This Allied victory will result in a lasting peace. There will be no longer any question as to a civilized people being dominated by a Foreign Power. The right of all people to dispose of themselves is the main issue of this struggle and it will be settled and settled right before the Allied armies lay down their arms. Russia has a great future and the Governments and the people whom we represent will not permit that future to be clouded or impaired by German presumption.

We expect to remain in Russia and to continue to represent the friendly sentiment of our countries toward you. Our Governments will recognize any form of Government you may adopt provided it is the choice of the entire people and provided furthermore it will offer resistance to our enemy who is your enemy also, and the enemy of all liberty loving people throughout the world. Russia has within borders more than sufficient products to feed and clothe her immense population, but if attributable to civil strife or ineffective transportation you are deprived of the necessities of life, we are willing and ready to divide our products with you, for the knowledge that you are suffering from hunger or nakedness would prevent our enjoyment of the material blessings of an all-wise providence.

[III.]

Note from Tchicherin to Dewitt C. Poole, Jr., American Consul, August 6, 1918.

(*New York Times*, August 15, 1918.)

Dear Mr. Poole:

At the time when Citizen Lenin, in a speech referring to the unjustifiable Anglo-French invasion, declared that the British and French were in fact at war with us and you came to ask whether peace or war existed between us and whether you were to remain with us, I replied that our people were still at peace with yours and that to enable you to continue acting as representative of the United States the same facilities would be granted you as heretofore.

This possibility still holds good as far as we are concerned, inasmuch as the interruption of cable communication by way of the Murman coast is the work of Great Britain, not ours. As the only possibility of communicating with your Government we have placed our wireless station at your disposal.

We therefore request you to inform your Government and peoples abroad that a completely unjustifiable attack and a pronounced act of violence is being committed upon us. We have done nothing to deserve such an attack. Our people want nothing but to live in peace and friendship with the masses and workers of all nations. Despite the existing state of peace Anglo-French armed forces have invaded our territory, taken our towns and villages by force, dissolved our workers' organizations, imprisoned their members and driven them from their homes without any reason possibly warranting these predatory acts.

Without a declaration of war and without the existence of a state of war, hostilities are opened against us and our national property is pillaged. Toward us no justice is observed and no law acknowledged by those who sent these invading troops against us, for we are the first in the world to establish a government for the oppressed poor. Barefaced robbery is held permissible against us.

These people, who did not declare war against us, act like barbarians toward us, but we, who represent the oppressed poor, are no barbarians like these invaders. Our retaliation against those who shoot the members of our Soviets does not take the shape of similar acts against representatives of these governments. The official Government representatives enjoy an immunity which is refused by the latter's official departments to our Soviet members.

While we take this attitude toward the official representatives of Great Britain and France we take into consideration your own urgent request, because we regard you as the representative of a nation which, to use your own words, will undertake nothing against the Soviets if we retaliate with precautionary measures against the warlike measures directed against us.

It is in pursuance of this that we intern the nationals of invading powers in concentration camps. We regard these nationals as civilian prisoners. We apply these precautionary measures only against the members of the property classes, who are our opponents. No such measures are taken against our natural allies, the workingmen of these same countries who happen to be here. The working classes of the whole world are our friends.

Precisely at this moment we say to these countries whose armies proceed with open violence against us, and we call out to their peoples, "Peace be to the homes of the poor!"

As you stated to us that your nation does not purpose to destroy the Soviets, we ask you now if you cannot tell us plainly what Great Britain wants with us. Is Great Britain's aim to destroy the most popular government the world has ever seen, namely, the councils of the poor and the peasants? Is her aim a counter-revolution?

In view of the acts referred to by me I must assume that this is true. We must believe that her intention is to re-establsh the worst tyranny in the world, namely, the hated tsarism, Or does she contemplate seizing any special town or territory we can name?

Remembering your kindness, I hope you will help us to elucidate these problems.

[112.]

Note from Tchicherin regarding the Departure from Russia of French and British, August 20, 1918.

(*Izvestia*, August 20, 1918.)

People's Commissary, Tchicherin, has sent the following telegram to the Minister from the Netherlands in Petrograd:

The offers which were made by us to the Governments of the Allies through the Neutral consular corps and which we transmitted by radio to Mr. Lindley in Archangel, and which we made collectively in view of the fact that the representatives of the Allies stated that they will leave only collectively, consist of the following:

The Allied citizens who have exercised diplomatic and consular functions, will have the opportunity to leave Russia on condition that our representative, Litvinov,[1] and all Russian citizens of official standing and with official commissions may return to Russia, and among them our agent in Christiania, Baitler, who was taken off a ship by the British and carried off by them while he was returning to Russia, and was on the way to Murmansk.

The officers and soldiers of the French Military Mission will be able to leave Russia when France will give the opportunity to the Russian soldiers who remained in that country to return to Russia by all possible routes, with the assistance of the International Red Cross and three members of the Russian Red Cross, who for this purpose should receive permission to enter France.

English and French citizens who were interned in Russia as civil prisoners as a means of protection and who are not criminals, will be liberated, and all others, except criminals, will remain at liberty on condition that no political repression against adherents of the Soviet Government should take place, either now or later, in the districts occupied by the Anglo-French and Czechoslovak troops, or in the Allied countries, and that all such measures which have already been introduced should be abolished.

Allied citizens will be permitted to leave Russia in exchange for the right of Russian citizens to leave Allied countries, including all those who are in the ranks of the British Army.

(signed)   TCHICHERIN,

[113.]

Statement by Trotsky, August 23, 1918.

AN AMERICAN LIE

(*Izvestia*, August 23, 1918.)

From the People's Commissarist of War and Marine, to all, all, all!

When in April the Japanese landing was being prepared in Vladivostok, the general staff in Tokio sent by Allied cables a statement that the Siberian railroad was threatened by the German and Austro-Hungarian war prisoners. I then sent to

[1] Maxim Litvinov, representative of the Soviet Government in London.

the Siberian line from Moscow, American and British officers, who were obliged to confirm officially that all rumors with regard to the threatening of the Siberian railroad by war prisoners were nothing but silly inventions.[1]

This fact is well known to the former Ambassador, Francis, and the former chief of the American Red Cross in Russia, Colonel Robins.

Now when the intervention by the Allies has become an established fact, the American Government picks up the Japanese lie and attempts to hand it to the world in a warmed-up condition.

According to the American statement, the intervention of the Allies is for the purpose of assisting the Czechoslovaks against the German and Austro-Hungarian war prisoners who are attacking them. The participation of these prisoners in the struggle against the Czechoslovaks is the most monstrous invention, as is the Japanese statement about the threat to the Siberian road from the Germans.

It is true that among the Soviet troops there are a certain number of former war prisoners, revolutionary socialists, who became Russian citizens, who are ready to fight against any kind of imperialism, no matter on what side it is. It must be said, however, that the internationalist soldiers of the Soviet army do not constitute more than 1/25 of the entire number of Soviet troops.

People's Commissary of War and Marine,
(signed)   L. TROTSKY,

[114.]

Resolution adopted at a Meeting of the All-Russian Central Executive Committee on September 2, 1918.

(*Izvestia*, September 3, 1918.)

The All-Russian Central Executive Committee expresses its deep indignation regarding the hideous attempt of the agent of the counter-revolution on the life of the leader of the working class and the peasant's poverty, Comrade Lenin, the most prominent representative of contemporary revolutionary socialism in the whole world.[2]

[1] See Documents 74 and 75.
[2] On August 30 an attempt was made on Lenin's life in Moscow. The following day Uritzki, Chairman of the Commission Extraordinary

The All-Russian Central Executive Committee sends him its wishes for speedy recovery. This unheard of attempt on the life most valuable to the world's proletariat, was prepared by the treacherous agitation of the renegades of socialism, inspired by the Black Hundred and paid for with the gold of Anglo-French imperialism.

In the person of Comrade Lenin, the Russian counter-revolution, which is led by the party of the Right S. R. and the staff of General Alexeev, wanted to destroy the great victories of the October revolution and to strike a heavy blow at the working class.

The All-Russian Central Executive Committee sincerely believes that the criminal attempts of the hirelings of the bourgeoisie will not bring confusion into the ranks of the revolutionary proletariat and will not weaken the struggle for the establishment of the socialist system and for the destruction of the counter-revolution.

The All-Russian Central Executive Committee appeals to the laboring masses to strengthen their organizations. At the same time, the All-Russian Central Executive Committee gives a solemn warning to all the serfs of the Russian and Allied bourgeoisie, warning them that for each attempt on the workers of the Soviet government and the upholders of the ideals of the socialist revolution, will be held responsible all the counter-revolutionists and all those that inspired them. To the White terror of the enemies of the Workers' and Peasants' Government, the workers and the peasants will reply by a mass Red terror against the bourgeoisie and its agents.

for Combating the Counter Revolution was murdered in Petrograd. The Commission issued a decree proclaiming "measures of terror" and laying down that every person found with a weapon in his hands would be immediately executed, while persons agitating against the Soviet Government would be arrested and interned. During the next two weeks a number of British and French citizens were arrested. At the meeting of the All-Russian Central Executive Committee which passed the above resolution, Tchicherin said in a speech that similar measures had not been adopted towards American citizens, because, "although the Government of the United States was compelled by its allies to agree to participation—so far nominal—in the intervention, its decision does not seem to us to be final" (*Izvestia*, No. 189, September 3, 1918).

[115.]

Official Statement by Soviet Government.

(*Izvestia*, September 3, 1918.)

THE CONSPIRACY OF ALLIED IMPERIALISTS AGAINST SOVIET RUSSIA.[1]

Official Statement:

To-day on the 2nd of September was liquidated the conspiracy, which was planned by Anglo-French diplomats, at the head of which was the Chief of the British Mission, Lockhart, the French Consul General Grénard, French General Lavergne and others. The purpose of the conspiracy was to organize the capture of the Council of People's Commissaries and the pronouncement of a military dictatorship in Moscow. This was to be attained by bribing Soviet troops.

The entire organization which was built on a basis of conspiracy, and which was acting by forged papers and bribery, has been disclosed.

Among other things, instructions were found, that in case of a successful overturn, forged secret correspondence should be published, this correspondence being between the Russian Government and the German Government, and forged treaties were to be manufactured for the creation of the proper atmosphere for renewing the war with Germany.

The conspirators acted under cover of diplomatic immunity and with certificates issued under the personal signature of the Chief of the British Mission in Moscow, Mr. Lockhart. Several copies of these certificates are at present in the hands of the special investigating commission.

It has also been established that through the hands of one of Lockhart's agents, a British Lieutenant, Riley, during the last week and a half, passed 1,200,000 rubles for bribery. The conspiracy was disclosed thanks to the reliability of those commanders of Soviet troops whom the conspirators offered to bribe.

[1] According to *Izvestia*, the purpose of this "conspiracy" was the seizure of the Council of People's Commissaries and their removal to Archangel. It was claimed that this was to be brought about by the bribing of Lettish troops, that on August 4 Mr. Lockhart met the Lettish commander Bersin in order to arrange matters (*Izvestia*, No. 189), that at subsequent meetings details were worked out, and that Bersin disclosed the whole conspiracy to the Government (*Izvestia*, No. 206).

At the secret headquarters of the conspirators an Englishman was arrested, but after being brought to the special investigating commission, he said that he was the British diplomatic representative, Lockhart. After the identity of the arrested Lockhart had been established, he was immediately released. The investigation is being carried out energetically.

[116.]

Statement by Tchicherin, September 7, 1918.

(*Izvestia*, September 7, 1918.)

At the time when the Russian Socialist Federated Soviet Republic through neutral powers was carrying on negotiations with the Governments of England and France regarding the exchange of diplomatic representatives as well as army men and civilians, it was disclosed that military and diplomatic representatives of England and France were taking advantage of their positions for the organization on the territory of the Russian Socialist Federated Soviet Republic of conspiracies directed to the arrest of the Council of People's Commissaries with the aid of bribery and propaganda among military units, the blowing up of bridges and food warehouses and trains carrying food. The facts which are at the disposal of the Government and which have been partially published already in the statements of the Extraordinary Investigating Commission and the Commissaries of the Northern Commune, establish, beyond doubt, the fact that the threads of the conspiracy met in the hands of the Chief of the British Mission, Lockhart and his agents. It was also established that the building of the British Embassy at Petrograd was practically turned into a headquarters of conspirators. Under such conditions, while being very anxious to sincerely and fully observe diplomatic immunity and the rules of international relations, the Government of the Russian S. F. S. R. has denied the opportunity of freedom of action to people who came to Russia as diplomatic and military representatives and who place themselves practically in a position of conspirators against the government of our country. The Government of the R. S. F. S. R. has been compelled to create such conditions for people convicted of conspiracies that they will be denied the opportunity to continue further activity—activity criminal from the point of view of international law. With the British and French troops advancing on the territory of the R. S. F. S. R. for the support of open rebellions against the Soviet power, and the diplomatic representatives of these powers creating an organization within Russia for the overturn of the State and the capture of power, the Government of R. S. F. S. R. was compelled to adopt the necessary measures of self-defense. All the interned representatives of the British and French bourgeoisie, among whom there is not a single workingman, will be immediately released, as soon as Russian citizens in England and France and in the districts occupied by allied troops and Czechoslovaks are not subjected any longer to repression and persecution. English and French citizens will be given the opportunity to leave immediately the territory of Russia, when the same opportunity is given to Russian citizens in England and France. French military officials will be given this opportunity as soon as Russian soldiers with the aid of the International and Russian Red Cross will be returned from France. Diplomatic representatives of both sides, and among them the chief of the conspirators, Lockhart, will simultaneously be given the opportunity to return to their countries.

Now, after the Government of the Soviet Republic adopted the above decisions, we have received from the British Government a radio informing us of the arrest of Comrade Litvinov and his staff. This event serves as an additional confirmation of the correctness of our actions and justification of our expectations, when we refused to allow the departure of Lockhart and his assistants from Russia before the departure of Comrade Litvinov from England.

And in this British radio as well as the radio statement of the French Government which was received at the same time, it is stated that in case of further detention under guard of British and French citizens, those Governments threaten individual repressions against all prominent Bolsheviks who may fall into their hands. This is not news to us, as such repressions have taken place in the district occupied by the Allies, including the shooting of Soviet employees. We adhere to our previous proposition, to cease repression only in case such repression is stopped on the side of the Allies, as we have already stated more than once. I repeat once more that the measures of precaution adopted by us concern exclusively the British and

French bourgeoisies and that we will not touch a single workingman.

People's Commissary of Foreign Affairs,
(signed) TCHICHERIN.

[117.]

Note from the British Foreign Secretary to Tchicherin, September 6, 1918.

(*Izvestia*, September 7, 1918.)

We have received information that an outrageous attack was made on the British Embassy in Petrograd, that the contents were partially looted and partially destroyed and that Captain Cromie who attempted to defend the Embassy was killed and his body horribly mutilated. We demand immediate satisfaction and severe punishment of all those responsible and those who participated in this abominable outrage.[1]

If the Russian Soviet Government will not give complete satisfaction or if violence be used against British subjects, the British Government will consider every member of the Russian Government individually responsible and will take measures to insure that all the governments of civilized nations shall consider them outside the law, and that there shall be no asylum for them to go to.

You have already been informed through Mr. Litvinov that His Majesty's Government was ready to do everything within its power for the immediate return of the representatives of Great Britain, and the representatives of the Russian Soviet Government to their respective countries, and a guarantee was given that as soon as the British officials were permitted to cross the Russian-Finnish frontier, Mr. Litvinov and his staff would be permitted to leave immediately for Russia. We have received information now that on the 29th of August a decree was issued in accordance with which all British and French citizens between the age of 18 and 40 are subject to arrest and also that official representatives of Britain were arrested on the trumped up charge of conspiracy against the Soviet Government.

His Majesty's Government in view of this considered it neces-

[1] This attack took place on August 31.

sary to subject Mr. Litvinov and his assistants to preventive arrest until all British subjects are liberated and receive permission for unhindered passage to the Finnish frontier under guarantees of complete immunity.[1]

(signed) BALFOUR.

September 6, 1918.

[118.]

Note from American Government to all the Associated and Neutral Governments, September 21, 1918.

(*New York Times Current History*, Vol. IX, Part 1, p. 287.)

This Government is in receipt of information from reliable sources revealing that the peaceable Russian citizens of Moscow, Petrograd, and other cities are suffering from an openly avowed campaign of mass terrorism and are subject to wholesale executions. Thousands of persons have been shot without even a form of trial; ill-administered prisons are filled beyond capacity, and every night scores of Russian citizens are recklessly put to death; and irresponsible bands are venting their brutal passions in the daily massacres of untold innocents.

In view of the earnest desire of the people of the United States to befriend the Russian people and lend them all that is possible of assistance in their struggle to reconstruct their nation upon principles of democracy and self-government, and acting therefore solely in the interest of the Russian people themselves, this Government feels that it cannot be silent or refrain from expressing its horror at this state of terrorism. Furthermore, it believes that in order to check the further increase of the indiscriminate slaughter of Russian citizens all civilized nations should register their abhorrence of such barbarism.

You will inquire, therefore, whether the Government to which you are accredited will be disposed to take some immediate action, which is entirely divorced from the atmosphere of belligerency and the conduct of war, to impress upon the perpetrators of these crimes the aversion with which civilization regards their present wanton acts.

[1] An agreement for exchange was finally arrived at and Litvinov left England September 25.

[119.]

Appeal by the All-Russian Provisional Government[1] to President Wilson, November 7, 1918.

(*New York Times Current History*, Vol. IX, Part I, p. 503.)

It is evident that the exit of Russia from the number of belligerents and the process of dismemberment which it is suffering has a deep influence on the fate of all the other countries. Furthermore, the problems of the future of Russia should be considered by Governments and nations of the universe as a problem of their own future. Russia will not perish. She is greatly suffering but not dead. Her national forces are regaining with remarkable quickness, and her effort to recover her unity and greatness will not cease until she attains this sublime aim.

Moreover, the reconstruction of powerful and prosperous Russia presents itself as a condition necessary to the maintenance of order and international equilibrium. It is therefore that the new Provisional Government, into whose hands has been intrusted the supreme power by the people of Russia, the regional Governments, the convention and committee of the members of the Constituent Assembly, the Zemstvos, and Municipalities addresses itself to the Allied Powers. It expects to receive their aid, and considers itself in the right to demand such help insistently.

It is to the head of the great American Democracy, recognized apostle of peace and fraternity of the nations, that it makes its appeal. All aid already extended to Russia by the Allies would be in vain if the new help should arrive too late, or in insufficient quantity. Every hour of delay threatens with innumerable calamities Russia, the Allies, and other nations.

[1] On September 24 a new Government was set up at Ufa by a conference attended by many members of the Constituent Assembly and presided over by Avskentiev, Social Revolutionary leader and former Minister of the Interior in the Kerensky Cabinet. It issued a manifesto to " Russian Ambassadors throughout the world " and to the Allied Governments. Early in November a fusion took place between this All-Russian Government and the Siberian Government, forming a new All-Russian Provisional Government with its seat at Omsk. By a coup d'état executed November 18-19, the Directorate of Five was overthrown and Admiral Kolchak, Minister of War and Marine, proclaimed himself Supreme Ruler.

[120.]

Letter from the Russian Soviet Government to President Wilson, dated October 24, 1918.

(Hearings on Bolshevik Propaganda before a Sub-committee of the Committee on the Judiciary, United States Senate, 65th Congress, 1919, p. 24.)

To the President of the United States of North America, Mr. Woodrow Wilson.

Mr. President:

In your message of January 8th to the Congress of the United States of North America, in the sixth point, you spoke of your profound sympathy for Russia, which was then conducting, single handed, negotiations with the mighty German imperialism. Your program, you declared, demands the evacuation of all Russian territory and such a settlement of all questions affecting Russia as will secure the best and freest co-operation of the other nations of the world in obtaining for her unhampered and unembarrassed opportunity for the independent determination of her political development and national policy, and assure her a sincere welcome into the society of free nations under institutions of her own choosing; and more than a welcome assistance of every kind that she may need and may herself desire. And you added that "the treatment accorded to her by her sister nations in the months to come will be the acid test of their good-will, of their comprehension of her needs as distinguished from their own interests, of their intelligent and unselfish sympathy."

The desperate struggle which we were waging at Brest-Litovsk against German imperialism apparently only intensified your sympathy for Soviet Russia, for you sent greetings to the Congress of the Soviets, which under the threat of a German offensive ratified the Brest peace of violence—greetings and assurances that Soviet Russia might count upon American help.[1]

Six months have passed since then, and the Russian people have had sufficient time to get actual tests of your Government's and your Allies' good-will, of their comprehension of the needs of the Russian people, of their intelligent unselfish sympathy. This attitude of your Government and of your Allies was shown

[1] See Document 65.

first of all in the conspiracy which was organized on Russian territory with the financial assistance of your French Allies and with the diplomatic co-operation of your Government as well— the conspiracy of the Czechoslovaks to whom your Government is furnishing every kind of assistance.

For some time attempts had been made to create a pretext for a war between Russia and the United States of North America by spreading false stories to the effect that German war prisoners had seized the Siberian railway, but your own officers and after them Colonel Robins, the head of your Red Cross Mission, had been convinced that these allegations were absolutely false. The Czechoslovak conspiracy was organized under the slogan that unless these misled unfortunate people be protected, they would be surrendered to Germany and Austria; but you may find out, among other sources, from the open letter of Captain Sadoul, of the French Military Mission, how unfounded this charge is. The Czechoslovaks would have left Russia in the beginning of the year, had the French Government provided ships for them. For several months we have waited in vain that your Allies should provide the opportunity for the Czechoslovaks to leave. Evidently these Governments have very much preferred the presence of the Czechoslovaks in Russia—the results show for what object—to their departure for France and their participation in the fighting on the French frontier. The best proof of the real object of the Czechoslovak rebellion is the fact that although in control of the Siberian railway, the Czechoslovaks have not taken advantage of this to leave Russia, but by the order of the Entente Governments, whose directions they follow, have remained in Russia to become the mainstay of the Russian counter-revolution. Their counter-revolutionary mutiny which made impossible the transportation of grain and petroleum on the Volga, which cut off the Russian workers and peasants from the Siberian stores of grain and other materials and condemned them to starvation—this was the first experience of the workers and peasants of Russia with your Government and with your Allies after your promises of the beginning of the year. And then came another experience: an attack on North Russia by Allied troops, including American troops, their invasion of Russian territory without any cause and without a declaration of war, the occupation of Russian cities and villages, executions of Soviet officials and other acts of violence against the peaceful population of Russia.

You have promised, Mr. President, to co-operate with Russia in order to obtain for her an unhampered and unembarrassed opportunity for the independent determination of her political development and her national policy. Actually this co-operation took the form of an attempt of the Czechoslovak troops and later, in Archangel, Murmansk, and the Far East, of your own and your Allies' troops, to force the Russian people to submit to the rule of the oppressing and exploiting classes, whose dominion was overthrown by the workers and peasants of Russia in October, 1917. The revival of the Russian counter-revolution which has already become a corpse, attempts to restore by force its bloody domination over the Russian people—such was the experience of the Russian people, instead of co-operation for the unembarrassed expression of their will which you promised them, Mr. President, in your declarations.

You have also, Mr. President, promised to the Russian people to assist them in their struggle for independence. Actually this is what has occurred: while the Russian people were fighting on the Southern front against the counter-revolution, which has betrayed them to German imperialism and was threatening their independence, while they were using all their energy to organize the defense of their territory against Germany at their Western frontiers, they were forced to move their troops to the East to oppose the Czechoslovaks who were bringing them slavery and oppression, and to the North—against your Allies and your own troops which had invaded their territory, and against the counter-revolutions organized by these troops.

Mr. President, the acid test of the relations between the United States and Russia gave quite different results from those that might have been expected from your message to the Congress. But we have reason not to be altogether dissatisfied with even these results, since the outrages of the counter-revolution in the East and North have shown the workers and peasants of Russia the aims of the Russian counter-revolution, and of its foreign supporters, thereby creating among the Russian people an iron will to defend their liberty and the conquests of the revolution, to defend the land that it has given to the peasants and the factories that it has given to the workers. The fall of Kazan, Symbyrsk, Syzran, and Samara should make it clear to you, Mr. President, what were the consequences for us of the actions which followed your promises of January 8th. Our trials helped to create a strongly united and disciplined Red

Army, which is daily growing stronger and more powerful and which is learning to defend the revolution. The attitude toward us, which was actually displayed by your Government and by your Allies could not destroy us; on the contrary, we are now stronger than we were a few months ago, and your present proposal of international negotiations for a general peace finds us alive and strong and in a position to give in the name of Russia our consent to join the negotiations. In your note to Germany you demand the evacuation of occupied territories as a condition which must precede the armistice during which peace negotiations shall begin. We are ready, Mr. President, to conclude an armistice on these conditions, and we ask you to notify us when you, Mr. President, and your Allies intend to remove troops from Murmansk, Archangel, and Siberia. You refuse to conclude an armistice, unless Germany will stop the outrages, pillaging, etc., during the evacuation of occupied territories. We allow ourselves therefore to draw the conclusion that you and your Allies will order the Czechoslovaks to return the part of our gold reserve fund which they seized in Kazan, that you will forbid them to continue as heretofore their acts of pillaging and outrage against the workers and peasants during their forced departure (for we will encourage their speedy departure, without waiting for your order).

With regard to other peace terms, namely, that the Governments which would conclude peace must express the will of their people, you are aware that our Government fully satisfies this condition, our Government expresses the will of the Councils of Workmen's, Peasants' and Red Army Deputies, representing at least eighty per cent of the Russian people. This cannot, Mr. President, be said about your Government. But for the sake of humanity and peace we do not demand as a prerequisite of general peace negotiations that all nations participating in the negotiations shall be represented by Councils of People's Commissaries elected at a Congress of Councils of Workmen's, Peasants', and Soldiers' Deputies. We know that this form of Government will soon be the general form, and that precisely a general peace, when nations will no more be threatened with defeat, will leave them free to put an end to the system and the clique that forced upon mankind this universal slaughter, and which will, in spite of themselves, surely lead the tortured peoples to create Soviet Governments, which give exact expression to their will.

Agreeing to participate at present in negotiations with even such Governments as do not yet express the will of the people we would like on our part to find out from you, Mr. President, in detail what is your conception of the League of Nations, which you propose as the crowning work of peace. You demand the independence of Poland, Serbia, Belgium, and freedom for the peoples of Austria-Hungary. You probably mean by this that the masses of the people must everywhere first become the masters of their own fate in order to unite afterwards in a league of free nations. But strangely enough, we do not find among your demands the liberation of Ireland, Egypt, or India, nor even the liberation of the Philippines, and we would be very sorry to learn that these people should be denied the opportunity to participate together with us, through their freely elected representatives, in the organization of the League of Nations.

We would also, Mr. President, very much like to know, before the negotiations with regard to the formation of a League of Nations have begun, what is your conception of the solution of many economic questions which are essential for the cause of future peace. You do not mention the war expenditures—this unbearable burden, which the masses would have to carry, unless the League of Nations should renounce payments on the loans to the capitalists of all countries. You know as well as we, Mr. President, that this war is the outcome of the policies of all capitalistic nations, that the governments of all countries were continually piling up armaments, that the ruling groups of all civilized nations pursued a policy of annexations, and that it would, therefore, be extremely unjust if the masses, having paid for these policies with millions of lives and with economic ruin, should yet pay to those who are really responsible for the war a tribute for their policies which resulted in all these countless miseries.

We propose, therefore, Mr. President, the annulment of the war loans as the basis of the League of Nations. As to the restoration of the countries that were laid waste by the war, we believe it is only just that all nations should aid for this purpose, the unfortunate Belgium, Poland, and Servia, and however poor and ruined Russia seems to be, she is ready on her part to do everything she can to help these victims of the war, and she expects that American capital, which has not at all suffered from this war, and has even made billions in profits out of it, will do its part to help these peoples.

But the League of Nations should not only liquidate the present war, but also make impossible any wars in the future. You must be aware, Mr. President, that the capitalists of your country are planning to apply in the future the same policies of encroachment and of super profits in China and Siberia, and that, fearing competition from Japanese capitalists, they are preparing a military force to overcome the resistance which they meet from Japan. You are no doubt aware of similar plans of the capitalist ruling circles of other countries with regard to other territories and other peoples. Knowing this, you will have to agree with us that the factories, mines, and banks must not be left in the hands of private persons, who have always made use of the vast means of production created by the masses of the people to export products and capital to foreign countries in order to reap super profits in return for the benefits forced on them, their struggle for spoils resulting in imperialistic wars. We propose, therefore, Mr. President, that the League of Nations be based on the expropriation of the capitalists of all countries. In your country, Mr. President, the banks and the industries are in the hands of such a small group of capitalists that, as your personal friend, Colonel Robins, assured us, the arrest of twenty heads of capitalistic cliques and the transfer of the control, which by characteristic capitalistic methods they have come to possess, into the hands of the masses of the people is all that would be required to destroy the principal source of new wars.

If you will agree to this, Mr. President—if the source of future wars will thus be destroyed, then there can be no doubt that it would be easy to remove all economic barriers and that all peoples, controlling their means of production, will be vitally interested in exchanging the things they do not need for the things they need. It will then be a question of an exchange of products between nations, each of which produces what it can best produce, and the League of Nations will be a league of mutual aid of the toiling masses. It will then be easy to reduce the armed forces to the limit necessary for the maintenance of internal safety.

We know very well that the selfish capitalist class will attempt to create this internal menace, just as the Russian landlords and capitalists are now attempting with the aid of American, English, and French armed forces to take the factories from the workers and the land from the peasants. But, if the

American workers, inspired by your idea of a League of Nations, will crush the resistance of the Russian capitalists, then neither the German nor any other capitalists will be a serious menace to the victorious working class, and it will then suffice, if every member of the commonwealth, working six hours in the factory, spends two hours daily for several months in learning the use of arms, so that the whole people will know how to overcome the internal menace.

And so, Mr. President, though we have had experience with your promises, we nevertheless accept as a basis your proposals about peace and about a League of Nations. We have tried to develop them in order to avoid results which would contradict your promises, as was the case with your promise of assistance to Russia. We have tried to formulate with precision your proposals on the League of Nations in order that the League of Nations should not turn out to be a league of capitalists against the nations. Should you not agree with us, we have no objection to an "open discussion of your peace terms," as your first point of your peace program demands. If you will accept our proposals as a basis, we will easily agree on the details.

But there is another possibility. We have had dealings with the President of the Archangel attack and the Siberian invasion and we have also had dealings with the President of the League of Nations Peace Program. Is not the first of these—the real President actually directing the policies of the American capitalist government? Is not the American Government rather a Government of the American corporations, of the American industrial, commercial, and railroad trusts, of the American banks —in short, a Government of the American capitalists? And is it not possible that the proposals of this Government about the creation of a League of Nations will result in new chains for the peoples, in the organization of an International trust for the exploitation of the workers and the suppression of weak nations? In this latter case, Mr. President, you will not be in a position to reply to our questions, and we will say to the workers of all countries: Beware! Millions of your brothers, thrown at each others throats by the bourgeoisie of all countries are still perishing on the battlefields and the capitalist leaders are already trying to come to an understanding for the purpose of suppressing with united forces those that remain alive, when they call to account the criminals who caused the war!

However, Mr. President, since we do not at all desire to wage war against the United States, even though your Government has not yet been replaced by a Council of People's Commissaries and your post is not yet taken by Eugene Debs, whom you have imprisoned; since we do not at all desire to wage war against England, even though the cabinet of Mr. Lloyd-George has not yet been replaced by a Council of People's Commissaries with MacLean at its head; since we have no desire to wage war against France, even though the capitalist Government of Clemenceau has not yet been replaced by a workmen's Government of Merheim, just as we have concluded peace with the imperialist government of Germany, with Emperor Wilhelm at its head, whom you, Mr. President, hold in no greater esteem than we, the Workmen's and Peasants' Revolutionary Government hold you, we finally propose to you, Mr. President, that you take up with your Allies the following questions and give us precise and business-like replies: Do the Governments of the United States, England, and France intend to cease demanding the blood of the Russian people and lives of Russian citizens, if the Russian people will agree to pay them a ransom, such as a man who has been suddenly attacked pays to the one who attacked him? If so, just what tribute do the Governments of the United States, England, and France demand of the Russian people? Do they demand concessions, that the railways, mines, gold deposits, etc., shall be handed over to them on certain conditions, or do they demand territorial concessions, some part of Siberia or Caucasia, or perhaps the Murmansk coast?

We expect from you, Mr. President, that you will definitely state what you and your Allies demand, and also whether the allowance between your Government and the Governments of the other Entente powers is in the nature of a combination which could be compared with a corporation for drawing dividends from Russia, or does your Government and the other governments of the Entente powers have each separate and special demands, and what are they? Particularly are we interested to know the demands of your French Allies with regard to the three billions of rubles which the Paris bankers loaned to the Government of the Czar—the oppressor of Russia and the enemy of his own people? And you, Mr. President, as well as your French Allies surely know that even if you and your Allies should succeed in enslaving and covering with blood the whole territory of Russia—which will not be allowed by our heroic revolutionary Red Army—that even in that case the Russian people, worn out by the war and not having sufficient time to take advantage of the benefits of the Soviet rule to elevate their national economy, will be unable to pay to the French bankers the full tribute for the billions that were used by the Government of the Czar for purposes injurious to the people. Do your French Allies demand that a part of this tribute be paid in installments, and if so, what part, and do they anticipate that their claims will result in similar claims by other creditors of the infamous Government of the Czar which has been overthrown by the Russian people? We can hardly think that your Government and your Allies are without a ready answer, when your and their troops are trying to advance on our territory with the evident object of seizing and enslaving our country.

The Russian people through the People's Red Army, are guarding their territory and are bravely fighting against your invasion and against the attack of your Allies. But your Government and the Governments of the other powers of the Entente undoubtedly have well prepared plans, for the sake of which you are shedding the blood of your soldiers. We expect that you will state your demands very clearly and definitely. Should we, however, be disappointed, should you fail to reply to our quite definite and precise questions, we will draw the only possible conclusion—that we are justified in the assumption that your Government and the Governments of your Allies desire to get from the Russian people a tribute both in money and in natural resources of Russia, and territorial concessions as well. We will tell this to the Russian people as well as to the toiling masses of other countries, and the absence of a reply from you will serve for us as a silent reply. The Russian people will then understand that the demands of your Government and of the Governments of your Allies are so severe and vast that you do not even want to communicate them to the Russian Government.

(signed) TCHICHERIN,
People's Commissary of Foreign Affairs,

[121.]

Statement by Tchicherin to Provisional Czechoslovak Government, November 1, 1918.

(The New York *Nation*, November 30, 1918.)

The Russian Workmen's and Peasants' Councils' Government, which represents large masses of the working population of Russia, and which in all its actions has always expressed its will to defend the interests of the laboring classes, this Russian Government declares solemnly to the Provisional Government of the Czechoslovaks that never has it even entered into their minds to deliver the Czechoslovaks, who have found a refuge in Russia, over to Austro-Hungarians. This is a baseless affirmation on the part of the counter-revolutionary calumniators. At the beginning of this year the Councils' Government agreed with the French and English Governments as to permission for the Czechoslovaks in Russia to go to France; but months and months passed, and France, in spite of her promise, did not furnish the ships for transporting these Czechoslovaks. In the meantime, agents of the French and English capitalistic Governments led the Czechoslovaks into error, and subjected them to counter-revolutionary influences. They put at their head Russian reactionaries, agents of the infamous old Tsarist régime. All measures which the Councils' Government was forced to take against the Czechoslovaks were merely measures of legitimate defense against the counter-revolutionary movement, which aimed at the deposition of the people's authority in Russia. The many victories won by the Red Army of revolutionary workmen and peasants of Russia over the Czechoslovak detachments of White Guards prove that the Czechoslovak detachments are powerless to depose the revolutionary Government of Russian workmen and peasants. The Councils' Government, in spite of the success of its forces, has no other wish than to terminate this useless shedding of blood, and declares to the Provisional Government of the Czechoslovaks that it is ready to allow the Czechoslovaks to cross Russia as soon as they have laid down their arms, and to give them a complete guarantee as regards security for their return home. The Councils' Government wishes to enter into direct negotiation with the Provisional Government of the Czechoslovaks, with a view to elaborating the conditions for the return home of those Czechoslovaks who are willing to go back to the territories which are now under the authority of the Czechoslovak Provisional Government of Prague. The Councils' Government will thank the Czechoslovak Government for a reply.

(signed) TCHICHERIN,
People's Commissary for Foreign Affairs.

[122.]

Protest by Tchicherin against intervention, sent out by Wireless, December 2, 1918.

(*Soviet Russia*,[1] December 13, 1919.)

To the Governments of Great Britain, France, Italy, and the United States of America:

The Government of the Russian Socialist Soviet Republic through which the great laboring masses themselves, the workers and the peasants are ruling, and which embodies their aspiration for the peaceful self-government of the toiling and producing people, who have no quarrel with the toilers of any other country, has learned that a British fleet is moving in the Baltic Sea towards Russian shores, that the ships of the Entente countries have been directed from Constantinople to the harbors of Crimea and the Southern Ukraine, and that the troops of those same countries have already crossed the borders of Bessarabia. The Russian Socialist Soviet Republic has never menaced or tried to invade the Entente countries; it only demanded to be left in peace, to develop itself on the lines which its people have chosen for themselves, contenting itself with influencing, by word and by example, their toiling brothers of other countries, and not to be interfered with by the great military powers which were carrying on the world war. Without any provocation from the Russian side, without any reason and without any shade of justification for their action, the armies of the Entente countries last summer invaded the borders of the Russian Socialist Soviet Republic, occupying its towns, seizing its villages and hamlets, ransacking the country and shooting down its best sons, and trying to advance into the heart of Russia, to crush its independence, and to drown the emancipa-

[1] Official Organ of the Russian Soviet Government Bureau in New York.

tion of its laboring masses in the blood of its defenders. The Entente troops were moved through the Far East for the support of the Czechoslovak and White Guards' counter-revolutionary mutinies, participating together with them in the mass massacres of workers, of peasants, of fighters for freedom, which were their constant deeds. British and French officers took a leading part in all the movements against freedom in whatever part of Russia they were devised; they were the principal authors and instigators of the dark subterranean conspiracies which aimed at taking by surprise the Soviet Government through base treachery and briberies and overthrowing it through its nearest servants, which nevertheless proved themselves to be incorruptible and faithful and turned to the discomfiture of the unmasked Entente plotters their treacherous attempts. After all these blows aimed at the liberty, at the life of the Russian laboring masses and of their popular Socialist Republic, the governments of the same Entente countries are now tightening their net against the ever-peaceful Russian Socialist Republic, which, far remote from any aggression against others, thinks only of defending itself against the aggressors. The plans of the Entente Governments are hidden in the dark. They have declared that their armed forces will protect in those regions which had been occupied by the German armies, the same social order which these German armies had protected. The armed forces of the Entente countries are coming to these regions as the enemies of the great popular masses in order to give support to their exploiters and to keep upright the old social régime which these popular masses wish to overthrow. Numerous utterances of responsible statesmen of the Entente countries prove that the governments of these countries have further reaching views and directly aggressive intentions against the independence, the freedom and the popular government of the Socialist Republic of the Russian laboring masses. The Soviets of the Russian workers and peasants have called out the youth of the people to rally around the banners of the Socialist Republic and to defend it to the last drop of their blood. At the moment when the Entente armies are crossing the borders and the Entente fleets nearing the shores of what was previously the Russian Empire, the Government of the Soviet Republic protests once more solemnly before the great popular masses of the Entente countries, before the deluded soldiers and sailors of their fleets, before their toiling brothers all over the world, against this wanton aggression, against this act of sheer violence and brutal force, against this attempt to crush the liberty, the political and social life of the people of another country. The Russian Republic has offered peace to the Entente countries, but the governments of the latter have left this offer unanswered, their answer is the present new aggression. The Socialist Soviet Republic is always ready, as before, to make peace; against attacks from without it relies upon its faithful and valiant Red Army; it makes responsible for the new bloodshed those who are coming to attack its borders and to continue their oppression in the occupied regions, and, with clear conscience, and pure intention, it answers the new menace of the governments of Great Britain, France, Italy, and the United States of America with this solemn protest.

(signed) TCHICHERIN,
The People's Commissary for Foreign Affairs.
December 2, 1918.

[123.]

Appeal by Litvinov to President Wilson, December 24, 1918.

(*Labor Leader.*)[1]

Mr. President:

In addition to the general peace offer recently addressed by the Soviet Government to the Allies, I formally informed to-day the Stockholm Ministers of the United States and of the Allied countries that I am authorized to enter into negotiations for a peaceful settlement of all questions making for hostilities against Russia. The principles proclaimed by you as a possible basis for settling European questions, your avowed efforts and intentions of making the settlement conform to the demands of justice and humanity, induce and justify me to send you this statement, inasmuch as most points of your peace program are included in the more extensive aspirations of the Russian workers and peasants, now rulers of their country.

It was they who first proclaimed and actually granted to nations the right of self-determination, who suffered most sacrifices in fighting Imperialism and militarism both at home and abroad, who dealt the severest blow to secret diplomacy. And it is partly for these innovations in politics that they have been,

[1] See also New York *Nation*, January 17, 1920.

fiercely attacked by the former ruling classes of Russia and their counterparts in other countries. To justify this attack a network of lies and calumnies has been woven round the activities of the Soviets and forged documents put into circulation.

Unfortunately, Allied statesmen accept all the monstrous accusations against the Soviets at their face value, without taking the trouble to check them. Whilst agents of anti-Soviet parties are allowed and encouraged to move freely in Allied countries and disseminate untruth, representatives of the accused side have never been allowed to put fully their case and to answer the charges made against them.

In fact, the chief aim of the Soviets is to secure for the toiling majority of the Russian people economic liberty, without which political liberty is of no avail to them. For eight months the Soviets endeavored to realize their aims by peaceful methods without resorting to violence, adhering to the abolition of capital punishment, which abolition had been part of their program. It was only when their adversaries, the minority of the Russian people, took to terroristic acts against popular members of the Government and invoked the help of foreign troops that the laboring masses were driven to acts of exasperation and gave vent to their wrath and bitter feelings against their former oppressors.

For the Allied invasion of Russian territory not only compelled the Soviets against their own will to militarize the country anew and to divert their energies and resources—so necessary to the economic reconstruction of Russia, exhausted by four years of war in the defense of the country—but also cut off the vital sources of foodstuffs and raw materials, exposing the population to most terrible privations, bordering on starvation. I wish to emphasize that the so-called "Red Terror"—which is grossly exaggerated and misrepresented abroad—was not the cause but the direct result and outcome of Allied intervention.

The Russian workers and peasants fail to understand how foreign countries, which never dreamed of interfering with Russian affairs when Tsarist barbarism and militarism ruled supreme, and even supported that régime, can feel justified in interfering in Russia now, when the working people themselves, after decades of strenuous struggling and countless sacrifices, succeeded in taking power and the destiny of their country into their own hands, aiming at nothing but their own happiness and international brotherhood, constituting no menace to other nations.

The Russian workers and peasants are determined to defend their dearly won power and liberties against invaders with all the means their vast country puts at their disposal, but mindful of the inevitable wanton loss of life and treasure on both sides, and wishing to avert the further ruining of Russia—which must result from the continuation of internal and external fighting —they are prepared to go to any length of concessions, as far as the real interests of their country are concerned, if they can secure thereby conditions enabling them to work out peacefully their social schemes.

I understand that the question of relations with Russia is now engaging the attention of Allied statesmen. I venture, then, to submit to you, Mr. President, that there are now only two courses open to them.

One is continued open or disguised intervention on the present or on a still larger scale, which means prolongation of war, further embitterment of the Russian masses, intensification of internal strife, unexampled bloodshed, and perhaps total extermination of the Russian bourgeoisie by the exasperated masses, final devastation of the country, and, in case of the interventionists after a long struggle obtaining their end, a White Terror eclipsing the atrocities of the Finnish White Guardists, the inevitable introduction of a military dictatorship, and the restoration of the monarchy, leading to interminable revolutions and upheavals, and paralyzing the economic development of the country for long decades.

The other alternative, which I trust may commend itself to you, is impartially to weigh and investigate the one-sided accusations against Soviet Russia, to come to an understanding with the Soviet Government, to withdraw the foreign troops from Russian territory, and to raise the economic blockade—soothing thereby the excited passions of the masses—to help Russia to regain her own sources of supply, and to give her technical advice how to exploit her natural richness in the most effective way, for the benefit of all countries badly in need of foodstuffs and raw materials.

The dictatorship of toilers and producers is not an aim in itself, but the means of building up a new social system under which useful work and equal rights would be provided for all citizens, irrespective of the class to which they had formerly belonged. One may believe in this ideal or not, but it surely gives no justification for sending foreign troops to fight against it, or for arming and supporting classes interested in the restoration of the old system of exploitation of man by man.

I venture to appeal to your sense of justice and impartiality.

I hope and trust, above all, that before deciding on any course of action you will give justice to the demand of *audiatur et altera pars.*

MAXIM LITVINOV,
Late Representative for Great Britain
of the Russian Federative Republic.
Stockholm, December 24, 1918.

[124.]

Statement by M. Pichon, French Minister of Foreign Affairs, in the Chamber of Deputies, December 29, 1918.

"The inter-allied plan of action," said M. Clemenceau in a telegram of December 13, "is not of an offensive character, but it simply interdicts to the Bolsheviks access to the Ukraine regions, the Caucasus, and Western Siberia, which are economically necessary to them for their endurance, and where the elements of Russian order are being organized.

"It is then a question at first of constituting and maintaining a defensive front before these regions, and especially in Eastern Russia. If an offensive effort is necessary to reduce Bolshevism, it should be executed later by Russian forces. It is important that you succeed in making the Russians realize this necessity, and that our momentary protection has for its only aim to permit them to organize themselves and acquire a material superiority over their adversaries.

"Your military action should, then, be based on a defensive plan and on the employment of economic forces, with shortening of the front, until the Siberian army is organized and instructed."

And in a subsequent telegram, dated December 21, M. Clemenceau confirmed these instructions, saying: "The plan of action of the Allies is to realize simultaneously the economic encirclement[1] of the Bolsheviks and the organization of order by the Russian elements."

[1] The French "cordon sanitaire."

The execution of this plan can be but slow and progressive, on account of reasons of effectives and the difficulties of transport.

[125.]

Letter from Litvinov and Vorovsky to Dr. Ludwig Meyer of Christiania: Semi-Official Statement with regard to Peace, January 10, 1919.

(London *Herald*, February 22, 1919.)

Stockholm, January 10, 1919.

Dear Comrade:

Referring to your letter of December 30, we very much regret to be unable to share your opinion as to the desirability and expediency at the present moment of a declaration by the Soviet Government containing the terms on which it would be prepared to conclude peace with the Allies. We feel sure that if the Allies, as the attacking party, formulate their demands, the Soviet Government will not fail to state clearly and in unmistakable terms to what extent these demands could be satisfied. So far the peace objects of the Allies, as regards Russia, have never been made known to the Soviet Government, either directly or indirectly. Moreover, no reply whatever has been given to the many peace overtures made both by the Central Soviet Government and by their representatives abroad, although in the statement to President Wilson of December 24, the possible changes in the external and internal policy of the Soviets were clearly outlined. The Soviet Government and ourselves are therefore of the opinion that as long as the Allies continue to show no sign of their willingness to enter into some kind of formal or informal negotiations no useful purpose would be served by any further peace proposals or declarations on the part of Russia. However, we shall gladly recapitulate in this letter our views on the possible peace terms as we expressed them during our conversation of December 25.

Lord Milner has recently declared one of the reasons of Allied intervention in Russia to be the protection of the so-called "Russian friends of the Allies," who may be exposed to reprisals in case the Soviet régime re-establishes itself in parts of Russia now occupied by the Allies. This apprehension should certainly not be in the way of an understanding with the Soviets, since the latter would be willing to give the Allies' friends the necessary guarantees for their safety and an amnesty for their past offenses. Irrespective of their line of policy in the past and of the social classes to which they previously belonged they would be given a fair chance of finding work within the Soviet System, according to their ability, education, and knowledge. It is our firm conviction that the discontinuance of foreign intervention would mean the cessation of civil war in Russia in its present form, and that there would be no necessity for any Press restrictions. We believe that when Russia is allowed to work under more normal conditions and the whole population has adapted itself to the new social system, an insignificantly small and ever diminishing part of the population will find itself excluded from active citizenship. But until this can take place the Soviet Republic must be allowed time and a fair chance to put into practice its principles and show what it can do for the Russian people.

With regard to Poland, Ukraine, and similar parts of the former Russian Empire it is and will be the policy of the Soviet Republic to abstain from any violation of the rights of these provinces to self-determination. The Soviet Republic must, however, at the same time insist on the non-interference with party or class strife in these provinces on the part of any other foreign powers. Pending a final settlement of the relations of these provinces with the Russian Republic, some arrangement should be secured regarding free railway, postal and telegraphic communication, exchange of goods, transit traffic, free use of ports, etc.

Russia needs for her economic reconstruction and development all the technical skill, experience, and material support which can be obtained from other countries. For that purpose, should an understanding with the Allies be arrived at, the Soviet Government would be willing to reconsider some of its decrees affecting the financial obligations of Russia towards other countries without infringing, however, the cardinal principles of its economic and financial policy. Special regard would be paid to the interests of small creditors abroad.

The Russian Government, as such, while anxious to continue to proclaim to the whole world its general principles and to combat the widely spread campaign of lies and calumnies directed against Soviets and their work, would certainly desist from carrying on any propaganda in the Allied countries, which could be construed as interference with their internal affairs. In connection with this, we must emphasize that no such propaganda has ever been carried on by the Soviets in any foreign country, except, perhaps, Germany.

The only demand the Soviet Republic has to put to the Allies is that they should discontinue all direct or indirect military operations against Soviet Russia, all direct or indirect material assistance to Russian or other forces operating against the Soviet Government, and also every kind of economic warfare and boycott.

These, as far as we remember, are the chief points touched upon during our conversation. We believe these views to reflect those of our Government.

You are entitled to make of this letter any use you may find expedient in the interest of peace between the countries concerned.

Yours truly,
MAXIM LITVINOV,
Formerly Russian Representative in London.
V. VOROVSKY,
Russian Representative in Stockholm.
To Ludvig Meyer, Esq.,
Advokat at the Supreme Court of Norway,
Christiania.

[126.]

Documents referring to the plan for Allied Supervision of the Chinese Eastern and Trans-Siberian Railways.

(*State Department Russian Series, No. 4*, pp. 3, 4.)

1.

THE JAPANESE AMBASSADOR AT WASHINGTON TO THE ACTING SECRETARY OF STATE, JANUARY 15, 1919.

(NOTE.)

Sir:

I have the honor to present to you, under instructions, a plan for the supervision of the Chinese Eastern and the Trans-Siberian Railways in the zone in which the allied forces are now operating and to request that you will be good enough to let me know whether it is acceptable to the Government of the United States.

Accept, sir, the renewed assurances of my high consideration.

K. ISHII.

(ENCLOSURE.)

PLAN FOR THE SUPERVISION OF THE CHINESE EASTERN AND THE TRANS-SIBERIAN RAILWAYS IN THE ZONE IN WHICH THE ALLIED MILITARY FORCES ARE NOW OPERATING.

(1) The general supervision of the railways in the zone in which the Allied forces are now operating shall be exercised in a special inter-allied committee which shall consist of representatives from each allied power having military forces in Siberia including Russia and the chairman of which shall be a Russian.

The following boards shall be created to be placed under the control of the inter-allied committee:

(a) A technical board consisting of railway experts of the nations having military forces in Siberia for the purpose of administering the technical and economic management of all railways in the said zone.

(b) An allied military transportation board for the purpose of co-ordinating military transportation under instructions of the proper military authorities.

(2) The protection of the railways shall be placed under the allied military forces. At the head of each railway shall remain a Russian manager or director with the powers conferred by the existing Russian law.

(3) The technical board shall elect a president, to whom shall be entrusted the technical operation of railways. In matters of such technical operation the president may issue instructions to the Russian officials mentioned in the preceding clause. He may appoint assistants and inspectors in the service of the board chosen from among the nationals of powers having military forces in Siberia to be attached to the central office of the board and define their duties. He may assign, if necessary, corps of railways experts to more important stations. In his assigning railway experts to any of the stations, interests of respective allied powers in charge of such stations shall be taken into due consideration. He shall distribute work among the clerical staff of the board, whom he may appoint at his discretion.

(4) The clerical staff of the inter-allied committee shall be appointed by the chairman of the committee, who shall have the right of distributing work among such employees as well as of dismissing them.

(5) The present arrangement shall cease to be operative upon the withdrawal of foreign military forces from Siberia, and all the foreign railway experts appointed under this arrangement shall then be recalled forthwith.

2.

MEMORANDUM AGREED UPON BETWEEN THE AMERICAN AMBASSADOR AT TOKIO AND THE JAPANESE MINISTER OF FOREIGN AFFAIRS, JANUARY 9, 1919.

First. That Viscount Uchida will forward the amended plan to Viscount Ishii with instructions to present it to the Department of State, and to explain that it is submitted with the understanding that Mr. Stevens be named as president (of the technical board).

Second. That the inter-allied committee shall be composed of one representative of each of the following Governments: China, France, Great Britain, Italy, Japan, Russia, and the United States, leaving question of Czecho-Slavs to be discussed.

Third. That each of the above-named Governments shall select one technical railway expert for membership on the technical board.

Fourth. That Mr. Stevens' selection as president shall not prevent his selection as a member of the technical board.

Fifth. That the Governments of Japan and the United States shall at once advise the above-named associated Governments of agreed plan, including the understanding in reference to the selection of Mr. Stevens, and request their adherence and cordial co-operation.

Sixth. That this plan shall be interpreted as a sincere effort to join the Chinese Eastern and Trans-Siberian Railways in the interest of the Russian people with a view to their ultimate return to those in interest without the impairing of any existing rights.

Seventh. That in trusting to Mr. Stevens as president the technical operation of these railways it is understood the Government of Japan and the Government of the United States are both prepared to give him the authority and support which will be necessary to make his efforts effective.

3.

ACTING SECRETARY OF STATE TO JAPANESE AMBASSADOR AT WASHINGTON, FEBRUARY 10, 1919.

(NOTE.)

Excellency:

I have the honor to acknowledge the receipt of your note of January 15, 1919, with which you presented to me January 16, 1919, under instruction from your Government, the plan of supervision of railways in the zone in which the allied forces are now operating in Siberia. I beg also to inform you that the memorandum handed by the American Ambassador at Tokio to Viscount Uchida, covering seven separate questions relating to the plan upon which the Ambassador and Viscount Uchida have reached a thorough understanding, as you mentioned to me, confirms the understanding which the department had already received from Ambassador Morris.

In notifying you of the acceptance by this Government of the general plan which you have presented, with due reservation as to any financial responsibility which may be involved and which, it is suggested, shall be the subject of further discussion, I wish to express my gratification that our two Governments have reached a cordial and clear understanding upon a matter which so much concerns the welfare of Russia. I wish also to inform you that this Government approves the memorandum agreed to by your Government with the American Ambassador at Tokio.

At the same time allow me to point out the clear understanding which this Government has as to the interpretation to be placed upon the word "interests" in the next to the last sentence of section 3 of the plan for the supervision of the railways. The United States understands that the word "interests" in this case is used as referring to the convenience of the respective allied powers and the United States, and not as implying any political or territorial rights or spheres of influence. As is so clearly stated in the memorandum to which I have referred above, the plan is to be interpreted as a sincere effort to operate the Siberian railway system in the interest of the Russian people, and I am already aware of the sincere and friendly purpose which your Government has in furthering this intention.

I may add that the American diplomatic representatives at London, Rome, Paris, and Peking are being instructed to-day to communicate formally to the Governments to which they are accredited our approval of the plan for the supervision of the railways and of the memorandum relating to the plan which have resulted from the negotiations between Viscount Uchida and the American ambassador at Tokio and to secure the approval and support of the respective Governments concerned. They have also been instructed to communicate their action to their Japanese colleagues.

Accept, Excellency, the renewed assurances of my highest consideration.

FRANK L. POLK.

[127.]

Reply by French Foreign Minister to the British Government's Suggestion with regard to Russia, January 5, 1919.

(*L'Humanité*, January 11, 1919.)

On January 5, 1919, the British Embassy sent me a British proposition, which also was sent to Rome, Washington, and Tokio, suggesting the sending of a message to the Government of the Soviets at Moscow, to the Governments of Admiral Kolchak at Omsk, General Denikin at Ekaterinodar, and Nicholas Tschaikovsky at Archangel, and also to all the other Governments constituted by the different Russian nationalities.

This message would invite all these Governments and all Russian parties completely to cease hostilities, violence, and reprisals and establish peace both among each other and with the neighboring States. This truce would be requested for the duration of the Peace Conference, one of the ends of which is to re-establish peace in Russia and the neighboring countries and bring the desired succor to the suffering populations.

In case the various Russian Governments, including that of the Soviets, should comply with this invitation, they would be permitted to send delegates to the Peace Conference.

While rendering full homage to the generous spirit of universal reconciliation with which the British Government was inspired in making this proposition, the French Government is unable to give its approval to such a suggestion, which fails to take into account the principles which have not failed to dominate its policy and that of the Powers in Russia.

The criminal régime of the Bolsheviks which does not represent in any degree that of a democratic Government, or furnish any possibility whatever of developing into a Government, since it is supported solely by the lowest passions of anarchial oppression, in negation of all the principles of public and private right, cannot claim to be recognized as a regular Government.

If the Allies were weak or imprudent enough to act thus, they would give the lie, in the first place, to the principles of justice and right which constitute their force and honor, and would give to the Bolshevik propaganda in the outside world a power and extension to which they would run the risk of being the first victims. The French Government, so far as it is concerned, will make no contract with crime.

By agreeing to recognize the Bolshevik Government we should give the lie to the policy—which the Allies have not ceased to sustain in agreement—of furnishing at all accessible points of Russia all the aid and succor which it is possible to give to the healthy, faithful, honest elements of Russia, in order to help them escape from the bloody and disorderly tyranny of the Bolsheviks and to reconstitute a regular Government by themselves.

It may be added that, aside from the Bolsheviks, the Allies can perfectly well admit the different Russian nationalities to present their claims. As regards the dangers which the menace of the Red armies threaten them, we should not cease to supply arms and money and even military support compatible with our aims.

Method and patience combined, together with the impossibility that any régime can last without a regular organization for maintaining provisioning, transport, order, credit, etc., will in the end overcome Russian internal anarchy. It may be prolonged for a certain time, but it can in no case possibly triumph definitely, and we shall continue resolutely to refuse it any recognition and to treat it as an enemy.

S. Pichon.

[128.]

Note from Tchicherin to the American State Department, January 12, 1919.

(New York *Nation*, January 17, 1920.)

On behalf of M. Chicherin, People's Commissar for Foreign Affairs, I am sending you the following statement:

A radio telegram from Washington, received via Lyons on the 12th of January, relates that a statement has been made by Senator Hitchcock, the Chairman of the Foreign Relations Committee, about the causes for the sending of American troops to Russia. The principal cause is said to have been a desire to prevent the establishment of a German submarine base in Archangel. Whether there ever has been such a cause or not, it does not exist any more.

In respect to the second alleged cause for the invasion, namely, that the intention was to safeguard Allied supplies in Archangel, I beg to remind you that even last year we had started negotiations for this purpose, and we are now still willing to enter into a satisfactory solution of this question. There can no longer be any danger of the supplies falling into German hands.

The third reason for the invasion was stated to be a desire to maintain an open way for diplomatic representatives traveling from and to Russia. I beg to call your attention to the fact that the best method to attain this aim would be to have an understanding with my Government. Mr. Francis, the American Ambassador, was quite free to return to his home and unhindered at the time he left Russia. Our only cause in asking him not to remain in Vologda was the great danger threatening his personal security, and we offered him particularly inviting quarters in or around Moscow.

The fourth alleged ground for invasion is the protection of the Czecho-Slovaks. Yet there has never been any obstacle to reaching an understanding about this issue with my Government. We have officially offered the Czecho-Slovaks free passage to their homeland through Russia on the condition that we should protect their safety. We have now reached a full understanding on this matter with Professor Max, the President of the Czecho-Slovak National Council in Russia. He has returned to Bohemia in order to communicate our proposition to the Bohemian Government.

Finally, Senator Hitchcock maintains that one reason for the invasion was to prevent the formation of any army composed of German and Austrian prisoners. The only now existing obstacle to the return of all war prisoners to their homelands is the presence of the Allied troops, or White Guards who are under the protection of the Allied troops. We therefore cannot understand why this should be a cause for a further maintenance of American troops in Russia.

Judging from statements contained in the above-mentioned radio telegram, some prominent members of the principal political party in the United States could not quite understand the reasons of Senator Hitchcock. They expressed their wish that American troops in Russia should be withdrawn as soon as possible. We share their wish to re-establish normal relations between the two countries, and we are ready to eliminate everything which may be an obstacle to such relations.

This is not the first time we are making an offer of this kind. In October we sent an offer of this character through the Norwegian Minister in Russia. A week later we made a similar offer through Mr. Christiansen, an attaché of the Norwegian Legation, at the time of his leaving Moscow. On the 3rd of November we invited the representatives of the neutral countries in Moscow and asked them to deliver a written proposition to the Allies, with the view to entering into negotiations which would put an end to the struggles against Russia. On the 26th of November the All-Russian Congress of Soviets declared to the Allies, and to the whole world, that Russia was willing to enter into peace negotiations. On the 23rd of December our representative, M. Litvinov, communicated once more with the Allied Ambassadors in Stockholm the desire of the Russian Government to reach a friendly settlement of all questions at issue. He also sent an appeal to President Wilson in London; thus the responsibility for the fact that no agreement has been thus far reached does not lie with us.

We have an opportunity to hear various American officers and soldiers express their astonishment at their being held in Russia, especially when we pointed out to such soldiers that the reason for their being in Russia seemed to be to put back on the shoulders of the Russian people the yoke which they have thrown off.

The results of these explanations of ours have not been unsatisfactory to our personal relations with these American citizens.

We hope that the desire for peace expressed by the above mentioned Senator is shared by the entire American Government and that the American Government will kindly name a place and a time for opening of peace negotiations with our representatives.

CHICHERIN,
People's Commissary for Foreign Affairs.
By MAXIM LITVINOV,
Representative of the Russian Government in Stockholm.

[129.]

Notes on Conversations held in the Office of M. Pichon at the Quai d'Orsay, on January 16, 1919: preliminary discussion regarding the Situation in Russia.

(Hearings before the Committee on Foreign Relations, United States Senate, 1919, Senate Doc. 106, p. 1235.)

Mr. Lloyd George commenced his statement setting forth the information in the possession of the British Government regarding the Russian situation, by referring to the matter which had been exposed recently in *L'Humanité*. He stated that he wished to point out that there had been a serious misconception on the part of the French Government as to the character of the proposal of the British Government. The British proposal did not contemplate in any sense whatever, a recognition of the Bolshevik Government, nor a suggestion that Bolshevik delegates be invited to attend the Conference. The British proposal was to invite all of the different governments now at war within what used to be the Russian Empire, to a truce of God, to stop reprisals and outrages and to send men here to give, so to speak, an account of themselves. The Great Powers would then try to find a way to bring some order out of chaos. These men were not to be delegates to the Peace Conference, and he agreed with the French Government entirely that they should not be made members of the Conference.

Mr. Lloyd George then proceeded to set forth briefly the reasons which had led the British Government to make this proposal. They were as follows:

Firstly, the real facts are not known.

Secondly, it is impossible to get the facts, the only way is to adjudicate the question; and

Thirdly, conditions in Russia are very bad; there is general mis-government and starvation. It is not known who is obtaining the upper hand, but the hope that the Bolshevik Government would collapse had not been realized. In fact, there is one report that the Bolsheviks are stronger than ever, that their internal position is strong, and that their hold on the people is stronger. Take, for instance, the case of the Ukraine. Some adventurer raises a few men and overthrows the Government. The Government is incapable of overthrowing him. It is also reported that the peasants are becoming Bolsheviks. It is hardly the business of the Great Powers to intervene either in lending financial support to one side or the other, or in sending munitions to either side.

Mr. Lloyd George stated that there seemed to be three possible policies:

1. Military intervention. It is true that the Bolshevik movement is as dangerous to civilization as German militarism, but as to putting it down by the sword, is there any one who proposes it? It would mean holding a certain number of provinces in Russia. The Germans with one million men on their Eastern Front only held the fringe of this territory. If he now proposed to send a thousand British troops to Russia for that purpose, the armies would mutiny. The same applies to U. S. troops in Siberia; also to Canadians and French as well. The mere idea of crushing Bolshevism by a military force is pure madness. Even admitting that it is done, who is to occupy Russia? No one can conceive or understand to bring about order by force.

2. A cordon. The second suggestion is to besiege Bolshevik Russia. Mr. Lloyd George wondered if those present realized what this would mean. From the information furnished him Bolshevik Russia has no corn, but within this territory there are 150,000,000 men, women, and children. There is now starvation in Petrograd and Moscow. This is not an health cordon, it is a death cordon. Moreover, as a matter of fact, the people who would die are just the people that the Allies desire to protect. It would not result in the starvation of the Bolsheviks; it would simply mean the death of our friends. The cordon policy is a policy which, as humane people, those present could not consider.

Mr. Lloyd George asked who was there to overthrow the Bolsheviks? He had been told there were three men, Denikin, Kolchak, and Knox. In considering the chances of these people to overthrow the Bolsheviks, he pointed out that he had received information that the Czecho-Slovaks now refused to fight; that the Russian Army was not to be trusted, and that while it was true that a Bolshevik Army had recently gone over to Kolchak it was never certain that just the reverse of this would not take place. If the Allies counted on any of these men, he believed they were building on quick-sand. He had heard a lot of talk about Denikin, but when he looked on the map he found that Denikin was occupying a little backyard near the Black Sea. Then he had been told that Denikin had recognized Kolchak, but when he looked on the map there was a great solid block of territory between Denikin and Kolchak. Moreover, from information received it would appear that Kolchak had been collecting members of the old régime around him, and would seem to be at heart a monarchist. It appeared that the Czecho-Slovaks were finding this out. The sympathies of the Czecho-Slovaks are very democratic, and they are not at all prepared to fight for the restoration of the old conditions in Russia.

Mr. Lloyd George stated that he was informed that at the present time two-thirds of Bolshevik Russia was starving.

Institutions of Bolsheviks are institutions of old Czarist régimes. This is not what one would call creating a new world.

3. The third alternative was contained in the British proposal, which was to summon these people to Paris to appear before those present somewhat in the way that the Roman Empire summoned chiefs of outlying tributary states to render an account of their actions.

Mr. Lloyd George pointed out the fact that the argument might be used that there were already here certain representatives of these Governments; but take, for instance, the case of Sazonoff, who claims to represent the Government of Omsk. As a matter of fact, Sazonoff cannot speak from personal observation. He is nothing but a partisan, like all the rest. He has never been in contact, and is not now in direct contact with the Government at Omsk.

It would be manifestly absurd for those who are responsible for bringing about the Peace Conference, to come to any agreement and leave Paris when one-half of Europe and one-half of

Asia is still in flames. Those present must settle this question or make fools of themselves.

Mr. Lloyd George referred to the objection that had been raised to permitting Bolshevik delegates to come to Paris. It had been claimed that they would convert France and England to Bolshevism. If England becomes Bolshevist, it will not be because a single Bolshevist representative is permitted to enter England. On the other hand, if a military enterprise were started against the Bolsheviks, that would make England Bolshevist, and there would be a Soviet in London. For his part, Mr. Lloyd George was not afraid of Bolshevism if the facts are known in England and the United States. The same applied to Germany. He was convinced that an educated democracy can be always trusted to turn down Bolshevism.

Under all circumstances, Mr. Lloyd George saw no better way out than to follow the third alternative. Let the Great Powers impose their conditions and summon these people to Paris to give an account of themselves to the Great Powers, not to the Peace Conference.

M. Pichon suggested that it might be well to ask M. Noulens, the French Ambassador to Russia, who had just returned to France, to appear before the meeting to-morrow morning, and give those present his views on the Russian situation.

President Wilson stated that he did not see how it was possible to controvert the statement of Mr. Lloyd George. He thought that there was a force behind this discussion which was no doubt in his mind, but which it might be desirable to bring out a little more definitely. He did not believe that there would be sympathy anywhere with the brutal aspect of Bolshevism, if it were not for the fact of the domination of large vested interests in the political and economic world. While it might be true that this evil was in process of discussion and slow reform, it must be admitted, that the general body of men have grown impatient at the failure to bring about the necessary reform. He stated that there were many men who represented large vested interests in the United States, who saw the necessity for these reforms and desired something which should be worked out at the Peace Conference, namely, the establishment of some machinery to provide for the opportunity of the individuals greater than the world has ever known. Capital and Labor in the United States are not friends. Still they are not enemies in the sense that they are thinking and resorting to physical force to settle their differences. But they are distrustful, each of the other. Society cannot go on that plane. On the one hand, there is a minority possessing capital and brains; on the other, a majority consisting of the great bodies of workers who are essential to the minority, but do not trust the minority, and feel that the minority will never render them their rights. A way must be found to put trust and co-operation between these two.

President Wilson pointed out that the whole world was disturbed by this question before the Bolsheviks came into power. Seeds need soil, and the Bolshevik seeds found the soil already prepared for them.

President Wilson stated that he would not be surprised to find that the reason why British and United States troops would not be ready to enter Russia to fight the Bolsheviks was explained by the fact that the troops were not at all sure that if they put down Bolshevism they would not bring about a re-establishment of the ancient order. For example, in making a speech recently, to a well-dressed audience in New York City who were not to be expected to show such feeling, Mr. Wilson had referred casually to Russia, stating that the United States would do its utmost to aid her oppressed people. The audience exhibited the greatest enthusiasm, and this had remained in the President's mind as an index to where the sympathies of the New World are.

President Wilson believed that those present would be playing against the principle of the free spirit of the world if they did not give Russia a chance to find herself along the lines of utter freedom. He concurred with Mr. Lloyd George's view and supported his recommendations that the third line of procedure be adopted.

President Wilson stated that he had also, like Mr. Lloyd George, received a memorandum from his experts which agreed substantially with the information which Mr. Lloyd George had received. There was one point which he thought particularly worthy of notice, and that was the report that the strength of the Bolshevik leaders lay in the argument that if they were not supported by the people of Russia, there would be foreign intervention, and the Bolsheviks were the only thing that stood between the Russians and foreign military control. It might well be that if the Bolsheviks were assured that they were safe from foreign aggression, they might lose support of their own movement.

President Wilson further stated that he understood that the danger of destruction of all hope in the Baltic provinces was immediate, and that it should be made very clear if the British proposal were adopted, that the Bolsheviks would have to withdraw entirely from Lithuania and Poland. If they would agree to this to refrain from reprisals and outrages, he, for his part, would be prepared to receive representatives from as many groups and centers of action, as chose to come, and endeavor to assist them to reach a solution of their problem.

He thought that the British proposal contained the only suggestions that lead anywhere. It might lead nowhere. But this could at least be found out.

M. Pichon referred again to the suggestion that Ambassador Noulens be called before the meeting.

Mr. Balfour suggested that it might be well to call the Dutch Consul, lately in Petrograd, if it was the desire of those present to hear the anti-Bolshevik side.

Baron Sonnino suggested that M. Scavenius, Minister of Denmark, would be able to give interesting data on the Russian situation.

Those present seemed to think that it might be desirable to hear what these gentlemen might have to say.

[130.]

Secretaries' Notes of a Conversation held in M. Pichon's Room at the Quai d'Orsay on Tuesday, January 21, 1919, regarding Situation in Russia.

(Hearings before the Committee on Foreign Relations, United States Senate, 1919, Senate Doc. 106, p. 1240.)

PRESENT

United States of America: President Wilson, Mr. R. Lansing, Mr. A. H. Frazier, Col. U. S. Grant, Mr. L. Harrison.

British Empire: The Right Hon. D. Lloyd George, the Right Hon. A. J. Balfour, Lieut. Col. Sir M. P. A. Hankey, K.C.B., Maj. A. M. Caccia, M.V.O., Mr. E. Phipps.

France: M. Clemenceau, M. Pichon, M. Dutasta, M. Berthelot, Capt. A. Potier.

Italy: Signor Orlando, H. E. Baron Sonnino, Count Aldrovandi, Maj. A. Jones.

Japan: Baron Makino, H. E. M. Matsui, M. Saburi.
Interpreter, Prof. P. J. Mantoux.

M. Clemenceau said they had met together to decide what could be done in Russia under present circumstances.

President Wilson said that in order to have something definite to discuss, he wished to take advantage of a suggestion made by Mr. Lloyd George and to propose a modification of the British proposal. He wished to suggest that the various organized groups in Russia should be asked to send representatives, not to Paris, but to some other place, such as Salonika, convenient of approach, there to meet such representatives as might be appointed by the Allies, in order to see if they could draw up a program upon which agreement could be reached.

Mr. Lloyd George pointed out that the advantage of this would be that they could be brought straight there from Russia through the Black Sea without passing through other countries.

M. Sonnino said that some of the representatives of the various Governments were already here in Paris, for example, M. Sazonoff. Why should these not be heard?

President Wilson expressed the view that the various parties should not be heard separately. It would be very desirable to get all these representatives in one place, and still better, all in one room, in order to obtain a close comparison of views.

Mr. Balfour said that a further objection to Mr. Sonnino's plan was that if M. Sazonoff was heard in Paris, it would be difficult to refuse to hear the others in Paris also, and M. Clemenceau objected strongly to having some of these representatives in Paris.

M. Sonnino explained that all the Russian parties had some representatives here, except the Soviets, whom they did not wish to hear.

Mr. Lloyd George remarked that the Bolshevists were the very people some of them wished to hear.

M. Sonnino continuing said that they had heard M. Litvinov's statements that morning. (That was the statement that Litvinov had made to Buckler[1] which the President had read to the council of ten that morning.)

The Allies were now fighting against the Bolshevists who

[1] Mr. Buckler had been sent to Stockholm and had secured from Litvinov a statement of the position of the Soviet Government.

were their enemies, and therefore they were not obliged to hear them with the others.

Mr. Balfour remarked that the essence of President Wilson's proposal was that the parties must all be heard at one and the same time.

Mr. Lloyd George expressed the view that the acceptance of M. Sonnino's proposals would amount to their hearing a string of people, all of whom held the same opinion, and all of whom would strike the same note. But they would not hear the people who at the present moment were actually controlling European Russia. In deference to M. Clemenceau's views, they had put forward this new proposal. He thought it would be quite safe to bring the Bolshevist representatives to Salonika, or perhaps to Lemnos. It was absolutely necessary to endeavor to make peace. The report read by President Wilson that morning went to show that the Bolshevists were not convinced of the error of their ways, but they apparently realized the folly of their present methods. Therefore they were endeavoring to come to terms.

President Wilson asked to be permitted to urge one aspect of the case. As M. Sonnino had implied, they were all repelled by Bolshevism, and for that reason they had placed armed men in opposition to them. One of the things that was clear in the Russian situation was that by opposing Bolshevism with arms, they were in reality serving the cause of Bolshevism. The Allies were making it possible for the Bolsheviks to argue that Imperialistic and Capitalistic Governments were endeavoring to exploit the country and to give the land back to the landlords, and so bring about a reaction. If it could be shown that this was not true, and that the Allies were prepared to deal with the rulers of Russia, much of the moral force of this argument would disappear. The allegation that the Allies were against the people and wanted to control their affairs provided the argument which enabled them to raise armies. If, on the other hand, the Allies could swallow their pride and the natural repulsion which they felt for the Bolshevists and see the representatives of all organized groups in one place, he thought it would bring about a marked reaction against Bolshevism.

M. Clemenceau said that, in principle, he did not favor conversation with the Bolshevists; not because they were criminals, but because we would be raising them to our level by saying that they were worthy of entering into conversation with us. The Bolshevist danger was very great at the present moment. Bolshevism was spreading. It had invaded the Baltic Provinces and Poland, and that very morning they received very bad news regarding its spread to Budapesth and Vienna. Italy, also, was in danger. The danger was probably greater there than in France. If Bolshevism, after spreading in Germany, were to traverse Austria and Hungary, and so reach Italy, Europe would be faced with a very great danger. Therefore, something must be done against Bolshevism. When listening to the document presented by President Wilson that morning, he had been struck by the cleverness with which the Bolshevists were attempting to lay a trap for the Allies. When the Bolshevists first came into power, a breach was made with the Capitalist Governments on questions of principle, but now they offered funds and concessions as a basis for treating with them. He need not say how valueless their promises were, but if they were listened to, the Bolshevists would go back to their people and say: "We offered them great principles of justice and the Allies would have nothing to do with us. Now we offer money, and they are ready to make peace."

He admitted his remarks did not offer a solution. The great misfortune was that the Allies were in need of a speedy solution. After four years of war and the losses and sufferings they had incurred, their populations could stand no more. Russia also was in need of immediate peace. But its necessary evolution must take time. The signing of the World Peace could not await Russia's final avatar. Had time been available, he would suggest waiting, for eventually sound men representing commonsense would come to the top. But when would that be? He could make no forecast. Therefore they must press for an early solution.

To sum up, had he been acting by himself, he would temporize and erect barriers to prevent Bolshevism from spreading. But he was not alone, and in the presence of his colleagues he felt compelled to make some concession, as it was essential that there should not be even the appearance of disagreement amongst them. The concession came easier after having heard President Wilson's suggestions. He thought that they should make a very clear and convincing appeal to all reasonable peoples, emphatically stating that they did not wish in any way to interfere in the internal affairs of Russia, and especially that they had no intention of restoring Czardom. The object of the Allies being to hasten the creation of a strong Government, they proposed to call together representatives of all parties to a Conference. He would beg President Wilson to draft a paper, fully explaining the position of the Allies to the whole world, including the Russians and the Germans.

Mr. Lloyd George agreed and gave notice that he wished to withdraw his own motion in favor of President Wilson's.

Mr. Balfour said that he understood that all these people were to be asked on an equality. On these terms he thought the Bolshevists would refuse, and by their refusal they would put themselves in a very bad position.

Mr. Sonnino said that he did not agree that the Bolshevists would not come. He thought they would be the first to come, because they would be eager to put themselves on an equality with the others. He would remind his colleagues that before the Peace of Brest-Litovsk was signed, the Bolshevists promised all sorts of things, such as to refrain from propaganda, but since that peace had been concluded they had broken all their promises, their one idea being to spread revolution in all other countries. His idea was to collect together all the anti-Bolshevik parties and help them to make a strong Government, provided they pledged themselves not to serve the forces of reaction and especially not to touch the land question, thereby depriving the Bolshevists of their strongest argument. Should they take these pledges, he would be prepared to help them.

Mr. Lloyd George inquired how this help would be given.

Mr. Sonnino replied that help would be given with soldiers to a reasonable degree or by supplying arms, food, and money. For instance, Poland asked for weapons and munitions; the Ukraine asked for weapons. All the Allies wanted was to establish a strong Government. The reason that no strong Government at present existed was that no party could risk taking the offensive against Bolshevism without the assistance of the Allies. He would inquire how the parties of order could possibly succeed without the help of the Allies. President Wilson had said that they should put aside all pride in the matter. He would point out that, for Italy and probably for France also, as M. Clemenceau had stated, it was in reality a question of self-defense. He thought that even a partial recognition of the Bolshevists would strengthen their position, and, speaking for himself, he thought that Bolshevism was already a serious danger in his country.

Mr. Lloyd George said he wished to put one or two practical questions to M. Sonnino. The British Empire now had some 15,000 to 20,000 men in Russia. M. de Scavenius had estimated that some 150,000 additional men would be required, in order to keep the anti-Bolshevist Governments from dissolution. And General Franchet d'Esperey also insisted on the necessity of Allied assistance. Now Canada had decided to withdraw her troops, because the Canadian soldiers would not agree to stay and fight against the Russians. Similar trouble had also occurred amongst the other Allied troops. And he felt certain that, if the British tried to send any more troops there, there would be mutiny.

M. Sonnino suggested that volunteers might be called for.

Mr. Lloyd George, continuing, said that it would be impossible to raise 150,000 men in that way. He asked, however, what contributions America, Italy, and France would make towards the raising of this Army.

President Wilson and M. Clemenceau each said none.

M. Orlando agreed that Italy could make no further contributions.

Mr. Lloyd George said that the Bolshevists had an army of 300,000 men who would, before long, be good soldiers, and to fight them at least 400,000 Russian soldiers would be required. Who would feed, equip, and pay them? Would Italy, or America, or France, do so? If they were unable to do that, what would be the good of fighting Bolshevism? It could not be crushed by speeches. He sincerely trusted that they would accept President Wilson's proposal as it now stood.

M. Orlando agreed that the question was a very difficult one for the reasons that had been fully given. He agreed that Bolshevism constituted a grave danger to all Europe. To prevent a contagious epidemic from spreading, the sanitarians set up a *cordon sanitaire*. If similar measures could be taken against Bolshevism, in order to prevent its spreading, it might be overcome, since to isolate it meant vanquishing it. Italy was now passing through a period of depression, due to war weariness. But Bolshevists could never triumph there, unless they found a favorable medium, such as might be produced by a profound patriotic disappointment in their expectations as to the rewards of the war, or by an economic crisis. Either might lead to revolution, which was equivalent to Bolshevism. Therefore, he would insist that all possible measures should be taken to set up this cordon. Next, he suggested the consideration of repressive measures. He thought two methods were possible; either the use of physical force or the use of moral force. He thought Mr. Lloyd George's objection to the use of physical force unanswerable. The occupation of Russia meant the employment of large numbers of troops for an indefinite period of time. This meant an apparent prolongation of the war. There remained the use of moral force. He agreed with M. Clemenceau that no country could continue in anarchy and that an end must eventually come; but they could not wait; they could not proceed to make peace and ignore Russia. Therefore, Mr. Lloyd George's proposal, with the modifications introduced after careful consideration by President Wilson and M. Clemenceau, gave a possible solution. It did not involve entering into negotiations with the Bolsheviks; the proposal was merely an attempt to bring together all the parties in Russia with a view to finding a way out of the present difficulty. He was prepared, therefore, to support it.

President Wilson asked for the views of his Japanese colleagues.

Baron Makino said that after carefully considering the various points of view put forward, he had no objections to make regarding the conclusion reached. He thought that was the best solution under the circumstances. He wished, however, to inquire what attitude would be taken by the Representatives of the Allied Powers if the Bolshevists accepted the invitation to the meeting and there insisted upon their principles. He thought they should under no circumstances countenance Bolshevist ideas. The conditions in Siberia east of the Baikal had greatly improved. The objects which had necessitated the despatch of troops to that region had been attained. Bolshevism was no longer aggressive, though it might still persist in a latent form. In conclusion, he wished to support the proposal before the meeting.

President Wilson expressed the view that the emissaries of the Allied Powers should not be authorized to adopt any definite attitude towards Bolshevism. They should merely report back to their Governments the conditions found.

Mr. Lloyd George asked that that question be further considered. He thought the emissaries of the Allied Powers should be able to establish an agreement if they were able to find a solution. For instance, if they succeeded in reaching an agreement on the subject of the organization of a Constituent Assembly, they should be authorized to accept such a compromise without the delay of a reference to the Governments.

President Wilson suggested that the emissaries might be furnished with a body of instructions.

Mr. Balfour expressed the view that abstention from hostile action against their neighbors should be made a condition of their sending representatives to this meeting.

President Wilson agreed.

M. Clemenceau suggested that the manifesto to the Russian parties should be based solely on humanitarian grounds. They should say to the Russians: "You are threatened by famine. We are prompted by humanitarian feelings; we are making peace; we do not want people to die. We are prepared to see what can be done to remove the menace of starvation." He thought the Russians would at once prick up their ears, and be prepared to hear what the Allies had to say. They would add that food cannot be sent unless peace, and order were reestablished. It should, in fact, be made quite clear that the representatives of all parties would merely be brought together for purely humane reasons.

Mr. Lloyd George said that in this connection he wished to invite attention to a doubt expressed by certain of the delegates of the British Dominions, namely, whether there would be food and credit enough to go round should an attempt be made to feed all Allied countries, and enemy countries, and Russia also. The export of so much food would inevitably have the effect of raising food prices in Allied countries and so create discontent and Bolshevism. As regards grain, Russia had always been an exporting country, and there was evidence to show that plenty of food at present existed in the Ukraine.

President Wilson said that his information was that enough food existed in Russia, but, either on account of its being hoarded or on account of difficulties of transportation, it could not be made available.

(It was agreed that President Wilson should draft a proclamation, for consideration at the next meeting, inviting all organized parties in Russia to attend a meeting to be held at some selected place such as Salonika or Lemnos, in order to discuss with the representatives of the Allied and Associated Great Powers the means of restoring order and peace in Russia. Participation in the meeting should be conditional on a cessation of hostilities.)

[131.]

President Wilson's Prinkipo Proposal at the Meeting of the Peace Conference, January 22, 1919.

The single object the representatives of the Associated Powers have had in mind in their discussions of the course they should pursue with regard to Russia has been to help the Russian people, not to hinder them, or to interfere in any manner with their right to settle their own affairs in their own way. They regard the Russian people as their friends, not their enemies, and are willing to help them in any way they are willing to be helped. It is clear to them that the troubles and distresses of the Russian people will steadily increase, hunger and privation of every kind become more and more acute, more and more widespread, and the more and more impossible to relieve, unless order is restored, and normal conditions of labor, trade, and transportation once more created, and they are seeking some way in which to assist the Russian people to establish order.

They recognize the absolute right of the Russian people to direct their own affairs without dictation or direction of any kind from outside. They do not wish to exploit, or make use of Russia in any way. They recognize the revolution without reservation, and will in no way and in no circumstances aid or give countenance to any attempt at a counter-revolution. It is not their wish or purpose to favor or assist any one of the organized groups now contending for the leadership and guidance of Russia as against the others. Their sole and sincere purpose is to do what they can to bring Russia peace and an opportunity to find her way out of her present troubles.

The Associated Powers are now engaged in the solemn and responsible work of establishing the peace of Europe, and of the world, and they are keenly alive to the fact that Europe and the world cannot be at peace if Russia is not. They recognize and accept it as their duty, therefore, to serve Russia in this great matter as generously, as unselfishly, as thoughtfully, and ungrudgingly as they would serve every other friend and ally. And they are ready to render this service in the way that is most acceptable to the Russian people.

In this spirit and with this purpose, they have taken the following action: They invite every organized group that is now exercising or attempting to exercise political authority or military control anywhere in Siberia, or within the boundaries of European Russia as they stood before the war just concluded (except in Finland) to send representatives, not exceeding three representatives for each group, to the Princes' Islands, Sea of Marmora, where they will be met by representatives of the Associated Powers, provided, in the meantime, there is a truce of arms amongst the parties invited, and that all armed forces anywhere sent or directed against any people or territory outside the boundaries of European Russia as they stood before the war, or against Finland, or against any people or territory whose autonomous action is in contemplation in the fourteen articles upon which the present negotiations are based, shall be meanwhile withdrawn, and aggressive military action cease. These representatives are invited to confer with the representatives of the Associated Powers in the freest and frankest way, with a view to ascertaining the wishes of all sections of the Russian people, and bringing about, if possible, some understanding and agreement by which Russia may work out her own purposes and happy co-operative relations be established between her people and the other peoples of the world.

A prompt reply to this invitation is requested. Every facility for the journey of the representatives, including transport across the Black Sea, will be given by the Allies, and all the parties concerned are expected to give the same facilities. The representatives will be expected at the place appointed by the fifteenth of February, 1919.

The proposal will be sent to-night by wireless to the interested parties.

[132.]

Note from the Soviet Government in reply to Prinkipo Invitation, February 4, 1919.

(New York *Nation*, January 17, 1920.)

To the Governments of Great Britain, France, Italy, Japan, and the United States of North America:

The Russian Soviet Government has learned, through a radiogram which contained a review of the press, of an invitation stated to have been addressed by the Entente Powers, to all de facto Governments of Russia, to send delegates to a conference on Princes' Islands.

As the Soviet Government of Russia has received no such invitation addressed to it, but has learned—and again through a radio review of the press—that the absence of an answer from the Soviet Government is interpreted as a refusal to reply to this invitation, the Russian Soviet Government desires to remove any false interpretation of its actions. On the other hand, in view of the fact that the foreign press systematically reports its actions in a false light, the Russian Soviet Government takes advantage of this opportunity to express its attitude with the utmost clearness and frankness.

In spite of the fact that both the military and internal conditions of Soviet Russia are constantly improving, the Soviet Government is so anxious to secure an agreement that would put an end to hostilities, that it is ready to enter at once into negotiations to this end, and, as it has more than once declared, is even willing in order to obtain such an agreement to make serious concessions, provided they will not menace the future development of Soviet Russia. In view of the fact that the power of resistance of the enemies which Soviet Russia has to fight depends exclusively on the aid which they receive from the Entente Powers, and that these are, therefore, its only real adversaries, the Russian Soviet Government addresses to these Powers a statement with regard to those questions on which it would consider such concessions possible in order to put an end to all conflicts with these Powers.

In view of the particular importance which is attached not only by the press, but also by the numerous declarations of the representatives of the Entente Governments to the question of Russian loans, the Soviet Government first of all declares its readiness to make concessions in this matter to the demands of the Entente Powers. It does not refuse to recognize its financial obligations to its creditors who are subjects of the Entente Powers, leaving the precise formulation of the manner in which this point is to be enforced to the special treaties the elaboration of which is to be one of the tasks of the proposed negotiations.

Secondly, in view of the difficult financial position of the Russian Soviet Republic and the unsatisfactory condition of its credit abroad, the Russian Soviet Government offers to guarantee the payment of interest on its loans by a certain amount of raw materials, which should be determined through a special agreement.

Thirdly, in view of the great interest which foreign capital has always evinced toward the question of the exploitation in its interests of the natural resources of Russia, the Soviet Government is willing to grant to subjects of the Entente Powers concessions in mines, forests, and other resources, which must be carefully formulated in such manner that the economic and social order of Soviet Russia shall be in no way violated by the internal regulations of these concessions.[1]

The fourth point which, in the opinion of the Russian Soviet Government, might be dealt with in the proposed negotiations is the question of territorial concessions, for the Soviet Government does not intend to insist on excluding from these negotiations the consideration of the question of annexation of Russian territories by the Entente Powers. The Soviet Government adds that the presence in the territory of the former Russian Empire, with the exception of Poland and Finland, of armed forces of the Entente or of forces which are maintained at the expense of the Governments of the Entente or receive financial, technical, military, or any other kind of support from them, should also be characterized as annexation.

As for points two and four, the scope of the concessions to which the Soviet Government will agree will depend on its military situation with regard to the Entente Powers, and this situation is at present constantly improving.

On the northern front the Soviet troops have just retaken the city of Shenkursk. On the eastern front they have temporarily lost Perm, but they have regained Ufa, Sterlitmak, Belebey, Orenburg, and Uralsk. As a result of this the railroad connection with Central Asia is at present in the hands of the Soviet Government. On the southern front they have recently taken the important railroad stations of Pavorino, Alexikovo, Uriupino, Talovaya, Kalatsh, and Begutchar, and thus control the railroads of this region, while the Ukrainian Soviet troops, advancing from Lugansk, threaten Krasnov's rear from the southeast. Local Soviet trops have taken Kharkov, Ekaterinoslav, Poltava, Kremenchug, Chernigov, Ovruch, and many other

---

[1] According to *The Russian Almanac*, 1919 (London, edited by N. Peacock), the following declaration was issued in Paris:

The representatives of Russia deem it their duty to declare, in order to avoid all misunderstandings, that no agreement made with Bolshevik authorities in regard to concessions or privileges will be recognized by the national authorities, and that all transactions concluded by foreigners with representatives of the Soviets will be considered null and void.

(Signed) PRINCE LVOV.   N. CHAIKOVSKY.
SAZONOV.   B. MAKLAKOV.

less important cities. White Russia, Lithuania, and Lettonia are almost entirely in the hands of the Soviet troops of these republics, including the large cities of Minsk, Vilna, Riga, Dvinsk, Mitau, Vindau, and others.

The remarkable improvement in the internal situation of Soviet Russia appears from the negotiations which the members of the former Constituent Assembly have begun with the Soviet Government. Their representatives, Rakitnikov (President of their Congress), Sviatizki (Secretary), Volski, Shmelev, Courevoy, Chernenkov, Antonov, all of whom are members of the Central Committee of the Social Revolutionary party, arrived in Moscow yesterday, February 3. These well-known Social Revolutionists have declared themselves with great emphasis against the Entente intervention in Russia.[1]

The improvement of the Soviet Government's relations with the elements formerly hostile to it in Russian society is indicated by the change of the attitude of the Mensheviki, whose conference has likewise protested against the Entente intervention and whose organ, *Vpered,* appears in Moscow without interference.[2] The general easing up of the former tension in the

[1] *L'Humanité* on January 22, 1919, published a declaration by the Deputies of the Constituent Assembly who took the initiative in organizing a Provisional Government at Ufa in the autumn of 1918.

" The struggle of the Revolutionary Socialists against the Bolsheviks was conducted against a power which was in direct contact with the oppressors of the Russian democracy,—namely the Germans.

" But now that Germany has been defeated and the victorious powers are intervening in Russia, this struggle assumes more and more the character of a support rendered, as it were, by the bourgeoisie of those countries to the reactionary Russian bourgeoisie.

" It has become necessary for us to abandon our struggle against the Bolsheviks. Kolchak's coup d'état at Omsk has finally thrown a clear light on the actualities of the situation. After this coup d'état the members of the Constituent Assembly secretly formed an Executive Committee and in accord with the resolutions of the congress this committee has begun to organize a struggle against Kolchak.

" It was decided to abandon the struggle against the Bolsheviks and to unite all forces in a common struggle against Kolchak and the Siberian reaction.

" Under the present circumstances the struggle against the Bolsheviks is in reality altered to a bloody civil war and a struggle against a party of workers and peasants. We are, therefore, making efforts to call all the troops attached to the Constituent Assembly away from the present front in order to direct them against Kolchak and to open preliminary negotiations with the Commander of the Bolshevik troops with the object of terminating the struggle and uniting all our strength against Kolchak." (Weekly Bulletin of the Bureau of Information on Soviet Russia, March 17, 1919.)

[2] *L'Humanité* published on March 5, 1919, a long manifesto which was

internal situation of Russia is shown by the abolition of the Local Extraordinary Commissions (for combating counter-revolution). And finally, the reports in the foreign press concerning the alleged unrest in Petrograd and other places are absolutely fabrications.

Emphasizing again that the situation of the Soviet Republic will necessarily affect the extent of the proposed concession, the Russian Soviet Government, nevertheless, stands by its proposal to enter into negotiations on the above-mentioned questions. As for the complaints frequently expressed in the Entente press with regard to the international revolutionary propaganda of the Russian Soviet Government, that Government declares that it is ready, if necessary, to include in the general agreement with the Entente Powers the obligation not to interfere in their internal affairs, pointing out, however, that it cannot limit the freedom of the revolutionary press.

On the above-mentioned basis the Russian Soviet Government is ready to enter into immediate negotiations on Princes Island or at any other place with all the Entente Powers or with individual powers of their number or with certain Rus-

---

issued in Moscow by the Central Executive of the Menshevik party. After referring to the Soviet Government's acceptance of the Prinkipo proposal and its abandonment by the Allies, the manifesto goes on to declare that "preparations for an Allied military campaign against Russia are in full swing."

"English and French Military missions are at this very moment everywhere in evidence; they are gathering together Russian counter-revolutionary forces, their presence being the occasion for all kinds of inhuman measures of repression—shootings, hangings, tortures. . . . Czechs, Ukrainians, Poles, Finns, Letts, etc., are all being pressed into an anti-Bolshevik police force, and are being encouraged in their design to seize portions of Russian territory for themselves.

"The masses of the Russian workers will defend themselves to the last against this series of dismemberments and against the forces of social reaction which cannot hope to gain power, except through the help of the Polish, Finnish, Rumanian, and Japanese reactionaries.

"Is the proletariat of western Europe going to allow these reactionary governments which are in power as the result of the world war, and have crushed their own working classes by a White Terror, to get together a force of international police, and with its aid to crush the working class throughout the world. . . . The Menshevik party appeals to all Socialist parties and to all trade unions to work for an agreement between the Entente and Lenin's government. . . .

"The Central Executive of the Menshevik party sincerely hopes that active intervention by the international proletariat will protect the Russian revolution from the blow which is being struck at it. Down with armed intervention! No interference with revolutionary Russia! Long live the unity of the proletariat in its international struggle." (Weekly Bulletin of the Bureau of Information on Soviet Russia, April 14, 1919.)

sian political groups, according to the wish of the Entente Powers. The Russian Soviet Government requests the Entente Powers to make known to it without delay the place to which it should send its representatives, as well as the time and the route.

CHICHERIN,
People's Commissary for Foreign Affairs.
Moscow, February 4, 1919.

[133.]

Replies of Non-Bolshevik Russian Governments to Prinkipo Invitation.[1]

(1)

REPLY OF LETTISH GOVERNMENT TO PRINKIPO INVITATION.

(*New York Times*, February 14, 1919.)

On January 22 the great Allied Powers assembled at the Peace Conference invited representatives of "every organized group that is now exercising or attempting to exercise political authority or military control anywhere in Siberia, or within the boundaries of European Russia as they stood before the war just concluded, except in Finland," to go to Princes' Islands, February 15, 1919, to confer with the representatives of the great Allied Powers.

Although from a political point of view the Provisional Government of Letvia is in a situation exactly similar to that of Poland and Finland, it finds itself, nevertheless, invited, according to an official declaration made by the Secretary General of the Peace Conference on February 10, 1919. In the name of the Provisional Lettish Government, the Lettish delegation has the honor to bring to the attention of the Peace Conference of Paris the following declaration:

"The Provisional Lettish Government will send three delegates to Princes' Islands, provided that all armed forces sent or directed by Russia against the Lettish State be withdrawn from Letvia and that all offensive military action cease.

Letvia announces its separation from Russia and announced

[1] The Georgian Government refused the invitation. The Soviet Ukrainian Government, the Government of the Crimea, and the Lithuanian Government accepted.

in January, 1919, at the Constituent Assembly of Russia (?), the constitution of an independent and sovereign Lettish State:

The Lettish delegation sent to the Peace Conference will participate in the conference at Prinkipo in order to:

I. Make peace with Russia, this peace to be recognized by the great Allied Powers.

II. Regulate, under the auspices of the great Allied Powers the political and economic affairs as they result from the separation of Letvia from Russia.

III. Make treaties in and take the necessary steps toward the establishment of States.

(signed) J. TSCHISTE."

(2)

REPLY OF THE ESTHONIAN GOVERNMENT TO THE PRINKIPO INVITATION

(*New York Times*, February 14, 1919.)

On January 22 the Peace Conference adopted a resolution by which the Governments established within the bounds of what was Russia before the war were asked to meet the representatives of the Allied Powers at Princes' Islands February 15. The resolution closed with a request for a reply to this invitation from the interested parties.

Therefore the Esthonian delegation considers it a duty to bring to the attention of the Peace Conference, in the name of the Esthonian Government, the following:

"The Esthonian people, by the intermediary of its National Council which springs from universal suffrage, determined to separate from Russia and thereupon proclaimed Esthonia an independent republic. The Government has been provisionally recognized by the English, French, and Italian Governments. Not only does the Esthonian Government exert its authority independent of any Russian Government, but for three months, after having organized a regular army, it has been at war with the Russian Soviet Communist Republic.

"Therefore, we in no wise consider ourselves a part of Russia, although we accept the invitation of the Allied Powers and of the United States to go to Princes' Islands. We believe that the participation of the representatives of Esthonia and of the Communist Republic of Russian Soviets of importance to the future relations between Russia and the Esthonian Republic."

(3)

NOTE HANDED THE PEACE CONFERENCE FEBRUARY 19, 1919, BY REPRESENTATIVES OF THE GOVERNMENTS OF SIBERIA, ARCHANGEL [1] AND SOUTHERN RUSSIA.

(*New York Times*, February 20, 1919.)

Highly appreciating the motives which inspired the Allies in their proposal of January 22, the above-mentioned Governments mark with satisfaction that the conference considers the reestablishment of order in Russia as an essential condition to durable peace in Europe, and gladly accepts the Allies' offer to collaborate in the interior pacification of Russia. After three years of fighting in which she loyally participated, and carried a considerable share of the common burden, Russia having been made powerless further to prosecute the war, can only in peace recuperate from her wounds; but such work of reconstruction is rendered impossible by the civil war which is being advocated and waged by the criminal usurpers, without regard for faith or law, whose despotism burdens a great part of Russia.

Aiming above all to put an end to the sanguinary tyranny of the Bolsheviki, the Russian political groups who have assumed the task of reviving our native land and restoring the State on true democratic bases would be grateful to the Peace Conference for the assistance which it desires to extend to this work of national reconstruction. They consider it as a certainty that everything which is done to restore to Russia, as soon as interior order is instituted, its place in the society of nations, will efficaciously serve at the same time the aims of justice, of humanity, and of international peace for which the conference is striving.

At the same time the united Governments of Russia are ready to put themselves at the disposal of the Allied Powers for the purpose of making known to them the actual situation of Russia and to seek in accord with them the means of remedy.

However, there cannot be any question of an exchange of ideas on this subject with the participation of the Bolsheviki, whom the conscience of the Russian people sees as traitors because they have betrayed the Russian cause and the cause of the

[1] A Paris dispatch dated February 21 announced that Nicholas Tchaikovsky, President of the North Russian Government, had consented to participate in the conference.

Allies in negotiating with the enemy; they have fomented anarchy, trampled the democratic principles which govern civilized countries, and maintained their power exclusively by terror. There is no conciliation possible between them and the national Russian groups. Any meeting would not only remain without effect, but might possibly cause to the Russian patriots' as well as to the allied nations an irreparable moral prejudice.

[134.]

Announcement of recognition of Poland by State Department, January 29, 1919.

(*New York Times*, January 30, 1919.)

The Provisional Government is accorded complete recognition in a telegram which Secretary Lansing has sent to Ignace Paderewski by direction of President Wilson. The message extending this full recognition follows:

The President of the United States directs me to extend to you as Prime Minister and Secretary for Foreign Affairs of the Provisional Polish Government his sincere wishes for your success in the high office which you have assumed, and his earnest hope that the Government of which you are a part will bring prosperity to the Republic of Poland.

It is my privilege to extend to you at this time my personal greetings, and officially assure you that it will be a source of gratification to enter into official relations with you at the earliest opportunity, and to render your country such aid as is possible at this time as it enters upon a new cycle of independent life will be in full accord with that spirit of friendliness which has in the past animated the American people in their relations with your countrymen.

[135.]

Note from the Russian Soviet Government to Italy, February 14, 1919.

(*Soviet Russia*, August 9, 1919.)

Up to the moment when the Italian Government actually broke with Russia, the Russian Soviet Government had been doing everything in its power to establish amicable relations with Italy.

There can be no opposition of interests between Russia and Italy. Nothing divides the Russian people from the Italian and, since the aggressive imperialistic policy of Czarism has ceased to menace the peace of the East and to instigate troubles in Slavic countries neighboring on Italy, nothing should trouble the harmony between the two cóuntries, and the Italian Government should refrain from any hostile action towards peaceful and democratic Russia, which is desirous of the friendship of all peoples.

Nevertheless, the contrary, alas! has happened. The Soviet Government has always treated the Italian representatives in Russia with the greatest consideration and courtesy, and has done all in its power to aid them when Italian prisoners who had escaped from Austria arrived in Moscow destitute of all that is necessary to exist. When the menace of Allied warships had forced the Soviet authorities in Archangel to introduce the state of siege in that city and a detachment of Italian soldiers had been arrested and brought by force to Moscow where the military authorities interned them in barracks, the Soviet government, after an inquiry necessitated by the abnormal and perilous situation in which Russia was situated, nevertheless freed all the Italian soldiers in question. When the Italian representatives desired to leave Russia—although the Soviet Government would have preferred to have them remain in Russia —they were treated with all possible respect and regard on the part of the Soviet Government, and all Italian subjects desiring to leave with them could do so without hindrance.

During the period when the Soviet Government was in constant relations with the Italian military attaché, General Romei, and the consul general in Moscow, Mr. Maioni, the representatives of the Soviet Government made constant efforts to make them see the ardent desire of Soviet Russia to live in peace with Italy. That was the time when the Entente representatives were striving to embroil Russia, ruined and bleeding from a thousand wounds, in a new war against Germany, which in view of Russia's situation at the time, with the enormous power of imperialist Germany not far from Moscow, would have meant certain ruin for Russia, an invasion by the imperialist German army and all the incalculable calamities involved in a foreign occupation and resulting from the oppression practiced by a German army upon her territory. It was impossible for Russia at such a moment to commit veritable suicide in this manner; the result would have been truly fatal for the unhappy Russian people. The representatives of the Soviet Government gave the representatives of Italy to understand that Soviet Russia had the best intentions towards Italy, that it requested nothing else but to live in peace with her as well as with other countries; and that moreover, when the Russian people would have recovered, the national organism would be reconstructed and filled with a new strength, then perhaps, if the circumstances should permit, the Russian people, with arms in their hands, would throw off the fetters which had been imposed upon them by the victorious German imperialism. The Soviet representatives even said that if the German army should invade the heart of Russia and put the Russian people before the prospect of subjection, the Russian Soviet Government would then address itself to all the powers of the Entente, asking that they come to its aid and propose to them a co-ordinated action against the German invader. But in the situation in which Russia found herself at the time, as long as this condition did not materialize, and as long as Germany should leave at peace all the extent of Russia which Germany did not occupy, the only possible policy for the Russian Soviet Government was that of peace, of peace at any price. How many times during these conversations with General Romei and with Mr. Maioni did the People's Commissary for Foreign Affairs try to make them understand that the Russian people in the terrible crisis through which it was passing could offer to the powers of the Entente no real assistance, and that to Russia itself incalculable harm would be involved in every imprudent action toward Germany. Internal reconstruction, creation of the national organs which were lacking in all spheres of Russian life, such was the task of the Russian Government at that moment, and peace, peace at any price, was the first condition of its existence.

Unfortunately, the representatives of Italy returned always to the same unreasonable demands, asking of Russia, which was unable to take up arms at that moment, to re-enter the field against Germany, then at the zenith of her military strength. The Red Army at that time was yet in an embryonic state; defenseless Russia could offer but a semblance of resistance to the terrific German force. In spite of that the Italian representatives demanded of the Soviet Government an impossibility, by asking defenseless Russia to reopen the war against the imperialist colossus, a victorious Germany.

Soviet Russia has done no wrong to the Italian people; Russia only refrained from beginning a new war that was beyond her power. This notwithstanding, the Italian Government has sent its armies against the Russian Soviet Republic. Italian contingents took part in the invasion of the northern provinces of Russia without any pretext and without a declaration of war; other Italian detachments appeared in the remote Siberian provinces of Russia which Russia was unable to defend against this danger. Now that the delegates of the Socialist-Revolutionary party, who had always been the adversaries of the Russian Soviet Government, faced by the barbarous and limitless reaction that is rampant in Siberia, thanks to the support of the Allies, have finally come to Moscow to seek a reconciliation with the Soviet Government against the terrible menace of the bloody counter-revolution—these delegates have declared, and the secretary of the ex-Constituent Assembly, Sviatizky, has published their statement in the *Izvestia* of February 6th, that the revolt of the peasants in the Marlinsk District of the province of Tomsk had been drowned in blood by Italian detachments stationed in these regions in order to keep the people under the yoke. Italian soldiers appeared in Siberia and in northern Russia in the rôle of judges of the Russian people. That is what we protest against with all our might and that is the state of affairs which we demand should stop.

Soviet Russia demands but one thing: that she be permitted to live in peace. She does not menace anybody, she has always sought the friendship of all peoples. The invasion of her territory by the Allied armies was provoked by no act on her part. Since then the Soviet Government has repeated many times its peace proposals to the representatives of the Entente through the neutral representatives in Moscow. The proposition to enter into peace parleys was addressed on November 3rd to the Italian Government at the same time as to the other Entente governments. On November 8th, the 5th Congress of the Soviets declared solemnly before the whole world that it had addressed to the Entente powers a proposition to enter into negotiations to put an end to the armed conflict with those powers. The same proposition was addressed on December 23rd, by the Russian representative at Stockholm, Litvinoff, to the representatives of the Entente countries resident in Sweden. Lastly, on February

4th, in the note sent out by wireless to the Entente governments, the Russian Soviet Government declared itself ready to make serious sacrifices with regard to its financial obligations, and also to furnish guarantees in the form of quantities of raw materials, as well as mining, forest, and other concessions and also some concessions in the sphere of territorial annexations. While these lines are being written, the Russian Soviet Government is still awaiting an answer from the Entente governments. We repeat once more that peace and friendship with all the peoples is the aim which Soviet Russia seeks to attain even at the price of serious sacrifices.

The pretext which was advanced by the Entente powers at the time when they entered upon the road of a hostile policy towards Soviet Russia was the armed struggle beginning at that time between the Soviet authorities and the Czecho-Slovak troops of Western Siberia. In reality the Soviet Government has displayed the greatest patience towards the Czecho-Slovaks and has taken recourse to rigorous measures only after the actions of the latter have made it impossible for the former to avoid using such measures. At the beginning of 1918, the Soviet Government consented to the departure of the Czecho-Slovaks, with their weapons, by the Vladivostok route. In the midst of a fully disarmed Russia, the Czecho-Slovak contingents, well organized, imbued with martial spirit, having at their disposal sufficient war materials and receiving considerable support from the Entente powers became soon a most serious menace to the internal safety of the Russian Soviet Republic. Animated by sentiments that were little favorable to the new régime in Russia, the Czech contingents manifested their sentiments more and more violently, taking possession by force of the rolling stock on the Russian railroads, which they lacked on account of the general disorganization of transportation, and seizing food stocks and provisions in the villages through which they were passing, and whose population was suffering from famine. Collisions took place between the Czecho-Slovaks and the local authorities, chiefly the railroad authorities. Soon their attitude with regard to the Soviet Government became decidedly hostile and seriously menacing. Where they met compatriots who were unwilling to follow their road, they committed the worst acts of violence against the latter. They also seized many camps inhabited by Czechs in various towns of interior Russia, such as Kirsanoff, where a certain number of Czechs were massacred by the Czecho-Slovak contingents. They were commanded by counter-revolutionary Czarist officers and, as the documents seized later on the Czecho-Slovak spies who fell into our hands have proved in an irrefutable manner, French agents systematically prepared, with the aid of gold distributed by them among the Czecho-Slovaks, the revolt which in their opinion was to deal a mortal blow to the people's revolution in Russia. The danger became so highly menacing that the towns of Western Siberia, especially after the disembarkation of the Japanese in the middle of April, which marked the beginning of the interventionist policy on the part of the Entente, demanded in a loud voice that the Czech contingents be directed by another road. The Soviet Government indicated to England and France that a journey by the way of Archangel and Murmansk would be much more desirable in the interest of the Czechs themselves. As Trotsky indicated in a lecture delivered by him in the middle of June, and published in the *Slovo Naroda* on June 18th, the situation after the occupation of Vladivostock by the Japanese became such that the departure by way of Archangel and Murmansk was the only possible way out for the Czecho-Slovaks. Unfortunately, England and France dragged on the negotiations in this matter which had been begun by Russia. As irrefutable proofs have later demonstrated, the Entente agents, at that time chiefly French agents, were systematically preparing the Czecho-Slovak revolt, while on the other hand they were arranging the counter-revolutionary government of the North of Russia and of certain parts of Siberia. Certain documents which fell into our hands later, contain precise data in regard to the activities of those French agents, supplied with very considerable sums of money, who scattered gold without stint.

When the proposition had been made to England and France to hasten the return of the Czecho-Slovaks by the northern maritime route, the English and the French Governments adopted in this connection a dilatory policy and dragged the matter on, week after week. In the meantime the Czecho-Slovaks occupied all railroad lines from Penza to Omsk, showing by their attitude their evidently hostile intentions with regard to the Russian Soviet Government. It was then that the latter, finding the situation irksome, took measures to free itself from the situation, and demanded from the Czecho-Slovaks that they give up the greater part of their arms, leaving them a certain quantity of rifles assigned for every echelon. The Czecho-Slovaks now responded with a mutiny; they raised the banner of revolt, seizing at once the towns in which they were, which at that time were completely denuded of armed forces. The Czecho-Slovaks made themselves at once masters of a very extensive region and of railroad lines that represent a vital necessity for communication between Russia and Siberia and for supplying the former with food, and began immediately, wherever they became masters, to overthrow the Soviet authorities and to replace them by the old bourgeois and capitalist authorities. The Omsk newspaper, *Delo Sibiri* of June 29th and the Kourgansk magazine *Svobodnaia Mysl* published a declaration of the chief of the French mission to the Czecho-Slovak insurgents, M. Alphonse Guinet, in which in the name of the French embassy he officially thanks the Czecho-Slovaks for their acts directed against the Russian Soviet Republic. He said that the French representative had maintained for some time continuous relations with the Soviet authorities, but that from this moment on they had changed their attitude and would support the Czecho-Slovaks in their military activity. On June 4th, the representatives of the Entente in Moscow, and among them Mr. Maioni, declared in the name of Italy to the People's Commissary for Foreign Affairs that their governments regarded the Czecho-Slovaks as an allied army under the protection of the Entente powers, and that they would view their disarmament as an act of hostility against those governments. On June 12th, the Soviet Government answered to this declaration that the disarmament of the Czecho-Slovaks could in no case be considered as a hostile act against the Entente powers, because Russia as a neutral power could not suffer on her territory armed forces not belonging to the armies of the Soviet Republic, and that the direct reason which made it absolutely necessary to disarm the Czechs was their counter-revolutionary insurrection, menacing with serious danger the safety of Soviet Russia. As the Soviet Government has explained in a note in question, the Czecho-Slovak insurrection started on May 26th at Tcheliabinsk, where they seized the railroad and stores of arms, overthrowing the Soviet authorities, and replacing them by counter-revolutionary authorities, which they afterwards repeated in Omsk, Novo-Nikolayevsk, later operating in intimate contact with the White Guards and with the former officers of the Czarist army. The Entente powers maintained their attitude of protection accorded to the counter-revolutionary Czech insurgents, asserting that the German Government had compelled Soviet Russia to adopt measures against them, whereas the German Government, on the contrary, began to pay attention to the actions of the Czechs only after their insurrection and after the Allies by their diplomatic action had transformed this question into a great political question of an international order.

Soon the whole region of the Czecho-Slovak occupation, which comprised an ever greater part of Siberia, became the field of a veritable orgy of the counter-revolution, of shooting and mass executions of workmen and peasants suspected of sympathies for the revolution, of summary massacres and courtmartials sentencing to death by wholesale. Tens of thousands of workmen and peasants filled the prisons of that region. A most brutal and bloody counter-revolution, under the protection of the armed forces of the Entente, soon embraced that immense region where the Czecho-Slovaks had prepared the ground for it, as well as in the North of Russia, where the English battleships had paved the way, menacing moreover the very existence of the Russian Soviet Republic and the popular revolution of the workers and peasants of Russia.

The activities of the Allied representatives became ever more systematic in inciting everywhere, where it was possible for them, riots, revolts, troubles, and in creating conspiracies, which they were able to do by generous distributions of money, thus paying for the most horrible crimes. Mr. René Marchand, correspondent of the *Figaro*, a person known to the president of the French Republic, Mr. Poincaré, in a letter dated August 22nd (September 4th) which fell into the hands of the Soviet authorities during a house search, tells the following:

"A semi-official gathering which I had occasion to attend recently, revealed to me in a most unexpected fashion, so far as I am concerned, a secret operation of a most dangerous nature. I allude to a private gathering held at the former Consulate General of the United States on August 23 and 24, if I am not mistaken. The former Consul General of the United States, Mr. Poole, and our Consul General were present there. Allied agents whose names I don't recall but whom I did not know personally attended the meeting.

"Undoubtedly, I hasten to state it, neither the American nor the French Consuls General have ever themselves made the slightest allusion to any hidden work of destruction; but incidentally I have been made aware of such a practice through the conversations of agents present among them.

"I have thus learned that an English agent was preparing the destruction of the railroad bridge which passes over the river Volkhoff, before the station of Zvanka. Now it is necessary only to glance at the map in order to see that the destruction of this bridge would be equivalent to the complete starving of Petrograd, which city would have found itself in fact cut off from any communication with the East, whence comes exclusively the grain of which it has already barely enough to live on. The author of the scheme himself recognized the full seriousness of the consequences of such an action and declares that he does not know yet whether he could put his project into execution.

"A French agent added to this proposition that he had already attempted to blow up the bridge of Tcherepovetz, which would have had the same consequence so far as food supply of Petrograd is concerned as the destruction of the Zvanka bridge, Tcherepovetz being also on the only line which keeps Petrograd in communication with the Eastern regions. Besides, there was the question of derailing the trains on different lines. One agent explained also that he was assured of co-operation among railroad men which was valuable but would prevent the use of certain instruments of destruction, as the railroad men who had been won over would consent only to operate against trains with war materials."

During the months of June, July, and August, everywhere in Russia, the agents of the Entente were fomenting insurrection. The Yaraslov riot took place after the visit of French officers. When the Commander-in-Chief Mouravieff revolted against the Soviet power, a proof was furnished to the government that he had received sums of money from England. All the mutinies that followed in various parts of Russia were plotted by invisible hands from a hidden center, and General Alexeieff, a professed partisan of England, whose subsidies furnish him with the means of existence, was named as the supreme chief of all the insurgents.

All this period of conspiracies fomented by agents of the Entente culminated in a huge conspiracy prepared by the English representative, Lockhart, who attempted to corrupt the Lettish Guards of the Kremlin in order to seize Lenin and Trotsky, who, in his opinion, would have to be immediately shot, and to replace the Soviet Government by a military dictatorship in close contact with the Orthodox Church and with all the blackest forces of a most terrible reaction. The unshaken devotion of the valiant Lettish revolutionists saved the Russian people from the calamity of losing Lenin and Trotsky, against whom this kidnapping game was directed, and revealed to the world the crimes which the English representative was secretly preparing.

The months of June, July, and August, 1918, constituted the most difficult period through which Soviet Russia has passed. The enemies hiding behind the corners attempted to stab from behind with a poisoned dagger the Russian Soviet Republic. All the forces of reaction working in the dark were set in motion, supported by a secret activity and the inexhaustible gold of the Entente. This was the moment when that which is called the red terror was developed in Soviet Russia. It was nothing but a case of elementary self-defense against the innumerable enemies who were assailing her from without and within. All the counter-revolutionary forces, former officers, capitalists, village usurers, did all in their power to join in overthrowing the revolutionary government of Russia in a union with the immense forces of the Entente and supported by the latter. Never indeed has the red terror attained the fabulous proportions that were assigned to it by the calumny which is rampant in the foreign press, never did any mass executions of former officers take place. In Petrograd, after the ex-officers were made to register, some of them who were dangerous were interned. In Moscow, the registered officers were released. The only mass execution, that of 500 persons in Petrograd, took place after the assassination of Ouritzky and the attempt on the life of Lenin, when the Petrograd proletarians were expecting every moment an uprising of the counter-revolutionary forces supported by the Entente. In Moscow, executions en masse have never taken place and all the death sentences passed in Moscow by the Extraordinary Commission during the entire past year barely exceed a total of one hundred. All the fantastic stories of mass shootings circulated by the international counter-revolutionary press belong to the domain of fable and there is no comparison between the number of these executions and the innumerable atrocities perpetrated by the bloody executioners of the counter-revolution in the regions of Allied occupation or by the army of Denikin in the South.

All the activity of the Entente against Soviet Russia, the

invasion in the north, in the east, in the south and latterly in the west, had as its result the cutting off of the food supplies from Central Russia, that is from the Russian Soviet Republic where a workers' and peasants' revolution is maintaining itself. That is what is being called the economic encircling; it is the lack of food which is one of the means of the counter-revolution by which it tries to force the Russian popular revolution to capitulate. Never has famine in Russia attained the fabulous proportions which were assigned to it by the campaign of calumnies which was systematically worked up during the past few months. Our situation as regards the food supply is difficult and painful, and it is only with the greatest efforts that we succeed in maintaining some food allowances to the people. But notwithstanding the privations that we have to undergo, we have thus far been victorious in this painful trial. The valiant Red Army, whose condition is becoming better from day to day, whose discipline is a most exemplary one, and for which numerous courses for instructors are preparing, with an unusual rapidity, increasing numbers of revolutionary officers coming from the ranks of the workers and the peasants, has by its heroic actions reconquered for Soviet Russia certain fertile regions which had always supplied with food the Center and the North of European Russia, which are so poor in foodstuffs. Our military force is developing successfully to greater proportions, while it is defending us against enemies who are still being supported by the Allied contingents and by the abundant war supplies furnished by them.

But still now as before our constant desire is peace with all peoples. In order to be able to enjoy its benefits we are now as ever ready to make serious sacrifices, which are mentioned in our note of February 4th, addressed to the powers of the Entente. We propose real advantages to the commerce and industry of the Western countries; we declare to the latter that their real interests will be served by the conditions which we propose. We believe that they ought for their own interest to consent to this and re-establish normal relations with us, so ardently desired by us. We hope that Italy, finally, which would seem to have no cause for hostility to Soviet Russia, will terminate its policy directed against us and will use her influence in the international deliberations of the Powers in order to aid us in the re-establishment of normal and peaceful relations with all the peoples and their governments, which is the

object of our desires. What we wish is peace and we hope that the Entente Powers will at last accede to our desire.
February 14, 1919.

[136.]

Text of Projected Peace Proposal prepared by Representatives of the Soviet Government, March 14, 1919.[1]

(Hearings before the Committee on Foreign Relations, United States Senate, 66th Congress, 1919, p. 1248.)

The allied and associated Governments to propose that hostilities shall cease on all fronts in the territory of the former Russian Empire and Finland on—[the date of the armistice to be set at least a week after the date when the allied and associated Governments make this proposal]—and that no new hostilities shall begin after this date, pending a conference to be held at—[the Soviet Government greatly prefers that the conference should be held in a neutral country and also that either a radio or a direct telegraph wire to Moscow should be put at its disposal]—on—[the conference to begin not later than a week after the armistice takes effect and the Soviet Government greatly prefers that the period between the date of the armistice and the first meeting of the conference should be only three days, if possible].

The duration of the armistice to be for two weeks, unless extended by mutual consent, and all parties to the armistice to undertake not to employ the period of the armistice to transfer troops and war material to the territory of the former Russian Empire.

The conference to discuss peace on the basis of the following principles, which shall not be subject to revision by the conference.

1. All existing de facto governments which have been set up on the territory of the former Russian Empire and Finland to remain in full control of the territories which they occupy at

[1] This paper was brought out from Russia by William C. Bullitt. Mr. Bullitt with Captain Walter Pettit of the Military Intelligence Division of the United States Army was sent to Petrograd by the American Commission to Negotiate Peace in the spring of 1919. The mission, accompanied by Mr. Lincoln Stephens left Paris on February 22d and arrived in Petrograd March the 8th. After interviews with Soviet officials, Mr. Bullitt left Russia March 15th. Captain Pettit remained in Petrograd until March 31st.

the moment when the armistice becomes effective, except in so far as the conference may agree upon the transfer of territories; until the peoples inhabiting the territories controlled by these de facto governments shall themselves determine to change their Governments. The Russian Soviet Government, the other soviet governments and all other governments which have been set up on the territory of the former Russian Empire, the allied and associated Governments, and the other Governments which are operating against the soviet governments, including Finland, Poland, Galicia, Roumania, Armenia, Azerbaidjan, and Afghanistan, to agree not to attempt to upset by force the existing de facto governments which have been set up on the territory of the former Russian Empire and the other Governments signatory to this agreement.[1]

2. The economic blockade to be raised and trade relations between Soviet Russia and the allied and associated countries to be re-established under conditions which will ensure that supplies from the allied and associated countries are made available on equal terms to all classes of the Russian people.

3. The soviet governments of Russia to have the right of unhindered transit on all railways and the use of all ports which belonged to the former Russian Empire and to Finland and are necessary for the disembarkation and transportation of passengers and goods between their territories and the sea; detailed arrangements for the carrying out of this provision to be agreed upon at the conference.

4. The citizens of the soviet republics of Russia to have the right of free entry into the allied and associated countries as well as into all countries which have been formed on the territory of the former Russian Empire and Finland; also the right of sojourn and of circulation and full security, provided they do not interfere in the domestic politics of those countries.[2]

Nationals of the allied and associated countries and of the other countries above named to have the right of free entry into the soviet republics of Russia; also the right of sojourn and of

---

[1] The allied and associated Governments to undertake to see to it that the de facto governments of Germany do not attempt to upset by force the de facto governments of Russia. The de facto governments which have been set up on the territory of the former Russian Empire to undertake not to attempt to upset by force the de facto governments of Germany.

[2] It is considered essential by the Soviet Government that the allied and associated Governments should see to it that Poland and all neutral countries extend the same rights as the allied and associated countries.

circulation and full security, provided they do not interfere in the domestic politics of the soviet republics.

The allied and associated Governments and other governments which have been set up on the territory of the former Russian Empire and Finland to have the right to send official representatives enjoying full liberty and immunity into the various Russian Soviet Republics. The soviet governments of Russia to have the right to send official representatives enjoying full liberty and immunity into all the allied and associated countries and into non-soviet countries which have been formed on the territory of the former Russian Empire and Finland.

5. The soviet governments, the other Governments which have been set up on the territory of the former Russian Empire and Finland, to give a general amnesty to all political opponents, offenders, and prisoners. The allied and associated Governments to give a general amnesty to all Russian political opponents, offenders, and prisoners, and to their own nationals who have been or may be prosecuted for giving help to Soviet Russia. All Russians who have fought in, or otherwise aided the armies opposed to the soviet governments, and those opposed to the other Governments which have been set up on the territory of the former Russian Empire and Finland, to be included in this amnesty.

All prisoners of war of non-Russian powers detained in Russia, likewise all nationals of those powers now in Russia to be given full facilities for repatriation. The Russian prisoners of war in whatever foreign country they may be, likewise all Russian nationals, including the Russian soldiers and officers abroad and those serving in all foreign armies to be given full facilities for repatriation.

6. Immediately after the signing of this agreement all troops of the allied and associated Governments and other non-Russian Governments to be withdrawn from Russia and military assistance to cease to be given to anti-soviet Governments which have been set up on the territory of the former Russian Empire.

The soviet governments and the anti-soviet governments which have been set up on the territory of the former Russian Empire and Finland to begin to reduce their armies simultaneously, and at the same rate, to a peace footing immediately after the signing of this agreement. The conference to determine the most effective and just method of inspecting and controlling this simultaneous demobilization and also the withdrawal of the troops and the cessation of military assistance to the anti-soviet governments.

7. The allied and associated Governments, taking cognizance of the statement of the Soviet Government of Russia, in its note of February 4, in regard to its foreign debts, propose as an integral part of this agreement that the soviet government and the other governments which have been set up on the territory of the former Russian Empire and Finland shall recognize their responsibility for the financial obligations of the former Russian Empire, to foreign States parties to this agreement and to the nationals of such States. Detailed arrangements for the payment of these debts to be agreed upon at the conference, regard being had to the present financial position of Russia. The Russian gold seized by the Czecho-Slovaks in Kazan or taken from Germany by the Allies to be regarded as partial payment of the portion of the debt due from the soviet republics of Russia.

The Soviet Government of Russia undertakes to accept the foregoing proposal provided it is made not later than April 10, 1919.

[137.]

Translation of Credentials sent by L. C. A. K. Martens to the State Department, March 19, 1919.

(Hearing on Russian Propaganda before a Sub-committee of the Committee on Foreign Relations, United States Senate, 66th Congress, 1920, p. 14.)

Russian Socialist Federated Soviet Republic,
People's Commissariat of Foreign Affairs,
Office of the People's Commissar, January 2, 1919.

No. 9/k.

Moscow, corner of Spiridonovka and Patriarch's Lane, house No. 30/1. Telephone No. 4-22-96.

It is hereby announced that Russian Citizen Ludwig Christian Alexander Carlovitch Martens, who resides in the United States of America, is appointed the representative of the people's commissariat of foreign affairs in the United States of America. G. CHICHERIN,
People's Commissary for Foreign Affairs.
F. SHENKIN,
Acting Secretary of the Office.

(Official seal of the people's commissariat for foreign affairs.)

[138.]

Memorandum sent to the State Department by L. C. A. K. Martens, March 19, 1919.

(Hearing on Russian Propaganda before a Sub-committee of the Committee on Foreign Relations, United States Senate, 66th Congress, 1920, p. 23.)

RUSSIAN SOCIALIST FEDERAL SOVIET REPUBLIC—A MEMORANDUM TO THE STATE DEPARTMENT OF THE UNITED STATES FROM THE REPRESENTATIVE IN AMERICA OF THE RUSSIAN SOCIALIST FEDERAL SOVIET REPUBLIC.

[The government of the Russian socialist federal soviet republic on January 2, 1919, appointed as its representative in the United States Mr. L. A. Martens. On Wednesday, March 19, 1919, Mr. Martens sent his official credentials to the State Department in Washington. The credentials were accompanied by the following memorandum dealing with the intentions of the government of Russia, as well as with the internal affairs of that country.]

The Russian socialist federal soviet republic was established on the 6th of November, 1917, by a spontaneous uprising of the toiling masses of Russia. Its government, the council of people's commissaires, is a government controlled by and responsible to all such members of the population of Russia as are willing to perform useful work, physical or mental. Those who, while not being unable to work, deliberately refuse to exercise their productive abilities, choosing to live on the fruits of the labor of other people, are eliminated from participation in the control of my government.

Under present conditions those who are willing to work for the common good number at least 90 per cent of the adult population in the area controlled by the soviets. All such people have full political and civic rights.

The basis for citizenship in Russia being industrial and economic rather than political, and the social system being of such a nature that every person engaged in useful social labor is bound to participate in public affairs, the percentage of people directly participating in the management of society in soviet Russia is higher than has been the case anywhere in the world hitherto. The Russian soviet republic affords thereby the widest possible field for a real expression of a conscious popular will. While the soviet government is a government of the working class, the abolition of exploitation of labor and the elimination thereby of class division creates a productive community in which all able inhabitants are bound to become useful workers who have full political rights. My government thus becomes the expression of fully 100 per cent of the people. It should also be noted that political rights are granted in Russia to every inhabitant engaged in useful work, even though he be not a citizen of Russia, but only temporarily working there.

The Russian socialist federal soviet republic was rapidly acclaimed by the vast majority of the laboring people throughout the former Empire of Russia. It has maintained itself in the face of manifold plots and opposition on the part of small groups of the former ruling classes, who in many cases enlisted foreign help and who employed the most unscrupulous methods in their fight against the soviet institutions. Yet nowhere in Russia could such elements of their own accord organize any noticeable resistance to the popular will as expressed by the soviet government. Only in sparsely populated outlying districts and in such of those districts where our opponents had access to foreign military help has it been possible for them to maintain any organized opposition and to wrest from the control of soviet Russia any territory. To-day, after 16 months of existence, the Russian soviet republic finds itself more securely established than at any previous time.

During the current year the soviet government has been particularly successful in retaking vast territories wrested from its control during the preceding months. By February, 1919, the soviet troops on the northern front had retaken the city of Shenkursk and adjoining territory. On the eastern front they have lost Perm, but they have regained Pereufa, Ufa, Sterlitamak, Bielebey, Orenburg, and Uralsk. The railroad connection with central Asia is at present in the hands of the soviet government. On the southern front they have taken the railroad stations of Pavorino, Alexikovo, Polovaya, Kalatsk, and Bogutchar, which have assured them of a control over the railroads of that region, while on the southeastern front the Ukrainian soviet troops threaten the army of Krasnov from Ugansk in the rear. In the Ukraine the soviet troops have acquired Kharkov, Yekaterinoslav, Poltava, Krementchug, Tchernigov, and Obrutch. In the Baltic provinces and in Lithuania the soviet power has been extended over a great part of the territory formerly occupied by the Germans, with the large cities of Minsk, Vilna,

Riga, Mitau, Dvinsk, Windau, and others in the control of adherents of the soviet.

The last-mentioned successes are largely due to the fact that after the evacuation by the German armies of the territories wrested from Russia during the war and by the peace treaty of Brest-Litovsk, which the soviet republic was forced to sign under duress, the workers in such territories everywhere are rising to support the ideals and the social order represented by the soviet republic.

The resentment against the former ruling classes, who did not hesitate to invite foreign military help against their own people, has evinced itself in an ever-increasing popular support of the soviet government, even among such people as at first were either hostile or indifferent to the soviet rule. Men and women of literary or technical training and of intellectual accomplishments are now in great numbers rallying to the support of the soviet government and co-operate with it in all administrative branches. The peasantry of Russia, the great majority of whom from the very outset was in favor of the workers' revolution, has become more consciously attached to our social system, realizing that in the support of the workers' republic lies the only guaranty for their remaining in control of the land which they have wrested from their former oppressors. The economic isolation of Russia, which so far has prevented the soviet government from adequately supplying the peasants with implements that they so badly need, is of course causing hardship among the peasantry: yet the peasants generally do not place the blame for this privation at the door of the soviet government, well realizing that it is due to the deliberate interference in the affairs of the Russian people by hostile groups, and that a remedy for this privation is not a weakening, but a strengthening, of the soviet power. They fully realize—and their experience in such instances where counter-revolutionary forces temporarily succeeded in overthrowing soviet institutions, clearly demonstrated the correctness of this realization—that an overthrow of the soviet rule, if possible at all, would lead to the establishment of a tyrannical, reactionary, bloody autocracy.

The remarkable improvement in the internal situation of soviet Russia appears from the negotiations which the members of the former constituent assembly have begun with the soviet government. Representatives of the former constituent assembly, such as Chernov, Rakitnikov, Sviatitzki, Volski, Bourevoy,

Chernenkov, Antonov, all of whom are also members of the central committee of the social revolutionary party, recently arrived in Moscow to participate in a conference with the soviet government with the view of giving support to our republic. This conference has led to an understanding whereby these well known social revolutionists and former bitter opponents have ceased their opposition and declared themselves with great emphasis against the Entente intervention in Russia.

An improvement of the soviet government's relations with the elements formerly hostile to it in Russian society is also indicated by the change of the attitude of the Mensheviki, whose conference has likewise protested against the Entente intervention.

The army of the Russian socialist federal soviet republic has been successfully organized and numbers to-day over a million men. A system of universal military training has been inaugurated which steadily supplies the army with accessions, with the view of creating a force numbering, by the end of the current year, 3,000,000 men. The forces of the government are led partly by officers of the former Russian armies who have proved their allegiance to the soviet government, and partly by officers developed from the rank and file by the military educational institutions established by my government. The commissariat of war has been successful in establishing and maintaining a strict discipline within the ranks of the army, a discipline not based on fear of punishment or on docile submission, but on the ardent conviction of the workers, from whose ranks the army is recruited, that it is their privilege as well as their duty to defend their social achievements against encroachments from any sources. This same conviction of the necessity of the defense of our revolutionary achievements has made it possible for us, in spite of all economic obstacles, efficiently to organize the production of military supplies.

The soviet government inherited a legacy of utter financial disruption, created by four years of war and a year of revolution. This state of affairs, and also the necessity of co-ordinating the financial system of Russia with the new industrial and economic system represented by my government, necessitated a complete reorganization of the financial institutions on the basis of common property rights. This reorganization, which aims at exchanging the money system for a system representing labor value, is still in the state of formation. Regardless thereof, the soviet government, in as far as financial relations with and obligations to other countries are concerned, is prepared to offer modes of financial transactions adapted to the financial system of other countries.

The period preceding the establishment of the soviet government also badly disrupted the machinery of production and distribution. The soviet government inaugurated a system of public control and ownership of industries. It has actually taken over many important branches of industry, and has established the control of the supreme council of national economy over all industries. Great handicaps have been faced because of the obstructionist methods of our opponents, lack of raw material and machinery, and because of the general confusion unavoidably coincident with the gigantic reorganization of the industrial life. In spite of these handicaps, various branches of industry have been re-established, even with an increase of productive efficiency. Many branches of industry, however, have not so far been able to recuperate, because of lack of raw material and lack of machinery. The needs of such industries offer a wide field for business transaction with Russia by other countries.

The state of railroad communications at the outset of the soviet régime was very unsatisfactory. The demands first of the demobilization of the old army and later of military operations against counter-revolutionary attacks taxed the capacity of our railroads and left little opportunity for reconstruction work in this field. The soviet government during the past year nevertheless has managed to build and to complete the building of about 2,000 versts of new railroads. It has also paid great attention to the construction of other means of communication, such as canals, roads, etc., and is at the present time planning work along these lines on a large scale, which will also offer great opportunities for foreign trade. The people of Russia, shut off for hundreds of years from the sources of popular education, have made it one of the main tasks of my government to reorganize the school system with the view of the greatest possible achievements in the field of popular education. In this respect extensive work has been carried on throughout Russia during the past year. Tens of thousands of new primary schools, vocational schools, workers' universities, and lecture courses, especially courses offering agricultural instruction, have been established and maintained at great expense on the part of the soviet government, and the field of the educational activities has been extended to include the making of the treasures of the arts and sciences as easily accessible to the people as possible.

All these efforts, incomplete as they still are, have nevertheless given the Russian people sufficient evidence of the earnestness of the desire and of the ability of the soviet government to fill the needs of the population and they have greatly contributed to the abatement of opposition. Inasmuch as opposition has ceased in the form of active resistance to the soviet government, it has become possible to lighten such extraordinary measures as censorship, martial law, etc.

Much prejudice has been created against the soviet government by the circulation of false reports about the nature of the institutions of and the measures undertaken by soviet Russia. One of the most frequent allegations has been that the rule of the soviets is one of violence and murder. In this connection I want to call your attention to the following passages in the note sent to the President of the United States on the 24th of December, 1918, by Maxim Litvinoff, on behalf of the soviet government in Russia:

". . . The chief aim of the soviets is to secure for the toiling majority of the Russian people economic liberty, without which political liberty is of no avail to them. For eight months the soviets endeavored to realize their aims by peaceful methods, without resorting to violence, adhering to the abolition of capital punishment, which abolition had been part of their program. It was only when their adversaries, the minority of the Russian people, took to terroristic acts against popular members of the government, and invoked the help of foreign troops, that the laboring masses were driven to acts of exasperation and gave vent to their wrath and bitter feelings against their former oppressors. For allied invasion of Russian territory not only compelled the soviets against their own will to militarize the country anew and to divert their energies and resources, so necessary to the economic reconstruction of Russia, exhausted by four years of war, to the defense of the country, but also cut off the vital sources of foodstuffs and raw materials, exposing the population to the most terrible privation, bordering on starvation.

" . . . I wish to emphasize that the so-called red terror, which is so grossly exaggerated and misrepresented abroad, was not the cause, but the direct outcome and result, of allied intervention. The Russian workers and peasants fail to understand how foreign countries, which never dreamt of interfering with

Russian affairs when czarist barbarism and militarism ruled supreme, and which even supported that régime, can feel justified in intervening in Russia now, when the working people themselves, after decades of strenuous struggling and countless sacrifices, have succeeded in taking the power and destiny of their country into their own hands, aiming at nothing but their own happiness and international brotherhood, constituting no menace to other nations."

In another passage of the same note Mr. Litvinoff states as follows:

". . . The best means for the termination of violence in Russia would be to reach a settlement which would include the withdrawal of all foreign troops from Russia and the cessation of direct or indirect assistance to such groups in Russia as still indulge in futile hopes of an armed revolt against the workers' government, but who by themselves alone would not think of such a possibility if they could not reckon on assistance from abroad."

The great work of social reconstruction inaugurated by the soviet government as the executors of the people's will has been hampered by the necessity of military defense against the opponents of our republic, and by the economic isolation of soviet Russia, which has been one of the weapons of their attacks, together with deliberate disruption of our means of communication with important food centers, as well as destruction of food stores; and all this has greatly increased the sufferings of our people. By tremendous efforts and by efficient consolidation of all economic means at its disposal, my government has been able to stave off the worst features of this situation. The fact that economic disruption, together with starvation, and lack of even the bare necessities of life, prevails so poignantly, and all the more in such parts of the former Russian Empire as have been for some time in the hands of the opponents of our republic and which have had contact with the outside world, clearly testifies that the soviet rule is much more capable of insuring means of existence to the people than any pretenders to the power in Russia.

In view of all that is stated above, I venture to say that the soviet government has given all such proofs of stability, permanence, popular support, and constructive ability as ever have been required from any Government in the world as a basis for political recognition and commercial intercourse. I am confident that people outside of Russia are becoming as convinced as the Russian people themselves of the futility of efforts to overthrow the soviet government. Such efforts lead only to unnecessary bloodshed, and, if successful in any part of Russia, lead to the temporary establishment of a bloody, monarchical autocracy, which cannot maintain itself and even the temporary existence of which will lead to bloodshed and misery.

Fully realizing that the economic prosperity of the world at large, including soviet Russia, depends on uninterrupted interchange of products between various countries the soviet government of Russia desires to establish commercial relations with other countries, and especially with the United States. The soviet government is prepared at once to buy from the United States vast amounts of finished products, on terms of payment fully satisfactory to the parties concerned. My government also desires to reach an agreement in respect to export from Russia of raw material needed by other countries and of which considerable surpluses exist in Russia. In order to re-establish the economic integrity of Russia and to insure uninterrupted commercial relations, the Russian workers and peasants, as Mr. Litvinoff stated in the above quoted note, "are prepared to go any length of concessions as far as the real interests of other countries are concerned, of course with the understanding that no agreements entered into should impair the sovereignty of the Russian people, as expressed by the Russian socialist federal soviet republic."

On the part of the Russian socialist federal soviet republic there thus exist no obstacles to the establishment of proper relations with other countries, especially with the United States. The soviet government of Russia is willing to open its doors to citizens of other countries for peaceful pursuit of opportunity, and it invites any scrutiny and investigation of its conditions, which I feel sure will prove that peace and prosperity in Russia —and elsewhere, in as far as the prosperity of Russia affects other countries—may be attained by the cessation of the present policy of non-intercourse with the soviet Russia, and by the establishment of material and intellectual intercourse.

Russia is now prepared to purchase in the American market great quantities of the following commodities, commensurate with the needs of 150,000,000 people: Railroad supplies, agricultural implements and machinery, tools, mining machinery and supplies, electrical supplies, printing machinery, textile manufactures, shoes and clothing, fats and canned meats, rubber goods, typewriters and office supplies, automobiles and trucks, chemicals, medical supplies, etc.

Russia is prepared to sell the following commodities: Flax, hemp, hides, bristles, furs, lumber, grain, platinum, metals, and minerals.

The Russian government, in the event of trade being opened with the United States, is prepared to place at once in banks in Europe and America, gold to the amount of $200,000,000, to cover the price of initial purchases.

To insure the basis for credits for additional Russian purchases in the United States, I suggest that detailed negotiations with my government will evolve propositions fully acceptable for this purpose.

I am empowered by my government to negotiate for the speedy opening of commercial relations for the mutual benefit of Russia and America, and I shall be glad to discuss details at the earliest opportunity.

L. A. MARTENS,
Representative in the United States of the
Russian Socialist Federal Soviet Republic.
S. NUORTEVA,
Secretary of the Bureau of the Representative.

[139.]

Letter from Dr. Nansen to President Wilson, April 3, 1919.

(Hearings before the Committee on Foreign Relations, United States Senate, 66th Congress, 1919, Senate Doc. 106, p. 1264.)

Paris, April 3, 1919.

My dear Mr. President:

The present food situation in Russia, where hundreds of thousands of people are dying monthly from sheer starvation and disease, is one of the problems now uppermost in all men's minds. As it appears that no solution of this food and disease question has so far been reached in any direction, I would like to make a suggestion from a neutral point of view for the alleviation of this gigantic misery on purely humanitarian grounds.

It would appear to me possible to organize a purely humanitarian commission for the provisioning of Russia, the foodstuffs and medical supplies to be paid for, perhaps, to some considerable extent by Russia itself, the justice of distribution to be guaranteed by such a commission, the membership of the commission to be comprised of Norwegian, Swedish, and possibly Dutch, Danish, and Swiss nationalities. It does not appear that the existing authorities in Russia would refuse the intervention of such a commission of wholly non-political order, devoted solely to the humanitarian purpose of saving life. If thus organized upon the lines of the Belgian Relief Commission, it would raise no question of political recognition or negotiations between the Allies with the existing authorities in Russia.

I recognize keenly the large political issues involved, and I would be glad to know under what conditions you would approve such an enterprise and whether such commission could look for actual support in finance, shipping, and food and medical supplies from the United States Government.

I am addressing a similar note to Messrs. Orlando, Clemenceau, and Lloyd George. Believe me, my dear Mr. President,
Yours most respectfully,
FRIDJOF NANSEN.
His Excellency the President,
11 Place des Etats-Unis, Paris.

[140.]

Reply of President Wilson, Premiers Clemenceau, Lloyd-George, and Orlando to Dr. Nansen, April 17, 1919.

(Hearings before the Committee on Foreign Relations, United States Senate, 66th Congress, 1919, Senate Doc. 106, p. 1269.)

Dear Sir:

The misery and suffering in Russia described in your letter of April 3 appeals to the sympathies of all peoples. It is shocking to humanity that millions of men, women, and children lack the food and the necessities which make life endurable.

The Governments and peoples whom we represent would be glad to co-operate, without thought of political, military, or financial advantage, in any proposal which would relieve this situation in Russia. It seems to us that such a commission as you propose would offer a practical means of achieving the beneficent results you have in view, and could not, either in its conception or its operation, be considered as having any other aim than the "humanitarian purpose of saving life."

There are great difficulties to be overcome, political difficulties, owing to the existing situation in Russia, and difficulties of supply and transport. But if the existing local governments of Russia are as willing as the Governments and people whom we represent to see succor and relief given to the stricken peoples of Russia, no political obstacle will remain.

There will remain, however, the difficulties of supply, finance, and transport which we have mentioned, and also the problem of distribution in Russia itself. The problem of supply we can ourselves hope to solve, in connection with the advice and cooperation of such a commission as you propose. The problem of finance would seem to us to fall upon the Russian authorities. The problem of transport of supplies to Russia we can hope to meet with the assistance of your own and other neutral governments whose interests should be as great as our own and whose losses have been far less. The problems of transport in Russia and of distribution can be solved only by the people of Russia themselves, with the assistance, advice, and supervision of your commission.

Subject to your supervision, the problem of distribution should be solely under the control of the people of Russia themselves. The people in each locality should be given, as under the régime of the Belgian Relief Commission, the fullest opportunity to advise your commission upon the methods and the personnel by which their community is to be relieved. In no other circumstances could it be believed that the purpose of this relief was humanitarian, and not political; under no other condition could it be certain that the hungry would be fed.

That such a course would involve cessation of all hostilities within definitive lines in the territory of Russia is obvious. And the cessation of hostilities would, necessarily, involve a complete suspension of the transfer of troops and military material of all sorts to and within Russian territory. Indeed, relief to Russia which did not mean a return to a state of peace would be futile and would be impossible to consider.

Under such conditions as we have outlined, we believe that your plan could be successfully carried into effect, and we should be prepared to give it our full support.

V. E. ORLANDO.
D. LLOYD GEORGE.
WOODROW WILSON.
G. CLEMENCEAU.

[141.]

The Soviet Government's Reply to the Nansen Offer.

(New York *Nation*, November 8, 1919.)

5/7/19.
To Mr. Fritjof Nansen,
   Hotel Continental,
      Paris.
Sir:

Your very kind message of April 17, containing your exchange of letters with the Council of Four, reached us only on May 4 by way of the Nauen wireless station, and was at once given to the People's Commissariat of Social Welfare for thorough examination. I wish in the name of the Russian Soviet Government to convey to you our heartiest thanks for the warm interest you manifest in the well-being of the Russian people. Great indeed are the sufferings and privations inflicted upon the Russian people by the inhuman blockade of the Associated and so-called neutral Powers and by the incessant wars forced upon it against its will. If left in peace and allowed free development, Soviet Russia would soon be able to restore her national production, to regain her economic strength, to provide for her own needs, and to be helpful to other countries. But in the present situation in which she has been put by the implacable policy of the Associated Powers, help in foodstuffs from abroad would be most welcome to Russia, and the Russian Soviet Government appreciates most thankfully your human and heartfelt response to her sufferings, and, considering the universal respect surrounding your person, will be especially glad to enter into communication with you for the realization of your scheme of help, which you emphasize as being purely humanitarian.

On this basis of a humanitarian work of help to suffering people, we would be desirous to do everything in our power to further the realization of your project. Unfortunately your benevolent intentions, which you yourself indicate as being based upon purely humanitarian grounds, and which, according to your letter, must be realized by a commission of wholly non-political character, have been mixed up by others with political purposes. In the letter addressed to you by the four Powers your scheme is represented as involving cessation of hostilities and of transfer of troops and war material. We regret very much that your original intentions have thus been fundamentally disfigured by the Governments of the Associated Powers. We need not explain to you that military operations which obviously have in view to change the external or internal conditions of the involved countries, belong wholly to the domain of politics, and that likewise cessation of hostilities, which means preventing the belligerent who has every reason to expect successes from obtaining them, is also a purely political act. Thus your sincerely charitable intentions have been misused by others in order to cover such purposes which are obviously political, with the semblance of an action originally humanitarian only. Being ready to lend every assistance to your scheme, so far as it bears the character you have ascribed to it in your letter, we at the same time do not wish to be the objects of foul play; and knowing that you in the same degree as ourselves mean business and wish really to attain the proposed aim, we would like to ask you whether this intermixture of heterogeneous purposes has been finally adopted by yourself. We expect that we will be able to make it clear to you that in order to realize your intentions this intermixture must be carefully avoided. You are no doubt aware that the cessation of the wars forced upon the Russian people is likewise the object of our most warm desire. It must be known to you that we have many times proposed to the Associated Governments to enter into negotiations in order to put an end to the present bloodshed, and that we have even agreed to take part in the conference at Prinkipo, notwithstanding the extremely unfavorable conditions proposed to us, and also that we were the only party to accept it. We responded in the same peace-loving sense to overtures made by one of the Great Powers. The Prinkipo conference was frustrated not by us but by our adversaries, the protégées of the Associated Powers, the counter-revolutionary Governments of Kolchak, Denikin, and the others.

These are the tools with the help of which the Entente Governments are waging war upon us and are endeavoring to attain our destruction; and wherever they are victorious their victory means the triumph of the most extreme barbarity and bestiality, streams of blood, untold sufferings for the laboring masses, and domination of the wildest reaction. Kolchak from the east, Denikin from the south, the Rumanian feudals, the most reactionary Polish and Finnish militarists, the German barons, and Esthonian White Guards from the west, and Russian White Guard bands from the north—these are the enemies whom the Entente Governments move against Soviet Russia, and against whom as against Entente troops we are carrying on a desperate struggle with ever growing success. The so-called Governments of Kolchak and Denikin are purely monarchical; all power belongs there to the wildest adherents of Czarism; extreme Czarist papers are in every way supported by them; Czarist hymns are constantly sung at their ceremonies; the so-called Constitution of Kolchak is in reality monarchical; among their soldiers they distribute only Czarist literature. Under the domination of Denikin the adherents of the Constituent Assembly are imprisoned or shot. Pogrom-making literature is being widely distributed by these so-called Governments, and whenever Jews come under their domination they are the object of the most horrible bestialities. In the west, the Polish legionaries and the troops of the Ukrainian counter-revolutionary Petlura, who are both supported and even directed by Entente officers, have perpetrated such massacres of Jews, which by far surpass the most horrible misdeeds of the Black Hundreds of old Czarism. As the Russian Red Cross in its appeal to the International Red Cross on April 28 elaborately states, whole villages, whole towns, were turned to ruins. Neither sex nor age was spared, and in numerous places the whole Jewish population was literally wiped out by these troops headed by Entente generals and officers. In the realms of Kolchak and Denikin everything that was gained by the peasants through the revolution is being taken back from them. Kolchak declares solemnly in his manifestoes that peasants must not have in their possession land taken by force from the nobility; he orders in his decrees that the seizure of the land of the gentry by the peasants should be prosecuted as a serious crime; he crushes the resistance of the peasants by wholesale massacres during which in some parts of Siberia many thousands of peasants were killed *en masse*. For the worker his domination means every possible persecution, oppression, wholesale arrests, and in many cases wholesale shootings, so that in some towns the workers were simply wiped out by the enraged ex-Czarist officers who are at the head of Kolchak's troops. The horrors perpetrated by these Kolchak officers defy every description, and their victims are innumerable, including all that is progressive, all that is free-thinking in Siberia. Inebriated officers are torturing, flogging, tormenting in every way the unfortunate laboring population under their dominion, and to be a worker means to be predestined to be the object of their brutalities.

These are the adversaries against whom we are engaged in a desperate struggle, and whom the Associated Governments are in every way supporting, providing them with war material, foodstuffs, financial help, military commanders, and political advisers, and on the north and east fronts sending their own troops to help them. In the hands of these barbarous bands Entente rifles and Entente cannon are sending death to the Russian workers and peasants struggling for their life and liberty. The same Entente Governments are the real source of the military supplies with the help of which our Polish, Rumanian, Finnish, and other adversaries from the west are uninterruptedly attacking us, and it was officially declared in the French Chamber of Deputies and in the British House of Commons that the policy of the Entente is now to send against Soviet Russia the armies of these nationalities. An American radio of May 6, sent from Lyons, says most emphatically that the Entente encourages the movement of the troops headed by the Russian counter-revolutionary general Judenitch, which presumably threaten Petrograd; that the Entente expects that the Bolsheviki will be forced to withdraw to Moscow, and that the Associated Governments intend in connection herewith to abandon your plan of revictualling Russia. While declaring that they have abandoned the idea of intervention, the Associated Governments are in reality carrying on the most reckless interventionist policy, and even the American Government, despite all the statements to the contrary published in the American press, seems at present to be wholly dominated by the implacable hostility of the Clemenceau Ministry against Soviet Russia.

This being the case we are in a position to discuss cessation of hostilities only if we discuss the whole problem of our relations to our adversaries—that is, in the first place, to the Associated Governments. That means to discuss peace, and to open real negotiations bearing upon the true reasons for the war waged upon us, and upon those conditions that can bring us lasting peace. We were always ready to enter into peace negotiations, and we are ready to do it now as before. We will be glad to begin discussing these questions, but, of course, directly with the other belligerents—that is, with the Associated Governments or else with the persons empowered by the latter. But it is, of course, impossible for us to make any concessions referring to these fundamental problems of our existence under the disguise of a presumably humanitarian work. This latter must remain purely humanitarian and non-political, and in this sense we will welcome every proposal from your side made to us in the spirit of your letter sent by you to the Council of Four on April 3. To these wholly non-political proposals we respond most gladly. We thank you most heartily for your good intentions. We are ready to give you every possibility of controlling the realization of such a humanitarian scheme. We will, of course, cover all the expenses of this work and the cost of the foodstuffs; and we can pay, if you desire, with Russian goods. But seeing that your original plan has been so unfortunately disfigured, and considering that the most complex and difficult questions thus created must first be thoroughly elucidated, we would suggest that you take the necessary steps to enable delegates of our Government to meet you and your collaborators abroad, and to discuss those questions, and we ask you kindly to indicate the time and the place for this conference between our delegates and the leaders of your Commission, and what guarantees can be obtained for the free passage of our delegates through countries influenced by the Entente.

CHICHERIN,
People's Commissary of Foreign Affairs.

[142.]

Statement by Secretary Lansing conveying recognition of Finland, May 7, 1919.[1]

(*New York Times*, May 8, 1919.)

In view of the fact that the people of Finland have established a representative Government, the Government of the United States of America declares that it recognizes the Government so constituted as the de facto Government of an independent Finland.

[1] A similar announcement had been made on behalf of Great Britain in the House of Commons the day before.

[143.]
Note from the Supreme Council to Admiral Kolchak, May 26, 1919.

(*New York Times*, June 13, 1919.)

The Allied and Associated Powers feel that the time has come when it is necessary for them once more to make clear the policy they propose to pursue in regard to Russia.

It has always been a cardinal axiom of the Allied and Associated Powers to avoid interference in the internal affairs of Russia. Their original intervention was made for the sole purpose of assisting those elements in Russia which wanted to continue the struggle against German autocracy and to free their country from German rule, and in order to rescue the Czechoslovaks from the danger of annihilation at the hands of the Bolshevist forces.

Since the signature of the armistice on November 11, 1918, they have kept forces in various parts of Russia. Munitions and supplies have been sent those associated with them at a very considerable cost. No sooner however did the peace conference assemble than they endeavored to bring peace and order to Russia by inviting representatives of all the warring Governments within Russia to meet them in the hope that they might be able to arrange a permanent solution of the Russian problem.

This proposal and the later offer to relieve the suffering millions of Russia, broke down through the refusal of the Soviet government to accept the fundamental condition of suspending hostilities while negotiations for the work of relief were proceeding.

Some of the Allied and Associated Governments are now being pressed to withdraw their troops and to incur no further expense in Russia on the ground that continued intervention shows no prospect of producing an early settlement. They are prepared however to continue their assistance on the lines laid down below, provided they are satisfied that it will really help the Russian people to liberty, self-government and peace.

The Allied and Associated Governments now wish to declare formally that the object of their policy is to restore peace within Russia by enabling the Russian people to resume control of their own affairs through the instrumentality of a freely elected constituent assembly, and to restore peace along its frontiers by arranging for the settlement of disputes in regard to the boundaries of the Russian State and its relations with its neighbors through the peaceful arbitration of the League of Nations.

They are convinced by their experience of the last twelve months that it is not possible to attain these ends by dealing with the Soviet Government of Moscow. They are therefore disposed to assist the government of Admiral Kolchak and his associates with munitions, supplies, and food to establish themselves as the government of all Russia, provided they receive from them definite guarantees that their policy has the same object in view as the Allied and Associated Powers.

With this object they would ask Admiral Kolchak and his associates whether they would agree to the following as the conditions under which they would accept continued assistance from the Allied and Associated Powers.

In the first place as soon as they reach Moscow that they will summon a constituent assembly elected by a free, secret, and democratic franchise, as the supreme legislature for Russia, to which the government of Russia must be responsible, or, if at that time order is not sufficiently restored, they will summon the Constituent Assembly, elected in 1917, to sit until such time as new elections are possible.

Secondly,—that throughout the areas which they at present control they will permit free elections in the normal course for all free and legally constituted assemblies, such as municipalities, Zemstvos, etc.

Thirdly,—that they will countenance no attempt to revive the special privilege of any class or order in Russia. The Allied and Associated Powers have noted with satisfaction the solemn declaration made by Admiral Kolchak and his associates, that they have no intention of restoring the former land system. They feel that the principles to be followed in the solution of this and other internal questions must be left to free decision of the Russian Constituent Assembly. But they wish to be assured that those whom they are prepared to assist stand for the civil and religious liberty of all Russian citizens and will make no attempt to re-introduce the régime which the revolution has destroyed.

Fourthly,—that the independence of Finland and Poland be recognized, and that in the event of the frontiers and other relations between Russia and these countries not being settled by agreement, they will be referred to the arbitration of the League of Nations.

Fifthly,—that if a solution of the relations between Esthonia, Latvia, Lithuania, and the Caucasian and Trans-Caspian territories and Russia is not speedily reached by agreement, the settlement will be made in consultation and co-operation with the League of Nations, and that until such settlement is made, the government of Russia agrees to recognize these territories as autonomous and to confirm the relations which may exist between their de facto Governments and the Allied and Associated Governments.

Sixthly,—that the right of the Peace Conference to determine the future of the Rumanian part of Bessarabia be recognized.

Seventhly,—that as soon as a government for Russia has been constituted on a democratic basis, Russia should join the League of Nations and co-operate with other members in the limitation of armaments and military organization throughout the world.

Finally,—that they abide by the declaration made by Admiral Kolchak on November 27, 1918, in regard to Russia's national debt.[1]

The Allied and Associated Powers will be glad to learn as soon as possible whether the government of Admiral Kolchak and his associates is prepared to accept these conditions, and also whether in the event of acceptance they will undertake to form a single government and army command as soon as the military situation makes it possible.

G. CLEMENCEAU.
LLOYD GEORGE.
ORLANDO.
WOODROW WILSON.
SAIONJI.

[1] (Russian Bonds Hearing before the Committee on Expenditures in the State Department on H. R. 132, Part I, 1919.)

The Chairman:—In this resolution it is charged that the bond-holders have used their influence and are still attempting to influence the retention of American troops in Russia, to the end that some agreement may be reached with whatever government is established there to recognize these bonds and to pay the principal and interest of the same. What do you know about that?

Mr. Polk:—No one has ever spoken to the department on the subject and it has not been necessary because we are as convinced as we can be that no government can exist in Russia that does not recognize its international obligations, and even the Bolshevik government has stated that it would recognize Russia's international obligations, so that it is not a live question.

[144.]

Admiral Kolchak's Reply to the Supreme Council, June 4, 1919.

(*New York Times*, June 14, 1919.)

The Government over which I preside has been happy to learn that the reply, as made public to-night, in regard to Russia, is in perfect accordance with the task which the Russian Government itself has undertaken, that government being anxious above all things to re-establish peace in the country and to assure our destiny in freedom by means of a constituent assembly. I appreciate highly the interest shown by the powers as regards the national movement and consider their wish to make certain the political convictions with which we are inspired as legitimate. I am therefore ready to confirm once more my previous declarations which I have always regarded as irrevocable.

1. On November 18, 1918, I assumed power and I should not retain that power one day longer than required by the interests of the country; my first thought at the moment when the Bolsheviki are definitely crushed will be to fix the date for the elections of the Constituent Assembly. A commission is now at work on direct preparation for them on the basis of universal suffrage. Considering myself as responsible for that Constituent Assembly I shall hand over to it all my powers in order that it may freely determine the system of government; I have, however, taken the oath to do this before the Supreme Russian Tribunal, the guardian of legality.

All my efforts are aimed at concluding the civil war as soon as possible by crushing Bolshevism in order to put the Russian people in a position to express its free will. Any prolongation of the struggle would only postpone that moment; the Government, however, does not consider itself authorized to substitute for the inalienable right of free and legal elections the mere establishment of the Assembly of 1917, which was elected under a régime of Bolshevist violence, and a majority of whose members are now in the ranks of the Soviet. It is through the legally elected constituent assembly alone which my Government will do its utmost to convoke properly, that there would belong the sovereign rights of deciding the problems of the

Russian State both in the internal and external affairs of the country.

2. We gladly consent to discuss at once with the powers all international questions, and in doing so shall aim at the free and peaceful development of the peoples, the limitation of armaments and the measures calculated to prevent new wars, of which the League of Nations is the highest expression.

The Russian Government thinks however that it could recall the fact that the final sanction of the decisions which may be taken in the name of Russia will belong to the Constituent Assembly. Russia cannot now and cannot in the future ever be anything but a democratic state where all questions involving modifications of the territorial frontiers and of external relations must be ratified by a representative body which is the national expression of the people's sovereignty.

3. Considering the creation of a unified Polish State to be one of the chief of the normal and just consequences of the world war, the Government thinks itself justified in confirming the independence of Poland proclaimed by the Provisional Russian Government of 1917, all the pledges and decrees of which we have accepted. The final solution of the question of delimiting the frontiers between Russia and Poland must however in conformity with the principles set forth here above, be postponed until a meeting of the Constituent Assembly. We are disposed at once to recognize the de facto government of Finland, but the final solution of the Finnish institution must belong to the Constituent Assembly.

4. We are fully disposed at once to prepare for the solution of the questions concerning the fate of the national groups in Esthonia, Letonia, Lithuania, and of the Caucasian and trans-Caucasian countries, and we have every reason to believe that a prompt settlement will be made, seeing that the Government is assuring at the present time the autonomy of the various nationalities. It goes without saying that the limits and conditions of these autonomous institutions will be settled separately as regards each.

Even in the case difficulties should arise in regard to the solution of these various institutions the Government is ready to have recourse to the collaboration and good offices of the League of Nations with a view of arriving at a satisfactory settlement.

5. The above principle implying the ratification of the

agreements by the Constituent Assembly, should obviously be applied to the question of Bessarabia.

6. The Russian Government once more repeats its declaration of the 27 November, 1918, by which it accepted the burden of the national debt of Russia.

7. As regards the question of internal politics which can only interest the Powers in so far as they reflect the political tendencies of the Russian Government, I make a point of repeating that there cannot be a return to the régime which existed in Russia before February, 1917. The provisional solutions which my Government has adopted in regard to the agrarian questions aim at satisfying the interests of the great mass of the population and are inspired by the conviction that Russia can only be flourishing and strong when the millions of Russian peasants receive all guarantees for the possession of the land.

Similarly as regards the régime to be applied to the liberated territories the Government, far from fearing obstacles in the way of the free elections of local assemblies, municipalities, and Zemstvos, regards the activities of these bodies and also the development of the people in self-government as the necessary conditions for the reconstruction of the country, and is already actually giving them its support by all the means at its disposal.

8. Having set themselves the task of re-establishing order and justice and insuring individual security to the population which is tired of trials and exactions, the Government affirms the equality before the law of all citizens without any special privilege (omission here) all shall receive without distinction of origin or religion, the protection of the state and of the law.

The Government whose head I am, is concentrating all the forces and all the reserves at its disposal in order to accomplish the task which it has set itself; and at this decisive hour I speak in the name of all national Russia. I am confident that Bolshevism once crushed, satisfactory solutions would be found for all questions which equally concern all those populations whose existence is bound up with that of Russia.

KOLCHAK.

[145.]

Acknowledgment by Supreme Council of Admiral Kolchak's Reply, June 12, 1919.

(*New York Times, June* 13, 1919)

The Allied and Associated Powers wish to acknowledge the receipt of Admiral Kolchak's reply to their note of May 26. They welcome the terms of that reply, which seem to them to be in substantial agreement with the propositions they had made and to contain satisfactory assurances for the freedom and self-government of the Russian People and their neighbors.

They are therefore willing to extend to Admiral Kolchak and his associates the support set forth in their original letter.

(signed) LLOYD GEORGE.
WILSON.
CLEMENCEAU.
MAKINO.

[146.]

Reply of President Wilson to a Senate Resolution concerning the American troops in Siberia, June 26, 1919.

(*State Department Russian Series, No. 4*, p. 5.)

For the information of the Senate and in response to the resolution adopted June 23, 1919, requesting the President to inform the Senate, if not incompatible with the public interest, of the reasons for sending United States soldiers to Siberia, the duties that are to be performed by these soldiers; how long they are to remain and generally to advise the Senate of the policy of the United States Government in respect to Siberia and the maintenance of United States soldiers there, I have the honor to say that the decision to send American troops to Siberia was announced to the press on August 5, 1918, in a statement from the acting Secretary of State.

This measure was taken in conjunction with Japan and in concert of purpose with the other Allied Powers, first of all to save the Czechoslovak armies which were threatened with destruction by hostile armies apparently organized by, and often largely composed of, enemy prisoners of war. The second purpose in view was to steady any efforts of the Russians at self-defense, or the establishment of law and order in which they might be willing to accept assistance.

Two regiments of Infantry with auxiliary troops, about 8,000 effectives, comprising a total of approximately 10,000 men, were sent under the command of Major General William S. Graves. The troops began to arrive at Vladivostok in September, 1918.

Considerably larger forces were dispatched by Japan at about the same time, and much smaller forces by other of the Allied Powers. The net result was the successful reunion of the separated Czechoslovak armies, and the substantial elimination in Eastern Siberia of the active efforts of enemy prisoners of war. A period of relative quiet then ensued.

In February, 1919, as a conclusion of negotiations begun early in the summer of 1918, the United States accepted a plan proposed by Japan for the supervision of the Siberian Railways by an international committee, under which committee Mr. John F. Stevens would assume the operation of the Russian Railway Service corps. In this connection it is to be recalled that Mr. John F. Stevens, in response to a request of the Provisional Government of Russia, went to Russia in the spring of 1917. A few months later he was made official adviser to the Minister of Ways of Communication at Petrograd under the Provisional Government.

At the request of the Provisional Government, and with the support of Mr. John F. Stevens, there was organized the so-called Russian Railway Service corps, composed of American engineers.

As originally organized the personnel of this corps constituted fourteen skeleton division units as known in this country, the idea being that these skeleton units would serve as practical advisers and assistants in fourteen different sections of the Siberian Railway, and assist the Russians by their knowledge of long haul problems as known in this country, and which are the rule and not the exception in Siberia.

Owing to the Bolshevist uprising, and the general chaotic conditions, neither Mr. Stevens nor the Russian Railway Service corps was able to begin work in Siberia until March, 1918. They have been able to operate effectively only since the railway plan was adopted in February, 1919.

The most recent report from Mr. Stevens shows that on parts

of the Chinese Eastern and Trans-Baikal Railway he is now running six trains a day each way, while a little while ago they were only able to run that many trains per week.

In accepting the Railway Plan (in February, 1919), it was provided that some protection should be given by the Allied forces. Mr. Stevens stated frankly that he would not undertake the arduous task before him unless he could rely upon support from American troops in an emergency. Accordingly, as provided in the railway plan and with the approval of the Inter-Allied committee, the military commanders in Siberia have established troops where it is necessary to maintain order at different parts of the line.

The American forces under General Graves are understood to be protecting parts of the line near Vladivostok and also in the section around Verkhne-Udinsk. There is also understood to be a small body of American troops at Harbin. The exact location from time to time of American troops, is, however, subject to change by the direction of General Graves.

The instructions to General Graves direct him not to interfere in Russian affairs, but to support Mr. Stevens wherever necessary. The Siberian Railway is not only the main artery for transportation in Siberia, but it is the only open access to European Russia to-day. The population of Siberia whose resources have almost been exhausted by the long years of war and the chaotic conditions which have existed there, can be protected from a further period of chaos and anarchy only by the restoration and maintenance of traffic on the Siberian Railway.

Partisan bands under leaders having no settled connection with any organized government, and bands under leaders whose allegiance to any settled authority is apparently temporary and transitory are constantly menacing the operation of the Railway and the safety of its permanent structure.

The situation of the people of Siberia, meantime, is that they have no shoes or warm clothing; they are pleading for agricultural machinery, and for many of the simpler articles of commerce upon which their own domestic economy depends, and which are necessary to fruitful and productive industry among them. Having contributed their quota to the Russian armies which fought the Central Empires for three and one half years, they now look to the Allies and to the United States for economic assistance.

The populations of Western Siberia and the forces of Admiral Kolchak are entirely dependent upon those railways.

The Russian authorities in this country have succeeded in shipping large quantities of Russian supplies to Siberia and the Secretary of War is now contracting with the great co-operative societies which operate throughout European and Asiatic Russia to ship further supplies to meet the needs of the civilian population. The Kolchak Government is also endeavoring to arrange for the purchase of medical and other Red Cross supplies from the War Department, and the American Red Cross is itself attempting the forms of relief for which it is organized.

All elements of the population in Siberia look to the United States for assistance. This assistance cannot be given to the population of Siberia, and ultimately to Russia, if the purpose entertained for two years to restore railway traffic is abandoned. The presence of American troops is a vital element in this effort. The services of Mr. Stevens depend upon it, and, a point of serious moment, the plan proposed by Japan expressly provides that Mr. Stevens and all foreign railway experts shall be withdrawn when the troops are withdrawn.

From these observations it will be seen that the purpose of continuance of American troops in Siberia is that we, with the concurrence of the great Allied Powers, may keep open a necessary artery of trade, and extend to the vast population of Siberia the economic aid essential to it in peace time, but indispensable under the conditions which have followed the prolonged and exhausting participation by Russia in the war against the Central Powers.

This participation was obviously of incalulable value to the Allied cause, and in a very particular way commends the exhausted people who suffered from it to such assistance as we can render to bring about their industrial and economic rehabilitation.

[147.]

Protest from Russian Soviet Government to the State Department, received through Swedish Channels, June 24, 1919.

(*New York Times*, July 2, 1919.)

The Commissariat for Foreign Affairs has learned with indignation of the arrest of Mr. Martens, its representative, in New

York. The Commissariat wishes to point out that all the Diplomatic and Consular representatives of the American Government in Russia, up to the departure in September last, have been treated by the Soviet authorities with the utmost courtesy, in spite of the fact that since June of last year the American Government openly sided with all the Russian and foreign dark forces, ranged against the workers and peasants of Russia with the sole object of crushing the great revolution and restoring the Czarist and bureaucratic capitalistic rule.

Even after American troops had landed on Russian territory and actively partaken in military operations against the Russian laboring people, not a single American citizen has been molested in Russia. Moreover American officials and journalists have been allowed admittance into Russia and accorded every courtesy and all possible facilities and privileges. The arrest of Mr. Martens is the more surprising and unjustifiable, as he acted openly as the representative of Soviet Russia without calling forth any objection or protestation on the part of the American Government.

The Russian Government feels that his arrest may not be an isolated case, but form part of a general persecution of Russian citizens loyal to their people's Government and demands the cessation of such persecutions and immediate release of Mr. Martens.

The Soviet Government expects to be accordingly informed at an early date and not to be compelled reluctantly to take reprisals against American citizens to be found on Russian territory.   TCHICHERIN,
People's Commissary for Foreign Affairs.

[148.]

Reply to Russian Protest cabled by Mr. Phillips, Assistant Secretary of State to American Legation at Stockholm, July 1, 1919.

(*New York Times*, July 2, 1919.)

Please inform proper Swedish authorities at once as follows:
The statement purporting to emanate from Moscow is wholly untrue. Mr. Martens has not been arrested, nor does this Government contemplate any action against law-abiding Russian citizens in this country. It is understood that Mr. Martens

claims official status as the representative of a régime at Moscow which the United States has not recognized as a Government. At the same time he is a German citizen, having voluntarily so declared himself when he entered this country in 1916.

This Government has not forgotten the unwarrantable arrest and detentions for months of Consul Tredwell and the illegal and unjustifiable imprisonment under severe hardships of Vice Consuls Durri and Leonard, contrary to the fundamental practice of civilized nations. Nor has it forgotten that an American citizen, Kalamatiano, has been held in prison at Moscow for months under sentence of death without proper trial and without opportunity for his Government to assist him.

The Government of the United States now views with grave concern the reported threat of the authorities at Moscow to take further illegal measures in the form of reprisals against American citizens in Russia.

Such a course if taken would be certain to arouse in the United States an overwhelming public sentiment of indignation against the authorities at Moscow responsible for such acts.

[149.]

Letter from Secretary Lansing to the Lithuanian National Council, on the Question of Recognition, October 15, 1919.

(*New York Times*, February 10, 1920.)

State Department,
Washington, October 15, 1919.

Gentlemen:

The Department has received your letters of October 2 and 9, 1919, on the subject of the provisional recognition of Lithuania.

The question of the future status of Lithuania has been given careful consideration. As you are aware, the Government of the United States is traditionally sympathetic with the national aspirations of dependent peoples. On the other hand, it has been thought unwise and unfair to prejudice in advance of the establishment of orderly, constitutional government in Russia the principle of Russian unity as a whole.

Accordingly, when the President, in common with the other heads of the allied and associated Governments, proffered Admiral Kolchak aid in bringing about in Russia a situation conducive to the establishment of orderly, constitutional government it was especially stipulated, inter alia, that failing an immediate agreement between Lithuania and the new Russian Government an arrangement would be made in consultation and cooperation with the League of Nations and that, pending such an arrangement, Russia must agree to recognize Lithuania as autonomous and to confirm the relations which might exist between the local Government of Lithuania and the allied and associated Governments.

Copies of the note to Admiral Kolchak and his reply are enclosed for your information.

It is believed that this arrangement assures the autonomous development of Lithuania, together with the other nationalities comprised within the former Russian Empire and wisely leaves to a future adjustment the determination of the relations which shall exist between them and the new Russian Government.

I am confident your council will recognize the justice of this attitude.

I am, Gentlemen,
Your obedient servant,
ROBERT LANSING.

[150.]

Note from the Allies to the German Government, inviting Germany to participate in the Blockade of Bolshevik Russia.

(*New York Times*, October 31, 1919.[1])

The President of the Peace Conference has been requested by the Conference to inform the neutral Governments of a deci-

[1] The same paper contains a London dispatch dated October 30, as follows:

"A wireless dispatch received from Berlin says Germany's reply to the Entente declines to participate in a blockade of Soviet Russia, because Germany does not believe the blockade would achieve the desired purpose.

"The dispatch adds that Germany, however, is prepared to assist in any measures against Bolshevism which are calculated to obtain the desired end.

"The German note argues that coercive measures by foreign countries are regarded in Russia as serving the interests of reaction, which is hated by all Russian democratic elements more than Bolshevism. Therefore, it is to be feared that a blockade will only produce favorable ground for the growth of Bolshevism.

"The note also points out that according to the articles of the League of Nations, circumstances at the present time would not justify a blockade."

sion taken by the Supreme Council of the allied and associated powers in regard to economic pressure which is to be exercised on Bolshevist Russia.

The German Government is asked to take measures similar to those indicated.

The avowed hostility of the Bolsheviki toward all Governments and their international program of revolution which they are spreading abroad constitute grave danger for the national security of all powers. Every increase of strength of the Bolsheviki would increase the danger and would be contrary to the desire of all peoples who are seeking to re-establish peace and social order.

It is in this spirit that the allied and associated Governments, after studying the commercial relations with Bolshevist Russia, find these relations, indeed, could only be effected through the agency of the chiefs of the Bolshevist Government, who, disposing at will of the products and resources which commercial liberty would bring them, would thereby achieve considerable increase in their tyrannical strength, which they are exercising over the Russian population.

Under these conditions the allied and associated Governments request the Swedish, Norwegian, Danish, Dutch, Finnish, Spanish, Swiss, Mexican, Chilean, Argentinian, Colombian, and Venezuelan Governments to be good enough to make an immediate agreement with them in measures to prevent their nationals from engaging in any commerce with Bolshevist Russia and to assure that this policy will be rigorously executed.

To refuse clearance papers to every ship going to Russian ports in the hands of Bolshevists or coming from said ports.

To establish similar measures for all merchandise destined to be sent to Bolshevist Russia by any other route.

To refuse passports to all persons going to Bolshevist Russia or coming from it, except through understanding with the allied and associated Governments.

It is the disposition, with a view to preventing banks from doing business with Bolshevist Russia, as far as possible to request refusal by each Government to its own nationals of facilities for correspondence with Bolshevist Russia by post, telegraph, or wireless.

The British and French warships in the Gulf of Finland

shall continue to change the route of ships bound for ports of Bolshevist Russia.[1]

[151.]

Reply by Mr. Phillips, Assistant Secretary of State, to Senator Wadsworth, November 4, 1919.

(*State Department Russian Series, No. 2.*)

In reply to your letter of October 20, 1919, concerning the so-called blockade of Petrograd, I beg to inform you that so far as the United States is concerned, no blockade exists. It is the present policy of this Government, however, to refuse export licenses for shipments to Russian territory under Bolshevik control and to refuse clearance papers to American vessels seeking to depart for Petrograd, the only remaining Bolshevik port. As you are aware, these measures cannot be continued after the ratification of peace unless there is new legislation.

The policy of non-intercourse with territory under Bolshevik control is based chiefly on two considerations. It is the declared purpose of the Bolsheviks in Russia to carry revolution throughout the world. They have availed themselves of every opportunity to initiate in the United States a propaganda aimed to bring about the forcible overthrow of our present form of Government.

They have at their disposal in Russia a large quantity of gold, being partly a residue of the former Russian gold reserve and partly a reserve of gold belonging to the Rumanian Government which was stored in Moscow for safe-keeping at the time of the German advance into Rumania. It is considered important that the Bolsheviks should not be given the means through commercial transactions to bring this gold into the United States where it could be used to sustain their propaganda of violence and unreason.

The second consideration relates to the control which the Bolsheviks exercise over the distribution of necessities. All foreign trade has been "nationalized." This means that there can be no dealing except with the Bolshevik authorities. Moreover, since the fall of 1918 the Bolsheviks have maintained a system of discrimination in the distribution of food. The population is divided into categories along occupational and class lines, and

[1] In the Note sent to neutral states the final paragraph was omitted.

receives food, so far as food may be available, in accordance with a scale which is adjusted with a view to the maintenance of the Bolsheviks in power and the fulfillment of their program for the extinction of the middle classes.

The rations given to members of the Red Army is estimated, in the official Bolshevik gazette of February 6, 1919, to be three times the average for the several categories of the civil population. It has seemed altogether inadmissible that food and other necessities of American origin should be allowed to become the means of sustaining such a program of political oppression.

The Government has not been unmindful of the material distress of many innocent people within the Bolshevik lines. An attempt was made last spring to provide for the relief of these people through the co-operation of a neutral commission to be headed by Dr. Nansen. The project failed because the Bolsheviks declined to agree to the cessation of hostilities which was considered an indispensable prerequisite.

The Department of State has subsequently studied other means by which necessities might be provided for the people of Central Russia without being used for purposes of political constraint and also class destruction. No feasible project has yet been found, but the problem continues to receive attention.

In the meantime provision has been made for the immediate relief of the people in any areas which may be freed from Bolshevik control as a result of current military operations. Stores of food estimated to be adequate for the relief of Petrograd for nearly one month were delivered to Russians by the American Relief Administration and are now at Viborg, Finland, whence they can be transported to Petrograd whenever that city may come under the control of authorities with whom it is possible to deal.

Definite arrangements have, moreover, been made with the United States Grain Corporation to provide further shipments of flour for this region, in the event of its liberation, and for the people in the north of Russia, which is under the control of a democratic government.

[152.]

Resolution of Congress of Soviets, December 5, 1919.

(The New York *Nation*, January 17, 1920.)

The Russian Socialist Federative Republic of Soviets desires to live at peace with all people, and to devote all its strength to internal constructive work, in order to perfect the production, transport, and public administration on the basis of a Soviet régime, to the work which has hitherto been hindered by the pressure of German imperialism and subsequently by the Entente intervention and the starvation blockade.

The Government of Workers and Peasants has many times proposed peace to the Entente Powers, notably on August 5, 1918, by means of a letter from the People's Commissariat for Foreign Affairs to the American Consul, Mr. Poole; on October 24 by a note to President Wilson; on November 3 to all the Entente Governments, by the intermediary of representatives of neutral countries; on November 7 in the name of the Sixth Congress of Soviets; on December 23 by a circular note addressed by Citizen Litvinov to the Entente representatives in Sweden, and subsequently by wireless messages on January 12 and 17, 1919; by a note to the Entente Governments on February 24; by a draft agreement drawn up on March 12 with Mr. Bullitt, President Wilson's delegate; and by a declaration made on May 7 by the intermediary of Mr. Nansen.

Completely approving these repeated steps, which have been taken by the Central Executive Committee, by the Council of People's Commissars, and by the People's Commissariat for Foreign Affairs, the Seventh Congress of Soviets once again confirms its unchanging desire for peace by proposing once more to all the Entente Powers—to Great Britain, France, the United States of America, Italy, and Japan, to all together and to each separately—immediately to commence peace negotiations, and charges the Executive Committee, the Council of People's Commissars and the People's Commissariat for Foreign Affairs systematically to continue this peace policy, taking all necessary measures for its success.

KALININ, President.
AVANESSOV, Secretary.

[153.]

Letter from Secretary Lansing to the Lithuanian Executive Committee, January 7, 1920.

(*New York Times*,[1] February 10, 1920.)

State Department,
Washington, January 7, 1920.

Gentlemen:

The receipt is acknowledged of your letter of December 30, 1919, by which you advise the Department that the so-called Provisional Government of the Republic of Lithuania has constituted your committee its diplomatic agent in the United States, and that your committee is prepared to perform all acts which are usually performed by the Embassies or Legations of Foreign Governments, in so far as this can be done consistently with the fact that the so-called Provisional Government of Lithuania has not been recognized by the United States.

You are informed that the Government of the United States not having recognized the so-called Provisional Government of Lithuania, it is not possible to attribute to your committee any diplomatic character.

The Government of the United States appreciates the difficult situation in which many Lithuanians find themselves as a result of the disruption of the Russian Government and is dis-

---

[1] A Washington dispatch dated February 9 in the same issue says:
"The fact that the documents are given out at this time is regarded as strongly indicating that the American Government's policy is being so shaped as to discourage any movement for the dismemberment of Russia, and that except as to the setting up of Finland and Poland as new Governments, the Government at Washington does not intend to recognize any of the many so-called republics or other Governments that have been set up within what was formerly the Russian Empire.

"Something like seventeen so-called Governments have been set up within what was formerly Russia in Europe and Asia. Among them are the so-called Governments of Esthonia, Livonia, Lithuania, Ukrainia, Georgia, Azerbaijain, and Eastern Karelia. A number of these new 'republics' have been seeking recognition from the United States. President Wilson and Secretary Lansing think it unwise and unfair to prejudice in advance of the establishment of orderly, constitutional Government in Russia, the principle of Russian unity as a while. For that reason they do not intend to accord recognition to any of these 'republics' other than Finland and Poland—which are recognized in the Treaty of Versailles— any more than they intend to grant recognition to the so-called Soviet Government."

posed to go to the utmost practicable limits to relieve them from its inconveniences. In the matter of passports it has been provided that persons of Lithuanian origin may depart from the United States on affidavits of identity and nationality, approved by the State Department in lieu of passports, when accompanied by the usual permits of departure.

The Department is glad to deal informally with individuals and groups of individuals which are acting disinterestedly in behalf of the Lithuanian people or any portion of them. Your committee, in common with other representative Lithuanian bodies, may therefore count upon the consideration of the Department in all matters which it may have occasion to take up with it, within the limitations set forth above.

I am, Gentlemen,
Your obedient servant,
ROBERT LANSING.

[154.]

Statement by the Secretary of State regarding the Withdrawal of American Military Forces from Siberia, January 16, 1920.

(*New York Times*, January 17, 1920.)

Decision of the United States Government to withdraw its troops from Eastern Siberia was announced by the Department of State to-day. Under instructions from his Government, the Japanese Ambassador at Washington, on December 8, invited the attention of the Secretary of State to the recent unfavorable development of the situation in Siberia, and inquired whether the United States proposed to maintain the status quo or to proceed to entire or partial withdrawal of its troops, or whether it was ready to send reinforcements in case of need.

Note to Japan.

The Secretary of State has communicated to the Japanese Ambassador the decision of this Government. The full text of the communication follows:

The Government of the United States has given the most careful consideration to the subject matter of the communication from the Japanese Government which was read to the Secretary of State by the Japanese Ambassador on the 8th day of December, and which concerns the recent unfavorable development of the military situation with which Admiral Kolchak's forces have been confronted, and which proposes three alternative courses for the allied and associated powers to take.

The Government of the United States agrees that for it to send a reinforcement of sufficient strength and to act on the offensive in co-operation with anti-Bolshevist forces is impracticable.

The Government of the United States believes that for it to continue to participate in guarding the districts now under allied military protection is also, under present conditions, impracticable, for the reason that an agreement to send reinforcements to such extent as may be required, with a view to maintain the status quo, might involve the Government of the United States in an undertaking of such indefinite character as to be inadvisable. The amount of reinforcement, which might become necessary for the execution of such an agreement might be so great that the Government of the United States would not feel justified in carrying it out.

Consideration has been given, therefore, to the alternative presented by the Government of Japan of entire or partial withdrawal. It will be recalled that the purposes of the expedition, as originally conceived by the United States and expressed in an aide memoire handed to the Japanese Ambassador at Washington, July 17, 1918, were, first, to help the Czechoslovak troops, which had during their retirement along the Siberian railway been attacked by the Bolsheviki and enemy prisoners of war in Siberia, to consolidate their forces and effect their repatriation by way of Vladivostok, and second, to steady any efforts at self-government or self-defense, in which the Russians themselves might be willing to accept assistance.

Not only are the Czechoslovak troops now successfully advancing into Eastern Siberia, but an agreement has been effected between the Governments of Great Britain and the United States providing for their repatriation from Vladivostok. American vessels will begin to arrive at that port by February 1 and a contingent of more than 10,000 Czechoslovak troops can be immediately embarked. It is expected that evacuation will proceed rapidly thereafter and from that date the first purpose for which American soldiers were sent to Siberia may be regarded as accomplished.

With respect to the second purpose, namely, the steadying of efforts at self-government or self-defense on the part of the Russians, the Government of the United States is impressed with the political instability and grave uncertainties of the present situation in Eastern Siberia as described in the aide memoire presented by the Japanese Ambassador December 8, and is disposed to the view that further military effort to assist the Russians in the struggle toward self-government may, in the present situation, lead to complications which would have exactly the opposite effect, prolonging possibly the period of readjustment and involving Japan and the United States in ineffective and needless sacrifices. It is felt accordingly to be unlikely that the second purpose for which American troops were sent to Siberia will be longer served by their presence there.

In view, then, of the fact that the main purposes for which American troops were sent to Siberia are now at an end, and of the considerations set forth in the communication of the Japanese Government of December 8, which subsequent events in Eastern Siberia have strengthened, the Government of the United States has decided to begin at once arrangements for the concentration of the American forces at Vladivostok with a view to their embarkation and departure immediately after the leaving of the first important contingent of Czechoslovak troops, that is to say, about February 1.

Careful consideration has also been given to the possibility of continuing, after the departure of the American troops, the assistance of American railway experts in the operation of the Trans-Siberian and Chinese Eastern Railways. It will be recalled that it is expressly stipulated in the plan for the supervision of these railways, which was submitted by the Japanese Ambassador at Washington, January 15, 1919, that the arrangement should cease upon the withdrawal of the foreign military forces from Siberia, and that all foreign railway experts appointed under the arrangement should then be recalled forthwith.

The experience of recent months in the operation of the railways under conditions of unstable civil authority and frequent local military interference furnishes a strong reason for abiding by the terms of the original agreement. Arrangements will be made accordingly for the withdrawal of the American railway experts under the same conditions and simultaneously with the departure of the American military forces.

The Government of the United States desires the Japanese Government to know that it regrets the necessity for this decision, but it seems to mark the end, for the time being at least, of a co-operative effort by Japan and the United States to assist the Russian people, which had of late begun to bear important results and seemed to give promise for the future. The Government of the United States is most appreciative of the friendly spirit which has animated the Government of Japan in this undertaking, and is convinced that the basis of understanding which has been established will serve in the future to facilitate the common efforts of the two countries to deal with the problems which confront them in Siberia. The Government of the United States does not in the least relinquish the deep interest which it feels in the political and economic fate of the people of Siberia nor its purpose to co-operate with Japan in the most frank and friendly way in all practical plans which may be worked out for the political and economic rehabilitation of that region.

It is suggested that the Government of Japan may desire to communicate to the other principal allied and associated Governments the substance of the aide memoire of December 8th. This Government will likewise make known to them the substance of the present communication.

[155.]

Announcement by the Supreme Council on Trade with Russia, January 16, 1920.

(*New York Times*, January 17, 1920.)

With a view to remedying the unhappy situation of the population in the interior of Russia, which is now deprived of all manufactured products from outside of Russia, the Supreme Council, after taking note of the report of a committee appointed to consider the reopening of certain trade relations with the Russian people, has decided that it would permit the exchange of goods on the basis of reciprocity between the Russian people and allied and neutral countries.

For this purpose it decided to give facilities to the Russian co-operative organizations which are in direct touch throughout Russia so that they may arrange for the import into Russia of clothing, medicines, agricultural machinery and the other necessaries of which the Russian people are in sore need, in exchange for grain, flax, etc., of which there is a surplus supply.

These arrangements imply no change in the policies of the allied Governments toward the Soviet Government.

[156.]

Supreme Council's Note to the Representatives of the Russian Central Co-operative Union regarding the Partial Lifting of the Blockade, January 26, 1920.

(*New York Times*, January 27, 1920.)

First— The allied Governments notify the Co-operative Union that they are disposed to authorize an exchange of products upon a basis of reciprocity between the Russian people and the allied and neutral countries, and they invite this union to export from Russia the surplus of its cereals, its foodstuffs and its raw materials with a view to exchanging them for clothing and other merchandise, of which Russia is in need.

It should be well understood that the value of the merchandise, the importation of which into Russia will be authorized, will be based on the value of the merchandise exported from Russia within a reasonable period.

Second— The Russian delegation at Paris will communicate immediately by wireless with the controlling committee at Moscow and will ask it if the co-operatives are ready to assume responsibility for handling these importations and these exportations, and if exchanges of this sort are practically possible. The representatives of the co-operatives at Moscow will determine immediately these questions.

Third— The Central Committee at Moscow will guarantee that the exportation of cereals, flax, etc., shall be authorized and that the necessary transportation facilities shall be furnished.

Fourth— As soon as certainty is reached in this matter the Central Committee at Moscow will inform Berkenheim (Alexander Berkenheim, Vice President of the All-Russian Union of Consumers' Societies) at Paris.

Fifth— The co-operative unions in foreign countries will then take measure to furnish Russian cereals and flax on condition that the co-operatives shall be advanced 25 per cent. of the value of the exports, either by direct contact or by British, French, or Italian financiers.

Sixth— The balance of necessary credits will be furnished in London or Paris by Russian resources or British, French, or Italian co-operatives, private banks, or traders.

Seventh—Goods purchased by the above credits will be loaded immediately in Black Sea or Baltic ports, risks of loss or conflagration being assumed by the Russian co-operatives.

Eighth— The Central Committee at Moscow will endeavor to supply at least four complete trains for the transportation of goods to and from the Black Sea ports. Should Moscow not succeed, the co-operatives in foreign countries will employ part of the credits for the purchase of freight cars and locomotives in the allied countries. In any case they will send motor trucks in order to help railroad transportation.

Ninth— As soon as the exportation of cereals, flax, and other raw materials from Russia has commenced effectively, the contracts referred to above will be considerably increased, in order, for instance, to reach a million tons of cereals, which would be the quantity available for export, in a little longer time.

[157.]

Authorization given by the Soviet Government to the Central Union of Russian Co-operatives to trade with Foreign Countries, February 2, 1920.

(*New York Times*, February 2, 1920.)

The Russian co-operatives' headquarters at Paris has received authorization from the Soviet Government to transact business with foreign countries. The announcement read as follows:

The Soviet Government permits the Central Union of Russian Co-operatives to enter into commercial relations with the co-operatives and business firms of Western Europe, America, and other countries.

The Soviet Government has given the Central Union all guarantees concerning the protection of goods exported and imported by the co-operatives.

The Central Union is ready to commence exchanges immediately.

The Soviet Government will allow to pass safely delegates coming to and leaving Russia whose names are furnished by the representatives of the Russian co-operatives of Central Europe.

[158.]

Statement by the Supreme Council, February 24, 1920.

(*New York Times*, February 25, 1920.)

If the communities which border the frontiers of Soviet Russia and whose independence or de facto autonomy they have recognized were to approach them and ask them for advice as to what attitude they should take with regard to Soviet Russia, the allied Governments would reply that they cannot accept the responsibility of advising them to continue war, which may be injurious to their own interests. Still less would they advise them to adopt a policy of aggression toward Russia. If, however, Soviet Russia attacks their legitimate frontiers the Allies will give them every possible support.

The Allies cannot enter into diplomatic relations with the Soviet Government, in view of their past experiences, until they have arrived at the conviction that the Bolshevist horrors have come to an end, and that the Government at Moscow is ready to conform its methods and diplomatic conduct to those of all civilized governments.

The British and Swiss Governments were both compelled to expel representatives of the Soviet Government from their respective countries because they had abused their privileges.

Commerce between Russia and the rest of Europe, which is so essential for the improvement of economic conditions, not only in Russia but in the rest of the world, will be encouraged to the utmost degree possible without relaxation of the attitude described above.

Furthermore, the Allies agree in the belief that it is highly desirable to obtain impartial and authoritative information regarding the conditions now prevailing in Russia. They have therefore noted with satisfaction the proposal before the International Labor Bureau, which is a branch of the League of Nations, to send a commission of investigation to Russia to examine into the facts. They think, however, that this inquiry would be invested with even greater authority and with superior chances of success if it were made on the initiative and conducted under the supervision of the Council of the League of Nations itself, and they invite that body to take action in this direction.

INDEX
[References are to pages.]

"Acid test," 72, 258, 260
Aims. *See* War aims.
Alexandrovitch, Michael, 2-3
Alexeieff, General, 314
Allied Ambassadors, Soviet Government's first note to, 44; note from Trotsky on suspension of armistice negotiations, 56; protest against repudiation, 78; removal from Vologda to Archangel, 230, 231
Allied Consuls, statement on remaining in Moscow, 230
Allies, note from Provisional Government as to a conference on war aims, 26; protest from military agents against violation of treaty, 49; note to diplomats from Soviet Government as to armistice negotiations, 51; armistice negotiations suspended for their definition of attitude, 56-57; note from Trotsky on peace negotiations with appeal to join, 61; agreement with Murman Regional Soviet, 232; protest from Tchicherin to Poole against hostile conduct, 246; conspiracy alleged by Soviet Government, September 3, 1918, 252; supervision of Siberian railways, plan, 276; charged with fomenting insurrection, 314; policy of non-recognition and non-intercourse with Soviet Government unchanged, 359, 361; *see also* Supreme Council
All-Russian Central Executive Committee, on the attempted assassination of Lenin, 250
All-Russian Congress of Soviets at Moscow, Wilson's cable and reply, 87, 89, 97; Gompers's cable, 88; proceedings as reported by Robins, 97, 102
All-Russian Convention of Soviets of Workers', Soldiers', and Peasants' Deputies. *See* Soviet Government

All-Russian Provisional Government (Omsk), appeal to President Wilson, 257
All-Siberian Soviet, 172; recognition desired, 176; guarantee as to armed prisoners, 179; memorandum given Hicks and Webster, 184
Ambassador from free Russia welcomed by Wilson, 31
America. *See* United States.
American Ambassador. *See* Francis, D. R.
American Ambassador at Tokio, 278, 279
American citizens in Russia, 347, 348
American Embassy at Vologda, 80
American Friends Society, 215
American Military Mission to Russia, 47-48; chief visits Trotsky, 55; on absence of officers with Gen. Kaledin, 58
American Mission to Russia, 23; aims explained by Lansing, 27; Root's address to Russia, June 15, 1917, 28; Root's statement to the press on its work, 32
American Railway Commission, 104, 107, 133, 220, 357
American Red Cross. *See* Red Cross
American troops in Russia, 238, 282
American troops in Siberia, 343; withdrawal, Secretary of State's statement, 355
Amnesty, 319
Anderson, Colonel, 103
Annexations, 300; old distinguished from new, 62
Annexations and indemnities, Gompers on, 15; Petrograd Soviet on, 17; Wilson's position, 25; Soviet Government on, 41, 45; Wilson's message on (Dec. 4, 1917), 57
Appeals from groups in Russia, 221
Archangel, 83, 122, 132, 155, 203, 213, 282; as port of trade, 213, 218, 219; Ambassadors' removal to, 230, 231; suitability for Am-

363

INDEX

bassadors, 232; uprising August 3, 1918, 242; reply of Government to Prinkipo proposal, 305
Armaments, reduction, 71, 341
Armed war prisoners in Siberia 104, 106, 109, 112, 115, 121, 123, 124, 125, 128, 139, 147; German origin of scare, 149; Irkutsk Soviet and, 167, 168; investigation by Hicks and Webster: record, 165-177; report, 177-186
Armistice, Soviet Government proposes, 43, 45; Soviet Government's note to Allies' diplomats as to beginning negotiations, 51; suspension of negotiations, 56
Army, reorganization by Soviet Government, 20, 101, 104, 107, 116, 124, 324
Associated Press, Kerensky interview, 39
Austria-Hungary, 72
Avskentiev, Mr., 257

Bakhmeteff, B. A., welcomed as ambassador by Wilson, 31; activity, 241
Balfour, A. J., 289, 290, 291, 293, 296; speech in Parliament on Japanese intervention, 89
Balkan states, 72
Baltimore, Md., address of President Wilson, April 6, 1918, 190
Baltic ports, 360
Berger, Victor, 19
Berkenheim, Alexander, 359
Bersin, Commander, 252
Berthelot, General, statement to General Dukhonin, 50
Bessarabia, 339, 342
Billings, Frank, 48
Black Sea, 298
Black Sea ports, 360
Blockade. *See* Economic blockade; commercial relations
Bogaevsky, Ataman, 121
Bolshevik leaders, 66
Bolshevik Revolution, 38
Bolsheviks, economic encirclement, 273; French Foreign Minister on, 281; Wilson on, 287; Lloyd George on, 284; as viewed by national Russian groups, 305; Foch's note to German Government on blockading, 349; propaganda in United States, 351; *see also* Soviet Government
Bonch-Bruevich, Vladimir, 44

Bonds. *See* Loans.
Brest-Litovsk, peace, 61, 68, 83, 258; negotiations begun, 56; peace signed, 79; Entente prime ministers protest against, 92; Francis on, 94; German "justice," 191; non-recognition by Allies, 232, 244-245
Briberies by Entente, 252, 253, 269
Bridges destroyed, 314
British Embassy in Petrograd, statement, Nov. 29, 1917, as to recognition of new government, 51, and reply, 52; conspiracies, 253; attack on and British protest, 255
British Foreign Secretary, note to Tchicherin protesting against attack on British Embassy in Petrograd, 255
British Government, Japanese intervention and, 195; declaration to the peoples of Russia, August 8, 1918, of assistance, 243
British troops, Murmansk, 227; protest from Tchicherin against movement, 229
Brotherhood of man, 25
Buchanan, George, 145
Buckler, Mr., 290
Bullard, Arthur, 57, 58
Bullit, W. C., 317, 353

Cadets, 178
Caldwell, J. K., 196, 197
Canada, 294
Capitalism, 262
Caucasian territories, 339, 342
Cecil, Lord Robert, 52
Cheidze, Mr., 19
Chicherin. *See* Tchicherin.
China, anxiety and conference over Russian troops, 128, 129, 170, 171, 176
Chinese Eastern Railway, 174, 183, 220, 345, 357
Chinese-Eastern and Trans-Siberian Railways, plan for Allied supervision, documents, 276
Chinese embargo, 160
Chita, 128, 168, 171, 178, 183
Christiania, 274, 276
Cieneros, Harrido, 46
Cipher messages, 161, 162, 163
Citizenship, Russian, 321
Class privilege, 338, 342
Clemenceau, Georges, 273, 290, 296,

INDEX

339, 343; on Bolsheviks, 291; reply to Nansen, 330
Coates (J. M.) Co., 215, 217
Colonial claims, 71
Commerce, Russian-American, 206, 208
Commercial relations, Russian foreign commérce, 206; opportunities, 325; Soviet Government's desire, 328; Supreme Council's blockade, 349; foreign trade " nationalized," 351; Supreme Council's announcement of January 16, 1920, 358; Soviet Government's authorization to Co-operative Union, February 2, 1920, 360; *see also* Economic relations.
Committee on Public Information, personnel, 57; relations with Soviet Government, 57, 67, 77; statements given out May 31, 1918, by Francis and by Lansing, 219, 221; statement to the press from American Ambassador, June 1, 1918, 223
Concessions, Bolshevik, not recognized by Russian nationals, 300
Congress of Soviets, Seventh, resolution, December 5, 1919, 353
Conspiracies, Allies charged with, 269, 314, 315
Constituent Assembly, promised, 1-2, 5, 21; convocation urged by government, Oct. 8, 1917, 37; expectation of Kerensky, 41; peace resolution adopted Jan. 18, 1918, 75; dissolution, 75, 77; negotiations with Soviet Government, 301, 324; Supreme Council and Kolchak on, 338, 340, 341
Constitutional Democrats, 178
Construction, enterprises in Russia for America, 211
Co-operative Union, Supreme Council's note, January 26, 1920, 359; Soviet Government's authorization of foreign trade, February 3, 1920, 360
Co-operatives, commercial relation through, 358, 359, 360
Cordon sanitaire, 273, 285, 294, 316
Corse, Frederick, 58
Cotton thread, 215
Council of Export Trade (Russian), 204, 210
Council of People's Commissaries, 44; *see also* Soviet Government; Tchicherin; Trotsky

Counter revolution, 260, 297, 301, 313; Far East conspiracy, 197; local government organizations, 225; Czechoslovaks and, 228; All-Russian Central Executive Committee's declaration, 250
Country of the North, proclamation, 242
Credentials of L. A. Martens, 320, 321
Credits, 360
Creel, George, cable from Sisson, December 18, 1917, 57; cable from Sisson desiring President to restate war aims, 67; cable from Sisson on use of Wilson's " acid test " speech in Russia, 74
Crimes, 303
Cromie, Captain, 255
Czarism. *See* Tsarism
Czechoslovak National Council, statement issued at Washington, July 27, 1918, 235
Czechoslovak Provisional Government, statement from Tchicherin, 267
Czechoslovak troops in Russia, 119, 225, 236, 237, 238, 240, 259, 261, 267, 282, 310, 312; disarming by Soviet Government, note of June 13, 1918, 224; assistance from America, 343; withdrawal from Siberia, 356

Dardanelles, 72
Dauria, 172, 173, 178
Davison, H. P., 113, 114, 127, 145; cable from Robins urging intercourse with Bolshevik Government, 60, with reply, 60; cable from Robins, March 26, 1918, on Red Cross work, 188; telegrams with Robins on Red Cross assistants, April 5, 1918, 189; cable to Robins on high value of his Red Cross work, 196; cables with Robins, April 25, 27, and May 9, 1918, about Red Cross work, 202, 204
Debs, Eugene, 265
Debts. *See* Loans; Repudiation
Demobilization, 319
Denikin, General, 286, 315, 333
Diamandi, Mr., 75
Dielo Nervda, 75
Diplomatic agents, letter from Lansing to Lithuanian National Council, 354

366 INDEX

Diplomats at Petrograd, protest over arrest of Rumanian Minister, 75
Distribution, 214; possibility and method in Russia, 217
Dora's Red Cross cargo, 155, 156
Drysdale, Walter, 121, 123, 131, 166, 168, 178
Dukhonin, General, 49; 53; statement from General Berthelot, 50; statement to, by Lieutenant-Colonel Kerth, 53; removal, 54
Duma, 1, 4
Durri, Consul, 348

Economic barriers, 71
Economic blockade of Russia, 272, 276, 318, 323, 327, 332, 353; Foch's note to German Government, 349; Supreme Council's note to Cooperative Union, January 26, 1920, 359
Economic Commission, aims as suggested by Robins, 213
Economic encirclement, 273, 285, 294, 316
Economic liberty, 271
Economic relations, Russian- American, plan sent by Lenin to Robins, May 14, 1918, 204-212; report of Robins to Secretary of State, July 1, 1918, 212-219; official statement from Washington, August 3, 1918, 237; *see also* Commercial relations
Elections, 338, 342
Emerson, Colonel, 127, 128, 133, 142, 221-222
Esthonia, 339, 341; reply to Prinkipo proposal, 304
Exchange of interned citizens, 249, 253, 254, 255, 256
Executions, mass, 315

Far East, conspiracy, 197
Finance, Russian, 324; *see also* Loans
Finland, 137, 140, 141, 145, 147, 300, 338, 341, 354; Red Cross work, 148; revolutionary leaders, 147, 150; leaders' protest against German militarism, 151; recognized by United States Government, 336
Finland, Gulf of, 350
Foch, Marshal, note to German Government as to blockading Bolshevik **Russia**, 349

Food supply, 316, 351; Nansen on, 329
Foreign commerce, Russian, 206
Fourteen Points of President Wilson, 71
France, will not recognize a Russian government capable of making a separate peace, 50; territory should be freed, 72; French agents and Czechoslovaks, 311
Francis, D. R., recognition of Provisional Government, 6; documents given Robins for use in certain contingencies (on recognition), 65, 66; cables to State Department warning against Japanese invasion, 84, 85; interview March 15, 1918, in which he declares he will not leave Russia, 94; certificate given Robins for Red Cross work, 95; correspondence in Vologda with Robins in Moscow, 96-164; message received from MacGowan at Irkutsk, 164; statement on Japanese intervention, 196; on non-intervention and standing by Russia, May 31, 1918, 219; on attitude of Amer ica, statement through committee on Public Information, June 1, 1918, 223; message to Tchicherin explaining removal to Archangel, 231; address to the Russian people August 9, 1918, on conditions of recognition, 244; unhindered in leaving Russia, 282
Fredericks, Baron, 108, 112, 186, 187
Freedom of the Seas, 71
French Foreign Minister, 280
French loan to Russia, 265
French Miliary Mission, 50; communication to Russian commander-in-chief, 59
French territory, 72
Friendship for Russia. *See* United States

General Staff. *See* Russian General Staff
Georgian Government, 303
" German peace," 92, 93
Germany, intrigues condemned by the United States, 24, 27, 58; greatness acknowledged by Wilson, 73; commercial penetration of Russia, 79, 80, 89; methods with other governments, 90; character condemned by Entente prime

ministers, 92; pledges and violation, 92; control commission in Petrograd, 108, 112, 114, 186, 187; justice toward, 191; exports to Russia before the war, 208; resentment in Russia, 216; asked by Foch to assist economic blockade of Bolshevik Russia, 349
Gold, reserves, 351; Rumanian, 351
Gompers, Samuel, message of sympathy to Petrograd Soviet, 14
Government of Autonomous Siberia, 197
Grain, 214
Graves, W. S., 344, 345
Great Britain, warned of Japanese intervention, March 5, 1918, 82; *see also* British, etc.
Groups in Russia, appeals from, 221; program and intentions, 241
Grénard, Consul General, 252
Guchkov, Mr., 12
Guinet, Alphonse, 312
Gurnberg, Alexander, 111

Harbin, 104, 125, 127, 168, 183, 201, 345
Hicks, W. L., 165
Hicks and Webster mission, 104, 105, 115, 124, 128, 139; record of investigation of armed war prisoner scare, 165-177; report, 177-184; memorandum given by Central Executive Committee of Soviets, 184
Hillquit, Morris, 19
Hitchcock, Senator, 282, 283
Horvat, Mr., 200
Hungarian military prisoners, 166, 170, 175, 179

Imperialism, 17, 18, 270; Japanese, 194
Indemnities. *See* Annexations and indemnities
Indigent persons, 77, 78
Industry, reorganization, 325
Interment, 315; British and French citizens, 249, 254
International Harvester Co., 110-111, 183, 215, 217
International Labor Bureau, 362
International Socialism, Trotsky and, 79, 82
International Socialist Congress at Stockholm, appeal for, from Petrograd Soviet, 18, 19, 22

Intervention, 275, 297, 302, 311, 335; military, 237; Trotsky's statement about, 249; America's participation, 250, 251; Tchicherin's protest to the Allies, December 2, 1918, 268; Litvinov on, 271, 272; Lloyd George on, 285; original puropse, 337; Wilson's message, June 26, 1919, to the Senate on Siberia, 343
Irkutsk, 124, 128, 178; Siberian Bolsheviks, 164; prisoners' camp visited, 169-170; anti-Bolshevik sympathies of consuls, 180
Irkutsk Soviet, 124
Ishii, K., 278; note to Acting Secretary of State January 15, 1919, 276
Italian soldiers in Russia, 309
Italy, 294; frontiers, 72; note from Soviet Government, February 14, 1919, 306-317
Izvestia, 110; position, 7; visit of Gen. Judson to Trotsky, 55; on Wilson's "acid test" speech, 74; on Japanese intervention, 135

Japan, Russian feeling against, 81, 82; declaration August 3, 1918, in conjunction with the United States, 239; plan presented through Japanese Ambassador at Washington for Allied supervision of Siberian railways, 276; United States concert with, 343, 344; note from United States Government on withdrawal of American troops from Siberia, 355; end of United States co-operative effort in Siberia, 358; *see also* Japanese intervention.
Japanese Ambassador at Washington, 276, 279, 355
Japanese intervention, warning from Lockhart to Great Britain, 82; Francis cables United States Department of State, 84, 85; Balfour on, 89; United States policy outlined, 99-100; Allied ambassadors' advise, 131; Russian press and, 136, 138; Central-Siberian Soviet and, 182; Soviet Government's statement, 194; Francis's statement as to Japanese and British landing at Vladivostok, 196; Soviet Government's complaint to Italy, 311; *see also* Vladivostok.

Japanese Minister of Foreign Affairs, 278
Jews, 334
Juan, Louis, communication to Russian commander-in-chief, 59
Judenitch, General, 335
Judson, W. V., letter to Russian General Staff on American supplies, 47; second letter to Russian General Staff, on sympathy for Russia, 48; visit to Trotsky, 55
Justice, 73

Kaiserism, Gompers on, 14, 15
Kalamatiano, Mr., 348
Kaledin, General, 58, 110, 121
Kalinin, President, 353
Kalpachnikoff, Colonel, 130, 131
Kamchatka fisheries, 199
Kato, Admiral, 134, 135, 139, 194, 196
Kerensky, Alexander, 20, 33, 36; Associated Press interview, 39
Kerth, Lieutenant-Colonel M., statements to Gen. Dukhonin, 53, and reply from Trotsky, 54; recall, 59
Knox, Senator, 286
Kola, 227
Kolchak, Admiral, 286, 301, 333, 346, 348, 349, 356; dictatorship proclaimed, 257; note from Supreme Council, 337; reply to Supreme Council, 340; support extended by Supreme Council, 343
Kolobov, M. A., 198, 200
Kornilov, General, 36, 152
Krasnoyarsk, 150, 177, 182
Krylenko, General, 50
Kulleroo, Mr., 151

Land question, 334, 338
Lansing, Robert, note on aims of American Mission to Russia, 27; cable to Robins, May 9, 1918, to return for consultation, 203; recognition of Finland, 336; letter to Lithuanian National Council on recognition, 348; letter to Lithuanian National Council on diplomatic agents, 354; *see also* State, United States Department of; United States Government
Latvia, 339, 341; reply to Prinkipo proposal, 303
Lavergne, General, 54, 59, 99, 252
League of Nations, 73, 338, 341, 362; Soviet Government's discussion, 262

Lee, Algernon, 19
Lemnos, 291, 296
Lenin, V. I., 96, 97, 102; chairman of new government, 44; telegram from Robins and reply on February 28, 1918, 80, 81; plan of economic relations with America, sent to Robins May 14, 1918, 204-212; attempt on his life, 250
Leonard, Consul, 348
"Letters from an American Friend," 113, 114
Lettish troops, 252
Letvia. *See* Latvia.
Lithuania, 289, 303, 339, 341
Lithuanian National Council, letter from Lansing on recognition, 348; letter from Lansing on diplomatic agents, 354
Lithuanians, passports, 355
Litvinov, Maxim, 249, 254, 255, 256, 290, 326, 327; appeal, December 24, 1918, to President Wilson, 270; letter (with Vorovsky) to Ludwig Meyer on peace terms, 274
Lloyd George, David, 339, 343; at Quai d'Orsay on peace in Russia, 284, 290; reply to Nansen, 330
Loans, Russian, 299, 320, 339, 342; Polk on, 339
Lockhart, R. H. B., 80; cable to British Foreign Office, March 5, 1918, warning of Japanese intervention, 82; letter to Robins with definite instances of Trotsky's willingness to work with Allies, 202; protest to from Tchicherin as to British armed troops at Murmansk, 226; asked by Tchicherin to disavow certain statements about intervention, 227; arrest and alleged conspiracy, 252, 253, 254; as conspirator, 314
Lvov, G. E., 10, 20, 33, 300

MacGowan, Mr., message to Francis from Irkutsk, 164
Machinery, Russian needs, 210
Maioni, Mr., 307, 308, 312
Makino, Baron, 290, 295, 343
Manchuria, 173, 174, 175, 179
Manchurian Railway, 183
Manifesto of Provisional Government, 4
Mannerheim, General, 140-141, 148
Manufactures, Russian needs, 210
Marchand, René, 313

INDEX 369

Marines, American, on Murman coast, 227
Marmora, Sea of, 298
Martens, L. A., credentials, with memorandum, sent to United States Department of State, 320, 321-328; protest of Soviet Government against alleged arrest, 346; reply of United States Assistant Secretary of State to Soviet Government as to alleged arrest, 347
Masaryk, T. G., 236
Mass executions, 315
"Mass terror," 251, 256
Massacres, 334
Matzievskaya, 173, 174, 175, 183
Max, Professor, 282
Mensheviks, 301, 302, 324
Meyer, Ludwig, 274, 276
Militarism, 270
Mlitary intervention, 237
Military stores, 211
Miliukov, P. N., note to Allies through Russian diplomats abroad, March 18, 1917, 2; reply to recognition of new government by the United States, 6; communication to Russian diplomats in Allied countries on durable peace, May 1, 1917, 11, 12; explanation to Soviet of his communication to diplomats, 12
Milner, Lord, 274
Minor, Robert, 154
Mirbach, Count von, 146, 231
Moonzund, 56
Moscow, National Conference, 36; situation, March, 1918, 103; bandits, 143; absurd press reports about ambassadorship, etc., 157, 158; mass executions, 315; cooperatives, 359; see also All-Russian Congress of Soviets
Moscow Soviet, elections, 148
Mouravieff, General, 314
Murman coast, American marines, 227
Murman region, 233, 235
Murmansk, 83, 107, 132, 145, 203; British troops, 227, 229
Murmansk Soviet, 230; agreement with Allies, 232

Nansen, Fridjof, 352, 353; letter to President Wison, 329; reply from, 330; Bolshevist reply to, 332
Nashe Slovo, 227, 228

National Conference in Moscow, message from Wilson, 36
National groups in Russia, position on Bolshevik concessions, 300; relation to Bolsheviks, 306
Neutral countries, Soviet Government's note, November 23, 1917, to certain representatives, 45; replies to Soviet Government's note, 46
New republics, recognition, 354
New York Call, 74
New York Life Insurance Co., 217
Nicholas, Emperor, renunciation of throne, 2
Niessel, General, 59, 99
"No annexations," etc. *See* Annexations and indemnities
Non-intervention, 221, 223; statement by Francis, May 31, 1918, 219; in internal affairs of Russia, 238; *see also* Intervention
Nuorteva, S., 329

Omsk, 150, 165, 168, 177, 182; All-Russian Provisional Government, 257; Sazonoff as representative, 286
Orjalsalo, Arne, 150
Orlando, V. E., 289, 294, 339; reply to Nansen, 330
Ouritzky (Uritzki), 250, 315

Paderewski, Ignace, 306
Passports, Stockholm Congress, 19; Lithuanians, 355
Peace, Petrograd Soviet's appeal of March 27, 1917, 7; Provisional Government's statement of its basis, 10, 11, 12; basis of durable, 13, 20; Soviet Government's decree, 41; Trotsky urges Allies to join negotiations, 61; program of the word's peace (Wilson's Fourteen Points), 71; Constituent Assembly resolution of Jan. 18, 1918, 75; danger of a peace without Russia, 245; *see also* Brest-Litovsk peace; Peace proposals, Soviet; Separate peace
Peace Conference, 280, 284, 287; Prinkipo proposal, 297; *see also* Supreme Council
Peace proposals, Soviet, 258, 268, 270, 274, 283, 309; text of proposal projected by Soviet Government, March 14, 1919, 317; Congress of Soviets enumerates, 353

370 INDEX

People's Commissaries. *See* Council of People's Commissaries
Perm, 165
Petrograd, Diplomatic corps' protest against arrest of Rumanian minister, 75; German control commission, 108, 112, 114, 186, 187; Red Cross supplies at work, 155; mass execution, 315; blockade, 351; *see also* British Embassy in Petrograd
Petrograd Soviet, proclamation to the peoples of the world, March 27, 1919, 7; message from Gompers, 14; appeal to Socialists of all countries, 16; call for International Socialist Congress, 18, 19, 22
Pettit, Walter, 317
Phillips, Mr., reply to Soviet protest as to arrest of L. A. Martens, 347; reply to Senator Wadsworth, 351
Pichon, S., statement, December 29, 1918, in the Chamber of Deputies, 273; reply, January 11, 1919, to British Government's suggestion as to Russia, 280; notes on discussions regarding Russia at his office, January 16, and 21, 1919, 284, 289
Platinum, 107, 109, 110, 112, 114, 129, 131, 132
Plebiscite, 42
Poland, 72, 93, 275, 289, 300, 338, 341, 354; announcement of recognition by United States Department of State, 306
Polk, F. L., note to Japanese Ambassador at Washington on plan for Siberian railway supervision, 279; on Russian bonds, 339
Poole, D. C., Jr., 230, 313; note from Tchicherin of appeal and protest against Anglo-French invasion, 246
Preliminary Parliament, 38
Princes' Islands (Prinkipo), 298, 333
Prinkipo proposal, 297; Soviet Government's reply, 298; replies of non-Boshevik Russian Governments, 303
Prisoners of war, 319; *see also* Armed war prisoners in Siberia
Production, decline in Russia, 205
Propaganda, 275, 276, 281, 302, 351

Provisional Council of the Republic, announcement, 38
Provisional Government of Russia, statement, March 18, 1917, of policy and principles, 1; membership, 1; foreign policy, 3; manifesto to Russian people, 4; recognition by the United States, 6; statement regarding the war, April 9, 1917, 9; declaration (of second) on May 18, 1917, 19; membership of second, 19, 20; note (of second) to Allies June 15, 1917, suggesting a conference on war aims, 26; statement to Allies August 1, 1917, on continuing the war, 33; declaration of last, Dec. 8, 1917, 36
Provisional Government of the country of the North, proclamation, 242
Prussian militarism, 14
Public Information. *See* Committee on Public Information
Publicity, policy of Soviet Government, 55; Wilson on, 70, 71

Quai d'Orsay, notes on discussions regarding Russia on January 16 and 21, 1919, 284, 289

Radek, Karl, 119
Radicalism, 216
Railroads, Siberia, supervision plan, 276; building, 325; *see also* American Railway Commission
Ransome, Arthur, 113
Raw materials, Russian, 209, 211, 299, 328, 360
Reciprocity, 358, 359
Recognition, of Soviet Government urged by Robins, 77; of new republics, 354
Red Army, 260-261, 265, 266, 267, 281, 308, 316; rations, 352
Red Cross, supplies for Russia, 48; certificate given by Francis to Robins, 95; Finland, 148; Soviet Government relations, 154; Soviet Government's statement to Robins, 188; cable from Robins to Davison, March 26, 1918, 188; telegrams between Robins and Davison, April 5, 1918, on assistants, 189; Davison's opinion of work of Robins, 196 cables between Davison and Robins, April 25, 27, and May 9, 1918, 202, 204

INDEX

Red terror, 251, 271, 315
Relief problem, 352
Repressions, 254
Reprisals, 347, 348
Republics, new, recognition, 354
Repudiation of Russia's debts, decree of Feb. 8, 1918, text, 77; protest of foreign ambassadors, 78
Resources, Russian, 214
Riga, 36
Riggs, Captain, 101, 103, 104, 111, 125, 126
Riley, Lieutenant, 252
Robins, Raymond, 48; cable to Davison urging intercourse with Bolshevik Government, 60, with reply, 60; documents from Francis for use in certain contingencies, 65, 66; cable to Thompson on the strength of Soviet Government, 76; cable to Thompson, February 15, 1918, urging commercial relations to prevent German commercial relations, 79; telegram to Lenin on February 28, 1918, and reply, 80, 81; informs Trotsky of appeal and protest against Japanese plans in Siberia, 86; thanked by Tchicherin, 89; certificate from Francis for Red Cross work, 95; confidence in Soviet Government, 116, 130-131; favors economic reconstructive program, 146, 150, 152-153, 154; communication, March 21, 1918, from Tchicherin denying rumored German control commissions, 186-187; statement from Soviet Government on Red Cross work in Russia, 188; cable to Davison, March 26, 1918, on Red Cross work, 188; telegrams with Davison on Red Cross assistants, April 5, 1918, 189; cable from Davison on high value of Robin's Red Cross work, 196; letter from Tchicherin, April 25, 1918, with enclosure showing counter-revolutionary conspiracy in Far East, 197; cables with Davison, April 25, 27, and May 9, 1918, about Red Cross work, 202, 204; cable from Lansing to return for consultation, 203; report to Secretary of State, July 1, 1918, on economic co-operation with Russia, 212-219
Robins, Mrs. Raymond, 127

Romei, General, 307, 308
Root, Elihu, address to Provisional Government June 15, 1917, 28; statement to the press on the work of the Mission to Russia, 32; speech in New York, August 12, 1917, 34
Ruggles, J. A., 85, 96, 104, 119
Rumania, 93
Rumanian gold, 351
Rumanian Minister, protest against his arrest, 75
Rumanian-Russian affairs, 118, 119
Russia, sympathy and friendship of America, 14, 27, 29, 36, 49, 94, 98; Tsar's Government, 34; Root on character and prospects, 35; "out of the war" reports, 39; exhaustion, 40; treatment by Allies the "acid test" of good will, 72; withdrawal from war, 79; American friendship continued in spite of difficulties, 219, 221; commission of investigation, 362
Russian Commander-in-Chief, communication from French Military Mission, 59
Russian diplomats abroad, note from Miliukov on March 18, 1917, 2
Russian Embassy at Washington, statement August 5, 1918, 241
Russian General Staff, letter from General Judson on American supplies, 47; second letter from General Judson, 48; protest from Allied military attachés against violation of treaty, 49
Russian Railway Service corps, 344
Russian Revolution, 17, 40; stage of control by necessities, 216
Russian Revolutionary Democracy, 17
Russian Socialist Federal Soviet Republic. *See* Soviet Government
Russian-American commerce, 206, 208
Russki Slovo, 57

Sadoul, J., 103
"Safe for democracy," 30
Saionji, 339
Salonika, 290, 291, 296
Samara, 214
Savings and savings banks, 78
Sazonoff, 286, 290, 300
Schools, 325
Secret diplomacy, 42, 270

INDEX

Secret treaties, Soviet Government abrogates, 43; Wilson on, 69, 70, 71
Self-determination of peoples, 270, 275; Provisional Government's position, 10, 12; Petrograd Soviet on, 17; in Allied countries, 62; Wilson on, 71
Self-government, 32, 357
Semenoff affair, 125, 128, 168, 170, 171, 173, 174, 183, 221
Separate peace (by Russia), 11, 20, 53, 63, 76; protest of Allies, 49; protest from the United States, 53
Serbian refugees, 144, 177
Serbian relief, 144, 147, 149
Shoes, 220
Siberia, Japanese intervention danger, 81; United States policy as to Japanese intervention, 99-100; republic, 119; counter-revolutionaries, 181; character of Soviets, 181; American attitude asked, 198, 199; Temporary Government, 241; plan of railway supervision, 276; reply of Government to Prinkipo proposal, 305; Wilson's message to the Senate, June 26, 1919, on intervention, 343; assistance to people, 345, 346 unfavorable situation, 355, 357; statement from Secretary of State on withdrawal of American troops, 355; *see also* Armed war prisoners; Japanese intervention
Siberian Bolsheviks, 164
Siberian Government, 197
Siberian railway, 167, 194, 236, 249
Siberian Railways, Japanese and American supervision, 344
Sisson, E. G., cable to Creel, December 18, 1917, 57; cable to Creel desiring President to restate war aims, 67; cable to Creel on use of Wilson's "acid test" speech in Russia, 74
Smolny, 55
Social reconstruction, 327
Social Revolutionists, 301
Socialism, Moscow All-Russian Congress of Soviets on, 89; Hungarian prisoners and, 180; among Siberian war prisoners, 181; radical modification, 216
Socialists, appealed to by Petrograd Soviet, 16
Sonnino, Baron, 289, 290, 293

Southern Russia, reply to Prinkipo proposal, 305
Soviet Government, *Izvestia* as organ, 7; adoption of proposition for beginning negotiations for peace, 41; first note to Allied Ambassadors, 44; note to neutral countries November 23, 1917, 45; replies from neutral countries to note, 46; note to Allies, diplomats regarding armistice negotiatons, 51; reply to statement of British Embassy, November 30, 1917, 52; independence of old government and its peace aim, 53; note on interference of Allied diplomats and agents, 54; policy of publicity, 55; question of American recognition, 65, 66; relations with Committee on Public Information, 57, 67, 77; strength after dissolution of Constituent Assembly, 76-77; American recognition urged, 77; note for American government, March 5, 1918, with inquiries, 81; Great Britain urged to support, 82, 84; United States attitude, 98, 102; Robins's confidence in, 116, 130-131; no organized Russian opposition to, 117, 118, 322, 326; power over Anarchists in Moscow, 143; United States urged to co-operate, 147, 150; Red Cross relations, 152; statement to Robins regarding Red Cross work in Russia, 188; desire for economic relations with America and plan, 204-212, 212-219; recognition not necessary to coperation, 216; American attitude to, as stated by Francis, June 1, 1918, 223; note regarding Czechoslovaks June 13, 1918, 224; official statement, September 3, 1918, of discovery of Allied conspiracy, 252; letter (through Tchicherin) to President Wilson, October 24, 1918, with discussion of peace terms, 258; New York organ, 268; reply to Prinkipo proposal, 298; note to Italy, February 14, 1919, with peace proposals and protest against Italian invasion, 306-317; text of projected peace proposal, March 14, 1919, 317; increasing popular support, 323, 324; territorial gains, 300, 322; reply to Nansen, 332; pro-

INDEX

test against alleged arrest of L. A. Martens, 346; Allied policy unchanged toward, 359, 361; authorization of foreign trade to cooperative union, February, 2, 1920, 360; *see also* Peace proposals; Tchicherin

Soviet of Workers' and Soldiers' Deputies, explanation from Provisional Government of Miliukov's communication to diplomats, May 4, 1917, 12; Executive Committee's appeal to preserve order, 13

Soviet Russia, 268

Soviets, Seventh Congress, resolution, December 5, 1919, 353

Spanish Ambassador's reply to Soviet Government's note of November 23, 1917, 46

Stal, Mr., 200, 201

State, United States Department of, on Russia being out of the war, 39; urged by Robins to continue intercourse with Bolshevik Government, 60; warned by Francis of Japanese invasion, 84, 85; Acting Secretary's correspondence with Japanese Ambassador, 276, 279; note from Tchicherin, January 12, 1919, 282; recognition of Poland, 306; credentials and memorandum from L. A. Martens, 320, 321-328; Assistant Secretary's cable to Stockholm in repy to Russian protest as to Martens, 347; Assistant Secretary's reply to Senator Wadsworth, 351; Secretary's statement on withdrawal of troops from Siberia, 355; *see also* Lansing, Robert

Steklov, Mr., 7

Stephens, Lincoln, 317

Stevens, J. L., 104, 108, 112, 127, 133, 142, 278, 344, 345, 346

Stockholm, 270, 274; International Socialist Congress, 18, 19, 22

Strenberg, military commissary, 106, 109, 124, 167, 168

Summers, Maddin, 58, 110, 122, 144, 147, 149

Supplies to Russia, American attitude, 47; Red Cross and, 48; manufactured materials and machinery desired, 124-125, 169, 183

Supreme Council at Paris, note to Kolchak, 337; support extended to Kolchak, 343; economic blockade of Bolshevik Russia, 349; announcement to Russia on January 16, 1920, 358; note to Cooperative Union, January 26, 1920, 359; statement as to commerce with Russia, February 24, 1920, 361; *see also* Peace Conference

Taxation, Second Provisional Government on, 21

Taylor, Graham, Jr., [Graham Romeyn Taylor] 57, 58

Tchaikovsky, Nicholas, 242, 305

Tcheliabinsk, 225, 312

Tcherepovetz bridge, 314

Tchicherin, George, telegram of thanks to Robins, 87; communication to Robins March 21, 1918, denying rumored German control commission in Petrograd, 108, 186-187; character, 138; letter to Robins, April 25, 1918, with enclosure showing counter-revolutionary conspiracy in Far East, 197; protest to Lockhart against British armed troops at Murmansk, 226; note to Lockhart asking disavowal of certain statements about intervention, 227; protest against movement of British troops, 229; note to the Consul General of the United States as to armed invasion by Allied troops, 229; note to Poole of appeal and protest against Anglo-French invasion, 246; note, August 20, 1918, permitting Allied citizens to leave Russia, 248; statement, September 7, 1918, as to exchanges and conspiracies, 253; statement to Czechoslovak Provisional Government, 267; protest, December 2, 1918, against intervention, 268; note to United States Department of State, January 12, 1919, dealing with American troops in Russia and peace terms, 282; *see also* Soviet Government

Tereshchenko, 26

Terrorism, 251, 256, 271, 315

Thacher, T. D., 77

Thompson, W. B., on American supplies, 48; cable from Robins on strength of Soviet Government, 76; cable from Robins urging commercial relations, 79

374 INDEX

Tokoi, Mr., 137, 147, 151, 278, 279
Tomsk, 178, 179
Trans-Baikal Railway, 345
Trans-Caspian territories, 339, 342
Trans-Siberian Railway, 357
Tredwell, R. C., 108, 348
Trotsky, Leon, 44, 46; note to Allies' diplomats as to armistice negotiations, 51; statement regarding note of Lieutenant-Colonel Kerth, 54; visit from General Judson, 55; note on suspension of armistice negotiations, 56; note to Allies on peace negotiations with appeal to join, 61; Brest-Litovsk peace and, 79; informed by Robins of appeal and protest against Japanese plans in Sberia, 86; on army organization, 106; instances of willingness to work with Allies, 202; Czechoslovaks disarming, 236; statement, August 23, 1918, as to Allied intervention and an American lie, 249
Tsarism, 1, 265, 266, 267, 271, 292, 334
Tschisti, J., 304
Turkish Empire, 72

Uchida, Viscount, 278, 279
Ufa, 257, 301
Ukraine, 218, 222, 275, 285, 303
United States, friendship and sympathy for Russia, 14, 27, 29, 36, 49, 94, 98; friendship in spite of difficulties, 219, 221
United States Government, asked by Soviet Government as to support, March 5, 1918, 81; policy on Japanese intervention in Siberia, 99-100; attitude to Soviet Government, 102, 335; official announcement, August 3, 1918, as to military and economic plans for Russia in co-operation with Japan, 237; note, September 1, 1918, to all associated and neutral governments, protesting against indiscriminate slaughter in Russian cities, 25; Soviet Government's characterization, 264; policy as to recognition of new republics, 354; see also Francis, D. R.; Lansing, Robert; State, United States Department of; Wilson, Woodrow
United States Grain Corporation, 352

Uritzki (Ouritzky), assassination, 250, 315
Ustrugov, Mr., 200, 201

Viatka, 165
Viborg, 352
Vladivostok, 81, 87, 196; Japanese landing incident, 134, 136, 140; shipments from, 142, 154; American consul involved in charge of conspiracy, 157, 158, 197; Soviet Government's view of Japanese landing, 194; reason given by the United States for occupation, 238; American troops' arrival, 344; Czechoslovak troops' embarkation, 356; American troops' departure, 357
Vladivostok Soviet, 135
Volga River, Czechoslovaks on, 236, 259
Volkhoff River, 314
Vologda, American Embassy at, 80; departure of Allied Ambassadors, 230
Vorovsky, V., 274, 276
Vpered, 301

Wadsworth, Eliot, 128
Wadsworth, Senator, reply from Mr. Phillips to letter on blockade, 351
War, determination of Provisional Government to continue, 33; " out of the war " reports about Russia, 39; Russia's withdrawal, 79
War aims, Wilson's note to Russia, May 26, 1917, 23; conference suggested to Allies by Provisional Government, 26; Root on, 30; restatement, 63; restatement from Wilson urged by Sisson, 67
War materials, 212
War prisoners, 319; *see also* Armed war prisoners in Siberia
Wardwell, A. D., 77, 132, 163
Washington Post, 39
Webster, W. B., 108, 147, 165; see also Hicks and Webster
Westnik, 57
White Guards, 137, 140, 145, 225, 267, 334
White terror, 251, 272
Wilcox, E. H., 7
Willard, Mr., 109
Williams, Harold, 83
Wilson, Woodrow, note to Russian Government May 26, 1917, on American war aims, 23; address

INDEX

of welcome to Bakhmeteff, 31; message to National Conference in Moscow, 36; message to Congress, December 4, 1917, 57-58; address to Congress, January 8, 1918, on Brest-Litovsk, etc., containing his Fourteen Points, 68; address of January 8, 1918, use and effect in Russia, 74; cable to Moscow Congress of Soviets, 87, and reply, 89, 97; address at Baltimore, April 6, 1918, on Liberty Loan and use of force against Germany, 190; appealed to by Omsk Government, 257; letter from Soviet Government, October 24, 1918, with discussion of peace terms, 258; promises as seen by Soviet Government, 260; appealed to, December 24, 1918, by Litvinov, 270; remarks at Quai d'Orsay on Russian conditions and proposition to invite various groups to confer, 287, 290; Prinkipo proposal, 297; letter from Nansen, 329, and reply to, 330; notes to Kolchak, 339, 343; message to the Senate, June 26, 1919, on intervention in Siberia, 343

Withdrawal of troops, 319, 337
Wright, J. B., 85

Yakovleff, Mr., 124, 128, 167, 168, 171, 180, 186
Yanson, Mr., 106, 124, 128, 167, 168, 171, 186, 198
Yaraslov riot, 314

Zvanka bridge, 314